W9-DAX-918

# the Pacific Crest

## Volume 1: California

Front cover photo by Esther Higgins
Maps by Jeff Schaffer
Drawings by Claudia Beck

ISBN: 911824-27-8
Library of Congress Card Catalog Number: 72-96122

# Trail

by Thomas Winnett

with

Jeffrey P. Schaffer

John W. Robinson

J. C. Jenkins

Andrew Husari

Acknowledgments

To put out a guide to 1650 miles of trail required a lot of input.

Without the late Clinton C. Clarke, there probably wouldn't be a Pacific Crest Trail.

Warren L. Rogers, who has all the files on the trail's history, contributed invaluable comment on the history chapter.

Dave Odell, Toby Heaton and the late Bilo Goddard told us about their trek from Mexico to Canada in 1972.

Walt Furen of the U.S. Forest Service kept us abreat of the Service's progress in creating the trail.

Karl Schwenke, Don Denison, Ron Felzer, Jim Barker and Myrsam Wixman provided field information that supplemented our own data.

Ken Ng's shuttle taxi helped us beat the winter snows.

Eleanor Smith typed up all the scraps we threw at her into one manuscript.

Rephah Berg again showed that she is a great copy editor.

Dharma Press gave us the use of their best typesetting skills.

Noelle Imperatore made the orange juice, the coffee and the ambience.

T.W.
J.P.S.
J.W.R.
J.C.J.
A.H.

## Other books by the authors

**by Thomas Winnett**

*Sierra North* (with Karl Schwenke)
*Sierra South* (with Karl Schwenke)
*The Tahoe-Yosemite Trail* (with Don Denison)
*Sierra Nevada Place Names Index* (with Don Denison)
*The Comstock Guide to California Backpacking*
*The Comstock Guide To Pacific Northwest Backpacking*
*Backpacking in the Wilderness Rockies*
*Tuolumne Meadows*
*Mt. Whitney*

**by John W. Robinson**

*Trails of the Angeles*
*San Bernardino Mountain Trails*
*Camping and Climbing in Baja*

**by Jeffrey P. Schaffer**

*The Pacific Crest Trail*
*Volume 2: Oregon-Washington*

# Contents

**Chapter**

1 History of the Trail .................. 1

2 Getting Ready to Hike the Trail ....... 5

Planning and Preparation
Backpacking Basics
Outdoor Courtesy
Land-use Regulations

3 Getting Ready to Appreciate the Trail . 19

Geology
Biology

4 Hiking the Trail..................... 39

5 The Trail ........................... 45

6 The Maps........................... 151

**Index**............................ 147

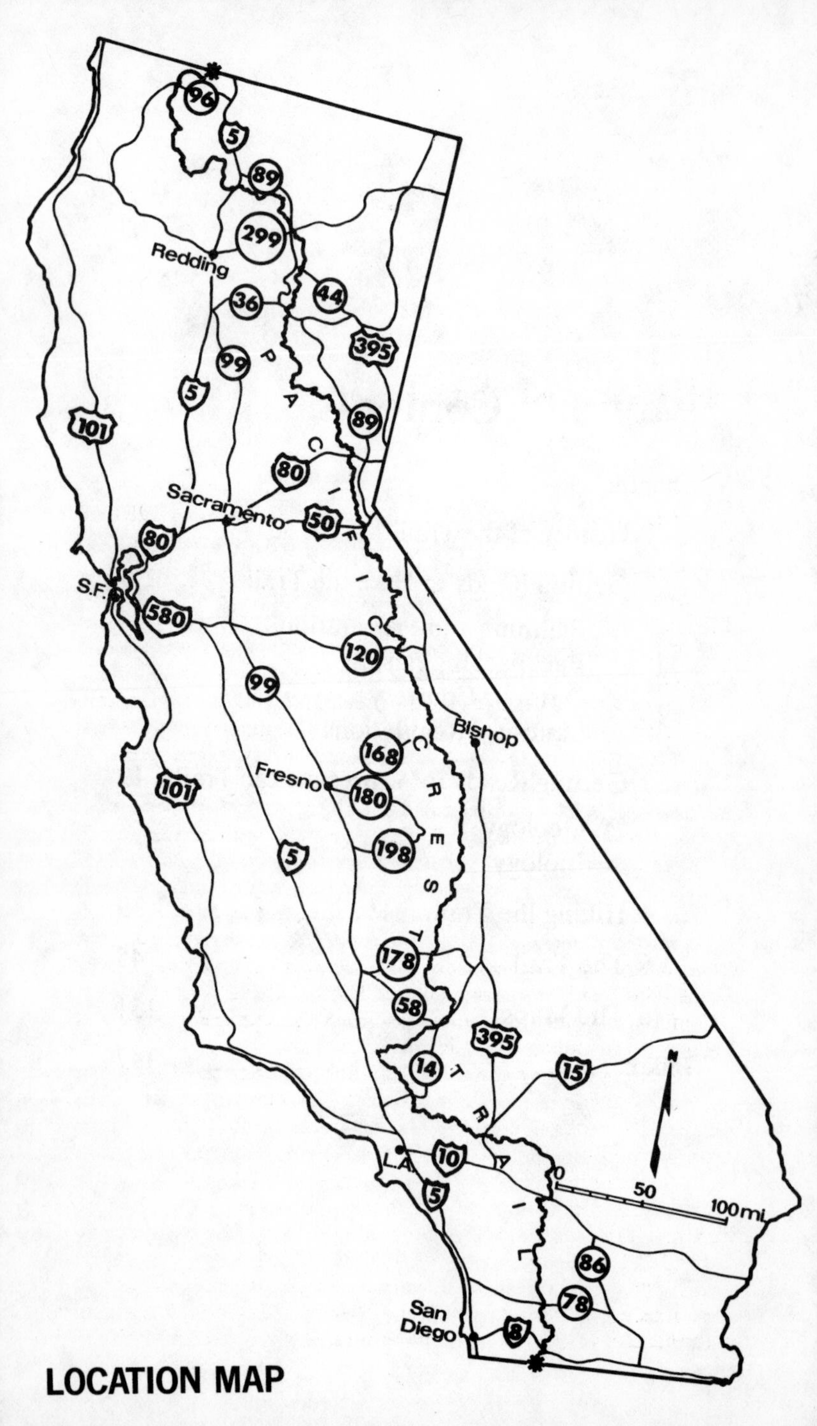


LOCATION MAP

# 1
# History of the Trail

The idea of a Pacific Crest Trail originated in the early 1930s, in the mind of Clinton C. Clarke of Pasadena, California, who was then chairman of the Executive Committee of the Mountain League of Los Angeles County. "In March 1932," wrote Clarke in *The Pacific Crest Trailway* (out of print), he "proposed to the United States Forest and National Park Services the project of a continuous wilderness trail across the United States from Canada to Mexico .... The plan was to build a trail along the summit divides of the mountain ranges of these states, traversing the best scenic areas and maintaining an absolute wilderness character."

The proposal included formation of additional Mountain Leagues in Seattle, Portland and San Francisco by representatives of youth organizations and hiking and mountaineering clubs similar to the one in Los Angeles. These Mountain Leagues would then take the lead in promoting the extension of the John Muir Trail northward and southward to complete a pathway from border to border. When it became evident that more than Mountain Leagues were needed for such a major undertaking, Clarke took the lead in forming the Pacific Crest Trail System Conference, with representatives from the three Pacific Coast states. He served as its President for 25 years.

As early as January 1935 Clarke published a handbook-guide to the PCT, giving the route in rather sketchy terms (the Trail goes east of Heart Lake, then south across granite fields to the junction of Piute and Evolution Creeks"–this covers about 9 miles).

In the summer of 1935–and again the next three summers–groups of boys under the sponsorship of the YMCA explored the route in relays, proceeding from Mexico on June 15, 1935, to Canada on August 12, 1938. This exploration was under the guidance of a YMCA secretary, Warren L. Rogers, who served as Executive Secretary of the Pacific Crest Trail System Conference (1932-1957) and who continues his interest in the PCT by currently serving on the Advisory Committee appointed by the Secretary of Agriculture.

Also in 1935, Clarke suggested to the Department of the Interior that the National Park Service construct the trail as a pathway connecting several national parks. Because so much of the land to be traversed was outside national parks, the Department declined. The trail's backers were then able to interest the U.S. Forest Service in constructing the trail. As early as 1920 the Forest Service had located and posted a trail from Mt. Hood to Crater Lake in Oregon, named the Oregon Skyline Trail. In 1928 the Forest Service began to study a high mountain route across Washington, and the reconnaisance of this trail was completed in 1935. In 1937, Region 6 of the Forest Service (Oregon and Washington) developed a design for PCT trail markers and posted them from the Canadian border to the California border.

Region 5 (California) did not follow this lead. In California, nothing beyond Clarks's rough description and generalized maps, published in hardback in 1945, appeared until the late 1960s, and anyone who wanted to walk or ride the PCT from Mexico to Oregon–or vice versa–was pretty much on his own for large portions of the 1600-mile distance. Clarke died in 1957, at age 84, confident that his dream would one day be fulfilled.

In 1965 the Bureau of Outdoor Recreation, a Federal agency, appointed a commission to make a nationwide trails study. The commission, noting that walking for pleasure was second only to driving for pleasure as the most popular recreation in America, recommended establishing a national system of trails, of two kinds–long National Scenic Trails in the hinterlands and shorter National Recreation Trails in and near metropolitan areas. The commission recommended that Congress establish four Scenic Trails–the already existing Appalachian Trail, the partly existing Pacific Crest Trail, a Potomac Heritage Trail and a Continental Divide Trail. Congress responded by passing, in 1968, the National Trails System Act, which set the framework for a system of trails and specifically made the Appalachian and the Pacific Crest trails the first two National Scenic Trails.

Meanwhile, in California, the Forest Service in 1965 had held a series of meetings about a route for the PCT in the state. These meetings involved people from the Forest Service, the Park Service, the State Division of Parks and Beaches, and other government bodies charged with responsibility over areas where the trail might go. These people decided that so much time had elapsed since Clarke had drawn his route that they should essentially start all over. Of course, it was pretty obvious that segments like the John Muir Trail would not be overlooked in choosing a new route through California. By the end of 1965 a proposed route had been drawn onto maps. (We don't say "mapped," for that would imply that someone actually had covered the route in the field.)

When Congress, in the 1968 law, created a citizens Advisory Council for the PCT, it was the route devised in 1965 which the Forest Service presented to the council as a "first draft" of a final PCT route. This body of citizens was to decide all the details of the final route; the Forest Service said it would adopt whatever the citizens wanted. The Advisory Council was also to concern itself with standards for the physical nature of the trail, markers to be erected along the trail, and the administration of the trail and its use.

In 1972 the Advisory Council agreed upon a route, and the Forest Service put it onto maps for internal use. Since much of the agreed upon route was cross-country, these maps were sent to the various national forests along the route, for them to mark a temporary route in the places where no trail existed along the final PCT route. This they did—but not always after field work. The result was that the maps made available to the public in June 1972 showing the final proposed route and the temporary detours do not correspond to what is on the ground in many places. A common flaw is that the Forest Service has shown a temporary or permanent PCT segment following a trail taken from a pre-existing Forest Service map when in fact there is no trail where it is shown on that map in the first place.

Perfect or not, the final proposed route was sent to Washington for publication in the Federal Register, the next step toward its becoming official. A verbal description of the route was also published in the Federal Register. But the material in the register does not give a center line which can be precisely and unambiguously followed; it is only a *route,* and the details in many places remain to be settled. Furthermore, much private land along the route remains to be acquired, or at least an easement secured for using it. It will be years before all this is done, and in our opinion decades before the final Pacific Crest Trail becomes a continuous, walkable, maintained trail from Mexico to Canada.

But meanwhile, it is possible to walk all the way, and we walked from Mexico to Oregon to obtain the information necessary to write an authentic guide to the California portion of the Pacific Crest Trail.

## The Ryback Caper

In 1971, in a new book called *The High Adventure of Eric Ryback,* young Ryback described walking from Canada to Mexico on the Pacific Crest Trail in 1970 (he was 18) and claimed to be the first person ever to walk the whole trail. There are strong reasons for doubting Ryback's claim that he walked from Canada to Mexico.

What is the evidence? According to Ryback's own figures, he covered 2500 miles of the PCT route in 129 days. But he mentions 11 layover days, which did not cover any miles along the route, and we have been told about others. One would infer there were other layover days, but assume only 11. Dividing 2500 miles by 118 days gives 21.2 miles per day that he must have averaged. Is this possible? Under what conditions?

Ryback stated at a press conference on November 18, 1970, in San Francisco that for the first month of his walk his boots never touched dirt because he was on snow all the time. In the book, he is mostly on snow the first month. At the press conference he also stated that much of his trek was cross-country because there were not trails where he wanted to go, and often an attempted route didn't work out, so that he had to backtrack. The same statement occurs many times in his book. To make up for any short-mileage days, due to snow, bushwhacking and backtracking, Ryback would have had to cover well over 21 miles per day when he was walking on snowless trail or road. My guess is 30 miles per day.

He states in his book that when his pack was full of food it weighed 80 pounds, and that when the food was all gone his pack weighed 40 pounds. Assuming he ate the food at a constant rate, his pack weighed an average of 60 pounds over the whole trip. He weighed 130 pounds, so his pack weighed on the average 46% of his body weight. Could an 18-year-old American boy carrying 46% of his body weight average 30 miles per day on mountain trails day after day after day?

Ryback did, evidently, get from Canada to Mexico in those 129 days. Perhaps he did so by walking and riding in cars. How else did he—for instance—go 65 miles in two days, slowed down not only by a pack but by a Forest Service official who was walking with him those two days? His best day was even more impressive, 87 miles from Big Bear Lake to Tahquitz Peak, including an elevation gain of 7000 feet!

We find the story incredible, and look forward to a believable book by someone else.

# 2

# Getting Ready to Hike the Trail

## Planning and Preparation

If experience with the John Muir Trail and the Tahoe-Yosemite Trail is any guide, 99.9% of the people who walk the PCT will not go from one end to the other without a break. But even one tenth of the California portion is more than 160 miles long, and a hike of that magnitude requires a lot of planning and preparation.

We hope some readers will walk the whole trail, Mexico to Canada. That would take more than five months, at least, and few people could do it all in the same year. You would have to start in early April. The California part takes more than three months. You should plan to do the hottest part, south of the Tehachapi Mountains, before June. Not far from there you enter the High Sierra, which is best in August in most years, but you will travel it in June if you started in April. In the northern Sierra, from Yosemite to Lassen, July is best, and north of Lassen June is best. North of Castle Crags and Interstate 5 there is not much of a drought or a snow problem, so you can do this part any time in the summer, though perhaps July is best. Clearly, if you travel the trail end to end, you cannot be in each area at its best time.

If you can't spare six months or so for the whole trail, decide how long you do have to spend. Then decide which part of the PCT you would like to see. Now, match up days available with overall mileage of that part of the PCT, using an estimate of:

- 20 miles a day if you are in top shape and don't want to see anything more than a blur
- 15 miles a day if you are in good shape and don't want to take any layover days
- 10 miles a day if you are in good shape and want to lay over every third day
- 10 miles a day if you are in fair shape and want to suffer

- 5 miles a day if you are in fair shape and want to enjoy yourself
- 2 miles a day if your companion is an attractive person of the opposite sex and you both enjoy wildflowers too.

After you decide which segment of the PCT you want to do, next comes the question of transportation. Buses are almost the only public transportation to places on or near the trail. Greyhound bus stops are listed at the end of this chapter. Instead you may choose to hitchhike. Or you might possibly take a car. A list of highways that cross or come close to the PCT appears at the end of this chapter.

Unlike round trips and loop trips, a hike along part of the PCT does not take you back to where you started. So if you take a car and leave it at the trailhead, you have a transportation problem. The solution may be any of several:

- walk back to where you started
- take a bus back to where you started
- hitchhike back to where you started
- arrange for someone to drop you off and pick you up
- arrange with another group to meet halfway along the trail and exchange car keys
- take at least two people and two cars, and leave one car at each end of your trek
- take a bicycle in your car, ride it to your trailhead, and after walking your section pick it up with the car
- abandon your car (this is quite illegal)

After you have decided on a solution to the car problem, write it down and put it in your pack. You might forget.

If you are going to be on the trail for more than a couple of weeks, you will want to have supplies waiting for you somewhere along the route. On the following pages is a list of places on or near the route where you can mail a package to yourself. Alternatively, you could drive there and leave the package with someone, if you can assure yourself in advance that the person will watch over it.

The main thing to mail yourself, of course, is food—nourishing, lightweight, backpacking food. You can also make a hidden cache along the trail, but that entails some risk. In addition, depending on the length of your trek, you may mail clothing, flashlight batteries, medicine and other consumable items. Then, if you are doing the whole trail from Mexico to Canada, you will use up about four pairs of boot soles, and unless you are a good cobbler, that will require mailing three pairs of boots to yourself. As for fuel, do not mail white gas, but you may mail butane or propane cartridges.

There are a few towns near the PCT which will perhaps have adequate supplies and equipment–Idyllwild, Mentone, Big Bear City, Mojave, South Lake Tahoe, Burney, Dunsmuir. However, even those towns may not have lightweight backpacking food. It is best to depend on post offices. A list of post offices on or near the trail appears at the end of this chapter.

Hikers who are used to the High Sierra or the Cascades may be out of the habit of worrying about water, since it is seldom far away, even in late summer. But dehydration can be a problem along parts of the PCT. The trail description mentions every place where you will have to hike more than five miles between watering spots. Of course, some years are wetter than others, and, moreover, if you are hiking in early summer, you can probably ignore most of these warnings.

## Backpacking Basics

Some hikers have emerged from the mountains with the scent of laurel and pine on their clothing and with dust on their boots, tired but enriched–both physically and mentally–by their wilderness experience. Others have stumbled out of the mountains exhausted, footsore, sunburned, dehydrated, chilled, with clothing and skin torn by thorny chaparral, or soaked to the bone by unexpected downpour, sadder but wiser for their ordeal. Some have had to be carried out. And a few have not come out.

An outing in the mountains can be many things–fabulous, pleasant, unpleasant, harrowing or disastrous. How it turns out depends to a large degree on the hiker himself–his preparation, his clothing and equipment, his physical condition, and his good sense.

Below is some basic advice that will help make your mountain trip an enjoyable and rewarding experience.

### Clothing

Mountain weather can vary considerably, even within a few hours. It is best to come prepared for both warm and cool temperatures with several layers of clothing–shirt, sweater and windbreaker, for example–that can be put on or peeled off as needed. This is particularly advisable for high-altitude trips.

Short pants may be satisfactory when walking a fire road or rambling through an open forest at middle elevations, but they are miserable for thrashing through chaparral. If any part of your trip is through chaparral, wear sturdy long pants.

Choice of headgear depends on the hiker. If you sunburn easily, you'll probably want a hat with generous brim. Since the weather may be threatening, bring raingear.

## Footgear

If your hike is short and on good trail, tennis shoes are adequate. But if your trip is long or over rough terrain, a pair of sturdy boots, preferably with lug soles, should be worn.

Proper shoe fit and close-fitting, heavy-duty socks are essential to prevent blisters and sore feet. A mistake in footwear can ruin your trip. Break in new boots on short walks before you attempt a long hike. If you blister easily, carry moleskin, and use it at the first hint of oncoming trouble.

## Food

Trail menus vary considerably, and there is little agreement among experts about what foods are best. However, what you eat may not be as important as how much you eat, and when. Small lunches and snacks along the trail are best, because exertion after a feast causes stomach and hiking muscles to compete for blood, and leads to indigestion and weakness.

On a hike liquid is as important as food. Without enough water, exertion and heat dehydrate the body surprisingly soon and cause marked muscular weakness. Unless you are hiking alongside a stream or in an area laced with runoff rills, carry a full canteen—two if the weather is hot and your walk is long. If you plan to do one of the drier PCT stretches, plan in terms of gallons rather than quarts. (See the data on water requirements on page 68).

## On the trail

Walking a mountain trail is not as simple as one might think. An enjoyable hike requires proper pace and rest stops, knowledge of the terrain, correct reading of trail signs and, above all, good judgment.

Unless you are training for the Olympics, a trail hike should not be a race to your destination. Start out slowly, easing your muscles into condition. Work up to the steady, rhythmic pace that suits you best. Your best trail speed is one at which you are working but not panting, and you feel you can continue almost indefinitely. When the trail steepens, shorten your steps but maintain your rhythm. Take short rests at moderate intervals, rather than stopping too frequently or too long at a time. If you are exceeding your ability, symptoms of exhaustion soon set in: sore or cramped leg muscles, profuse sweating, pounding pulse, headache, dizziness, redness of the face. Not only do these lessen your enjoyment, but a tired hiker is more accident-prone. The rambler who rushes up the trail, then collapses in a panting heap, is usually overtaken before long by the leisurely hiker. "Who goes into the mountains fast, comes out last," says an old proverb.

Stay on the trail. Short cuts not only break down the trail (see **Outdoor Courtesy** below) but can lead you astray. Probably the greatest temptation is to cut switchbacks–but sometimes the last zigzag doesn't zag, and you find yourself stumbling down a steep talus slope to nowhere, or thrashing through thorny brush in the wrong direction. When you finally realize your mistake, you are faced with the unpleasant necessity of churning back up the loose talus or beating through an ocean of chaparral–a painful, time-consuming object lesson in mountain sense.

## Off the trail

On slopes of loose talus or scree, tread lightly; even the most careful walker cannot avoid dislodging a few rocks or triggering a slide. Solid-looking boulders may be precariously balanced; you must be ever-ready to leap nimbly aside when a foothold suddenly gives way.

Stream crossing is an art mastered by few, and rare is the hiker who has never dampened his boots. If you cannot find a dry crossing–a series of steppingstones or a strategically located log –you must wade. It is better to wade the widest part of the stream, where the water is shallower, and the current is slower. If the streambed rocks are smooth, wade across barefoot. If they are sharp-edged, remove your socks and wear your boots across. Then drain your boots, dry your feet, and replace socks and boots.

Hiking over snow can be a pleasure if the grade is gentle and the snow firm but not icy. It can be tedious if the sun has softened the snow so much that you break through at every step. And it can be extremely dangerous if the slope is steep and the snow icy, as it often is in higher elevations during winter and early spring. If you plan to snow-hike, a pair of lug-soled boots are a necessity, preferably treated with a water-proof wax and worn with gaiters (waterproof leggings covering the upper part of the boot and part of the pant leg) to keep your feet dry. (An ice ax, and knowledge of how to use it, is a requirement for steep snow slopes. Serious climbing on snow and ice, requiring ice ax, crampons and rope, is only for skilled mountaineers. If you are interested, the Sierra Club offers a mountaineering course.)

## Backpacking equipment

As long as your pack weight is below 20 or 25 pounds, a rucksack is usually big enough and relatively comfortable. For long trail trips or for comfort with heavy loads, it is hard to beat the rectangular aluminum-and-nylon frame pack, which has attained great popularity in recent years. Whichever type you use, a waistband is important to place most of the weight on the hips rather than the shoulders.

For a good night's rest, you need a good sleeping bag. Down is the most efficient material for keeping you warm, but down bags are expensive. "All-feather" bags are about 80% as warm as down, and dacron bags about 66% as warm—per weight unit of filling. In late spring or summer below 8000 feet, chances are that nights will be mild, and a cheaper bag will be adequate. Otherwise, better go with down. "Mummy" and rectangular-shaped bags each have their adherents. Some people cannot tolerate the close fit of the mummy style, despite its thermal and weight advantages.

Other backpacking essentials include warm clothing, raingear, plastic ground cloth, air mattress or foam pad, utensils, cooking gear, flashlight, first-aid kit, snakebite kit, matches and toilet paper. During rainy season (winter and early spring) better tote a waterproof tent or—much less expensive—a plastic "tube tent" with nylon line.

## Emergencies

The first rule for survival in any outdoor emergency—be it losing your way, injury, snakebite, storm or fire—is common sense: make a calm, reasoned judgment of the situation and act accordingly. The biggest threat to survival is panic. Panicky hikers have been known to throw away their supplies and wander aimlessly for miles. According to mountain-rescue experts, 8 out of 10 survival-situation fatalities could have been prevented if the hiker had known survival techniques and had used common sense.

Getting lost is by far the most common crisis faced by hikers. If you ever face this prospect, awareness of several basic rules should spare you unnecessary strain, fatigue or injury, and maybe even your life. The minute you realize you are lost, stop and appraise the situation. If you are reasonably certain of your general location and have map and compass, try to retrace your steps, looking always for footprints and familiar landmarks. You may want to climb a nearby high point to survey the terrain for landmarks. Never take what you think is a "short cut" over unfamiliar terrain; you stand a chance of becoming hopelessly tangled in thorny chaparral or slipping down an unstable slope. If you are uncertain of your whereabouts, stay put. Never try to find your way at night. If you've told people where you were going, a search will be made, probably the next day. Try to stay warm by huddling against a tree, or if necessary by using branches, bark or pine needles to build a primitive shelter. Don't search extensively for food; water is far more critical. To attract help from the air (search-and-rescue teams make much use of the helicopter nowadays) hang out bright-colored clothing or other objects, but *do not* under any circumstances start a fire–you could burn down the forest, endangering your life and the lives of many others. A common distress signal is three signs, visible or audible, repeated at intervals–for example, three bright objects placed in a row or three shouts. If you manage to find your way out on your own, immediately notify the Forest Service, Park Service, or Sheriff's Office so that the search can be ended.

The best way to avoid being trapped in a storm is to stay out of the mountains when the weather is threatening. If you are caught in a sudden blizzard at higher elevations, descend as rapidly as you can with safety, but don't start down unfamiliar slopes that might lead to dropoffs or to box canyons. Stay off ridges and open saddles, where wind velocity often becomes extreme. At lower elevations in Southern California, your worry is water rather than snow and wind. Warm summer thunderstorms can drop more than 10 times as much water as a cold Sierra storm of the same size. Stay clear of canyon bottoms and gullies that may flash-flood. If you're on the trail, stay on it. If you try a short cut, your anxiety to get out, combined with the decreased visibility, could get you hopelessly lost. If you can't make it out, seek shelter in the hollow of a tree or under a rock overhang, away from the raging stream.

Fire in the California mountains can be a fearful thing. Chaparral, especially when it's tinder-dry in late summer and early fall, burns with unbelievable intensity, and wind can cause a brush fire to rampage at enormous speeds. If you see a fire in the mountains, even one that seems a safe distance away, get out fast and notify the Forest Service or other authorities–the fire could be upon you before you realize it. If you are confronted by a close-at-hand brush fire, you must act fast. Determine the wind direction—fire moves much more raidly downwind—and move laterally from that direction. Seek slopes and gullies where chaparral is sparse or absent—the fire may pass around these pockets. Or seek the refuge of a stream, preferably where brush does not crowd the banks. Many California forest and brush fires are caused by human carelessness, so make sure that no one in your party contributes to this tragic destruction.

## Outdoor Courtesy

Traveling a wild trail, away from centers of civilization, is a unique experience. It brings intimate association with nature—communion with the earth, the forest, the chaparral, the wildlife, the clear sky. A great responsibility accompanies this experience—the obligation to keep the wilderness as you found it. Being considerate of the wilderness rights of others will make the mountain adventures of those who follow equally rewarding.

As a wilderness visitor, you should become familiar with the rules of wilderness courtesy outlined below.

### Trails

Never cut switchbacks. This practice breaks down trails and hastens erosion. Take care not to dislodge rocks that might fall on hikers below you. Improve and preserve trails, as by clearing away loose rocks (carefully) and removing branches. Report any trail damage and broken or misplaced signs to a ranger.

### Off trail

Restrain the impulse to blaze trees or to build ducks where not essential. Let the next fellow find his way as you did.

### Campgrounds

Spread your gear in an already-cleared area, and build your fire in a campground stove. Don't disarrange the camp by making hard-to-eradicate ramparts of rock for fireplaces or windbreaks. Rig tents and tarps with line tied to rocks or trees; never put nails in trees. For your campfire, use fallen wood only; do not cut standing trees nor break off branches. Use the campground latrine. Place litter in the litter can or carry it out. Leave the campground cleaner than you found it.

### Fire

Fire is a great danger in the mountains, especially in southern California; act accordingly. Smoke only in cleared areas along the trail where a sign authorizes it. Report a mountain fire immediately.

### Litter

Along the trail, place candy wrappers, raisin boxes, orange peels, etc. in your pocket or pack for later disposal; throw nothing on the trail. Pick up litter you find along the trail or in camp. More than almost anything else, litter detracts from the wilderness scene. Remember, you can take it with you.

### Noise

Boisterous conduct is out of harmony in a wilderness experience. Be a considerate hiker and camper. Don't ruin another's enjoyment of the wilderness.

### Good Samaritanship

Human life and well-being take precedence over everything else—in the wilderness as elsewhere. If a hiker or camper is in trouble, help in any way you can. Indifference is a moral crime. Give comfort or first aid; then hurry to a ranger station for help.

## Land-use Regulations

The California portion of the PCT passes through national parks, national forests, state parks, land administered by the Bureau of Land Management and private land. All these areas have their own regulations, which you ignore only at your risk—risk of physical difficulty as well as possibility of being cited for violations.

On private land, of course, the regulations are what the owner says they are. The same is true on Indian lands. In particular, don't build a fire on private land without the owner's written permission.

Regulations on U.S. Bureau of Land Management land are not of major consequence for users of this book, since the route passes through only about 40 miles of it, mostly in the Tehachapis and southeast of San Gorgonio Wilderness. Fire permits are not required on desert lands in the public domain below 3500 feet elevation in southern California.

The Forest Service and the Park Service, for good reason, have more regulations. These are not uniform throughout the state, or as between the two services. We list below the Forest Service and Park Service regulations that *are* uniform along the trail, plus some that are peculiar to the Park Service. Special regulations in particular places are mentioned in the trail description when it "arrives" at the place.

1. ***Wilderness permits,*** which also serve as fire permits, are required to enter the Salmon-Trinity Primitive Area and all Wilderness areas, and for overnight stays in the back country of the National

Parks. They may be obtainted free on application from an area's headquarters or its ranger stations. If you intend to hike through several areas, write the Forest or Park in which you plan to start and request a National Park Service-U.S. Forest Service Joint-Use Wilderness Permit. If you are hiking the entire PCT, write Cleveland National Forest. The permit will be valid for the entire stretch. (See the list of headquarters at the end of this chapter.)

2. If you are hiking only in non-Wilderness and non-Park areas, you will still need a *campfire permit.* In northern California these are issued for the entire year. They may be obtained free at offices or stations of the U.S. Forest Service, U.S. Bureau of Land Management or California Division of Forestry.

In southern California within the Cleveland, San Bernardino and Angeles National Forests, a special campfire permit is necessary for each visit. Obtain this permit free from an office or station in the National Forest you are visiting.

Permits are not required in the public domain below the 3500′ elevation within the counties of Mono, Inyo, Kern, Los Angeles, San Bernardino, Riverside, San Diego and Imperial.

Campfire permits require each party to carry a shovel. If you don't build any fires but use only gas stoves, then you can leave the shovel behind but you'll still need the permit. A stove is particularly recommended for the high country, where dead and down wood is scarce. Rotting wood should be preserved, since it enriches the soil and and hosts organisms which larger animals feed on.

3. A California *fishing license* is required for all persons 16 years old or older who fish. The limit is 10 trout per day, with some exceptions, given in the state Department of Fish and Game regulations.

4. *Destruction,* injury, defacement, removal or distrubance in any manner of any natural feature or public property is prohibited. This includes:

a. Molesting any animal, picking flowers or other plants;
b. Cutting, blazing, marking, driving nails in, or otherwise damaging growing trees or standing snags;
c. Writing, carving or painting of name or other inscription anywhere;
d. Destruction, defacement or moving of signs.

5. *Collecting specimens* of minerals, plants, animals or historical objects is prohibited without written authorization, obtained in advance, from the Park Service or Forest Service. Permits are not issued for personal collections.

6. *Smoking* is not permitted while traveling through vegetated areas. You may stop and smoke in a safe place.

7. Pack and saddle *animals* have the right-of-way on trails. Hikers should get completely off the trail, on the downhill side if possible, and remain quiet until the stock has passed.

8. It is illegal to cut *switchbacks.*

9. Use *existing campsites* if there are any. If not, camp away from the trail and at least 100 feet from lakes and streams, on mineral soil or unvegetated forest floor–never in meadows or other soft, vegetated spots.

10. *Construction* of improvements such as rock walls, large fireplaces, bough beds, tables, and rock-and-log stream crossings is prohibited.

11. *Soap* and other pollutants should be kept out of lakes and streams. Use of detergents is not recommended, since they affect the water detrimentally.

12. *Toilets* should be in soft soil away from camps and water. Dig a shallow hole and bury all.

13. You are required to *clean up* your camp before you leave. Tin cans, foil, glass, worn-out or useless gear, and other unburnables must be carried out.

14. *National Parks but not Forests* prohibit dogs and cats on the trail and prohibit carrying or using firearms.

## Greyhound Bus Stops

### South to North

Palm Springs
Cabazon
Acton Jct.
Gorman
Tehachapi
Mojave
Lone Pine
Independence
Bishop
Rock Creek
Mammoth Lakes Jct.
Lee Vining
Yosemite Valley (local bus to Tuolumne Meadows)
South Lake Tahoe
Seasonal stops along Lake Tahoe west shore
Truckee
Quincy
Belden
Dunsmuir
Mt. Shasta
Ashland, Oregon

(Schedules change, of course. Check in advance to make sure which days the buses stop. Other bus lines may have additional or connecting schedules.)

## Highways That Cross or Come Near the Route

### South to North

State Highway 94
Interstate 8
San Diego County Highway S1
State Highway 78
State Highway 71
State Highway 74
Interstate 10
State Highway 38
State Highway 173
State Highway 138
Interstate 15
Angeles Crest Highway
Interstate 14
State Highway 138
Tehachapi-Willow Springs Road
State Highway 14 (US 6)
State Highway 178
State Highway 155
State Highway 120
State Highway 108
State Highway 4
State Highway 88
State Highway 50
Interstate 80
State Highway 49
State Highway 70
State Highway 32
State Highway 36
State Highway 44
State Highway 299
State Highway 89
Interstate 5
Whiskeytown–Callahan Road
Cecilville–Callahan Road
Sawyers Bar–Etna Road
State Highway 96
Interstate 5 (Ore.)

## Post Offices Along or Near the Route

### South to North

* = recommended for use

Some stations are seasonal. The best pickup time is weekdays 1-4 p.m. Hours of most are 9-12 and 1-5 or longer. Some are open Saturday mornings. Address your package to:

Yourself
General Delivery
P.O., state, ZIP
HOLD UNTIL (date)

Tecate 92080
* Campo 92006
* Mt. Laguna 92048
* Warner Springs 92086
* Anza 92306
* Cabazon 92230
White Water 92282
* Big Bear City 92314
Big Bear Lake 92315
Lake Arrowhead 92352
* Wrightwood 92397
* Acton 93510
* Lake Hughes 93532
* Monolith 93548
Tehachapi 93561
Mojave 93501
Cantil 93519
Lake Isabella 93240
Wofford Heights 93285
Kernville 93238
* Weldon 93283
Casa Vieja (see trail description)
Lone Pine 93545
Independence 93526
Cedar Grove 93633
Big Pine 93513
Bishop 93514
Mono Hot Springs 93642
* Red's Meadow 93546
Mammoth Lakes 93546
June Lake 93529
* Tuolumne Meadows 95389
* Lake Alpine 95235
Markleeville 96120
Woodfords 96120
Fallen Leaf 95716
S. Lake Tahoe 95705
Little Norway 95721
* Echo Lake 95721
Squaw Valley 93646
* Soda Springs 95728
* Sierra City 96125
* La Porte 95981
Meadow Valley 95956
Quincy 95971
* Belden 95915
* Old Station 96071
Hat Creek 96040
Cassel 96016
* Burney 96013
* Dunsmuir 96025
Castella 96017
* Sawyers Bar 96027
Etna 96027
* Seiad Valley 96086
* Ashland (Ore.) 97520

## Government Administrative Headquarters

### South to North

Cleveland National Forest
3211 5th Avenue
San Diego, CA 92103

San Bernardino N.F.
144 North Mountain View
San Bernardino, CA 92408

San Jacinto Wilderness
see San Bernardino N.F.

San Gorgonio Wilderness (alternate route)
see San Bernardino N.F.

Cucamonga Wilderness (alternate route)
see San Bernardino N.F.

Angeles National Forest
150 South Los Robles Avenue
Pasadena, CA 91101

Sequoia National Forest
900 West Grand Avenue
P.O. Box 391
Porterville, CA 93528

Sequoia National Park
Three Rivers, CA 93271

Kings Canyon National Park
Three Rivers, CA 93271

John Muir Wilderness
Inyo National Forest
2957 Birch Street
Bishop, CA 93514

Sierra National Forest
Federal Building
1130 "O" Street
Fresno, CA 93721

Minarets Wilderness
Inyo National Forest
2957 Birch Street
Bishop, CA 93514

Yosemite National Park
Box 577
Yosemite, CA 95389

Toiyabe National Forest
111 North Virginia Street
Reno, NV 89503

Stanislaus National Forest
175 South Fairview Lane
Sonora, CA 95370

Eldorado National Forest
100 Forni Road
Placerville, CA 95667

Desolation Wilderness
see Eldorado N.F.

Tahoe National Forest
Highway 49 & Coyote
Nevada City, CA 95959

Plumas National Forest
159 Lawrence Street
Quincy, CA 95971

Lassen National Forest
707 Nevada Street
Susanville, CA 96130

Lassen National Park
Mineral, CA 96063

Shasta-Trinity N.F.
1615 Continental Street
Redding, CA 96001

Salmon-Trinity Alps Primitive Area
see Shasta-Trinity N.F.

Klamath National Forest
1215 South Main
Yreka, CA 96097

Marble Mountain Wilderness
see Klamath N.F.

Rogue River National Forest
Medford, OR 97501

# 3
# Getting Ready To Appreciate the Trail

## Geology

It is very likely that the California section of the Pacific Crest Trail is unequaled in its diversity of geology. Many mountain trails cross glacial and subglacial landscapes, but which ones also cross arid and semi-arid landscapes? Some parts of your trail will have perennial snow; others are always dry. Precipitation may be more than 80 inches per year in places, less than 5 in others. In each of the three major rock classes–igneous, sedimentary and metamorphic–you'll encounter dozens of rock types. Because the PCT provides such a good introduction to a wide spectrum of geology, we have added a liberal dose of geologic description to the basic text. You start among granitic rocks at the Mexican border, and then we inform you of every new major rock outcrop you'll encounter along your trek northward. We hope that by the end of your journey you'll have developed a keen eye for rocks and that you'll understand the relations between the different rock types. Since we assume that many hikers will have only a minimal background in geology and its terminology, we'll try to cover this broad subject for them in the next few pages. Those wishing to pursue the subject further should consult the list of references at the end of this chapter.

### ROCKS

First, you should get acquainted with the three major rock classes: igneous, sedimentary and metamorphic.

#### Igneous rocks

Igneous rocks came into being when the liquid (molten) rock material (*magma*) solidified. If the material solidified beneath the earth's surface, the rock is called *intrusive,* or plutonic, and a body of it is a *pluton*. If the material reached the surface, and erupted as *lava,* the rock is called *extrusive,* or volcanic.

**Intrusive rocks.** The classification of an igneous rock is based on its texture, what minerals are in it, and the relative amounts of each mineral present. Since intrusive rocks cool more slowly than extrusive rocks, their crystals have a longer time to grow. If, in a rock, you can see an abundance of individual crystals, odds are that it is an intrusive rock. These rocks may be classified by crystal size: fine, medium or coarse-grained, to correspond to average diameters of less than 1 millimeter, 1-5, and greater than 5.

Some igneous rocks are composed of large crystals (*phenocrysts*) in a matrix of small crystals (*groundmass*). Such a rock is said to have a *porphyritic* texture. The Cathedral Peak pluton, which is well exposed on Lembert Dome at the east end of Tuolumne Meadows in Yosemite National Park, has some feldspar phenocrysts over four inches long. High up on the dome these phenocrysts protrude from the less resistant groundmass and provide rock climbers with the holds necessary to ascend the dome.

The common minerals in igneous rocks are quartz, feldspar, biotite, hornblende, pyroxene and olivine. The first two are light-colored minerals; the rest are dark. Not all are likely to be present in a piece of rock; indeed, quartz and olivine are never found together. Intrusive rocks are grouped according to the percentages of minerals in them. The three common igneous groups are *granite, diorite* and *gabbro.* Granite is rich in quartz and potassium feldspar and usually has only small amounts of biotite. Diorite is poor in quartz and rich in sodium feldspar, and may have three dark minerals. Gabbro, a *mafic* rock (rich in magnesium and iron), lacks quartz, but is rich in calcium feldspar and pyroxene, and may have hornblende and olivine. You can subdivide the granite-diorite continuum into granite, quartz monzonite, granodiorite, quartz diorite and diorite. These rocks, which are usually called "granitic rocks" or just plain "granite," are common in the Sierra Nevada and in most of the other ranges to the south. Since it is unlikely that you'll be carrying a polarizing microscope in your backpack, let alone a great deal of mineralogical expertise in your head, your best chance of identifying these granitic rocks lies in making educated guesses based upon the following table.

| rock | color | % dark minerals |
|---|---|---|
| granite | creamy white | 5 |
| quartz monzonite | very light gray | 10 |
| granodiorite | light gray | 20 |
| quartz diorite | medium gray | 30 |
| diorite | dark gray | 40 |
| gabbro | black | 60 |

At first you'll probably estimate too high a percentage of dark minerals, partly because they are more eye-catching and partly because they show through the glassy light minerals. If the intrusive rock is composed entirely of dark minerals (no quartz or feldspar), then it is an ultramafic rock. This rock type, which can be subdivided further, is common along the trail section northwest of Interstate 5 at Castle Crags State Park.

**Extrusive rocks.** Extrusive, or volcanic, rocks are composed of about the same minerals as intrusive rocks. *Rhyolite, andesite* and *basalt* have approximately the same chemical compositions as granite, diorite and gabbro, respectively. As with the intrusive rocks, these three volcanics can be subdivided into many groups so it is possible to find ordinary rocks with intimidating names like "quartz latite porphyry"–which is just a volcanic rock with quartz phenocrysts and a composition in between rhyolite and andesite.

Texture is the key feature distinguishing volcanic from plutonic rocks. Whereas you can see the individual crystals in a plutonic rock, you'll have a hard time finding them in a volcanic one. They may be entirely lacking, or so small, weathered and scarce that they'll just frustrate your attempts to identify them. If you can't recognize the crystals, then how can you identify the type of volcanic rock? Color is a poor indicator at best, for although rhyolites tend to be light gray, andesites dark gray, and basalts black, there is so much variation that each can be found in any shade of red, brown or gray.

One aid to identifying volcanic rock types is the landforms composed of them. For example, the high silica ($SiO_2$) content of rhyolite makes it very viscous, and hence the hot gases in rhyolite magma cause violent explosions when the magma nears the surface, forming *explosion pits* and associated rings of erupted material (*ejecta*). For the same reason a rhyolite lava flow (degassed magma) is thick, short, and steep-sided and may not even flow down a moderately steep slope. The Mono and Inyo craters, north of Devils Postpile National Monument, are perhaps the best examples of this volcanic rock in California. You will find very little of it along the trail.

You'll become very familiar with andesite, such as the flow that makes up the Devils Postpile. Most of the six-sided columnar flows you'll be encountering north of it will also be andesite. The landform characteristically associated with andesite is the *composite cone,* or volcano. Mt. Shasta and some of the peaks in the Lassen area, including Lassen Peak, are good examples. These mountains are built up by alternating flows and ejecta. In time *parasitic vents* may develop, such as the cone called Shastina on Mt. Shasta, and the composition of the volcano may shift to more silica-rich *dacite* rock, an intermediate between rhyolite and andesite, which gives rise to tremendous eruptions, like several at Lassen Peak.

The least siliceous and also the least explosive of volcanic rocks is basalt. A basaltic eruption typically produces a cinder cone, rarely over 2000 feet high, and a very fluid, thin flow. When in Lassen Volcanic National Park, take the alternate route up to the rim of the Cinder Cone. From this vantage point you can see what an extensive, relatively flat area its thin flows covered. Contrast this with Lassen Peak, to the west, with its steep-sided massive bulk armed with protruding dacite domes.

## Sedimentary rocks

We often think of rocks as being eternal–indeed, they do last a long time. But even the most resistant polished granite eventually succumbs to the effects of physical and chemical weathering. Next time you're in an old stone granite building, take a look at the steps, even the inside ones. Chances are you'll notice some wear. Constant traffic may account for some of it, but even more may be attributed to their use on rainy days and to repeated cleanings with solutions. In most environments, chemical wear is greater than physical wear. Granite rocks solidified under high pressures and rather high temperatures within the earth. At the surface, pressure and temperature are lower and the rock's chemical environment is different, and in this environment it is unstable. The rocks weather and are gradually transported to a place of deposition. This place may be a lake in the High Sierra, a closed basin with no outlet such as the Mono Lake basin, an open structure such as the great Central Valley, or even the continental shelf of the Pacific Ocean. The rocks formed of the sediment that collects in these basins are called sedimentary rocks.

Most sedimentary rocks are classified by the size of their particles: clay that has been compacted and cemented forms *shale*; silt forms *siltstone,* and sand forms *sandstone.* Sandstone derived from granitic rock superficially resembles its parent rock, but if you look closely, you'll notice that the grains are somewhat rounded and that the spaces between the grains are usually filled with a cement, usually calcite. Pebbles, cobbles and boulders may be cemented in a sand or gravel matrix to form a *conglomerate.* If the larger particles are angular rather than rounded, the resulting rock is called a *breccia.*

*Limestone,* another type of sedimentary rock, is formed in some marine environments as a chemical precipitate of dissolved calcium carbonate or from fragments of shells, corals and foraminifers. The individual grains are usually microscopic. If the calcium in limestone is partly replaced, the result is *dolomite.*

Since the PCT attempts to follow a crest, you'll usually find yourself in an area being eroded, rather than in a basin of deposition, so you'll find very ephemeral sediments or very old ones. The young ones may be in the form of alluvium, talus slopes, glacial moraines or lake sediments. The old ones are usually resistant sediments that the intruding granitic plutons bent (*folded*), broke (*faulted*) and changed (*metamorphosed*).

## Metamorphic rocks

A volcanic or sedimentary rock which undergoes enough alteration (metamorphism) due to heat and pressure that it loses its original characteristics becomes a *metavolcanic* or *metasedimentary* rock. Metamorphism may be slight or it may be complete. A shale undergoing progressive metamorphism becomes first a *slate,* second a *phyllite,* then a *schist.* The slate resembles the shale but is noticeably harder. The schist bears little resemblance and is well-foliated with flaky minerals such as biotite or other micas clearly visible.

*Hornfels* is a hard, massive rock, common in parts of the High Sierra, formed by contact of an ascending pluton with the overlying sediments. It can take on a variety of forms. You might find one that looks and feels like a slate, but it differs in that it breaks across the sediment layers rather than between them.

*Gneiss* is a coarse-grained metamorphic rock with the appearance of a layered granitic rock. *Quartzite* is a metamorphosed sandstone and resembles the parent rock. The spaces between the grains have become filled with silica, so that now if the rock is broken, the fracture passes through the quartz grains rather than between them as in sandstone. Metamorphism of limestone yields *marble,* which is just a crystalline form of the parent rock. Check out Marble Mountain when you reach it.

**Glacial erratic boulder**

*Don Masulis*

# GEOLOGIC TIME

You cannot develop a feeling for geology unless you appreciate the great span of time that geologic processes have had to operate within. A few million years' duration is little more than an instant on the vast geologic time scale (see Geologic Time Table). Within this duration a volcano may be born, die and erode away. Several major "ice ages" may come and go.

A mountain range takes longer to form. Granitic plutons of the Sierra Nevada first made their appearance in the late Jurassic, and intrusion of them continued through most of the Cretaceous, a span of 60 million years. Usually there is a considerable gap in the geologic record between the granitic rocks and the sediments and volcanics that they intrude–often better than 100 million years.

## GEOLOGIC TIME TABLE

| Era | Period | Epoch | Began (years ago) | Duration (years) |
|---|---|---|---|---|
| Cenozoic | Quaternary | Holocene | 12,000 | 12,000 |
| | | Pleistocene | 3,000,000 | 3,000,000 |
| | Tertiary | Pliocene | 11,000,000 | 8,000,000 |
| | | Miocene | 25,000,000 | 14,000,000 |
| | | Oligocene | 40,000,000 | 15,000,000 |
| | | Eocene | 60,000,000 | 20,000,000 |
| | | Paleocene | 70,000,000 | 10,000,000 |
| Mesozoic | Cretaceous | *Numerous* | 135,000,000 | 65,000,000 |
| | Jurassic | *epochs* | 180,000,000 | 45,000,000 |
| | Triassic | *recognized* | 225,000,000 | 45,000,000 |
| Paleozoic | Permian | *Numerous* | 280,000,000 | 55,000,000 |
| | Carboniferous | | 345,000,000 | 65,000,000 |
| | Devonian | *epochs* | 400,000,000 | 55,000,000 |
| | Silurian | | 440,000,000 | 40,000,000 |
| | Ordovician | *recognized* | 500,000,000 | 60,000,000 |
| | Cambrian | | 570,000,000 | 70,000,000 |
| Pre-cambrian | No formally accepted chronostratigraphic units; oldest rocks are about 3 billion years old; Earth is about 4½ billion years old. | | | |

## GEOLOGIC HISTORY

With the aid of a geologic section, like the one on the next page, we can reconstruct the geologic history of an area. Our example represents an idealized slice across the Sierra Nevada to reveal the rocks and their relations.

Through dating methods that use radioactive materials, geologists can obtain the absolute ages of the two granitic plutons, the andesite flow and the basalt flow, which would likely be Cretaceous, Pliocene and Holocene. The overlying, folded sediments intruded by the plutons would have to be pre-Cretaceous. The metabasalt could be dated, but the age arrived at may be for the time of its metamorphism rather than for its formation. A paleontologist examining fossils from the marble and slate might conclude that these rocks are from the Paleozoic Era.

Before metamorphism the Paleozoic slate, quartzite, metabasalt and marble would have been shale, sandstone, basalt and limestone. The shale-sandstone sequence might indicate marine sediments being deposited on a continental shelf, then on a coastal plain. Lack of transitional rocks between the shale and the sandstone leads us to conclude that they were eroded away, creating a gap in the geologic record. We then have an *unconformity* between the two *strata* (layers), the upper resting on the *erosional surface* of the lower. The basalt, shale and limestone sequence indicate first localized volcanism followed by a marine then a shallow-water environment.

These Paleozoic rocks remained buried and protected from erosion for eons of time until the intrusion of granitic plutons, associated with regional uplift. Radiometric dating would show that the quartz monzonite pluton was emplaced before the granodiorite pluton. Field observations would verify this sequence because the latter intrudes the former as well as the overlying sediments. During this period of mountain building, the Paleozoic rocks became folded, metamorphosed and often faulted.

As the range continued to grow, erosion removed much of the Paleozoic rocks, cut into the granodiorite and rounded the topography. Then in the Pliocene volcanic eruptions to the east spewed andesite flows westward down the gentle valleys. In our geologic section, a remnant of a flow, resting on the bottom of a granitic valley, is preserved today as a high ridge.

Uplift quickly followed this volcanism as faults developed along the east side of the range, and it tipped westward. This tipping caused the andesite flow to have a steeper apparent gradient than it had when it solidified. These faults were mostly more or less vertical, unlike the horizontal direction of the right-lateral San

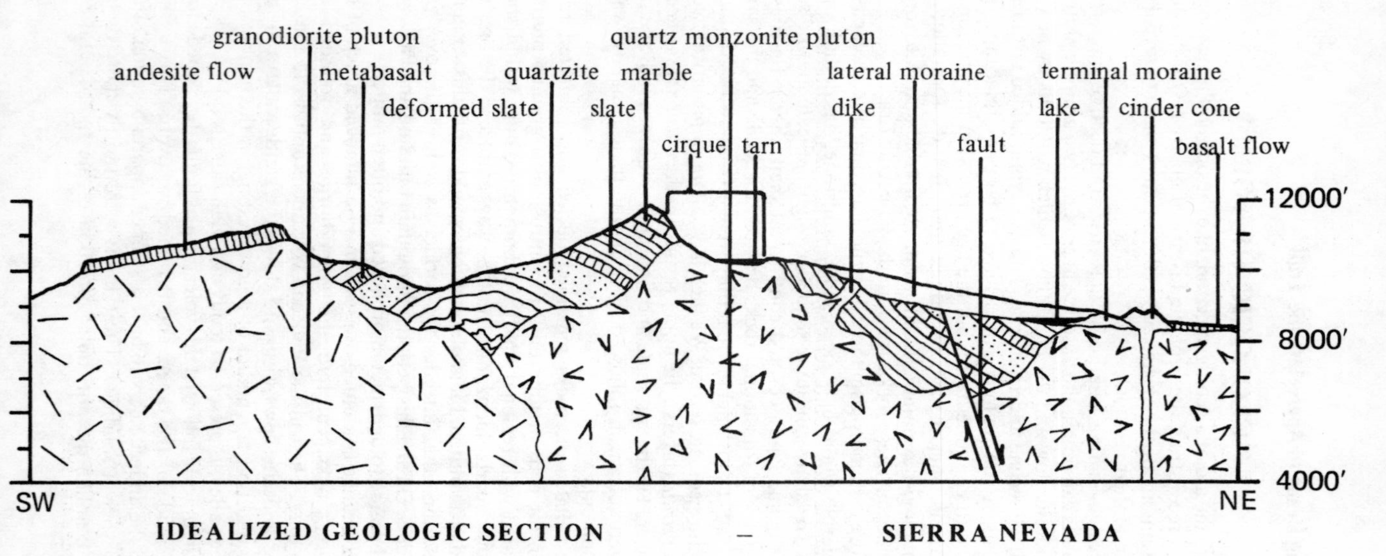


IDEALIZED GEOLOGIC SECTION – SIERRA NEVADA

Andreas Fault (during an earthquake, objects on the opposite side of the fault appear to shift to the right). Most faults exhibit a combination of vertical and horizontal movement. Since the fault in this section does not offset the lateral *moraine,* it must have stopped its activity before the Pleistocene. (Note that this is not a true section, since it has a dimension of width: the lateral moraine alongside the canyon floor, included for illustrative purposes, is really beneath the plane of the paper.)

During the Pleistocene epoch, glaciers carved and scoured the canyon east of the high peak, and they deposited massive boulders and other debris along their sides and end. Today we see this preserved evidence of glaciation as lateral and terminal moraines. The steep-walled *cirque* and its bedrock lake (tarn) together with a moraine-dammed lake, are further signs of glaciation.

After this Ice Age a cinder cone erupted and partly overlapped the terminal moraine, thereby indicating that it is younger. A radiometric date would verify its youth. Erosion is attacking the range today, as it did in the past, ever seeking to reduce the landscape to sea level.

When you encounter a contact between two rocks along the trail, you might ask yourself: Which rock is younger? Which older? Has faulting, folding or metamorphism occurred? Is there a gap in the geologic record? When you can begin to answer these questions, you'll feel a great satisfaction as you slowly solve this great geologic jigsaw puzzle.

## Recommended Reading

American Geological Institute, *Dictionary of Geological Terms,* Garden City: Dolphin Books, 1962.

Bailey, Edgar H., ed., *Geology of Northern California* (California Division of Mines and Geology, Bulletin 190). Sacramento: California Division of Mines and Geology, 1966.

Brown, Vinson, and David, Allan, *Rocks and Minerals of California,* 2nd rev. ed. Healdsburg: Naturegraph, 1964.

Oakeshott, Gordon B., *California's Changing Landscapes.* San Francisco: McGraw-Hill, 1971.

Pough, Frederick H., *A Field Guide to Rocks and Minerals,* 3rd ed. Boston: Houghton Mifflin, 1960.

Putnam, William C., *Geology,* 2nd ed. New York: Oxford University Press, 1971.

Sharp, Robert P., *Geology: Field Guide to Southern California.* Dubuque: William C. Brown, 1972.

Shelton, John S., *Geology Illustrated.* San Francisco: W. H. Freeman, 1966.

# Biology

One's first guess about the Pacific Crest Trail–a high adventure rich in magnificent alpine scenery and sweeping panoramas–turns out to be incorrect along some parts of the trail. The real-life trail hike will sometimes seem to consist of enduring many repetitious miles of hot, dusty roads, battling hordes of mosquitoes, or slogging up seemingly endless switchbacks. If you find yourself bogged down in such unpleasant impressions, it may be because you haven't developed an appreciation of the natural history of this remarkable route. There is a great variety of plants and animals, rocks and minerals, landscapes and climates along the PCT, and the more you know about each, the more you will enjoy your trek.

Even if you don't know much about basic ecology, you can't help noticing that the natural scene along the Pacific Crest Trail changes with elevation. The most obvious changes are in the trees, just because trees are the most obvious–the largest–organisms. Furthermore, they don't move around, hide, or migrate in their lifetime, as do animals. When you pay close attention, you notice that not only the trees but the shrubs, flowers and grasses also change with elevation. Then you begin to find altitudinal differences in the animal populations. In other words, there are different *life zones*. Of 7 zones, ranging from tropical at the tip of Florida to arctic in northern Alaska, 6 are found in California.

When you ascend San Gorgonio Mountain from its southern base, you pass through all the same zones that you would if you walked from southern California north to Alaska. It turns out that 100 feet of elevation are about equivalent to 17 miles of latitude. This means that, in terms of the life, walking north from Devils Postpile National Monument to the northern border of Lassen Volcanic National Park, 200 miles north, is like ascending about 1200 feet. Therefore, if you started your hike in the mosquito-infested lodgepole forest at Devils Postpile and walked north on the level to the Lassen Park area, you should finish 1200 feet above the forest. In reality, you start in the lodgepole forest, drop 1200 feet overall, and end up in a lodgepole forest anyway, inhabited by droves of mosquitoes.

We can also correlate change in elevation with change in time of year, using the ratio of one day = 100 feet. If the mosquitoes hatch on June 23 at Susie Lake in Desolation Wilderness, they should hatch on June 24 at Heather Lake, which is 100 feet higher. Obviously, a careful planner could spend his whole summer in a cloud of mosquitoes, if he could average a northward hike of 17 miles a day. More felicitously, he could watch a single species of flower, such as corn lily, bloom every day.

## FLORA

A professional botanist, if he had the time and energy, could identify perhaps 3000 plant species along the PCT route. Other hikers may discover "only" a couple hundred species; and some will just see trees, bushes and flowers. If you can spare the luxury of an additional 10 ounces, then obtain a copy of *Sierra Nevada Natural History,* which identifies over 270 plants and 480 animals. Not only does it provide identifying characteristics of species; it also describes their habitats and gives other interesting facts. Its title is misleading, for it is applicable to about 75% of the PCT route: Mt. Laguna, the San Jacinto, San Bernardino and San Gabriel mountains, and from the Sierra Nevada north to the Oregon border.

**Wildflowers.** Limitations of space prevent us from listing the hundreds of common wildflower species you'll encounter along the trail. Furthermore, the ephemeral nature is such that most species will be in bloom for only a fraction of the growing season. For example, if you were to look for flowers at three-week intervals around the Quail Meadows area (7800′), which is about the midpoint on the John Muir Trail, here is a partial list of what you might find:

| June 30 | July 20 | August 10 |
|---|---|---|
| corn lily | buckwheat | evening primrose |
| Douglas phlox | clarkia | fireweed |
| false solomon's seal | groundsel | meadow goldenrod |
| larkspur | mountain hemp | meadow hosackia |
| monkey flower | red columbine | phacelia |
| paintbrush | rock cress | scarlet gilia |
| penstemon | rose everlasting | Sierra forget-me-not |
| pussy paws | Sierra rein-orchis | tiger lily |
| streptanthus | western mtn. aster | yarrow milfoil |
| wall flower | wild geranium | yellow cinquefoil |

**Trees you will have to know.** There are 4 decision points mentioned in this guidebook for which the route is not evident and you will have to recognize a particular tree species in order to stay on route. We mention each species a number of times before you arrive at its decision point; this gives you an opportunity to become familiar with it. The 4 species and points in question are:

*silver pine* – Round Valley, north of Soda Springs
*red fir* – Basin Peak slopes, north of Round Valley
*Jeffrey pine* – Emigrant Trail, Lassen National Park
*lodgepole pine* – Lake Helen area, west of Castle Crags

Identifying them is quite easy, since all the "guidepost" trees are large and mature.

The silver pine has a checkerboard bark pattern and finger-length needles in clumps of 5's or 4's. This majestic tree has slender, tapered, slightly curved cones 6 to 8 inches long.

The deeply corrugated, dark red bark of the red fir makes this tree easy to identify. Short, upcurving needles grow on the branchlets. Its fist-sized cones, as on all true firs, perch atop the branches rather than hang from them, as pine and Douglas-fir cones do.

Can you identify a tree with your nose? Yes! Stick it in a deep furrow of the suspected tree. A pleasant aroma of vanilla or butterscotch identifies the Jeffrey pine. Three long needles per bunch, and robust, canteloupe-sized cones are additional characteristics.

If you've reclined against a scaly, thin-barked tree, then stood up with a sap-covered back, chances are you've identified a lodgepole pine, which, like the incense cedar of lower elevations, is an adverse canopy to camp under. This rarely impressive tree has diminutive features compared to the other three species in question. Rarely over 100 feet tall, it has a thin-barked, narrow trunk, small, wide cones, and short needles in groups of two.

The more trees you get to know, the more you will appreciate your hike. The same can be said about the minerals, rocks, animals and other plants. Nevertheless, since trees are very conspicuous, approachable and readily identified, it would be worth your effort to include a copy of the *California Tree Finder,* 1½ ounces light, with your equipment. Over 60 of its trees and large shrubs can be found along the trail.

**Plant geography.** Every plant (and every animal) has its own *range, habitat* and *niche.* Some species have a very restricted range; others, a very widespread one. The Sequoia, for example, occurs only in about 30 small groves at mid-elevations in the western Sierra Nevada. It flourishes in a habitat of tall conifers growing on shaded, gentle, well-drained slopes. Its niche–its role in the community–consists in its complex interaction with its environment and every other species in its environment. Dozens of insects utilize the Sequoia's needles and cones, and additional organisms thrive in its surrounding soil. The woolly sunflower, on the other hand, has a tremendous range: from California north to British Columbia and east to the Rocky Mountains. It can be found in brushy habitats from near sea level up to 10,000 feet.

Some species, evidently, can adapt to environments and competitors better than others. Nevertheless, each is restricted by a complex interplay of *climatic, physiographic* (topography), *edaphic* (soil) and *biotic* influences.

**Climatic influences.** Of all influences, temperature and precipitation are probably the most important. Although the mean temperature tends to increase toward the equator, this pattern is camouflaged in California by the dominating effect of the state's highly varied topography. Temperature decreases between 3° and 5.5° F for every 1000-foot gain in elevation, and vegetational changes reflect this cooling trend. For example, the vegetation along San Gorgonio Pass in southern California is adapted to its desert environment. Annuals are very ephemeral; they quickly grow, blossom and die after heavy rains. Perennials are succulent or woody, have deep roots, and have small, hard or waxy leaves —or no leaves at all. Only the lush cottonwoods and other associated species along the dry streambeds hint at a source of water.

As you climb north up the slopes of San Gorgonio Mountain, not only does the temperature drop, but the annual precipitation increases. On the gravelly desert floor below, only a sparse, drought-adapted vegetation survives the searing summer temperatures and the miserly 10-inch precipitation. A doubled precipitation on the mountainside allows growth of chaparral, here a thick stand of whitebark soapbloom, birchleaf mountain mahogany, Gregg's ceanothus and great-berried manzanita. By 7000 feet the precipitation has increased to 40 inches, and the moisture-loving conifers—first Jeffrey pine, then lodgepole pine and white fir—predominate. As the temperature steadily decreases with elevation, evaporation of soil water and transpiration of moisture from plant needles and leaves are both reduced. Furthermore, up here the precipitation may be in the form of snow, which is preserved for months by the shade of the forest, and even when it melts is retained by the highly absorbent humus (decayed organic matter) of the forest soil. Consequently, an inch of precipitation on the higher slopes is far more effective than an inch on the exposed, gravelly desert floor.

**Physiographic influences.** As we have seen, the elevation largely governs the regime of temperature and precipitation. For a *given* elevation, the mean maximum temperature in northern California is about 10° F less than that of the San Bernardino area. Annual precipitation, however, is considerably more; it ranges from about 20 inches in the Sacramento Valley to 80 inches along the higher slopes, where the snowpack may last well into summer. When you climb out of a canyon in the Feather River country, you start among live oak, poison oak and California laurel, and ascend through successive stands of Douglas fir and black oak, incense cedar and ponderosa pine, white fir and sugar pine, then finally red fir, lodgepole and silver pine.

The country near the Oregon border is one of lower elevations and greater precipitation which produces a wetter-but-milder climate that is reflected in the distribution of plant species. Seiad Valley is hemmed in with forests of Douglas fir, tan oak, madrone and canyon live oak. At higher elevations, mountain chaparral and knobcone pine cover your route. When you reach Cook and Green Pass (4750′) you reach a forest of white fir and noble fir. To the east, at higher elevations, you encounter weeping spruce.

A low minimum temperature, like a high maximum one, can determine where a plant species lives, since freezing temperatures can kill poorly adapted plants by causing ice crystals to form in their protoplasm. At high elevations, the gnarled, grotesque trunks of the whitebark, limber and foxtail pines give stark testimony to their battle against the elements. The wind-cropped, short-needled foliage is sparse at best, for the growing season lasts but two months, and a killing frost is possible in every month. Samples of this subalpine forest are found on the upper slopes of the higher peaks in the San Jacinto, San Bernardino and San Gabriel mountains and along much of the John Muir Trail. Along the High Sierra crest and on the summits of Mt. Baldy and San Gorgonio Mountain, all vestiges of forest surrender to rocky, barren slopes pioneered only by the most stalwart perennials, such as alpine willow and alpine buttercup.

Other physiographic influences are the *location, steepness, orientation* and *shape* of slopes. North-facing slopes are cooler and tend to be wetter than south-facing slopes. Hence, on north-facing slopes, you'll encounter red-fir forests which at the ridgeline abruptly give way to a dense cover of manzanita and ceanothus on south-facing slopes. Extremely steep slopes may never develop a deep soil or support a coniferous forest, and of course cliffs will be devoid of vegetation other than crustose lichens, secluded mosses, scattered annuals and perhaps a tenacious weather-beaten Sierra juniper.

**Edaphic influences.** Along the northern part of your trek, at the headwaters of the Trinity River and just below Seiad Valley, you'll encounter outcrops of serpentine, California's official state rock. This rock weathers to form a soil poor in some vital plant nutrients but rich in certain undesirable heavy metals. Nevertheless, there are numerous species, such as leather oak, that are specifically or generally associated with serpentine-derived soil. There is a species of streptanthus (mustard family) found only in this soil, even though it can grow better on other soils. However, experiments demonstrate that it cannot withstand the competition of other plants growing on these soils. It therefore struggles, yet propagates, within its protected environment. Another example is at Marble Mountain, also in northern California, which has a local assemblage of plants that have adapted to the mountain's limey soil.

A soil can change over time and with it, the vegetation. If a forest on a slope is burned, the organic layer on the forest floor is destroyed, leaving only charred stumps as tombstones. With no protective cover, the rest of the soil is soon attacked by the forces of erosion. This mute landscape may still receive as much precipitation as a neighboring slope, but its effective precipitation is much less; it will take years to make a recovery. Herbs and shrubs will have to pioneer the slope and slowly build up a humus-rich soil again.

**Biotic influences.** In an arid environment, plants competing for water may evolve special mechanisms besides their water-retaining mechanisms. The creosote bush, for example, in an effort to preserve its limited supply of water, secretes toxins which prevent nearby seeds from germinating. The result is an economical spacing of bushes along the desert floor.

Competition is manifold everywhere. On a descending trek past a string of alpine lakes, you might see several stages of plant succession. The highest lake may be pristine, bordered only by tufts of grass between the lichen-crusted rocks. A lower lake may exhibit an invasion of grasses, sedges and pondweeds thriving on the sediments deposited at its inlet. Corn lilies and lemmon willows border its edge. Farther down, a wet meadow may be the remnant of a past lake. Water birch and lodgepole pine then make their debut. Finally, you reach the last lake bed, recognized only by the flatness of the forest floor and a few boulders of a recessional moraine (glacial deposit) that dammed the lake. In this location, a thick stand of white fir has overshadowed and eliminated much of the underlying lodgepole.

When a species becomes too extensive, it invites attack. The large, pure stand of lodgepole pine near Tuolumne Meadows has for years been under an unrelenting attack by a moth known as the lodgepole needle-miner. One of the hazards of a pure stand of one species is the inherent instability of the system. Within well-mixed forests, lodgepoles are scattered and the needle miner is not much of a problem.

Unquestionably, the greatest biotic agent is man. For example, he has supplanted native species with introduced species. Most of California's native bunchgrass is gone, together with the animals that grazed upon it, replaced by thousands of acres of one-crop fields and by suburban sprawl. Forests near some mining towns have been virtually eliminated. Others have been subjected to ravenous scars inflicted by man-made fires and by clear-cutting logging practices. The Los Angeles basin's smog production has already begun to take its toll of mountain conifers, and Sierra forests may soon experience a similar fate. Wide-scale use of pesticides has not eliminated the pests, but it has greatly reduced the pests' natural predators. Through forestry, agriculture and urban practices, man has attempted to simplify nature, and by upsetting its checks and balances has made it unstable. Along the Pacific Crest Trail, you'll see areas virtually unaffected by man as well as areas greatly affected by man. When you notice the difference, you'll have something to ponder as you stride along the quiet trail.

## FAUNA

We have seen how plants adapt to a variety of influences from the environment and from other species. Animals, like plants, are also subject to a variety of influences, but they have the added advantage of mobility. On a hot summer day, a beetle under a scant cover of chaparral can escape the merciless sun by seeking protection under a loose rock or under a mat of dried leaves.

Larger animals, of course, have greater mobility and therefore can better overcome the difficulties of the environment. Reptiles, birds and mammals may frequent the trail, but they scatter when you—the intruder—approach. At popular campsites, however, such as those in Yosemite, the animals come out to meet you, or more exactly, to obtain your food. Of course, almost anywhere along the trail you may encounter the ubiquitous mosquito, always looking for a free meal. But in popular campsites you'll meet the robin, the Steller jay, the Clark nutcracker, the mule deer, the Allen, lodgepole and alpine chipmunks, the golden-mantled and Belding ground squirrels, and at night, the black bear. You may be tempted to feed them, or they may try to help themselves, but please protect them from your food—they will survive better on the real, "organic" food Mother Nature produces. Furthermore, an artificially large population supported by generous summer backpackers may in winter overgraze the vegetation. In the three following examples, we'll take a closer look at population dynamics.

**Mule deer.** This large mammal can be found along the entire California section of the Pacific Crest Trail except for the temporary Tehachapi bypass through the western Mojave Desert. Mule deer, like other herbivores, do not eat every type of plant they encounter, but tend to be quite specific in their search for food. They typically browse the new vegetation on oaks, ceanothus, bitterbrush, cherries and silk tassel; seasonally they may also consume grasses and forbs. Together with other herbivores, parasites and saprophytes (organisms feeding on decaying organic matter), they take care of a small portion of the 100 billion tons of organic matter produced annually on the earth by plants.

Mule deer face a considerable population problem: they have lost some of their predators. With the arrival of "civilized" man in California, the wolves and the grizzly bears were exterminated. In their places, coyotes and black bears have increased in numbers. Coyotes, however, feed principally on rabbits and rodents, and only occasionally attack a fawn or a sick deer. Black bears occasionally kill fawns. The mountain lion, a true specialist in feeding habits, preys mainly on deer. This magnificent animal, unfortunately, has been unjustly persecuted by man, and now many deer that are saved from the big cat are lost to starvation and disease. The California deer population, over one million individuals today, is in poorer health overall than it was a century ago. California's increasing human population compounds the problem. The expansion of settlements causes the big cats to retreat farther, which leaves them farther from the suburban deer. Forests must be logged to feed this expansion of cities, and then the logged-over areas sprout an assemblage of shrubs that are a feast for the deer. The deer population responds to this new food supply by increasing. But then the shrubs mature or the forest grows back, and there is less food for the larger deer population. The larger herd is faced with starvation. The ever-increasing brush fires in California produce the same feast-followed-by-famine effect.

**Porcupine.** Your chances of seeing this large, lumbering rodent are fairly slim except perhaps during a night visit in its search for salt. Otherwise, it keeps to itself and is rarely seen by the hiker, even though it inhabits Douglas-fir, ponderosa-pine and lodgepole-pine forests. If you happen to notice a conifer with a ring of bark missing, chances are the bark was gnawed off by a porcupine that was dining on the tree's succulent inner bark. By girdling the cambium layer beneath the bark, the porcupine can kill a tree. If the porcupine population gets out of hand–say, due to a decrease in its predators–then it can inflict considerable damage to a forest.

The porcupine has only one *effective* natural enemy, the fisher. This relative of the skunk became valued for its fine pelt earlier in our century, when women's fashions dictated long fur coats. When trapping exterminated the fisher over much of its range, the pine marten and other smaller carnivores partly filled its niche. None, however, was able to control the porcupine population. Hence loggers waged their own war against these "pesky" rodents. Lately, due to a shift in fashions away from fur, the fisher has made the start of a comeback in the forests of California and other states. In the absence of man's interference, the porcupine problem is now slowly getting back under control, and these reclusive rodents can get back to just trimming the forest without tearing it down.

**Western rattlesnake.** The thought of suddenly encountering one of these reptiles may raise fear in the hiker's mind as he goes cross country over a rocky, brush-covered slope. Indeed, your chances of meeting one greatly increase when you go cross country through rocky or streamside terrain below the red-fir forest belt. Our guide does take you through several miles of cross country and considerably more miles of vegetated, little-used trail. Nevertheless, the danger is not great, because rattlesnakes make an effort to get out of your way. While one of the authors was surveying a potential climbing route up a brush-dotted cliff, a rattler made good its escape by slithering between his feet before being seen. The only danger lies in confronting a rattler before it has a chance to escape. Walk cautiously when in rocky, brushy or streamside areas and when stepping over fallen logs.

The western rattlesnake and other rattlesnakes frequent virtually every type of habitat below the red-fir forest belt. Together they do a significant job in checking the populations of ground squirrels, other rodents and the smaller rabbits. Man, typically, has instigated campaigns to eradicate the rattlesnake and other predators such as hawks and coyotes, thereby causing eruptions in the rodent population (and problems for the ranchers who pushed for such measures). One rattlesnake extermination program carried out in the 1960s eliminated the conspicuous, noisy rattlers, and left the silent ones to breed. A population developed in which the snakes would strike before buzzing. Luckily, most of the rattlers that you might encounter along your PCT route will be glad to get out of your way and will let you know if you get too close for comfort.

In each of the three studies above, each animal has a specific role to perform in its community. A fluctuation in its population will cause a fluctuation in the other species it usually feeds upon or that feed upon it. In each case, man has tried to exterminate a species and in each case an unsuspected adverse result has occurred. As man increasingly asserts his influence over nature, he will have to learn to work within its framework, for he, like any other species, is an integral part of it.

## Recommended Reading

Brown, Vinson, and George Lawrence, *The California Wildlife Region,* Healdsburg: Naturegraph, 1965.

Burt, William H., and Richard P. Grossenheider, *A Field Guide to Mammals,* 2nd ed. Boston: Houghton Mifflin, 1964.

Ingles, Lloyd G., *Mammals of the Pacific States.* Stanford: Stanford University Press, 1965.

Jaeger, Edmund C., and Arthur C. Smith, *Introduction to the Natural History of Southern California.* Berkeley: University of California Press, 1966.

Munz, Philip A., *California Mountain Wildflowers.* Berkeley: University of California Press, 1963.

Munz, Philip A., *California Spring Wildflowers.* Berkeley: University of California Press, 1961.

Munz, Philip A., and David D. Keck, *A California Flora.* Berkeley: University of California Press, 1959.

Murie, Olaus, *A Field Guide to Animal Tracks.* Boston: Houghton Mifflin, 1954.

Odum, Eugene P., *Fundamentals of Ecology,* 3rd. ed. Philadelphia: W. B. Saunders, 1971.

Peterson, P. Victor, *Native Trees of Southern California.* Berkeley: University of California Press, 1966.

Peterson, Roger T., *A Field Guide to Western Birds,* 2nd ed. Boston: Houghton Mifflin, 1961.

Raven, Peter H., *Native Shrubs of Southern California.* Berkeley: University of California Press, 1966.

Stebbins, Robert C., *A Field Guide to Western Reptiles and Amphibians.* Boston: Houghton Mifflin, 1966.

Storer, Tracy I., and Robert L. Usinger, *Sierra Nevada Natural History.* Berkeley: University of California Press, 1963.

Sudworth, George B., *Forest Trees of the Pacific Slope.* New York: Dover, 1967.

Watts, Tom, *California Tree Finder.* Berkeley: Nature Study Guild, 1963.

# 4

# Hiking The Trail

## Our Route Description and Maps

The heart of this book is the words and maps that describe the route of the Pacific Crest Trail from Mexico to Oregon. The route is basically the one chosen by the federal government, particularly the Forest Service, and announced to the world in tentative form in June 1972. We covered every inch of the route in 1972 in order that we could map and describe it exactly. In a few places, we found the government route impossible to follow, as at Tejon Ranch, where armed guards bar the way. In some other places, we describe alternate routes that we think are much preferable to the government route in that area–and we describe the government route as well. In some places, we describe a trailless cross-country route because although the government says a trail is there, it isn't.

The 127 maps in this book show the topography, being based on United States Geological Survey topographic maps. They also show the proposed Pacific Crest Trail. The proposed trail is by law to be all trail; the route is not supposed to follow any road. However, since the proposed Pacific Crest Trail is far from complete, our maps show several kinds of routes: the PCT where it exists; the proposed PCT where it is yet unbuilt; temporary routings to bypass these unbuilt sections via 1) trail, 2) road, or 3) cross country; and alternate routes via trail and road along the general route of the PCT. These maps are the most accurate maps of the PCT available, because we covered every inch of the route. The government maps, unfortunately, have many errors. Similarly, our mileages are the most accurate ones available.

The verbal description of the 1646 miles from Mexico to Oregon first of all tells you how to find your way. There are thousands of choice points, and many of them are totally unsigned. So far only a few of them have a PCT sign. At every choice point (printed in **boldface type**) we tell you whether to turn left or right, or go straight ahead, and we state what compass direction right or left is.

We also name the trails and roads at every junction and give the elevation of the junction. Where the trails have numbers, we give those too. For junctions near settlements, we give the distance to the settlement, and we tell you how far it is to the *next* settlement. Between junctions, our description tells whether you will be ascending or descending, and how steeply. It gives your compass heading and the elevations of features you cross, such as creeks, roads and passes. It tells which roads you follow are paved (all others are of course dirt). We give the distance between two consecutive points on the trail to the nearest tenth of a mile. Along the alternate routes we also include a running total. A separate table at the end of this chapter gives the cumulative distance from the Mexican border to 77 major points.

In the trail description, numbers in the margin indicate what maps to refer to. Our verbal description of the route also tells something about the country you are walking through—the landmarks, the geology, the biology (plants and animals), the geography, and sometimes a bit of history. After all, you're not hiking the Pacific Crest Trail just to rack up the miles/make your pedometer click/prove your man(woman)(child)hood.

## Following the Trail

The "Pacific Crest Trail" is sometimes trail, sometimes road and sometimes cross country. Quite naturally, you want to stay on the route. For that purpose, we recommend relying on the route description and maps in this book. To be sure, there are various markers along the route—PCT emblems and signs (blue and white), California Riding and Hiking Trail posts (brown and yellow) and signs (orange and blue on tree trunks), metal in the shape of diamonds and discs nailed to tree trunks, plastic ribbons tied to branches, and blazes and ducks. (A blaze is a place on a tree trunk where bark has been removed. Typically a blaze is about 4–6 inches in its dimensions. A duck is a small rock placed on a very large boulder or a pile of several small rocks whose placement is obviously unnatural.)

Our route descriptions depend on these markers as little as possible because they are so ephemeral. They get destroyed by loggers, packers, motorbikers, hikers, wilderness purists, bears and other agents. Furthermore, the blazes or ducks you follow, not having any words or numbers, may or not mark the trail you want to be on.

One way to find a junction is to count mileage from the previous junction. If you know the length of your stride, that will help. We have used yards for short horizontal distances because one yard approximates the length of one long stride. Alternatively, you can develop a sense of your ground speed. Then, if it is 1½ miles to the next junction and your speed is 2¼ miles an hour, you should be there in ⅔ hour, or 40 minutes. Be suspicious if you reach an unmarked junction sooner or later than you had expected.

## California Pacific Crest Trail—Cumulative Mileage

| | South to North | Distance between Points | North to South |
|---|---|---|---|
| Mexican border | 0.0 | 16.3 | 1646.3 |
| Kitchen Creek Camp | 16.3 | 27.0 | 1630.0 |
| Green Valley | 43.3 | 15.3 | 1603.0 |
| State Highway 78 | 58.6 | 19.0 | 1587.7 |
| Warner Springs | 77.6 | 30.6 | 1568.7 |
| Anza | 108.2 | 19.3 | 1538.1 |
| State Highway 74 | 127.5 | 15.1 | 1518.8 |
| Strawberry Cienaga Trail | 142.6 | 30.2 | 1503.7 |
| Interstate 10 | 172.8 | 28.7 | 1473.5 |
| North Fork Meadow | 201.5 | 23.0 | 1444.8 |
| Big Bear City | 224.5 | 24.5 | 1421.8 |
| Deep Creek | 249.0 | 16.8 | 1397.3 |
| State Highway 138 | 265.8 | 16.9 | 1380.5 |
| Interstate 15 | 282.7 | 15.1 | 1363.6 |
| Wrightwood | 297.8 | 15.7 | 1348.5 |
| Vincent Gap | 313.5 | 23.7 | 1332.8 |
| Cloudburst Summit | 337.2 | 18.5 | 1309.1 |
| Mill Creek Summit | 355.7 | 23.5 | 1290.6 |
| Acton | 379.2 | 26.5 | 1267.1 |
| San Francisquito Canyon Road | 405.7 | 33.9 | 1240.6 |
| Quail Lake Fire Station | 439.6 | 23.7 | 1206.7 |
| Rosamond Boulevard | 463.3 | 22.7 | 1183.0 |
| Mojave | 486.0 | 18.2 | 1160.3 |
| Cantil | 504.2 | 17.7 | 1142.1 |
| Kelso Valley Road | 521.9 | 19.2 | 1124.4 |
| Bright Star Mine Road | 541.1 | 19.4 | 1105.2 |
| Weldon | 560.5 | 16.1 | 1085.8 |
| Cannell Meadow Trail | 576.6 | 33.2 | 1069.7 |
| Jordan Hot Springs Trail | 609.8 | 24.7 | 1036.5 |
| Siberian Pass | 634.5 | 12.1 | 1011.8 |
| John Muir Trail | 646.6 | 13.5 | 999.7 |
| Forester Pass | 660.1 | 21.5 | 986.2 |
| Woods Creek Crossing | 681.6 | 28.7 | 964.7 |
| Middle Fork of the Kings River | 710.3 | 30.8 | 936.0 |
| Florence Lake Trail | 741.1 | 22.2 | 905.2 |
| Mono Creek | 763.3 | 31.3 | 883.0 |
| Devils Postpile National Monument | 794.6 | 20.6 | 851.7 |
| Donohue Pass | 815.2 | 12.4 | 831.1 |
| Tuolumne Meadows Camp | 827.6 | 14.4 | 818.7 |

## Cumulative Mileage – Concluded

| | South to North | Distance between Points | North to South |
|---|---|---|---|
| Summit Pass Trail | 842.0 | 14.4 | 804.3 |
| Hetch Hetchy Trail | 864.1 | 22.1 | 782.2 |
| Bond Pass Trail | 878.2 | 14.1 | 768.1 |
| State Highway 108 | 897.9 | 19.7 | 748.4 |
| Wolf Creek Lake | 911.2 | 13.3 | 735.1 |
| State Highway 4 | 939.8 | 28.6 | 706.5 |
| Old State Highway 88 | 968.6 | 28.8 | 677.7 |
| State Highway 50 | 982.4 | 13.8 | 663.9 |
| General Creek Trail | 1002.6 | 20.2 | 643.7 |
| Whisky Creek Camp | 1028.4 | 25.8 | 617.9 |
| Soda Springs | 1049.1 | 20.7 | 597.2 |
| Jackson Meadow Recreation Area | 1074.0 | 24.9 | 572.3 |
| State Highway 49 | 1089.0 | 15.0 | 557.3 |
| Johnsville-Gibsonville Road | 1112.4 | 23.4 | 533.9 |
| Quincy-LaPorte Road | 1128.5 | 16.1 | 517.8 |
| Hartman Bar | 1160.0 | 31.5 | 486.3 |
| Bucks Summit | 1178.8 | 18.8 | 467.5 |
| Belden Town | 1198.0 | 19.2 | 448.3 |
| Humbug Summit | 1216.7 | 18.7 | 429.6 |
| State Highway 32 | 1235.2 | 18.5 | 411.1 |
| Warner Valley Campground | 1263.5 | 28.3 | 382.8 |
| Badger Flat | 1273.9 | 10.4 | 372.4 |
| Hat Creek Rim Fire Lookout | 1302.3 | 28.4 | 344.0 |
| Burney Falls State Park | 1329.1 | 26.8 | 317.2 |
| Summit Lake Road | 1342.3 | 13.2 | 304.0 |
| Grizzly Peak Fire Lookout | 1369.9 | 27.6 | 276.4 |
| Squaw Valley Road | 1395.1 | 25.2 | 251.2 |
| Interstate 5 | 1411.6 | 16.5 | 234.7 |
| Panther Rock Road | 1431.7 | 20.1 | 214.6 |
| Trinity River Trail | 1450.7 | 19.0 | 195.6 |
| Whiskytown-Callahan Road | 1463.2 | 12.5 | 183.1 |
| Cecilville-Callahan Road | 1491.8 | 28.6 | 154.5 |
| Sawyers Bar-Etna Road | 1507.1 | 15.3 | 139.2 |
| Marble Trail | 1527.8 | 20.7 | 118.5 |
| Kelsey Trail | 1549.6 | 21.8 | 96.7 |
| Seiad Valley | 1579.9 | 30.3 | 66.4 |
| Cook and Green Pass | 1595.4 | 15.5 | 50.9 |
| Oregon border | 1619.1 | 23.7 | 27.2 |
| Ashland Mountain Interchange | 1646.3 | 27.2 | 0.0 |

# 5

# The Trail

The temporary route begins on the Mexican border just south of the small town of Campo. (The permanent route will eventually begin near Tecate, 10 miles west.) To reach the start of the temporary route, drive from San Diego east on State Highway 94 to Campo, 50 miles, then turn south on Rancho del Campo Road, passing the U.S. Border Patrol Station, to the border fence, 1.8 miles. It is advisable to state your intentions at the Border Patrol office (open 9 a.m. to 4 p.m. daily), because people wandering in the border area are subject to interrogation.

**See maps 1 2**

**Mexican border (2770 – 0.0).** Follow the road north through semi-arid chaparral and oak country. The road becomes paved as you enter Campo, where water and supplies are available. Your next permanent water source will be at Cameron Ranger Station, 11.8 miles farther. Your next supply center will be at Mt. Laguna Village, 27 miles farther. Pass the Border Patrol Station on your right and reach **State Highway 94 (2570 – 1.8).** Turn right (northeast) and follow this paved highway north to **Buckman Springs Road (2620 – 1.5).** Turn left (northwest) and follow this paved road through a shallow oak-dotted valley, passing the intersection of Morena Village Road (2776 – 1.5), to an unmarked junction with the

**Cameron Road (3082 – 2.0).** Turn right (east) and follow this road as it curves north through low, chaparral-covered granite hills, passing ranch houses. You cross a saddle (3425 – 1.2), descend into Cameron Valley, dotted with stately live oaks, and enter Cleveland National Forest. The road curves east, then north to **Interstate 8 (3300 – 4.0).** Turn left (west) and follow this busy paved highway to

**Cameron Ranger Station (3250 – 1.2).** Water is available here. Turn right (north) just past the ranger station and follow Road 15S17 as it climbs rocky, chaparral-covered slopes, crosses an unnamed pass (3990 – 2.7), and drops to Kitchen Creek Camp

---

**Left: co-author Robinson at the border** *John W. Robinson*

(3820 – 0.4). Here you have your first encounter with metamorphic rocks—these are pre-Cretaceous metasediments. If you can walk 16 miles the first day, this makes an ideal overnight camp. The campground is nestled in a narrow valley and shaded by live oaks. Water is available in all but the driest months from adjacent Yellow Rose Spring. It's a good place to rest, for most of the next 10 miles are uphill and shadeless. Your next water will be at Mt. Laguna, 12.0 miles farther. From the campground, continue north along the road, following the west bank of sluggish Kitchen Creek, to a junction with the

**Fred Canyon Road (4200 – 1.4).** Turn right (northeast) and follow the road to Cibbets Flat (4240 – 0.4), in a small oak-shaded valley. You then follow it southeast over a divide (4400 – 0.7) and northeast down into Fred Canyon (4340 – 0.5), shaded by oaks (water only during the rainy season). Rest here, for the next 6 miles are uphill and shadeless. Your route now climbs high on the ridge between Fred and Antone canyons, through scraggly chaparral, with panoramic views south to the Mexican border. After passing a junction (5675 – 5.1) with the road ascending from Thing Valley, you enter a shallow valley spotted with live oaks and Jeffrey pines and reach Quail Springs Meadow (5950 – 1.9), a grassy flat just past Thunder Valley Road surrounded with pine-
2 clad hills. You are now well up in the Laguna Mountains, a
welcome change from the semi-arid foothill country you have
3 been traversing since leaving the Mexican border. Continue north,
passing a side road west to Morris Ranch (5990 – 0.4), through the forest, to a junction with the

**Desert View Road (5990 – 1.2).** You are now entering the Mt. Laguna Recreation Area of Cleveland National Forest. Turn right (northeast) and follow the road 400 yards, then go left (north) onto a trail that passes through a shady forest of Jeffrey pine and black oak to the backside of Burnt Rancheria Campground (6000 – 0.4). Water is obtainable here. One-half mile northwest of here is the village of Mount Laguna, with a store and post office. Your next supplies and permanent water will be at Warner Springs, 49 miles ahead. From the backside of the campground, continue on a delightful forest trail to the

**Desert View Picnic Area (6000 – 0.8),** just south of the Desert View spur road. You have a superb view over Anza-Borrego Desert to the Salton Sea. Here your trail ends. Follow the road west to **San Diego County Highway S1 (5980 – 0.1).** Turn right (north) and follow this paved road to **Laguna Rim Trail access road (5650 – 2.3),** opposite the access road to Horse Heaven Group Campground. Turn right (east) and follow the road as it winds through the pine forest, curving north to

**Laguna Rim Trail (5700 – 0.5).** Follow the trail north along the eastern rim of the Laguna Mountains, through dense chaparral, with fine views down over the desert. The trail crosses a ridge and descends, paralleling the highway for a short distance, to Highway S1 and a junction opposite **Road 15S23 (5440 – 1.4).** Follow this road, paved at first but soon becoming dirt, west through an open forest of black oak and Jeffrey pine to **Road 15S13 (5580 – 0.9).** Turn right (northwest) and follow this road as it descends through an open forest, then climbs along a chaparral-mantled ridge, with superb views west over the Cuyamaca country, to **Road 14S04 (4790 – 3.4).** Turn sharp right (north) and follow this road as it descends to Indian Creek (4640 – 0.3). Water flows here only during the rainy season. Cross the creekbed and continue north along the road to Deer Park (4720 – 0.4). This little oak-shaded flat is a good place to rest after your 3 miles through open chaparral, but no water is available.

Your route now continues north on 14S04, curves northwest through a little valley spotted with live oaks, passes La Carcel ranch house, and reaches a junction with Indian Potrero Road ("Deer Park Road" on the map) (4590 – 0.9). Continue straight ahead (northwest) to a locked gate at the boundary of Cuyamaca Rancho State Park (4640 – 0.1). Cross the gate and continue northwest along the road to a junction with the

**Harvey Moore Trail (4920 – 1.5).** Turn right (north) and follow 3
this new footpath down slopes covered with chaparral, oak and 4
pine, then cross Harper Creek (4280 – 1.2), with water only in the rainy season, and head west down into **Green Valley (4190 – 1.2),** a broad basin, verdant with lush grasses, containing the headwaters of the Sweetwater River.

If your water is low, it is best to head southwest on Green Valley Road to the **Cold Spring Trail (4200 – 0.4).** Take this west over a low ridge, then northwest up to **Cold Spring (4320 – 1.4 – 1.8).** If it is dry, hike up State Highway 79 northwest 2 miles to Paso Pichacho Campground, where you can take in a mini-museum as well as loading up on water. One mile north on 79 you'll pick up a spur road east to Horsemen's Group Camp. Otherwise, head northeast on the Cold Spring Trail to the **temporary PCT (4400 – 1.2 – 2.6).**

The temporary PCT crosses the creek and heads right (north) on the Green Valley Trail 50 yards to an intersection with the **Stonewall Creek Trail (4130 – 0.2 ).** Follow this forest trail north along trickling Stonewall Creek and pass just east of the granitic Stonewall Peak to the backside of Horsemen's Group Camp (7710 – 3.5), a campground under scattered pines (no water). Your trail now leaves the forest, crosses rolling grassland to the southeast edge of Cuyamaca Reservoir (this end usually dry), and follows the reservoir basin northeast to **Sunrise Highway S1 (4666 – 2.3).** Cross the highway, pass through the gate with the PCT marker, and follow a trail east around a sagebrush-covered hill, then north through a shallow valley to **Mason Valley Truck Trail (4660 – 1.4).** Turn right and follow this dirt road east, descending to

**Chariot Canyon Road (3860 – 1.3).** Turn left (north) and follow this eroded road down Chariot Canyon, passing numerous 19th century mining prospects located along the contact between granitic and metamorphic rocks. You are now descending the east rampart of the Cuyamaca Mountains into desert country, noticeable in the vegetation change (sagebrush, mesquite, creosote bush) and rising temperatures. After several miles you reach an **unnamed fork (3360 – 3.6).** Turn right (northeast) and start down a road, then a PCT-marked trail (3260 – 0.8) to **State Highway 78 (2538 – 2.2).** Cross the highway, pass through the PCT-marked gate, and walk north along the road through Valle de San Felipe, passing the white houses of San Felipe Ranch to

**San Felipe Valley Road (2506 – 3.4).** Cross the highway and follow the PCT-marked trail northwest, generally paralleling this paved road about 10 yards back. You are also paralleling the Earthquake Valley Fault, which is along the base of the San Felipe
4 Hills on your right. Gradually ascend the long San Felipe Valley,
5 first through low desert vegetation, then through scattered live
oaks which provide welcome shade as you approach the tiny
6 settlement of San Felipe (no supplies) (3477 – 7.1). Your route
crosses an unnamed saddle (3557 – 0.7), then descends to **Montezuma Valley Road (3330 – 0.8).** Cross this road and proceed north on a PCT-marked dirt road through cattle-grazing land and over low, chaparral-covered hills, with a view of Cal Tech's Mt. Palomar telescope dome on the northwest horizon, to

**Warner Springs (3132 – 7.0).** Here, under stately oaks, is a hot-spring resort, restaurant, general store and post office. This is a good place to rest for the long climb ahead. Your next water hole will be at lower Twin Lake in 17.1 miles, and your next supply center will be in Anza, 31 miles distant. To continue north, take the paved State Highway 79 out of town, then pick up the PCT-marked trail that parallels it on the right side to **Agua Caliente Creek (2940 – 1.3),** usually dry. Here the trail leaves the highway and turns northwest, crosses a slight rise, then drops to **Lost Valley Road (9S05) (3120 – 0.4).** Turn right (northeast) and start up this road. You now begin a long, shadeless ridge ascent through oceans of ribbonwood and manzanita. In your view south you can see where ephemeral streams are incising through the Pliocene nonmarine sediments of Valle de San Jose and transporting them west into Lake Henshaw. Continue up Lost Valley Road to

**Road 9S02 (3989 – 4.4).** Turn right (north) and take this narrow roadway up over the crest of the ridge (4430 – 1.6) and down to Lost Valley Spring (4390 – 0.2). Water from this mountainside spring is available for humans only after rainy seasons; a Forest Service sign warns that water in the tank is fit only for wildlife and vehicles. Use Halazone tablets or boil the water, if desperate. You will welcome the oaks and pines here, the first shade since leaving Agua Caliente Creek. Continue north along the dirt road that soon turns into a trail, which crosses a gentle divide and then drops to the headwaters of the **San Luis Rey River (4430 – 1.7).** Water is available here in the springtime only. Turn left (northwest) along a poor dirt road and follow it past the Whistling Winds Ranch (4400 – 1.7), through a gate, and into the broad, shallow Chihuahua Valley. Walk north, then west on Chihuahua Valley Road, passing scattered live oaks, to

**Mitchell Road (4167 – 2.5).** Turn right (north) and follow the road to a fork (4160 – 0.8), then go left (west) through a gate and follow the roadway west, then north over a sage-covered divide (4516 – 1.3) and down into Cooper Canyon to lower Twin Lake (4080 – 1.2). This polluted cattle pond is a permanent water source if you have Halazone tablets. Good water is available in
Anza, 13.5 miles ahead. Continue north on Cooper Cienega Truck **6**
Trail up Iron Spring Canyon, over a divide (4924 – 3.8) and down **7**
into sage-covered Durasna Valley (4330 – 1.7). Continue north to
a fork, then right (northeast) past small ranches of the Cahuilla **9**
Indian Reservation to the paved **10**

**State Highway 71 (3942 – 6.5).** Turn right (east) to Anza (3918 – 1.5), with a grocery store and post office. Your next supplies and permanent water will be in the Lake Hemet area, 23 miles farther. Continue east on the highway to **Table Mountain Truck Trail (4160 – 3.0).** Turn left (north) through the gate, and follow this road northwest along the San Jacinto Fault past a ranch house to **Road 7S07 (4155 – 0.3).** Turn right (northeast) and climb up this eroded dirt road, crossing into San Bernardino National Forest to

**Thomas Mountain Fire Road (4966 – 1.7).** Turn left (northwest) and walk up this ridgetop roadway through ribbonwood, scrub oak and occasional pinyon pines, with splendid views of Anza Valley to the south and the San Jacinto high country to the north. You finally enter a Jeffrey pine forest and reach Tool Box Spring Camp (6150 – 4.7). To the right (east) and down 0.3 mile is Tool Box Spring (usually water). Continue up the fire road, through a splendid forest of pine, incense cedar, and live oak to Thomas

Mountain Camp (6620 – 1.9) (no water). Your road now descends the northwest slope of Thomas Mountain and turns east to a junction with

**State Highway 74 (4378 – 7.7).** Turn left (northwest) and follow the highway, passing the fenced-in Lake Hemet and a general store to **Herkey Creek Camp (4400 – 1.7),** usually crowded with car campers. Your next permanent water will be at Strawberry Cienaga in the San Jacinto Wilderness, 14.4 miles ahead. The next store will be in Cabazon, near San Gorgonio Pass, 38 miles distant. Cross to the north edge of the campground and pick up an unmarked trail leading north, then northwest to a junction with the

**May Valley Road (5S21) (5080 – 2.7),** lined with pines and live oaks. Turn right (northwest) and walk up this road to a junction with **South Ridge Trail (5440 – 0.9),** marked by a large Forest Service sign that indicates *Tahquitz Peak, 6.* Turn right (northeast) and follow this forested trail up the long south ridge, steep in places, to Tahquitz Peak (8828 – 6.0). You are now well up in the San Jacinto Wilderness. From the Forest Service lookout on top, you are rewarded with a breathtaking panorama of this forested high country. Take the trail northeast, then north down to **Saddle Junction (8080 – 1.8),** a 5-way trail junction. Go north on the trail marked *San Jacinto Peak.* You climb through a forest of pine and fir, pass the sign *Mt. San Jacinto Wilderness State Park,* and reach
10 the **Strawberry Cienaga Trail (9030 – 2.0).**

11

* * * *

**Here you have a choice of two routes.** The alternate, more scenic, high route is via Wellmans Cienaga, San Jacinto Peak, and Little Round Valley Trail Camp. If you wish to take this route, then continue straight ahead (north), rounding the head of Willow Creek basin, through chinquapin and manzanita to Wellmans Cienaga (9200 – 0.5), a mountainside marsh lined with streamlets of cold water. Your trail continues up to

**Wellman Divide (9620 – 0.7 – 1.2)** and a trail junction. The right branch goes down to Round Valley Trail Camp, 1 mile. Go left (north) through an open forest of lodgepole pine, passing another junction (10,000 – 0.8) with a trail coming up from Round Valley. Your trail now switchbacks up through a dense thicket of chinquapin and manzanita to the southwest ridge of San Jacinto Peak and the

**San Jacinto Peak Trail (10,500 – 1.2 – 3.2).** A side trip right (northeast) takes you ¼ mile past the stone shelter cabin to the summit of San Jacinto Peak (10,804) for one of the outstanding views in southern California. The steep streams on the north and east slopes are etching into the retreating crest of this fault-block mountain, gradually destroying its older, gentle-sloped erosion surface, which is obvious to the south and east. Your route now descends northwest to Little Round Valley Trail Camp (9850 – 0.9), with water, then continues down the west slopes of San Jacinto Peak, passing Boggy Meadow, and rejoins the permanent PCT route at the junction of the Fuller Ridge Trail (9230 – 0.9 – 5.0).

*  *  *  *

11

The permanent PCT route turns left on the Strawberry Cienaga Trail. Follow it west to Strawberry Cienaga (8720 – 1.0), a marsh laced with cold streamlets, sometimes dry by late summer. Continue west, contouring the south slope of Marion Mountain to a junction with the

**Deer Springs Trail (7900 – 1.6).** Turn right (north) and follow this well-established trail around the west slopes of Marion Mountain, through dense stands of pine, fir and incense cedar to Deer Springs Trail Camp (8800 – 2.4), with your last permanent water until Cabazon, 20 miles farther. From here your trail climbs northeast to the **Fuller Ridge Trail (9230 – 0.5),** where the alter-

**On the Wellmans Cienaga Trail** *John W. Robinson*

nate route over San Jacinto Peak rejoins the permanent PCT route. Turn left (northwest) and follow this new trail down Fuller Ridge, first on the southwest side, then across a notch to the northeast side, with superb views down over San Gorgonio Pass, to

**Black Mountain Road (7750 – 4.2).** Turn left (west) and follow the road past Fairview Point down to Black Mountain Group Campground (7350 – 1.5), with water only after seasons of abundant rainfall. Continue down the road through a forest of pine and incense cedar to the **Hurley Flat Trail (7290 – 0.9).** The sign here reads *Pacific Crest Trail.* Turn right (north) and follow this trail as it descends moderately, first through forest, then down slopes of open, scraggly chaparral to Hurley Flat (3500 – 6.0). You pass behind Twin Pines Guest Ranch to **Road 3S05 (3450 – 0.7),** the old "Hall Grade" built for lumbering in 1876. Turn right (north) and follow this narrow dirt road as it switchbacks down arid slopes past mine shafts that penetrate the metamorphic rock near its contact with granite. The road continues its descent to the desert floor and crosses the San Gorgonio River (1675 – 4.2), usually a stark, dry, wide, boulder bed with only very seasonal water. You will welcome the shade of some cottonwoods along this wash. Continue north on 3S05 to its end at

**Esperanza Avenue (1690 – 0.5),** on the south edge of the town of
Cabazon, located on a great alluvial fan built with sediments
11 transported down from Millard Canyon to your north. Notice how
12 this alluvial fan has edged the San Gorgonio River southward
against the San Jacinto Mountains. Turn right (east) and follow
13 the avenue, marked by the familiar brown and yellow posts of the
California Riding and Hiking Trail, to Broadway Street (1665 – 0.4). One mile north is central Cabazon, with water, a store and post office. The next stores will be in Big Bear City, 59 miles distant. Continue east to an **unnamed dirt road (1600 – 1.3),** marked by a CRHT sign, and leading left (northeast). Follow this road across the dry, sandy wash of the San Gorgonio River to **Elm Street (1570 – 0.7).** Take this road north to its end just south of the railroad tracks, where you intersect an unnamed **railroad frontage road (1630 – 0.8).** Turn right (east) and follow this very poor dirt road alongside the fence, paralleling the railroad to a **railroad and highway underpass (1320 – 3.5),** just before the Verbenia Avenue highway overpass you see ahead. Turn left (north) and cross under the railroad tracks and Interstate 10, following CRHT posts, then go right (east) on a road to

**Verbenia Avenue (1365 – 0.3).** To your right is an ARCO service station, with soft drinks and your last permanent water until Forks Spring, 21.0 miles farther. Cross the avenue, heading east, to Tamarack Road (1365 – 0.1). Continue east on this dirt road, which drops to 1185 feet, the lowest PCT elevation in California, as it parallels Interstate 10 on the north side to **Whitewater Canyon (1425 – 2.9).** Turn left (north) on Whitewater Canyon Road and ascend the broad, boulder-filled arroyo. The side canyon on your left, just before Bonnie Bell, lies along the east-west trace of the Banning Fault, which separates igneous and metamorphic rocks to its north from Pleistocene sediments to its south. Pass occasional cottonwoods that offer welcome shade and finally reach an

**Unmarked trail (2120 – 4.7),** just south of Whitewater Trout Farm, the oasis of green trees you see just ahead. Your trail heads northwest, crosses the boulder-filled Whitewater River (just a trickle in early summer, sometimes a raging torrent after spring rains), turns north, recrosses the river bottom, climbs northeast over a divide (3020 – 3.9) and drops to Cat Claw Flat (2880 – 0.5), on the usually dry West Fork of Mission Creek. Your trail now ascends another brush-covered divide (3563 – 1.3) and descends to Mission Creek (3040 – 1.7). You follow the boulder bed of this major drainage, with the high peaks of the San Gorgonio Wilderness looming above on your left, up to Forks Spring (4800 – 6.8), at the junction of the South and North Forks of Mission Creek (always water). Your trail now makes the long, hot climb up the North Fork, partly along the stream, partly high on the north slope
to bypass narrows. You enter the back door of San Bernardino **13**
National Forest, reach the welcome shade of Jeffrey pine and
white fir, and finally arrive at North Fork Meadow (7750 – 6.5). **14-A**
Water is usually available here until midsummer. Continue up the **15-A**
trail to its junction with **Road 1N30Y (6840 – 0.2),** recently bulldozed.

* * * *

**Here you again have a choice of routes.** The alternate route is more spectacular than the temporary route since it goes through the San Gorgonio Wilderness and includes an ascent of San Gorgonio Mountain. If you wish to take this route, turn left (west) on 1N30Y and cross the low divide to another junction, then go left again (southwest) to the roadend just above

**Fish Creek Meadows (7980 – 1.5),** a grass-covered flat where Fish Creek makes a right-angle turn. Take the trail marked *San Gorgonio Wilderness* and proceed west along upper Fish Creek. The trail climbs along the left slope above the creek bed and finally contours over to Fish Creek Trail Camp (8580 – 1.7)–several cleared flats amid rocky terrain, shaded by a canopy of white firs. Water flows year-round in the stream here. Your trail now climbs the broad slopes of Grinnell Mountain into a forest of lodgepole pine, crosses the saddle (9780 – 3.2) between Lake and Grinnell peaks, and contours southwest to a junction with the

**Dry Lake-North Fork (Whitewater) Meadows Trail (9800 – 0.9 – 7.3).** Turn right (west) and follow the trail up to **Mine Shaft Saddle (9900 – 0.3 – 7.6).** Here you intersect the Sky High Trail leading southeast up San Gorgonio Mountain. Turn left and take this trail, following numerous switchbacks up glacial till on the northeast slope of the mountain, then climbing around to the south slope to a junction with the

**San Bernardino Peak Divide Trail (11,250 – 3.3 – 10.9).** You are now above timberline, and the vista is magnificent. A ¼ mile summit trail east gets you to the top of San Gorgonio Mountain (11,502), the highest peak in southern California. The rocks here are quartz monzonite, a granitic rock rich in silica. Those north and below the slope are mostly gneiss. To the southwest, in Mill Creek Canyon, is the trace of the north branch of the San Andreas Fault. Back at the trail junction, turn west and follow the divide trail around the south slopes of Jepson and Charlton peaks, among lodgepole pines, down to Dollar Lake Saddle (9970 – 3.7). Here is a trail camp, but no water. Continue west on the divide trail, passing the lateral trail left to High Meadow Springs (water, ¼ mile), around the north side of Shields Peak, to a **trail fork**
15-A **(10,220 – 2.6 – 17.2).** Go right (WNW) to Trail Fork Springs (10,400 – 0.3), emitting ice-cold water. Here is a trail camp shaded
16 by lodgepoles. Continue west, rejoining the fork of the divide trail (10,400 – 0.7) that goes high on the north slope of Anderson Peak, then ascend to within a few yards of the summit of San Bernardino East Peak (10,691 – 0.5). You now dip to a forested saddle, ascend to near the summit of San Bernardino West Peak, drop west down the ridge, then turn north and drop steadily to Limber Pine Springs (8680 – 2.9). Limber Pine Trail Camp is ¼ mile farther down the trail. Your trail continues down the northwest slopes of the San Bernardino Peak massif, passing a side trail to Manzanita Springs (0.1 left), leaves the west end of the San Gorgonio Wilderness, and drops steeply to

**Angelus Oaks (5780 – 5.2 – 26.8),** formerly called Camp Angelus. Here, across State Highway 38, is a store and post office. Take the dirt road past the post office to the Filaree Flat Trail, and follow the latter down through a Jeffrey pine forest, across the Santa Ana River (4380 – 1.9), where fording may be a problem in late spring, to **Santa Ana Road (1N09) (4730 – 0.4 – 29.1).** Turn left (west) and follow it across Tertiary sandstone to **Seven Pines Road (4070 – 2.8 – 31.9).** Turn right (northeast) and follow this road through Seven Pines to a junction with the

**Siberia Creek Trail (4980 – 2.8 – 34.7).** Turn left (northwest)

**San Gorgonio ridge** *John W. Robinson*

and follow this footpath across fire-burnt slopes to Siberia Creek and down to Siberia Creek Trail Camp (4790 – 4.2), with water. This is one of the nicest trail camps in the San Bernardinos, nestled alongside the singing creek under a verdant canopy of white alder, live oak, and big-cone spruce. Continue northwest, crossing Bear Creek and ascending fire-scorched slopes to trail's end at the paved

**Rim of the World Highway (State Highway 18)** 16
**(6850 – 2.7 – 41.6).** Turn left (west) and follow the highway down 17
to **Snow Valley (6700 – 0.7 – 42.3),** a popular ski resort. About 18
100 yards beyond the Snow Valley Picnic Area, turn right (northwest) onto the **Green Valley Trail (6690 – 0.3 – 42.6).** Follow this trail up through beautiful stands of pine, fir and incense cedar to **Little Green Valley (7300 – 1.3 – 43.9),** site of a YMCA camp.

Continue northeast on jeep tracks, over the forested ridge and down to

**Green Valley (6900 – 2.4 – 46.3),** a popular summer resort with a public campground, stores and post office. Green Valley Lake has a swimming beach that will tempt you. Follow Green Valley Lake Road west to **Road 3N16 (6730 – 1.2 – 47.5).** Turn right (north) and take this road through the forest down past several junctions to

**Crab Flats Campground (5840 – 4.4 – 51.9)** (no water). Take the road that leads northwest at the campground entrance, going right at a fork in ¼ mile, and follow it down to Deep Creek (4625 – 3.2). Cross the creek and rejoin the permanent PCT route as you reach **Road 2N95 (4690 – 0.3 – 55.4).**

* * * *

If you wish to take the temporary PCT route from North Fork Meadow, be sure you are well-stocked with water to last until Big Bear City, 23 miles farther. Turn right (northeast) and follow Road 1N30Y, going right at an unmarked fork, up and around a forested ridge to

**Mission Creek-Heart Bar Creek Divide (8160 – 0.6).** Here you
turn right (north) and follow the trail, marked by CRHT posts,
over a slight rise and down into the head of Heart Bar Creek
18 (7840 – 1.0). Descend the creek, heading northwest, first on trail
14-A and then on jeep tracks. (The creek is usually dry by early
summer.) The route eventually curves north then soon reaches
15-B **Coon Creek Road (7100 – 2.1).** Turn right (northeast) and follow
it across Coon Creek (usually a trickle of water until midsummer),
then up to a junction with the **Onyx Summit Trail (7920 – 3.1).**
Turn left (northeast) at the CRHT marker and follow the forested
trail north over a ridge (8780 – 1.4), across the head of Cienaga
Seca Creek, and up to

**Onyx Summit (8443 – 3.6),** separating the waters of the Santa Ana River to the west from those that flow east into the Colorado Basin. This is the high point of the PCT in the San Bernardinos. The main vegetation here is juniper, mountain mahogany, white fir, Jeffrey pine and rabbit brush. As your trail descends north, then northwest, notice the influence of the desert on this side of the divide–pinyon pine and sagebrush become predominant. Your trail leaves Arrastre Creek, continues northwest across pinyon-dotted flats, becomes a dirt road, and passes alongside **Deadmans Lake (7240 – 4.9),** a small, stagnant waterhole at the foot of Deadmans Ridge, which is a block of Paleozoic quartzite. Follow the road west, then north over the low west end of Deadmans Ridge and down to **Woodlands (6850 – 2.6),** a real estate development. Turn left (west) on State Lane and proceed through the pines to **State Highway 38 (6870 – 0.6).** Turn right (northwest) and follow this paved road into

**Big Bear City (6770 – 2.9),** with stores and post office. Your next permanent water will be from Holcomb Creek, 12.4 miles farther; your next supplies will be in Wrightwood, 73 miles farther. Continue on Highway 38, turning north on Green Way Drive, then southwest on North Shore Highway to **Van Dusen Canyon Road (6770 – 1.5).** Turn right (north) and follow the road up Van Dusen Canyon, veering northwest to

**Holcomb Valley (7352 – 4.2),** a pine-dotted basin once the scene of a frenzied gold rush. Along this road you started in Mesozoic quartz monzonite and walked along Paleozoic limestone followed by granite porphyry, then finally ended in Paleozoic quartzite. Heavy minerals were concentrated near the contact of the intruding granitic rocks here and the overlying Paleozoic sediments. The next stretch of road has a similar rock sequence. At Road 3N08 turn left (west) and follow it to Holcomb Valley Campground (7350 – 0.1) (no water). Continue west on this road, passing Hitchcock Ranch and the grassy bowl of Holcomb Valley proper (7239 – 1.3), climbing the slopes above Holcomb Creek, passing Hitchcock Spring (water into early summer), then dropping back beside the creek to **Road 3N14 (6525 – 5.3).** Obtain water from
Holcomb Creek, then turn right (northwest) and follow this road **15-B**
over a slight rise (6822 – 0.8) and down to **17**

**Big Pine Flat (6824 – 1.6).** Here, under Jeffrey pines, is a public
campground with water and a ranger station. Just southeast of the **18**
campground, go southwest on Road 3N16 to an unmarked junction with the

**Holcomb Creek Trail (6560 – 1.3),** where jeep tracks lead right (southwest). If you continue on 3N16 to 3N27, you've gone 0.3 mile too far. Take the jeep tracks, which soon become a trail, down the tributary canyon, under pinyon-spotted slopes, to Holcomb Creek (5300 – 3.7). Your trail turns west and parallels the creek on the north side, climbs the slope to bypass rocky narrows, drops back along the creek, passes a junction with the Cox Creek Trail (5240 – 0.6), crosses to the south bank of the stream, and reaches Holcomb Trail Camp (5220 – 0.2), on a pine-shaded bench. Water is available from the creek. Your trail now climbs the forested slopes south of Holcomb Creek, passes a junction with the Crab Flats Trail (5300 – 0.3), contours along the mountainside, then drops into the canyon of Deep Creek (4590 – 3.6). Cross the stream (this could be difficult in spring) and follow the trail, then dirt road, up to **Road 2N95 (4700 – 0.5).** Go left (southwest) 50 yards on the road, then turn right and follow the trail up

verdant Little Bear Creek, a sylvan sanctuary of incense cedar, black oak and pine. Your trail winds along the north bank of the little creek, then, just before reaching a messy logging camp, turns right (northwest) and climbs to **Road 2N25 (5200 – 2.0).** Turn left (southwest) and follow the road up to North Shore Campground (5380 – 0.5), with water–better refill here. Continue west on the road, past a hospital, to

**State Highway 173 (5210 – 0.4).** If your supplies are low, you can turn left (south), then head west over to stores on the southwest shore of Lake Arrowhead. Virtually every road heading north or west from this shore will eventually take you back to the temporary route. Turn right (north) on 173 and follow this road as it curves west, then contours north on the west slopes of Willow Creek Canyon. Just before the road turns west to leave the canyon, you reach the **CRHT-posted trail (4870 – 2.9),** on your left. Head west on it through hilly pine country, above the highway, then parallel it to **Road 2N33 (4871 – 2.0),** opposite Rock Camp Ranger Station. Turn left (west) and follow the road down to Grass Valley Creek (4700 – 0.8), shaded by black oak and pine (water until early summer). Continue west on the road to **Road 2N34 (4900 – 1.1).** Turn left (south) and follow it up along the forested crest of Tunnel 2 Ridge, with good views of the west-end country of the San Bernardinos and out over the desert, to an
**unnamed junction (5480 – 3.1),** marked by a CRHT post. Turn 18
right (west) and follow jeep tracks down the forested ridge to 19

**Valley of the Moon Road (2N38) (4700 – 2.2).** Turn right
(northwest) and follow it down into Miller Canyon (3800 – 2.5). 20-A
As you descend through the forest, it gradually changes from 21
Douglas fir, ponderosa pine, incense cedar and black oak to a drier
forest with increasing amounts of live oak. Cottonwood and 22
broad-leaf maple are found along the creeks. Continue west, above the south bank of the East Fork of the West Fork of the Mojave River, which usually has water nearly year-round, to a junction with

**State Highway 138 (3640 – 0.8).** This highway has been recently relocated on the south slope of Miller Canyon to get around the new Silverwood Reservoir of the California Water Project. The old trail is now under water and a new one is yet to be constructed, so you must follow the paved highway west. In 2.8 miles you reach a drinking fountain, then 2.8 miles farther, at a turnout with a good view east of Silverwood Reservoir, you reach another one. This will be your last water until Cajon Canyon, 11.3 miles ahead. Continue the gentle ascent north to a broad ridge, then northwest down to Summit Valley (3240 – 6.9), at the foot of the San Bernardinos' north-slope, semi-arid country of sagebrush and scat-

---

**Left: Holcomb Creek** *John W. Robinson*

tered oaks. Follow State Highway 138 west through broad Horsethief Canyon to **Little Horsethief Junction (3370 – 1.9).** A sign points south to Little Horsethief Ranch. Follow the jeep tracks south up to a trail on a **ridge (3470 – 0.5)** separating Horsethief Canyon from Little Horsethief Canyon. Turn right (west) and follow this ridge trail to its junction with the **jeep tracks (3780 – 1.5).** Continue west, passing just south of Cajon Pass, down to a reunion with

**State Highway 138 (3515 – 3.0).** Turn left (northwest) and follow the road as it curves southwest gently down to an unmarked junction with the **Crowder Canyon Trail (3200 – 1.9).** This is at a junction of two dry washes just as the road begins to climb west. Turn left (south) and take the trail down the brushy, granite-walled canyon to

**Cajon Canyon (2980 – 1.2),** where you intersect Interstate 15 just south of a relocated historical marker that commemorates the 1849 pioneers of the Santa Fe and Salt Lake trails. Cross under the freeway through a concrete box culvert, where dirty but permanent water is available (Halazone tablets strongly recommended). Your next water will be at Wrightwood, 15.1 miles distant. Turn left (southeast) and follow a narrow road between tracks and freeway to a junction (2950 – 0.3) with a road leading
right (west), then southwest to a junction with **Road 3N77Y**
22 **(2950 – 0.3).** Turn left (south) and follow this road, crossing the
23 Southern Pacific Railroad tracks, then climb over a brush-covered
ridge and descend past Lost Lake, in the San Andreas Fault Zone,
24-A to **Lone Pine Canyon Road (2720 – 3.6).**

24-B

* * * *

25-A

26-A **Here you have a choice of routes.** The alternate, more scenic, high route is via Lytle Creek, Cucamonga Wilderness, Baldy Notch, Mt. San Antonio and Blue Ridge. To take it, proceed southwest on Applewhite Road (2N53) up over Lower Lytle Creek Ridge, curving west, then northwest to

**Applewhite Campground (3350 – 3.3),** on the North Fork of Lytle Creek. Water is available here. Turn left (southeast) on Lytle Creek Road and follow it as it curves southwest, passing numerous summer homes, to **Middle Fork Road (3000 – 1.5 – 4.8).** Turn right (west) and follow this road up the Middle Fork of Lytle Creek to the beginning of the **Middle Fork Trail (3999 – 3.0 – 7.8),** marked by a wooden sign on your right. Take this trail up the north slope above the boulder-strewn streambed, through scrawny chaparral, into a forest of live oak, spruce and pine to the boundary of Cucamonga Wilderness (4640 – 1.5). Your trail continues west, now under the canopy of the main mountain forest, to Third Crossing Trail Camp (5260 – 0.9), a primitive campsite where the trail crosses the bubbling Middle Fork of Lytle Creek, your last permanent water on this alternate route. You now climb southwest above the south branch of the Middle Fork to Comanche Trail Camp (6280 – 1.5), alongside the small creek, shaded by tall pines. From here your trail climbs westward moderately up to

**Icehouse Saddle (7580 – 1.8 – 13.5),** a major trail fork on the western boundary of the Cucamonga Wilderness, well up in the San Gabriel high country. Turn right (north) and follow the delightful ridge trail through open stands of pine, fir and incense cedar, across the slopes of "The 3 T's" (Timber, Telegraph, and Thunder mountains), with continuous vistas, then descend down jeep tracks to Baldy Notch (7802 – 4.6), a popular ski resort (seasonal restaurant). Follow the dirt road northwest up the divide, passing the top of a ski lift, to the beginning of the Devil's Backbone (8580 – 1.3), a precipitous, knife-edge ridge. The trail starts along the backbone, then climbs around the south slope of Mt. Harwood through a thinning forest cover of lodgepole pine, and emerges above timberline to climb moderately to the summit of

**Mt. San Antonio (Old Baldy) (10,064 – 2.0 – 21.4),** a tapered
expanse of boulders, barren of vegetation, the high point of the
San Gabriel Mountains. Your vista can be magnificent since half **26-A**
of southern California spreads out before you, but often it is **27**
buried under an extensive layer of brown smog. Turn north and
descend a hardly recognizable trail to the saddle (8680 – 0.7) **29**
between Baldy and Dawson Peak, then pick up a distinct trail that **30**
climbs over the west shoulder of Dawson (9450 – 0.6), drops to a
saddle, ascends the west slope of Pine Mountain (9480 – 1.1), and **25-B**
drops down the ridge to another saddle (8180 – 1.4), then climbs **26-B**
to **Blue Ridge Road (8310 – 0.1 – 25.3).** Turn left (west) and
follow the road along Blue Ridge to its junction with the **Acorn** **28**
**Canyon Trail (8250 – 1.0 – 26.3),** where you rejoin the PCT route.

* * * *

If you wish to take the temporary PCT route, then turn right (northwest) and follow the gravel road up the long, straight chamise-covered valley of Lone Pine Canyon–arid, hot and shadeless. Pray that the San Andreas Fault does not choose this occasion to move; you are walking directly on top of it. Granitic rocks lie to its northeast, metamorphic rocks to its southwest. Your road becomes paved as you continue into the upper canyon. Finally you reach the welcome shade of a few pines and cross Lone

Pine Summit (6078 – 9.4). Your road continues northwest down to the forest community of

**Wrightwood (5840 – 1.5)** (stores and post office). Your next water will be at Guffy Campground, 5.4 miles farther; your next supplies, however, won't be until Acton, a very long 81 miles farther. Walk west through the town to **Acorn Road (6080 – 1.2).** Turn left (south) and follow the road to its end in Acorn Canyon, where you meet the **Acorn Canyon Trail (6800 – 1.2).** Take this trail steeply up the ridge between Acorn and Heath canyons through a forest of ponderosa pine, sugar pine and white fir to a junction with the **Blue Ridge Road (8250 – 2.0).** Turn right (northwest) and follow the ridgetop trail, marked with CRHT posts, into Angeles National Forest and up to Guffy Campground (8250 – 1.0) (water). The next permanent water will be at Little Jimmy Spring, 20.0 miles distant. Your trail continues northwest along Blue Ridge, paralleling the road and often intersecting it, through an open forest of pine and fir, with spectacular vistas down into the gorge of the San Gabriel River, to Blue Ridge Campground (7910 – 2.8) (no water). Continue northwest on the CRHT-posted pathway down to the

**Angeles Crest Highway (7345 – 2.4).** Cross the highway and follow the ridgetop trail northwest to **Grassy Hollow Campground**
**(7320 – 1.1)** (no water). Your route now follows Road 3N26 west
28 along the forested ridge, then south down to the Angeles Crest
30 Highway at **Vincent Gap (6585 – 4.0).** Cross the highway, heading
southwest, and take the forest trail that switchbacks up the steep
31 ridge of Mt. Baden-Powell. This well-traveled pathway starts in
32 live oak and Jeffrey pine, passes through belts of white fir and
lodgepole pine, and, high on the ridge, reaches clusters of aged,
33-A gnarled limber pine, cousin of the bristlecone pine. After 2500 feet
of climbing, you reach a junction with the

**Baden-Powell Summit Trail (9200 – 3.7).** Mt. Baden-Powell's 9399-foot crown is ¼ mile to the left. You go right and follow the crest trail down the ridge, leaving the Paleozoic metamorphic rocks behind and hiking along the older Precambrian metaigneous rocks west to granitic rocks. Hike around the upper slopes of Mt. Burnham, Throop Peak and Mt. Hawkins, passing the side trail down to Lily Spring (8520 – 4.0), to Windy Gap (7588 – 1.8). Follow the trail northwest to Little Jimmy Spring (7450 – 0.2), just below the trail, where there is always a seepage of water. Your next permanent water will be at Little Rock Creek, 8.1 miles ahead. Continue on the trail, largely through granitic terrain, to Little Jimmy Trail Camp (7430 – 0.1)—no water, but a delightful forested campground of Jeffrey pine, sugar pine and white fir, favored by Boy Scouts. Continue west along jeep tracks, then trail,

**Limber pines on Baden-Powell Trail** *John W. Robinson*

down to **Islip Saddle (6700 – 2.5)** on the Angeles Crest Highway. Cross the highway and take the trail that leads northwest up the southeast ridge of Mt. Williamson to the crest of the ridge, then descends southwest back down to the

**Angeles Crest Highway (6720 – 3.4).** Cross the highway and take a trail that parallels it southwest to a point opposite **Eagles Roost Picnic Area (6640 – 0.7).** Cross the highway and follow the Rattlesnake Trail down into the upper reaches of Little Rock Creek (6080 – 1.4), crossing the sparkling stream, then following the north slope through delightful forest country and finally dropping back alongside the creek to a junction with the **Burkhart** 33-A
**Trail (5640 – 2.4).** Turn left (southwest), cross the creek, and 33-B
follow the trail up Cooper Canyon to a junction with the **Cooper Canyon Trail (5720 – 0.3).** You may be tempted to pause here in this verdant sanctuary of forest and fern. Turn right (west) and follow the trail up forested Cooper Canyon to **Cooper Canyon Trail Camp (6210 – 1.4)** (stream water). This will be your last water until Mill Creek Summit, 20.3 miles ahead. Take Road 3N02 up to the Angeles Crest Highway at

**Cloudburst Summit (7018 – 1.8).** Walk west along the highway

70 yards, then take the trail that goes left (west) down into Cloudburst Canyon, paralleling the highway. You cross the highway and follow below it on the north side, then recross, following above it on the south slope to **Three Points (5911 – 5.0),** where you rejoin the highway. Walk east 50 yards to the intersection of Horse Flat Road, then turn left (northwest) and follow the latter around and across chaparral-coated ridges, under scattered Jeffrey pines, passing side roads to Bandido and Horse Flats campgrounds, and descend to **Alder Saddle (5561 – 4.8),** on the divide between Alder Creek and the South Fork of Little Rock Creek. You now follow the road (3N17) northwest up the long, hot, shadeless slopes of Pacifico Mountain to a saddle (6440 – 3.7), then drop on steep switchbacks to

**Mill Creek Summit (4910 – 5.0),** where you meet Angeles Forest Highway. To your left is a picnic area with a drinking fountain. Your next water will be at Deer Spring, 10.1 miles farther. Cross the highway and start up the trail, heading north, just left of the Mt. Gleason Road. Your trail climbs the long east ridge of the Mt. Gleason massif, through chaparral and Jeffrey pine, paralleling the road first on one side, then the other. Road crossings are marked by CRHT posts. You veer westward, then southwest as you climb higher on the ridge, passing just left of the
33-B U.S. Army's Mt. Gleason Military Reservation (a former Nike
missile base). Your route then climbs the forested east slope of Mt.
34 Gleason itself, joins the road (6080 –7.5), and finally reaches a
35 high point on the southeast ridge (6240 – 0.9) of Mt. Gleason. The
large white dome on top is an Air Force radar installation. Your route now descends northwest on Santa Clara Divide Road, passing a side road left (6300 – 0.6), which heads southwest, then north, to Deer Spring in 1.1 miles. This spring will be your last water until Acton, 14.5 miles distant. Backtrack, or go cross country up to the road, then follow the route northwest to Messenger Flats Campground (5840 – 1.4), shaded by tall Jeffrey pines (no water). Continue down the road, heading west through chaparral country, to

**Moody Canyon Road (5440 – 1.3).** Turn right (north) and start the long, mostly shadeless descent down the north flank of the San Gabriels. Your road winds down the mountainside to Perspiration Point (4160 – 4.0), well named, where a cement monument commemorates the CCC boys who built this steep fireroad back in 1934. Continue down the dusty road to Magnetic Spring (3900 – 0.8), just east of the road, with water seeping in all but the driest months. Your route continues to follow Moody Canyon Road down to **Power Line Road (3450 – 1.2),** where a sign warns of a locked gate ahead. Turn right (northeast) and follow the power

line to **Arrastre Canyon Road (3245 – 1.4).** Turn left (north) and descend it through chamise and juniper down into Soledad Canyon to **Crown Valley Road (2624 – 3.2).** Turn right (northeast)
and follow this paved road to the small town of 35

**Acton (2698 – 1.2),** with a store and post office. The next stretch is a long, dry one—36 miles to Lake Hughes (water and supplies). Follow Crown Valley Road north out of town to a junction with

**Approaching Acton** *John W. Robinson*

**Escondido Canyon Road (2710 – 0.4).** Turn left (west) and follow it northwest to **Ward Road (3050 – 3.0).** Turn right (north) and take it across the Interstate 14 overpass to

**Sierra Highway (3110 – 0.3).** Take this paved road northwest, then west, over a shallow divide (3390 – 1.7) to a junction with an **unnamed dirt road (3150 – 1.0),** marked with a CRHT post. Turn right and follow this road 0.1 mile north, then west to its junction with **Anthony Road (2920 – 1.2).** Turn right (north) and take this road up Letteau Canyon, curving northwest, then west to Anderson Ranch (3180 – 2.3), shown on the topographic map as *Annan Ranch,* shaded by oaks and cottonwoods. Continue west on the dirt road, climbing a brush-covered slope to a junction with **Trail 14W02 (3350 – 1.3).** Turn right (north) and follow this footpath up the shadeless, chaparral-covered slope to the top of **Sierra Pelona (4470 – 2.3),** a bare, wind-swept ridge. Turn left (west) and follow the ridgetop fire road for ⅓ mile, then go right (northwest) down the trail, passing the side trail left to the *world's largest canyon live oak,* just a charred hulk due to a recent fire). Then you cross the Martindale Canyon Fire Road as you drop to a junction with the

**Bouquet Canyon Road (3200 – 2.7).**The Clearwater and San
Francisquito faults merge together just east of Bouquet Reservoir
and run east along this road. Mesozoic granite is to the north,
35 Paleozoic Pelona schist to the south. Paleocene marine sediments
36 underlie the reservoir, between the two faults. Cross the road and
walk 50 yards left (west) to a fence and a trail. You still have 17 dry
37 miles to Lake Hughes. If you can't make it, head west along the
road for 1½ miles, then west on Spunky Canyon Road, which takes you along the north shore of the reservoir, then climbs north over a low saddle and descends to Spunky Canyon Campground, a good place to rest. The road then heads northwest past Green Valley to San Francisquito Canyon Road. Follow this highway northeast up to a saddle and back to the route. If your water supply is adequate, turn right (north) and follow the trail alongside the fence, passing scattered oaks, up a small valley, then steeply up a ridge to

**Leona Divide Fire Road (4240 – 2.1).** Turn left (northwest) and follow the bare ridgetop road as it winds its tortuous way through manzanita, chamise, and occasional mountain mahogany and scrub oak to **San Francisquito Canyon Road (3700 – 8.2).**

* * * *

**You now have a choice between two undesirable routes.** Farther north, the permanent *and* temporary PCT routes were routed by the Forest Service to run northeast along the crest of the Tehachapis. Armed guards of the giant Tejon Ranch will make sure you don't. If you wish to parallel these routes, you can do so by following roads northeast through Antelope Valley and the western Mojave Desert to the town of Mojave. If you have had trouble on the last dry stretch, then you should not attempt our revised temporary route with its 46-mile hot, dry, shadeless, forced march through the desert. Our recommended alternate route is to turn right (northeast) and follow the paved San Francisquito Canyon Road down into Leona Valley to

**Elizabeth Lake Road (3402 – 0.8).** Turn left (north) and follow it past small homes, shaded by a few pines and cottonwoods, to **Johnson Road (3331 – 0.8 – 1.6).** Go right (east) and climb gently over Johnson Summit, following this paved road as it descends into Antelope Valley, then turns north and becomes **110th Street (2880 – 3.3 – 4.9).** Follow the road as it heads due north across the flat valley floor. Clusters of juniper, tamarisk and cottonwood offer occasional shade. You cross State Highway 138 (2487 – 7.9) and continue straight north, finally reaching **Avenue A (2486 – 3.0 – 15.8).** Turn right (east) and follow this dirt road past the alfalfa fields of the Dennis Bar X Ranch to a junction with

**90th Street (2433 – 2.1 – 17.9).** Turn left (north) and follow this road into the outskirts of Willow Springs (2455 – 3.0). Here, at the
junction with Rosamond Boulevard, is a gas station and cafe– **37**
food and water available, your last until Mojave, 18.8 miles ahead. **44**
Continue north on 90th Street (Tehachapi–Willow Springs Road), now paved, rounding Willow Springs Butte on your right, then eventually curving northwest (3000 – 6.5) and gently climbing up to a reunion with the temporary PCT route along the aqueduct (3140 – 1.5 – 28.9).

* * * *

The other revised temporary PCT route, 41 miles longer than its alternate, crosses San Francisquito Canyon Road and continues west up the Leona Divide Fire Road, which traverses the north slopes of Grass Mountain, passes several junctions with roads leading down both sides of the ridge, then descends to the small community of

**Lake Hughes (3320 – 9.0),** with a store, post office, and lots of live oaks for welcome shade. Your next water will be at Quail Lake County Fire Station, 24.9 miles farther. Your supplies have to last all the way to Mojave, 71 miles farther. Head south on Elizabeth Lake Canyon Road to a junction with the

**Sawmill-Liebre Road (3240 – 0.3).** Turn right (west) and follow this dirt road up onto the long hogback ridge of Sawmill Mountain. Vistas are far-reaching, particularly north across the golden-brown Antelope Valley to the distant Tehachapis, but there is no shade for the first 8 miles. Finally you reach a few black oaks and spruces and a junction with the Burnt Peak Road (5250 – 10.5). Continue northwest on the main divide road, paralleling the San Andreas Fault in the valley below you to your right, then reach a side road to Sawmill Campground (5300 – 1.4), 0.1 mile down to your right (no water). Now you are in a rich forest of California black oak, big-cone spruce and ponderosa pine, a welcome change from the long miles of shadeless walking. Your road now drops down the west slope of Sawmill Mountain to Artmore Saddle (4710 – 1.9). Continue west on your crest road, which climbs the long ridge of Liebre Mountain to Bear Campground (5390 – 3.5), down to your left, shaded by oaks (no water). Continue west on Liebre Mountain, under beautiful black oaks, to Tent Rock Campground (5350 – 4.7), to your right (again no water). Your route now continues west, rounding Sandberg Point at the west end of Liebre Mountain, and reaches an **unmarked trail (5250 – 0.5),** leading down the ridge to your right (northwest). Follow this trail down to a junction with the **Old Ridge Route Road (4195 – 1.5).** Turn right (north) and follow this old highway down to

**37** **Quail Lake County Fire Station (4020 – 0.6).** This will be your
**38-A** last water for the next 47 miles, until you reach the town of
**38-B** Mojave. You might consider the following government figures,
arrived at by subjects operating under *optimal* experimental con-
**39** ditions. Without water you can survive only 2 days at 120°F if you
**40** stay in one spot, 5 days at 100°F, and 9 days at 80°F. If you walked
during the day, you will survive only one third as long. If you rest
**41** during the day, but *hike* at night, then these figures become 1, 3,
**42** and 7 days, with 12, 33, and 110 miles being covered. At 100°F, the
mid-figure, you'll add about 20 miles to your cumulative night-
**43** hiking miles for every gallon of water you carry. Since you have 46 miles of hiking through mostly shadeless desert, you should take about 3 gallons of water. If you determine that you are running short around the midpoint, you can head east to Willow Springs and refill. In order to conserve your water, you should consider hiking at night or during the early morning hours. Use a flashlight, even on moonlit nights–rattlesnakes take advantage of the cool night too. One more word of caution: you'll lose plenty of salt on this hot stretch, so make sure you have an adequate supply of salt tablets. Our route now continues north down the Old Ridge Route, leaving the Angeles National Forest, then crossing the San Andreas Rift Zone at a junction with

**State Highway 138 (3380 – 2.4).** If your supplies are low, better head west 7 miles to Gorman on Interstate 5 and resupply. Otherwise, turn right (east) and follow the highway along the south edge of Antelope Valley to a junction with **280th Street (3037 – 6.5),** just past the Mettler Valley development. Turn left (north) and follow the road across the bottom of Antelope Valley, crossing the east branch of the California Aqueduct, to a junction with **Gaskell Avenue (3064 – 3.5).** Turn right (east) and take this road through the shadeless valley to the

**Los Angeles Aqueduct (3080 – 2.3)** (underground) bringing water south from Owens Valley. Turn half-left (northeast) and follow the dirt road that parallels the cement top of the aqueduct to an **unnamed road junction (3120 – 6.3),** just before the aqueduct tunnels into the hillside. Go right (southeast) and follow the road around the foot of the hills to a junction with the terminal end of **Rosamond Boulevard (2870 – 2.7),** about 0.4 mile before you cross under the Edison Company power lines, which head southeast across Antelope Valley. If your supplies are low, then follow this road 9 miles due east to Willow Springs, restock, then head north on the recommended alternate route. If you are still in good shape, continue along your road northeast to Cottonwood Creek (2950 – 1.9), a broad, dry wash coming down from the Tehachapis, where you meet a maze of roads and jeep tracks
branching in all directions. Here a 1½ mile detour northwest up to 43
the West Antelope Aqueduct Station will reward you with water 44
and perhaps a spot to camp. Otherwise, continue northeast until
you rejoin the **Los Angeles Aqueduct (3130 – 1.7).** Turn right 45
(east) and follow the road that parallels the cement roof of the aqueduct, passing occasional Joshua trees, to a junction with 110th Street (3140 – 6.5), heading north, distinctive because it is paralleled by tall telephone poles. Continue northeast along the aqueduct to

**Tehachapi-Willow Springs Road (3140 – 1.8),** a paved highway, and the junction with the recommended alternate route. Continue your aqueduct-side tramp, either along the new aqueduct, covered but marked by a line of white-capped pipes extruding from the earth, or along the old one, a sidewalklike cement slab through sand and sagebrush. The usual plethora of wheel tracks depart for everywhere and nowhere, but you won't have any problem staying on route. The railroad spur that you cross (3170 – 5.3) heads west up toward a cloud of dust emanating from Creal Mine, which the California Portland Cement Company operates to extract pre-Cretaceous limestone. You'll soon reach paved **Oak Creek Road (3160 – 0.9).** Turn right (east) and trace its path into Mojave to meet

**State Highway 14 (2782 – 4.3),** also paved. Water, phones, restaurants, and motels are here. The post office is three blocks east of Highway 14 on Belshaw, the street just north of White's Cafe. Your next water and supplies will be at Cantil, 18.2 miles distant. Turn left on Highway 14 (U.S. 6 on the map) and head north a block or so, then leave it and tread the ties of Southern Pacific Railroad's seldom-used Inyokern line. If the day is a hot one, the stench from the oiled ties may drive you to walk the dirt road parallelling the tracks on the east side. The advantage that this route has over following Highway 14 north is twofold: you don't have the noisy 60-mile-an-hour traffic or its carbon monoxide fumes to contend with, and you also get a unique perspective of the Sierra crest which you can't see from 14. Beyond the Marine Corps Air Station, the Randsburg-Mojave Road (2684 – 6.9) crosses our tracks. After another hot, monotonous stretch you cross Phillips Road (2395 – 5.8). Continue north past the new alfalfa fields of Fremont Valley, which contrast startlingly with the chalky magenta-orange Pliocene nonmarine sediments at the mouth of Jawbone Canyon. Just after the road turns northwest (2195 – 3.7), you cross the left-lateral Garlock Fault, which extends from the San Andreas Fault east to the Death Valley Fault. Keep an eye out for the reappearance of Highway 14 to your left. Cross the tracks, intervening desert, and highway to Tokiwa's gas station and res-
45 taurant at

46 **Cinco (2135 – 1.2).** Farther north along the main highway is a
store (2110 – 0.9) and the Cantil post office. Your next water will
47 be at Skyline Ranch in Kelso Valley, 18.1 miles ahead. You won't find a dependable source of supplies until you reach either Weldon or Lake Isabella, roughly 55 miles distant. Continue northwest on the highway across a dry wash, turning left (west) onto paved

**Jawbone Canyon Road (2170 – 0.4)** as it passes under two big siphons of the Los Angeles Aqueduct. Just before you come to a cliff almost touching the south side of the road, a spur road leads south to secluded campsites in a box canyon. Grayish-green rock identifies the outcrop of Blue Point, a remnant of Miocene basalt and pyroclastics, just above an unmarked junction with sandy

**Hoffman Well Road (2550 – 4.8).** Property-owners between Jawbone Canyon and the Sequoia National Forest boundary (20 miles farther) prohibit camping. Turn right (north) here and start north, then take the left fork upon reaching the Alphie Spring Road (2650 – 0.8). It's a stiff pull up through groves of Joshua trees to reach abandoned Hoffman Well (3650 – 3.6), then a reunion with

**Jawbone Canyon Road (3815 – 0.5),** now a dirt road. Turn right

---

**Right: Los Angeles aqueduct** *J.C. Jenkins*

(north) and hike past a junction with Butterbread Canyon Road (4000 – 0.6), remaining on the more heavily traveled road as it curves west. The spacious basin of Kelso Valley comes into view as you top a saddle (4830 – 3.3) on the southwest shoulder of granitic Butterbread Peak. Your road now descends Pleistocene sediments into the valley to a junction with the Kelso Valley Road (3970 – 3.7). Water and limited supplies are available at the Skyline Ranch store, just north on this road. The next permanent water will be at a spring 16.0 miles distant. Your road curves sharply south 300 yards past this junction, then begins a gentle ascent northwest to Cottonwood Creek (4705 – 5.0), which flows through early summer. Now the Geringer Grade reacquaints you with digger, pinyon, Jeffrey and ponderosa pines, mountain juniper, red and white fir, and ultimately western white pine as you toil up short, steep hairpin curves into the Piute Mountains, topping out at the boundary of Sequoia National Forest (6250 – 2.1). Campsites on this ridge abound in sweeping views and cooling, pine-scented breezes. Logging is underway, and development of a new network of roads is proceeding apace in the Greenhorn (Piutes) and Cannell (Kern Plateau) Districts traversed by the Pacific Crest Trail. Trails are obliterated in some places, in others confusingly hard to find. To stay on the route here (the road is now
marked 29S01), take every well-travelled road to the right. Hike
47 past the Gwynne Mine Road (6510 – 3.1), an organizational
48 camp, a decrepit sawdust burner, and other relics of the area's
mining era until you come to a junction with

49 **Piute Mountain Road (28S01) (6250 – 3.5)** at the site of
50 Claraville, a boom camp for gold miners in the 1870's. Turn left
(west) and wade through the dust of this gentle grade. Just before
51 the road forks west, search the hillside to your left for a cattle
trough and spring (6620 – 1.9). Turn right (north) onto **Woolstalf Road (26S01) (6680 – 0.1)** through piquant French Meadow, ascending past a Weldon Meadow spur road (6750 – 0.7) to **Bright Star Mine Road (7515 – 2.8).** During its heyday, this mine yielded a million dollars in gold.

* * * *

**At this junction a 40-mile alternate route is possible.** It has the advantages of abundant drinking water, good bathing in hot and cold water, and all the facilities you'll need. If you miss having people to talk to or your supplies are running low, then follow the mine road to the start (7520 – 0.3) of the Bright Star Trail (34E34), which heads north-northwest along a ridge before descending to

**Erskine Creek Road (27S01) (4340 – 4.2 – 4.5).** Pursue this road as it winds down-canyon through pre-Cretaceous metamorphic rocks. Spur roads lead up to mines located in limestone metamorphosed by the underlying intrusive granite. Where the canyon opens up (2870 – 6.0), the road becomes paved, like all the roads you will now walk along, and descends gently past Kern Valley High School to **State Highway 178 (2490 – 2.5 – 13.0).** Turn right (northeast) and walk past Scovern Hot Springs into the small settlement of Lake Isabella. Here are telephones, a store, a post office, and a junction with

**Burlando Road (State Highway 155) (2500 – 0.7 – 13.7).** Turn left (west) and follow this road past numerous campgrounds, some with good bathing beaches, along the west shore of Lake Isabella. Continue straight ahead past Evans Road (State Highway 155) (2660 – 6.8), where the name of our route changes to Wofford Boulevard. Wofford Heights (2660 – 0.2) proffers a handful of stores, motels and cafes, and a post office. Leaving town, your road skirts upper Lake Isabella, a parched dustbowl summer and fall, and on its way to Kernville passes a golf course. Everything a hiker could ask for–almost!–is here. Leave Wofford Boulevard at **Circle Park (2700 – 3.9 – 24.6)** and curve east across the Kern River to the Kernville post office, the U.S.F.S. Cannell District Ranger Station, and a junction with **Kern River Road (2700 – 0.6 – 25.2).** Turn left (northwest) and follow this road to
meet the 51

**Cannell Trail (33E49) (2760 – 1.4 – 26.6),** which starts along 52
the west slopes of a small but obvious hill of metamorphic rock.
Turn right (northeast) and ascend the trail to a saddle (3660 – 1.2), 53
then go down and east to a road (3490 – 0.3). A steep 4000′ ascent 54
through open chaparral looms ahead. This, combined with the prospect of no available water for 10 miles, makes a stop at Cannell Creek to tank up on water advisable. Cross the Rincon Fault, leaving metamorphic rocks behind, and begin your long climb up the trail over granitic rocks, switchbacking at times, to a saddle (5240 – 2.6), then east up a ridge to

**Cannell Meadow Trail (33E32) (5600 – 0.8 – 31.5).** Turn left (east) and follow this trail up the ridge, soon gaining the welcome canopy of a coniferous forest. The grade becomes gentler as your trail curves northeast to Pine Flat and **Road 24S12 (7360 – 3.2 – 34.7).** Follow this road north along the eastern fringes of Cannell Meadow to a junction with **Road 24S50 (7560 – 3.1 – 37.8).** Turn left (north) and walk along it until you reach Cannell Creek and a reappearance of the **Cannell Meadow Trail (33E32) (7570 – 0.7 – 38.5).** Turn right (northeast) and parallel selectively logged Cannell Creek before climbing east to a saddle (8450 – 1.2). A brief descent northward brings you to

**Cherry Hill Road (22S01) (8210 – 0.8 – 40.5),** and a reunion with the temporary PCT route.

*   *   *   *

The temporary route turns east at the junction with the Bright Star Mine Road and follows Woolstalf Road (28S25) as it loops around the head of Bright Star Creek, then contours forested slopes to a saddle (7130 – 2.8). Here the road ends for all but jeep, motorcycle, and foot travel. Quite recently, this country has been selectively logged. Once the Forest Service removes the slash and stumps after the logging is done, the land looks quite presentable, not the eyesore that clear-cut logging practices would leave. As you start your descent north, you might try to find well-hidden Steve Spring, somewhere down the north side of this ridge and within a ¼ mile radius of the trail signs. More dependable water can be found in Woolstalf Creek below the meadow. Just before you reach Woolstalf Meadow, an old green-and-white trail sign indicates a junction with

**Dry Meadows Trail (34E31) (6570 – 0.8). Again, you have a choice.** The Greenhorn District's temporary PCT route involves a long, circuitous, and almost never used path to Dry Meadows (6200 – 5.5), then over a broad saddle (6580 – 1.1) and down a
**54** steep, rocky trail, with no available water except when the snow-
**50** pack has been heavy. You then have a tangle of wheel tracks
(3770 – 2.6) to thread down to a right turn on **Highway 178**
**58** **(2625 – 3.4).** The only nice thing about it is that it comes out at a KOA campground with a store and showers. From here, proceed east on 178 past a store and motel to Fay Ranch Road (2651 – 3.2).

*   *   *   *

A better alternative is to take the Woolstalf Trail (34E32) straight ahead, around the fenced confines of Woolstalf Meadow, and leave the jeep road (6490 – 0.7) to cross the creek at a spring and fine campsites. Look for blazed trees to find the route, and always take the trail rather than the road where there's a choice. Our trail runs down a nose, keeping left at a lateral, crosses Woolstalf Creek again (5750 – 1.4), and plunges off the plateau to become a road at Roberts Ranch (3750 – 2.7). Tread softly or ask permission to cross private land to join the

**Kelso Valley Road (3160 – 1.9 – 6.7).** There's usually water in willow-fringed Kelso Creek. Turn left (north) and descend along it very gently to **Kelso Creek Road (2990 – 2.7 – 9.4).** Kelso Valley

Road angles northwest here, but your route saunters north on Kelso Creek Road to meet **State Highway 178 (2680 – 4.6 – 14.0).** Turn left (west) and follow this cottonwood-shaded corridor to the Weldon post office at **Fay Ranch Road (2651 – 1.3 – 15.3),** where you rejoin the temporary PCT route.

* * * *

Weldon is the last settlement you'll see along the route for 232 miles to Reds Meadow, near Devils Postpile National Monument. Until then you will have to take lateral trails out to settlements to obtain supplies. Your next water will be along the upper reaches of Fay Creek, about 12 miles ahead. Turn right (north) on Fay Ranch Road and follow it a level two miles across the South Fork Kern River and its broad valley, then ascend Fay Creek's alluvial fan to

**Quarter Circle Five Ranch (3800 – 4.9).** Signs at its entrance read *No trespassing, hunting, or fishing–under penalty of law.* Hikers are allowed to pass through as long as they inform the ranch foreman of their intentions. He's also an excellent source of advice for Kern Plateau travel. Cross Fay Creek, turn right along a fence, then right again at a green corrugated shed. The foreman's house is diagonally across the road from this shed. Pick up the trail here (4180 – 1.1), ducking into a gully, rounding a nose, and
crossing a pipeline. Your route, now a cattle driveway, shoots **58**
straight up this ridge. Once secure on the Kern Plateau, you'll pass
a junction with the Bartolas Country Trail (6780 – 3.8) before **50**
touching the end of Cherry Hill Road (22S01) (6800 – 0.5). Con- **53**
tinue northwest through Little Cannell Meadow (6900 – 0.5) and
up a low ridge, where you'll encounter Fay Creek again **54**
(7420 – 1.1), and parallel it up to

**Cannell Meadow Road (7640 – 0.9)** at Long Meadow. Just north up this road you join the **Cherry Hill Road (22S01) (7850 – 0.4)** and ascend it past Road 24S13 (7830 – 0.4) and Little Buck Meadow (8080 – 1.8) to a junction with the **Cannell Meadow Trail alternate route (8220 – 0.7).** The next gentle ascent, which may seem to the hiker to be just another grind up one more hill, is really an invitation to easy walking. From the saddle (8340 – 0.5), your descent is light on the muscles and an aura of holiday transforms the landscape. At your feet, the wind ripples through the rye stalks of deep-dish Big Meadow like crème de menthe syrup over vanilla ice cream. Pass Big Meadow South Loop (7960 – 1.0) and skirt the meadow's western margin to leave the Cherry Hill Road on the

**Main Summit Trail (33E32) (7750 – 1.5),** just after crossing Salmon Creek. Over the low rim of hills to the east in Domelands

Wilderness, notable for obelisks, monoliths, solitude, and rattlesnakes. Follow the trail north along the meadow's edge to Big Meadow North Loop (23S07) (7810 – 0.8). From here, a long, protracted ascent along the trail to Sherman Pass looms ahead, following the trace of the Durrwood Fault. Trail 34E12 (8030 – 0.8), Siretta Peak pass (8820 – 1.0), Deadwood Meadow and Trail 34E13 (8760 – 0.4), Mosquito Meadow (8800 – 2.0), Round Meadow (9000 – 1.0), and Durrwood Meadows (8820 – 1.6) pass by to the cadence of the hiker's stride. The Sherman Pass Road is slated for construction as soon as an agreement for cooperative construction between the Forest Service and the company intending to log the Bonita-Paloma country is signed. The alignment of this trans-Sierra road will roughly parallel or obliterate our trail between Durrwood and Curliss Meadows. Continue north through the western white pine and red fir up to Sherman Pass (9150 – 0.7), where a two-mile spur trail northwest along the ridge to 9909′ Sherman Peak makes an interesting side trip. From its summit you can see the long, straight Kern River Canyon, which has eroded along an inactive fault zone. From the pass, descend to a low ridge (8500 – 1.3), then down to intersect the **North Meadow Trail (8340 – 0.5).** Occasional stands of incense cedar freckle the face of this country, which is scheduled to be shaved all the way north to Beach
54 Meadows within the next 10 years. Turn right (east) and continue
55 along Trail 34E09 as it crosses the Trout Creek Trail (33E28)
(8210 – 0.4), veers northeast, and climbs over a low, broad saddle to

**Curliss Meadows Guard Station (8400 – 1.2).** The Sherman Pass Road from the east has been pushed through as far as Palóma Meadows, 1.2 miles east of here. Turn left (north) and follow Trail 34E01 over a slight divide to **Bonita Meadows (8300 – 1.5).** The old guard station here is another of the relics from the days before the invasion of roads on the Kern Plateau, when each station was an outpost in the wilderness, by horseback a day's ride apart. Turn right (east) and follow the Bonita Creek Trail as it drops down a steep, rocky course beside the creek to a junction with **Rattlesnake Creek Trail (34E07) (7430 – 1.6).** California black oak and mountain whitethorn put in an appearance here. Turn left (north) and descend this trail along the creek to the **Beach Meadows Trail (7230 – 0.8),** on your right. Switchback up it to a saddle (7800 – 1.0), then continue north over undulating topography to the

**Beach Meadows Guard Station (7720 – 5.5).** Tracking PCT shields, leave the guard-station road just before it joins wider Road 21S19, and head west on a trail, crossing Beach Creek before

---

**Right: Beach Meadow** *Toby Heaton*

ascending to **Lion Meadows Road (20S42) (7860 – 0.5).** Do not follow the trail running up beside Beach Creek–logging has obliterated it in places. Instead, proceed west on the Little Horse Meadows Trail (34E02), then up a spur ridge and over to Little Horse Meadows (8320 – 1.5), a good campsite. From here, a gentle grade prevails up past lodgepole-fringed Osa Meadows (8480 – 2.8) to an intersection with the Manzanita Knob Road (20S25) (8590 – 0.5). A pleasant up-canyon stroll beside a flowery brook is disrupted by the appearance of yet another logging road (8440 – 0.9). A short pull through a selectively logged tract brings you to a road and a saddle at the nominal boundary of Inyo National Forest (9050 – 0.4).

Administration of Inyo forest lands is divided across the Toowa Range. The southern half is controlled by Sequoia National Forest, which allows and provides for jeep and motorcycle traffic, while Inyo has always held a more wilderness-oriented philosophy. People with stock should take care, for with few exceptions the temporary PCT route is open to motorcycles throughout Sequoia lands. Motorcyclists rationalize their obnoxiously loud whine as "letting off steam"–it wouldn't occur to them that they are ruining the healing quiet that so many with city-jangled nerves come to the mountains for. They make your winding descent northeast to Casa Vieja Meadows resemble a
55 banked highway. A few hundred yards beyond a spur trail to a
56 public pasture is Ninemile Creek and a left-handed junction with the

**Jordon Hot Springs Trail (34E19) (8310 – 1.5).** Just beyond, a jeep trail crosses the grasslands east to Casa Vieja Guard Station. Supplies may be picked up here, provided you've mailed your parcel at least a month before arriving, addressed to

Yourself
c/o District Ranger
Box 6
Kernville, California 93238
Attn.: Pacific Crest Trail – Casa Vieja Guard Station
Date you plan to be here.

Write the district ranger beforehand to verify that this service is still being offered, and for the earliest date supplies can be picked up at Casa Vieja.

Beginning the long, gentle grade up over the Toowa Range, your trail keeps to the woods, avoiding a cattle-cropped panhandle of Casa Vieja Meadows. Crumbling granite bosses, a picturesque northerly view of Kern Peak, and a dalliance in the mud of Lost Trout Creek (8460 – 1.4) pass the time until a sign where the Beer Keg Trail (34E17) (8520 – 1.1) branches off indicates *Long*

*Canyon Creek,* with good campsites. Hereafter the trail becomes hard to follow. In 300 yards cross to the left bank of this creek and parallel it eastward to a *TRAIL* sign. Just across the creek you'll see a new mileage sign where the Big Dry Meadows Trail (8620 – 0.6) takes off south. Stay on the left (north) bank and keep a sharp eye out for the PCT shield at the edge of the woods to your left. Here the tread resumes, running up to join a spur of the Beer Keg Trail (8640 – 0.1). Your way proceeds north up-valley parallel to a jeep road across the creek. A new trail, indistinct at first, bypasses fenced private property surrounding the building on the map. Look for the new *TRAIL* sign and PCT shield at the far end of a clearing and to your left, uphill. Beyond a step-across brook, the trail is best followed by using PCT shields and diamonds as blazes. More distinctly now, your path heads through "Dancha Desert" to the welcome relief of a sign prohibiting further motorcycle travel, and you reach a saddle (9460 – 2.8) at the end of the Long Canyon grade. The descent, steep at first, eases and levels to meet the South Fork Trail (8800 – 1.9) coming up from Monache Meadows. Nearly straight corridors through scrubby forest lead on to perennial Strawberry Stringer and fine campsites around Lacey's Cow Camp (8610 – 0.9). Just beyond is a junction with the

**Strawberry Meadows Trail (35E10) (8635 – 0.3).** Templeton
Mountain, the Tertiary andesitic dome on your right, nearly fills **56**
the floor of ancient Toowa Valley, a feature that once extended from the present course of the Kern River east past the present Sierra crest (the crest has been slowly migrating westward). Turn left (northwest) beside dry Strawberry Creek, where the

**Redrock Creek Trail (8650 – 0.4)** branches off to scale the Toowa Range. You should take the right fork, crossing the sandy creekbed. The great, gritty flats of Templeton Meadows are a small remnant compared to the vast sweep the Toowa Valley once commanded. The rounded mountains and stream-cut valleys here are typical of much of the Sierra Nevada before glaciation. Shortly after crossing a seldom-used airstrip, you come to a junction with the unmaintained Mulkey Meadows Trail (35E06) (8635 – 1.0) and a lateral south from the Redrock Creek Trail. The new Cottonwood Creek roadend is 11½ miles by way of Mulkey Meadows and Trail Pass, although cattle grazing has made the trail indistinct until after it leaves Ramshaw Meadows. After crossing Movie (8630 – 0.4) and Lewis (8640 – 0.7) Stringers, your trail climbs over a low ridge and skirts the edge of Ramshaw Meadows past a crumbling granite keyhole to Kern Peak Stringer (8715 – 2.7). An unmaintained trail departs here for the panoramic views atop 11510′ Kern Peak, the first glaciated peak you've seen unless you took the alternate route in the San Bernardinos that ascended San Gorgonio Mountain. Your trail's gentle ascent of cinder-cone slopes to a drift fence offers fine vistas eastward of the isolated hump of Olancha Peak behind Ramshaw Meadows, the picture framed by contrasts of the orange pumice on your right, old white granite on your left, and the glistening green pine needles that filter the view. Continue up along the banks of the trickling South Fork Kern River and past a pleasant campsite to a junction with the

**Golden Trout Creek Trail (8885 – 1.2).** Turn right (north) and pass a guard station to a ditch marking the remains of The Tunnel (8890 – 0.2). At one time South Fork ranchers attempted unsuccessfully to divert Golden Trout Creek here. A glance at the topographic map reveals the oddity of this place, as both creeks trace an acute "x" that has been sliced perpendicularly by a low ridge. The South Fork Kern River has captured the Tunnel Meadow drainage, which, until geologically recent time, used to flow west into Golden Trout Creek. A lateral to Tunnel Air Camp, a popular fly-in resort for fishermen and hunters, peels off to the right here. Beyond a gaging station is a ditch through the pumice, another defunct enterprise of the South Fork ranchers, and a junction (9080 – 1.2) with a second lateral to Tunnel Air Camp.
56 Golden Trout Creek skewers beads of emerald meadows and
offers delightful camping and fishing. Ford the creek here and
57 ramble up its west side, past a lateral to Rocky Basin Lakes
(9820 – 1.8). Soon, Big Whitney Meadow (9680 – 1.0) and the raw, ragged peaks of the glaciated High Sierra will break into view. The junction of a second lateral to Rocky Basin Lakes (9680 – 1.2) offers a public pasture, a campground, and the knockout whiff and residue of cattle grazing in action. Farther still is the Cottonwood Pass Trail (35E05) (9780 – 0.3), departing eastward. Unnecessarily gentle switchbacks frustrate your waterless ascent to **Siberian Pass (10,920 – 3.5),** on the border of Sequoia National Park, and a junction with the Upper Rock Creek Trail.

* * * *

A spectacular alternate route is available here for mountaineers competent on third-class rock who are planning to climb Mt. Whitney. Proceed north on the Siberian Pass Trail, across the barren sandflats of two prongs of what's called Siberian Outpost, and over a watershed divide among a smattering of lodgepole and foxtail pines to meet the **Army Pass Trail (10,800 – 1.8).** Turn left (northwest), descend slightly and turn right (north) on the

**Rock Creek Trail (10,700 – 0.3 – 2.1).** Your way idles in a

speckled band of meadows en route to a sparkling lake (10,795 – 0.5) at the foot of The Major General, a figure so imposing that it took a glacier to polish his boots. Campsites are best on the south-shore peninsula. The wildflowers, lake waters, and granite spires here are the most dazzling of any segment of the Pacific Crest Trail you've encountered since the Mexican border. Here the trail ends; your route-to-come is cross-country and well-ducked. Skirt the lake's east shore, picking up random footpaths. Cross the inlet stream, clambering beside it up a chute to a shallow pond (11,200) shown on the topo map. Contour northward along the 11,200′ level, boulder-hopping the talus. Across the outlet
stream of Iridescent Lake, some nice timberline campsites 57
(11,200 – 2.0) have been leveled in the woods. Looking due north, 65
you can see how The Miter earned its name. Proceed northwest, ascending smooth shoulders and ledges of granite to Sky Blue Lake (11,600 – 0.5). Camping is fair on exposed lakeshore gravels. Leave the lake from its north shore, where a rock rib is more easily surmounted the farther west you attack it. Cross a stream, keeping close to the west side of it as you resume a northerly course. Skirt the lake on its east side. Getting to Arc Pass from here is a matter of slogging up slopes of sand. A stunning view of the Whitney crest–and your descent route–awaits you at the pass (12,900 – 2.5).

North from Siberian Pass *Toby Heaton*

Descent from this pass is tricky; the granite is crumbling and some fine mountaineers have fallen to their deaths here, caught off guard. Do not descend straight down from the pass–a hidden dropoff lurks below. Instead, traverse east on treacherous ledges, descending slightly to a prominent chute coming down from Mt. Irvine. Stay close to the rocks along the right (north) side of the chute. A large cairn on your right and ducks mark where you leave the chute to avoid another dropoff. Work your way down ledges and cracks systems to rejoin the chute, and boulder-hop over talus to the fair camp spots at the eastern tip of Consultation Lake (11,650 – 1.2). These aren't usually as squirming with people as the flats a half-mile beyond at Trail Camp. Traverse east, crossing the outlet stream and climbing through stately corridors of rock, to meet the

**Mt. Whitney Trail (11,945 – 0.4 – 9.2).** Over 100 switchbacks have been chisled into the grade up to 13,777′ Trail Crest. Shortly beyond is a junction with the **John Muir Trail (13,560 – 3.0 – 12.2).** Turn right (north), staying on the Mt. Whitney Trail. A row of gendarmes, a few mild switchbacks, a few hundred tourists . . . and you've made the summit of the highest peak in the United States outside of Alaska, **Mt. Whitney (14,494 – 2.0 – 14.2).** When you're ready to come down, backtrack to the junction of the

**John Muir Trail (13,560 – 2.0 – 16.2)** and turn right (west). A
65 moderate descent brings you face-to-face with 13,184′ Mt. Hitch-
66 cock and the cirque containing the Hitchcock Lakes. You can tell
where the "high-water mark," or trim line, of the glacier that
57 scooped out this bowl was–all the avalanche chutes on the
northeast face of Mt. Hitchcock terminate at it. For those who will take lumps in their mattress, campsites have been fashioned everywhere imaginable along this trail. Camping has been prohibited at Timberline Lake. People who won't take their lumps will find better sites where firewood and good fishing abound near the

**Crabtree Ranger Station. (10,640 – 6.5 – 22.7).** Just beyond, at a trail fork, keep to the right and ascend a gentle slope to meet the **Pacific Crest Trail (10,880 – 0.9 – 23.6).**

* * * *

At the Siberian Pass trail junction you turn left (west) onto the sandy, open expanses of Siberian Outpost. Enjoying fine views of the Mt. Whitney country, you make several easy fords of Siberian Pass Creek as the timber cover thickens, lodgepole joining foxtail, while you descend gently. Lodgepole is an old friend by now, but foxtail is a new, fascinating species found mainly in the high southern Sierra near timberline. The descent finally steepens, and you switchback down to a meadowy, flowery

**Junction near Rock Creek (9700 – 5.0).** The PCT turns left (west) past the Rock Creek Patrol Cabin, fords Rock Creek (no problem if there's a log) and swings north to climb steeply up the canyon wall on a gravelly-sandy path. After the climb, you ford Guyot Creek (10,350 – 1.9) and climb around boulders to a forested saddle (11,020 – 1.1), then descend to the large sandy basin called Guyot Flat. On this large flat the sand is very deep, and not much grows here. Beyond Guyot Flat you rollercoaster for several mostly forested miles, then drop steeply toward Whitney Creek. On this stretch you will have your first views of the west, or "back," side of Mt. Whitney (14,494), which from this angle looks long and flat-topped, and is fluted by many avalanche chutes on its great west slope. You pass a minor trail that goes west to the Kern River as you descend to Whitney Creek (10,329 – 3.3) and a good campsite. A shortcut trail leads northeast from here to Crabtree Ranger Station on the John Muir Trail. (15 miles east is Whitney Portal, a roadend 13 miles west of Lone Pine, where supplies may be had.) Continuing north, the PCT rises steeply into foxtail-pine forest to meet the

**John Muir Trail (10,860 – 0.8).** This trail, a major segment of the PCT, runs 212 miles from Yosemite Valley to the top of Mt.
Whitney, and as of this writing it is more famous than the PCT, 57
but that may not be true in a few years. You will be on the Muir 66
Trail until you are almost at Reds Meadow, 146 miles ahead. Leaving the foxtail forest–ghostly on an overcast day–you skirt what the map calls Sandy Meadow and ascend to a high saddle (10,964 – 1.9). The trail winds among the huge boulders of a glacial moraine on the northwest slope of Mt. Young and brings you to excellent viewpoints for scanning the main peaks of the Kings-Kern Divide and the Sierra crest from Mt. Barnard (13,990) north to Junction Peak (13,888). You descend moderately, making several easy fords, and then switchback down to

**Wallace Creek (10,390 – 1.6),** where the High Sierra Trail goes left (west) toward the roadend near Giant Forest and a lateral trail goes east to Wallace Lake. The Wallace Creek ford, just north of the overused campsites, is difficult in early season. Now your sandy trail climbs up to a forested flat, crosses it, and reaches the good campsite at the ford of Wright Creek (10,800 – 1.0). You then trace a bouldery path across the ground moraines of Wright Creek glacier and rise in several steps to Bighorn Plateau. Views from the plateau are indeed panoramic, including the first view that the southbound hiker would have of Mt. Whitney. An unnamed grass-fringed lake atop the gravelly, lupine-streaked pla-

teau makes for great morning photographs westward. Now the PCT descends gently down the talus-clad west slope of Tawny Point, past many extraordinarily dramatic foxtail pines. At the unnamed lake beside the trail there are fair campsites, but hardly any wood. At the foot of this rocky slope, a trail goes southwest to the Kern River, and in 200 yards you come to the formidable ford of

**Tyndall Creek (10,920 – 4.0).** At the ford, the Shepherd Pass Trail goes off to the right. On the west side of the creek are many, many highly used campsites–a good place not to camp. Your trail makes a short climb to the junction with the **Lake South America Trail (11,270 – 0.7),** passes some campsites and rises above timberline. As you tackle the ascent to the highest point on the PCT, you wind among the barren basins of high, rockbound (but fishy) lakes to the foot of a great granite wall, then sweat up numerous switchbacks, some of which are literally cut into the rock wall, to

**Forester Pass (13,200 – 4.3)** on the border between Sequoia and Kings Canyon National Parks. Wearing your wind garment, you will enjoy the well-earned, sweeping views from this pass before you start the (net) descent of 9000 feet to Canada. Down the switchbacks you go (unless they are buried under snow), rolling past the steep west shore of Lake 12,248 and thrice fording Bubbs Creek. You reach timber, ford Center Basin Creek, pass the
Center Basin Trail (10,520 – 4.0) and then ford more branches of **66**
Bubbs Creek. Campsites of various quality are located near some **67**
of these fords, and wood is scarce, as it is almost everywhere along the Muir Trail. Continuing down the east side of Bubbs Creek, you reach

**Vidette Meadow (9600 – 3.0),** long a favorite camping spot in these headwaters of the South Fork of the Kings River. High use has made the place less attractive, but its intrinsic beauty has not been lost, and the mighty Kearsarge Pinnacles to the north have lost only a few inches of height since Sierra Club founders like Joseph Le Conte camped here seventy years ago. As of this writing, camping is limited to one night in one place from here to Woods Creek crossing. A summer ranger is here to assist traffic flow. Beyond the meadow, the trail to Cedar Grove goes west (14 miles to scanty supplies) and the PCT turns north (9550 – 0.7) to fiercely attack the wall of Bubbs Creek Canyon. You pause for breath at the Bullfrog Lake junction (10,530 – 1.7) and then finish off the tough climb to a broad, sandy saddle that contains the

**Junction of the Charlotte Lake and Kearsarge Pass trails (10,720 – 0.7).** There are modest supplies 9 miles east at the Kearsarge roadend in Onion Valley. The Muir Trail traverses high above Charlotte Lake, veers eastward, and brings you to the foot

---

**Left: Mt. Whitney from Bighorn Plateau** *Jim Barker*

of the wall that is notched by Glen Pass. It is hard to see where a trail could go up that precipitous blank wall, but one does, and after very steep switchbacks you are suddenly at Glen Pass (11,978 – 2.3). The view north presents a barren, rocky, brown world with precious little green of tree or meadow visible. Yet you know by now that not far down the trail, there will be plenty of willows, grasses, wildflowers and eventually groves of lodgepole, foxtail and whitebark pines. To be sure you get there, take special care on your descent over loose rock from Glen Pass. When you are about 300 vertical feet above Rae Lakes, you will see why Dragon Peak (12,995) has that name. Where the 60 Lakes Trail turns off to the west (10,500 – 2.2) your route crosses the isthmus between two lakes, passes the Dragon Lake Trail (10,560 – 0.3), and then skirts the east shore of Rae Lakes past a summer ranger station. As of this writing, wood fires are not allowed between Glen Pass and the Baxter Pass Trail. Your trail passes more campsites which dot the shores of three unnamed lakes on the South Fork of Woods Creek. At the outlet of the third, the unsigned, unmaintained Baxter Pass Trail (10,200 – 3.5) heads northeast. From here you descend gently down open, lightly forested slopes, crossing several good-sized though unnamed tributaries. The reward for all this descent is the chance to start climbing again at

67 **Woods Creek Crossing (8492 – 3.1),** made via log, where the
68 campsites are good but much used. A ranger is stationed here in summer. There is no water problem as you slog up the valley of Woods Creek, what with the main stream near at hand and many tributaries to jump, hop or wade. West of well-shaped Mt. Cedric Wright (12,372) the trail passes an area where Woods Creek has eroded a box canyon in the highly jointed rock. After the junction of the **Sawmill Pass Trail (10,400 – 3.6)** the grade abates and the traveler reaches the alpine vale where this branch of the Kings River has its headwaters, bounded by big-as-life peaks on 3½ sides. With one long, last spurt you top Pinchot Pass (12,110 – 4.2) and devour the view of the entire headwaters of the South Fork of the Kings with one flick of your eyes. The PCT swoops down into the lake-laden valley below, past Lake Marjorie, to the **Bench Lake Trail junction (10,750 – 3.0).** Just beyond, you pass a trail leading east to Taboose Pass, then another after 1.1 miles, just beyond a ford. After 200 yards you cross the South Fork and meet the

**South Fork Trail (10,040 – 1.5).** You veer right (northeast) and cross several unnamed tributaries that can slow you down at the height of the melt, then ford the infant South Fork near some good campsites. East of the trail, on the Sierra crest, looming Cardinal

**Right: Fin Dome over Dollar Lake** *Thomas Winnett*

Mountain (13,397) is named for red but is in fact half white and half black, in a strange mixture. You cross grassy flats and hop over numerous branches of the headwaters of the South Fork of the Kings River. Every camper can have his own lake or lakelet in this high valley–though the campsites are a bit austere.

The ascent finally steepens to reach Mather Pass (12,100 – 5.2), named for Stephen Mather, first head of the National Park Service. The view ahead is dominated by the 14,000′ peaks of the Palisades group, knifing sharply into the sky. Your trail now makes a knee-shocking descent to the poor-to-fair campsites at long, blue Palisades Lakes (10,600 – 4.0). Wood is scarce here. Knees rested, you descend again, down the "Golden Staircase" cut into the cliffs of the gorge of Palisade Creek. This was the last part of the Muir Trail to be constructed, and it is easy to see why. Beyond multibranched Glacier Creek you arrive at Deer Meadow (8870 – 3.5), which is more lodgepole forest than meadow, but pleasant enough. Here an unmaintained trail goes south to Amphitheater Lake. The downhill grade continues, less steeply, across the stream draining Palisades Basin and several small streams to reach the

**Middle Fork of the Kings River (8000 – 3.7).** Turning right (north) you ascend past a series of falls and chutes along the river to Grouse Meadows, a serene expanse of grassland with good
68 campsites in the forest along the east side. Up the canyon, you
69 encounter repeated evidence of great avalanches crashing down
the immense canyon walls and wiping out stands of trees. The trail
70 crosses turbulent **Dusy Creek (8690 – 3.4)** on a steel bridge and
71 encounters the junction of the Bishop Pass Trail, where there is a
ranger station manned in summer. The route upcanyon ascends between highly polished granite walls, past lavish displays of a great variety of wildflowers. The trail passes through sagebrushy Little Pete and Big Pete Meadows, and swings west to assault the Goddard Divide and search out its breach, Muir Pass. Up and up the rocky trail winds, passing the last tree long before you reach desolate Helen Lake–named, along with Wanda Lake to the west, for John Muir's daughters. This east side of the pass is under snow throughout the summer in some years. Finally you haul up at Muir Pass (11,955 – 7.5), where a stone hut honoring Muir would shelter you in a storm. The views from here of the solitary peaks and the lonely lake basins are painted in the many hues of the metamorphic rocks that make up the Goddard Divide. From the hut your trail descends gently past Lake McDermand and Wanda Lake, which has fair campsites near the outlet. (Wood fires are banned from Muir Pass to Evolution Lake.). You then ford Evolution Creek (11,420 – 1.9) and switchback down into the

**Evolution Lake** *Andy Husari*

Sapphire Lake basin. The land here is nearly as scoured as when the ice left it, and the aspect all around is one of newborn nakedness. To the east is a series of tremendous peaks named for Charles Darwin and other major thinkers about evolution, and the next lake and the valley below it also bear the name "Evolution." The trail fords the stream at the inlet of this lake (10,850 – 2.9), skirts the lake, which has some campsites in clumps of stunted whitebark pines, and then drops sharply into Evolution Valley. The marvelous meadows here are the reason for re-routing the trail through the forest, so the fragile grassland can recover from over-tromping by the feet of earlier backpackers and horsepackers. At McClure Meadow is a summer ranger station. After several tributary fords on boulders or logs, you cross Evolution Creek (9240 – 7.8) any way you can and descend steeply to the bridge across the South Fork of the San Joaquin River (8470 – 1.5). Past numerous campsites, you recross on another bridge and roll on down and out of Kings Canyon National Park at the bridge crossing of **Piute Creek (8050 – 4.1),** where the Piute Pass Trail goes east. The Pacific Crest Trail continues down the South Fork Canyon to a junction with the

**Florence Lake Trail (7890 – 1.7),** where it veers right and
climbs the canyon wall, passing two lateral trails to Blaney
71 Meadows. You can refill your cooling system at Senger Creek
(9740 – 3.8), between the two, and enjoy the highline stroll past
72 Sally Keyes and Heart lakes to Selden Pass (10,900 – 4.2). There
73 are many campsites on the lakes north of this pass, the better ones
reached by going off the Muir Trail to, for instance, Lou Beverly or Sandpiper Lake. At Rosemarie Meadow (10,000 – 2.5) trails depart for Rose Lake and Lou Beverly Lake, and farther down (9530 – 1.4) a trail leads east up the East Fork of Bear Creek. To ford Bear Creek when the wade-across trail ford just before this junction is too high, go down below the outlet stream from Orchid Lake. You cross Hilgard Creek (9300 – 1.2) on logs, passing the Lake Italy Trail, and continue through the mixed forest cover to the place called Kip Camp (8840 – 2.4) on maps. Due to overuse, this camp is no more. The PCT then climbs over Bear Ridge, an unglaciated Pliocene erosion surface, to

**Mono Creek (7750 – 6.7),** crossed via bridge, and campsites at Quail Meadows. Six miles west by trail is a resort with limited supplies. (Supplies at Reds Meadow are 30 miles distant.) You head east, pass the Mono Creek Trail (8270 – 1.7), and then head north to make one hell of a climb on south-facing slopes. Water for drinking is no problem, but in early season watch your step at the first ford of Silver Pass Creek. This exhausting ascent preclimaxes

---

**Right: Silver Pass Creek** *Toby Heaton*

at Silver Pass (10,700 – 5.3), and then tops out at a glorious viewpoint on the Silver Divide (10,900 – 0.3). The descending route encounters the Goodale Pass Trail (10,550 – 1.1), wades the outlet of Helen Lake (collectors of lakes named "Helen" do well on the PCT) and makes a relentless descent to the beautiful valley of Fish Creek (9130 – 2.7), where there are good campsites not far from the junction with the Cascade Valley Trail. Beyond a bridge over Fish Creek (9130 – 0.2) you turn northeast up to Tully Hole (9520 – 1.1), a well-flowered grassland at the junction of the McGee Pass Trail with good campsites. The PCT climbs north up a band of Mesozoic metavolcanics which sweep east and grade into the Paleozoic metasediments of the domineering Red Slate Mountain (13,163). At Lake Virginia (10,314 – 1.9) there are some exposed campsites. In early season you will have to wade across the head of the lake. Your trail jogs over one ridge to Purple Lake (9900 – 1.8), where there are good campsites and a junction with a trail to Cascade Valley, and around another ridge to the

**Duck Lake Trail (10,150 – 2.3),** leading north. During dry seasons fill your canteen in Duck Creek. The PCT slants northwest high above Fish Creek, veers north to ford the branches of Deer Creek, forges on through Upper Crater Meadow (side trail to Mammoth Pass) and reaches the good campsites at Crater Meadow (8800 – 8.4). Here the eventual route of the PCT goes
73 left, but you stay on the Muir Trail (temporary PCT). The reason
74 the PCT does not stay on the Muir south of Reds Meadow is not
clear. North of there, the reason probably is to bypass some of the
75 most heavily used lakes in the wilderness High Sierra. Beyond another trail to Mammoth Pass, the Muir Trail swings down toward Reds Meadow, where there is a resort with the last supplies before Tuolumne Meadows, 35 miles ahead. However, contrary to Forest Service maps, the Muir Trail does not go through the resort: a rerouting has put it south of the civilization here, so that it does not cross a road anywhere south of Tuolumne Meadows. West of the resort you come to

**Devils Postpile National Monument (7600 – 4.5)** with its indeed monumental rock cliff. When this Pleistocene andesite flow cooled, it fractured into a hexagonal pattern, forming a bundle of long, vertical rock columns ("posts") that are mostly six-sided in cross section. Glaciers polished the top of the formation, so that it looks like a bathroom floor with huge tiles. Piled at the foot of the outcropping are hundreds of broken-off hexagonal "posts," forming the "postpile." Beyond this landmark you cross the

**Middle Fork of the San Joaquin River (7540 – 0.5),** on a sturdy bridge. Leaving the Monument at the north end of a large meadow, you make a steep ascent through deep, dusty pumice, a product of explosions of the geologically recent Inyo Craters, a few miles northeast. Shortly before Minaret Creek, find logs north of the trail ford, and continue up to

**Johnston Meadow (8120 – 2.0)** to thread the lake-dotted east slopes of Volcanic Ridge, high above the Middle Fork. Deadman Pass, across the canyon, is mantled with glacial till about 3 million years old. The age of this deposit caused geologists to move the beginning of the Pleistocene (Ice Age) from 1 million back to 3 million years B.P. (Before Present). You switchback down to beautiful Shadow Lake (8750 – 5.9), a classic case of chronic
congestion that may have to be declared off limits for a while. You **75**
should camp elsewhere even if it isn't. Your route ascends
westward up Shadow Creek Canyon, then turns right (north) at **76**
the

**Ediza Lake Trail junction (9030 – 1.1).** You climb 1000′ and then descend 500′ to the outlet of Garnet Lake (9680 – 2.4), another overused gem of the Minarets high country. Over the next ridge is the most dramatic of these lakes, Thousand Island Lake (9834 – 2.0). When the wind isn't blowing (twice a year) one can capture great photographs of Banner Peak (12,945) and much of the Ritter Range reflected in the clear lake waters. At the outlet,

0.2 miles farther, we are back on the route of the permanent PCT, which already exists as trail from here back to Agnew Meadows. From the outlet to Island Pass (10,200 – 2.0) most of the Muir Trail is not where the maps show it, having been rerouted in the Sixties. Your route descends to cross the branches of Rush Creek (campsites), passing trails to Davis Lakes and Waugh Lake. The route then climbs above timberline, swings west, negotiates some switchbacks, and *voila!* you are in Yosemite, at

**Donohue Pass (11,056 – 4.7),** where the view is worth a sip of wine, if you've been hoarding some since Reds Meadow. (Camping in Yosemite back country is allowed anywhere if you use a stove, but campfires are restricted to designated fire sites, and fires are restricted to established fire rings at the designated sites.) On the steep descent bordered by many flowery alpine meadows, you hop across the infant Tuolumne River twice, then cross it on a bridge. This segment is often under snow in early season. The trail levels off at a Lyell Fork base camp (9000 – 3.9) at the head of the long, long meadow down which the river meanders. This glaciated, wide, straight canyon is a boon for those who like to stare at the scenery and not have to watch the underfooting all the time. In lodgepole forest, you pass the Evelyn Lake Trail (8880 – 3.0) and the Rafferty Creek Trail (8700 – 4.2) before turning right to cross the river on a bridge and arrive at

76 **Tuolumne Meadows High Sierra Camp (8750 – 1.3).** Having
77 done almost the whole Muir Trail, you deserve a shower, and they
are available in the camp. Less than 2 miles west on the highway is
78 the summertime grocery store and post office. (The next supplies are 76 miles ahead at Leavitt Meadows Resort.) Your route goes west past maintenance buildings, employees' tent tops and a ranger station, crosses State Highway 120 (8595 – 1.1) and follows the oiled road that leads down the north side of Tuolumne Meadows, the largest subalpine meadows in the Sierra. As you pass the lower slopes of Lembert Dome on the north, notice how the glacier polished the stoss (back) side and plucked the lee (front) side. Erratic boulders carried by the glacier have been deposited all around your path. In these granite boulders note the large feldspar crystals that characterize the Cathedral Peak pluton, which intruded this area. Past the stables, the road becomes dirt, and shortly beyond it ends in a parking area (8590 – 0.8) by the river, near the Sierra Club camp. Here, beside a dilapidated shack housing a natural soda spring (bring Kool-Aid or Tang for soft drinks) you come to mile 0.0 of the Tahoe-Yosemite Trail (it works both ways). You go over the hill and down the river, making easy fords of Delaney and Dingley Creek. Two bridges cross and recross the river to bring you to

---

**Right: Lyell Glacier, Yosemite** *Jim Barker*

**Glen Aulin (7840 – 4.5),** where a High Sierra Camp might sell candy bars and does serve meals (reservations often required). The river trail goes west, but you ascend long, straight Cold Canyon, where the stream may not flow in late season, to the McCabe Lakes Trail (9210 – 7.1). Here you turn north and dip into Virginia Canyon, where you cross McCabe Creek and Return Creek on logs and encounter the Summit Pass Trail (8550 – 0.9). Then the PCT climbs to cross Spiller Creek and skirt Miller Lake (9480 – 3.4). As you drop down into Matterhorn Canyon, the corrugated "washboard" of northern Yosemite begins to take shape in your mind. Good campsites are near the wading ford, by the junction of the Burro Pass Trail (8490 – 1.9). Your trail swings southwest, then scrambles steeply up beside Wilson Creek, which it finally crosses on its way west to Benson Pass (10,140 – 4.2). You wind among house-size boulders west of the pass, making a two-stage descent to island-dotted Smedberg Lake (9220 – 2.2). Groves of lodgepole and whitebark pine surround the lake, and you are likely to find a great silence here, for you are in the heart of the largest roadless area in California. The fame of the Pacific Crest Trail may bring other campers to this lake, but you can surely be by yourself if you hike a little way off the trail in any direction.

Continuing toward Canada, you pass trails to Rodgers Lake and
Pate Valley, and descend a badly eroded path to a ford of Piute 78
Creek. Just beyond it is the short lateral (7590 – 3.9) to Benson 79
Lake, a fine place to lay over and enjoy the sandy beach and the
often good fishing. If you brought your canoe or sailboat, you can 80
even use it on the blue waters, for this is one of several lakes in Yosemite National Park where the authorities permit boats. The PCT climbs over the next ridge on the washboard, called Seavey Pass (9150 – 2.5), and descends to the junction with the **Buckeye Pass Trail (8910 – 0.6).** From the junction you float down a groove in the washboard for several miles, a groove called Kerrick Canyon, to the junction with the

**Hetch Hetchy Trail (7960 – 3.4)** and wade Rancheria Creek. Look for your trail on the far side of the well-developed campsite north of the creek. The PCT takes you over another ridge, plunges across Stubblefield Canyon Creek (7740 – 2.0) and despite your protests hauls you up to the top of Macomb Ridge. Find the route through the meadows atop the ridge by watching for ducks. At the west foot of the ridge, you ford Tilden Canyon Creek and meet the **Tilden Lake-Tiltill Valley Trail (8390 – 2.4).** About 200 yards north, your route turns west off this trail. You skirt several lakelets, one of which might be just right for swimming, and descend to

**Wilma Lake (7980 – 1.5)** with campsites. Here you turn right (north) on the Jack Main Canyon Trail and, passing the Tilden

---

**Left: Potter Point in Lyell Canyon** *Jim Barker*

Lake Trail (8140 – 1.5), make the long ascent up Falls Creek, past scattered primitive campsites all ablaze with flower colors in early season. For the first few miles early-season fords can be a problem, but after Grace Meadow, with its good campsites, the environment is higher and drier all the way to the unsigned junction with the

**Bond Pass Trail (9400 – 6.7).** You turn right (east) and after an almost level, tarn-dotted mile in lodgepole forest reach Dorothy Lake (9400 – 0.9), which has many good campsites. The trail skirts the north shore through subalpine forest and tops Dorothy Lake Pass (9560 – 0.8) on the border of Yosemite Park. From here you descend past Stella, Bonnie and Harriet lakes, ford Cascade Creek twice on boulders, and about ½ mile beyond the second ford arrive at a junction with the recently constructed

**Cinko Lake Trail (9000 – 2.4),** where you veer left (west). This trail segment was one of the first parts of the PCT to be constructed after the proposed final route was adopted in 1972. You pass three tarns, descend to cross an unnamed stream on a log bridge, and ascend under lodgepole and hemlock past an unmapped tarn. Here the trail veers north to Cinko Lake (9210 – 1.5), which has several fair-to-good campsites. From the lake you descend gently to a level meadow, at the far side of which the trail meets the

**West Fork of the West Walker Trail (9150 – 0.6),** and you turn
**80** right (northeast) onto it. Just at the edge of the forest, you descend
**81** on alternately sandy, rocky and granite-slab underfooting to a
boulder ford of the stream. Trucking on down under generally dense lodgepole pine, mixed with some silver pine, you soon come to a junction with the

**Long Lakes/Chain of Lakes trails (8600 – 1.8).** The Forest Service map shows the final PCT going high on the cliffs west of here, but it is doubtful that it will. The volcanic rocks that make up these cliffs are just a page of a great volcanic story which unfolds before you as the Sierra Nevada slowly and sporadically gives way to the Cascades. From the junction you dip to ford the West Fork of the West Walker and strike out across cow-infested meadows separated by overdeveloped cowmen's camps in clumps of lodgepole. Near the largest of these (8530 – 1.0), a trail goes east toward Fremont Lake and Leavitt Meadows. At this writing the temporary PCT is easy to lose across these meadows, but easy to find again if you maintain a course almost due north. At an unsigned junction where a tree is blazed " X " veer left and cross a small meadow that has a 60-foot-high granite prominence just east of it. Beyond this meadow at a Y, take the left-hand fork and in a few steps arrive at

**Kennedy Canyon Creek (8530 – 0.7).** Ford the creek on boulders and turn left upstream on the north side, avoiding the

---

**Right: North of Dorothy Lake** *Thomas Winnett*

trail that goes north down the main canyon. Your trail climbs moderately, staying above the creek's gorge, for a long mile as it fords several tributaries, some of which are the cause of very wet meadows. The trail is hard to follow across a sage-dotted, rocky runoff course, and you should *not* cross the main creek just beyond here but should look for the trail farther up along the north bank. Near timberline you come to the last (in midseason) flowing water (9200 – 2.3). From here to the saddle at the head of Kennedy Canyon the trail becomes increasingly faint, then nonexistent, but it is easy to see where to climb to reach the

**Saddle between Kennedy Canyon and Kennedy Creek Canyon (9650 – 0.7),** on the Sierra crest. Here the route meets a road and turns right (north) onto it. This most unfortunate road leads from Leavitt Lake south for more than 15 miles to a series of mining claims in the Emigrant Basin Primitive Area. A bill now before Congress would delete from wilderness status a long corridor centered on the road, creating a "dagger" into the heart of what is otherwise the largest roadless area in California. To avoid following the road, the final Pacific Crest Trail is shown on maps following a hair-raising route up the north wall of Kennedy Canyon and down around Ski Lake. Similarly, north of Leavitt Lake the final route is supposed to cling to the cliffs below Leavitt Peak, but it will take a lot of money to build it. The PCT follows this obscene
81 road as it switchbacks up pink volcanic rocks near the Sierra crest, above timberline, to a saddle west of Point 10850 (10,600 – 2.4), where a locked gate bars the way to vehicles not on mining business. (Strangely, jeepsful of families on Labor Day fun outings take this road deep into the Emigrant wilderness; the lock must have many keys.) From this saddle the road descends steeply through subalpine forest to

**Leavitt Lake (9560 – 1.5).** Wood is scarce around the lake's campgrounds. It is possible to drive an ordinary car on the dirt road from Highway 108 to a point about 0.4 mile above the sign that identifies Leavitt Lake and gives its elevation. The PCT goes down this dirt road, crossing several unnamed tributaries, and passing some campsites in the lodgepole groves, to

**State Highway 108 (8450 – 3.1).** There are meager supplies 6 miles east at Leavitt Meadows Resort (next supplies at Markleeville on State Highway 4, 56 miles distant). Here the route turns left (west) and follows this blacktop road past Sardine Meadow to a **jeep road junction (9100 – 2.5)** 1.5 miles east of Sonora Pass. You turn onto this well-graded road, passable to most cars, and follow it across the heads of creeks that feed the West Walker River, with almost constantly sweeping views of the glaciated canyon below you, to a bridge over Wolf Creek, just beyond which you meet the

**Pickel Meadow Road (8320 – 6.5).** You turn left (west) on this dirt road, which in 2.3 miles becomes trail. The route threads several fine meadows with good campsites before climbing steeply up to shallow, troutless Wolf Creek Lake (10,100 – 4.3). So many frogs and pollywogs live here that trout wouldn't have room anyway. Via an easy ascent from the lake, you gain Wolf Creek Lake Saddle (10,280 – 0.5). From here the temporary PCT descends into White Canyon, carved by the East Fork of the Carson River. In less than a mile you are back on the permanent PCT, although the "trail" down some stretches of the canyon can't be seen, and you must stay on course by finding tree blazes, red ribbons, ducks, and occasional clumps of PCT signposts. You ford the river six times on this descent, and the lower fords could be difficult in early season. In this canyon are some very large and well-executed if primitive carvings on lodgepole and aspen trees, done–judging from the associated names–by Basque sheepherders with a lot of free time. Just past the meadowy junction with the

**Soda Springs Trail (7100 – 10.6),** you ford the East Carson, go back along the river and enter Golden Canyon. You ascend the sometimes steep canyon trail past some virgin forests of lodgepole and Jeffrey pine, red fir and Sierra juniper. The grass, however, is
not virgin–cows have seen to that. Partway up, carved on a mature 81
lodgepole, is another of those stylized, primitive, probably Basque
carvings, this one of a horrendous, devouring woman with small 82
breasts and large, pointed teeth. Good campsites recur on flat spots in this deep canyon. The stiff climb ends at a trail junction at the

**Head of Golden Canyon (8930 – 3.4),** where you turn north onto the permanent PCT. After a short ascent to a saddle, you skirt the base of volcanic cliffs on the west, keeping just above the willow-choked marshy areas where Murray Canyon Creek has its wellsprings. The trail is not easy to stay on, but a northerly course will take you past the west side of a round andesite eminence that is a good beacon. Past this landmark, the path is again evident, and you stroll over a high ridge with excellent views in all directions of granite walls and volcanic pinnacles, blanketed by pine, hemlock and fir, to

**Wolf Creek Saddle (8790 – 3.4).** The Murray Canyon Trail branches right here, signed *Falls Meadow.* From this saddle you make a gentle descent northwest on long switchbacks across open slopes dotted with lodgepole and sagebrush. The volcanic rocks on these slopes present a tremendous variety of shapes and textures, giving you some insight into the infrastructure of the volcanic heights visible up and across the valley of Wolf Creek. Your trail

**Eroded flow south of Ebbetts Pass** *Thomas Winnett*

descends into groves of silver pine, aspen, red fir and Sierra juniper, and comes to an **unmarked junction (7750 – 1.5),** where you take the right-hand fork. Soon the trail levels off in Wolf Creek Meadows, where there are some fair cowmen's campsites and year-round stream water. (All these "Wolf" names around here would seem to mean the area once had a lot of wolves, but it remains unproved that they ever lived in the High Sierra.) Just past a tall snowcourse marker with a series of crossbars to measure snow depth, you find a dirt road and come to an intersection, where a **road (7690 – 0.2)** leads left up the canyon to Asa Lake. You turn right (north), wade Wolf Creek and come to a Y (7750 – 0.3), where the PCT goes left on a faint old road. You walk almost on the level in dense red-fir forest to a ford of Bull Creek and in 200 yards reach a

**Junction (7800 – 0.9),** where the PCT, plain trail now, turns left (west) up Bull Creek Canyon. The trail ascends on a moderate grade, well-shaded, past Table Rock, an extraordinary natural outdoor table that looks as if it were poured concrete embedded in the base of a large lodgepole pine. You then come to an easy boulder ford of Bull Creek and continue the moderate, shaded ascent, reaching the unsigned junction of the Bull Lake Trail, (8670 – 1.7), which goes left. You continue your upward slog to the foot of Bull Canyon Meadow, where the kind of damage that stock grazing under the "Multiple Use" program does to the delicate Sierra highlands is all too evident. You ford Bull Creek once again and, lacking a distinct trail across the meadow, head for the willow patch above the northwest corner of the meadow, bound for the saddle to the left of that corner. You will find the trail again to the right of the grove of lodgepoles at the head of the meadow. Now you climb in earnest, taking in the fragrant odor of pennyroyal when the slope is in sun, to a whitebark-and hemlock-dotted

**Saddle (9470 – 0.8)** between Bull and Nobel canyons. On the north side there is a short, steep descent to open fields of sagebrush and whitebark pine, in view of Nobel Lake to the north. If the trail
is hard to see, simply head for the slope above the west shore of 82
Nobel Lake (8840 – 0.6). On this slope you swing left and descend 83
a short, steep, bad trail almost to a stream before turning right (ignoring the trail that goes up this little canyon). Your northbound trail descends moderately through the last of the volcanic rock you have been treading for miles and enters granite, where the sandy trail surface is that decomposed granite called *gruss.* At the foot of the moderate descent is a boulder ford of Nobel Creek, from where you make a long, gentle descent of Nobel Canyon, crossing 4 all-year tributary streams about a half mile apart. Then you hop to the west side of Nobel Creek on boulders and finish this trail segment on almost level sandy underfooting under moderately dense Jeffrey pine, white fir and quaking aspen, arriving at

**State Highway 4 (7280 – 4.7)** at the end of the last road switchback above Silver Creek Campground, not in the campground as the topo map indicates. The temporary PCT goes down Highway 4 past the campground to an **unsigned dirt road (6700 – 2.3)** that leads up Raymond Meadows Creek Canyon. (Supplies can be obtained in Markleeville, 11.8 miles north on Highway 4; Sorenson's Resort is still 33 miles distant.) You climb steeply up this road, with the creek playing happily among the granite boulders below, to a **road junction (7200 – 0.6)** at a switchback, where you turn right and enjoy great views across Silver Creek to Silver Mountain. (All these "Silver" names are remnants of the tremendous mining action at the town called Silver Mountain, in the 1860s one of the largest towns in the Sierra, but now collapsed and forgotten.) Several switchbacks later you level off, come to a saddle, and begin the descent to Pennsylvania Creek (7200 – 1.6).

Beyond the creek, you are free of vehicles, due to geography, not regulations, and you climb freely up an abandoned logging road that has an earth dam across it about every 25 yards to fight erosion and prevent vehicle passage. About 170 yards from the creek, you turn left at a junction and climb steeply for ¼ mile, then veer left and continue up the abandoned logging road. At a logged-over area (7800 – 0.8) the abandoned road ramifies into many laterals all of which dead-end among the down trees and stumps. From here, there is no trail, so proceed first to the shallow saddle (7800 – 0.8) near the head of the logged area, then turn west and climb the ridge that separates Pennsylvania Creek from Raymond Canyon Creek. Wind westward along this ridge, almost on top of it most of the time. When you approach the slope up to the farthest east outlier of Raymond Peak, veer right, through the trees, and contour over until you are directly below the saddle where the steep northeast side of Raymond Peak becomes much less steep.
83 There are a number of trees in this saddle. Climb to this saddle to find the

**Temporary PCT (8840 – 2.4).** To the left, 0.3 mile up, is Raymond Lake, with fair campsites marred by junk from motorbikers. To the right is your route. From the saddle you can see the high peaks just south of Lake Tahoe, and a few yards farther on there are sweeping views that include these and more peaks. Across the deep canyon, the many switchbacks you will soon have to labor up dare you to fly across. To the left is a hunk of mind-blowing geology–the north face of Raymond Peak. The billowy marble-fudge configuration of this volcanic formation is enhanced by a great variety of pinks, magentas, tans, browns and reds in the rock wall, and by the greens of plants growing up some of the draws, and even the yellows of flowers on these plants, surprisingly bright at this distance. Following the long, gently graded switchbacks, you drop into an almost pure red-fir forest and eventually reach an easy ford of Raymond Lake Creek (7600 – 3.0). Now you have to go right back up the north slope of the canyon to a saddle (8200 – 1.1) in the colorful volcanic ridge that borders the drainage of Raymond Creek. Two switchback legs down bring you to the

**Pleasant Valley Trail junction (7840 – 0.6).** Here you turn left and ascend gently through pleasant forest to cross Raymond Creek, then climb to where a road comes in on the right, and step onto it. This road crosses a little saddle and descends to a parking area (8100 – 0.8) which some ordinary vehicles can reach southbound from Blue Lakes. Now on level road, you see through the trees Wet Meadow Reservoir, which is more meadow than reservoir, and hike along through white fir, lodgepole and willows to a **road junction (8010 – 1.2).** Turning right, the route soon passes the road to Lower Sunset Lake (8700 – 0.7) and after two miles passes Tamarack Lake. This dusty, waterless stretch of temporary PCT continues to the **junction (8000 – 3.0)** with a road that connects with Highway 88. You turn left on the dirt road to a **junction (8050 – 1.2)** with the road to Twin Lakes, then turn north toward Blue Lakes, passing Lower Blue Lake Campground almost immediately. The rough, overused, summer-crowded dirt road contours above the Blue Lakes basin past Middle Creek Campground (8080 – 1.4), Upper Blue Lake Damsite Campground (8100 – 0.4) and Blue Lake Campground (8150 – 1.2). You will not find these campgrounds idyllic or secluded, but they do have views, water, and possibly a few scraps of wood left over from the bonfires that typify the trailer-camper's "wilderness experience."

Leaving this social hub behind, you climb steeply on narrower dirt road through a moderate forest cover of red fir, hemlock and
silver pine to a ridge crest (8870 – 0.8), from where a side road **83**
leads northeast to Lost Lakes. You continue toward Red Lake, **84**
undulating high above Upper Blue Lake with excellent views west down Summit City Canyon and northwest to looming Elephants Back, with the contrasting steep right-hand and gentle left-hand slopes. At about timberline you reach a

**Saddle (8900 – 1.6)** from where a trail takes off down Summit City Canyon, connecting with the Tahoe-Yosemite Trail. You descend north down the dirt road, soon passing from gray granite to pink volcanic rock. Across the canyon to the west it is the same: Elephants Back is pink, but just south of it the mountain is granite. Some of us never tire of the juxtaposition of volcanic and granitic rock that is so common in the High Sierra between northern Yosemite and Echo Summit. Not only do they differ in color, but they erode differently, and so have contrasting shapes and forms. Just beyond a logged red-fir forest is Forestdale Creek (7900 – 1.5), with some fair campsites and an unsigned road leading right (east). Your route goes gently downgrade into a valley and through aspen groves past a stockmen's cabin to

**Old State Highway 88 (7790 – 1.8).** (Supplies are 6½ miles northeast at Sorenson's Resort on new State Highway 88.) Your route turns left (west) up the old blacktop highway, past a barricade, and winds up the old Red Lake Grade to Carson Pass (8572 – 1.6). Here is where John C. Fremont, with Kit Carson as his scout, made the first winter crossing of the Sierra by white men. They damn near froze. (Supplies are 5 miles west at Caples Resort. The next supplies are 15 miles ahead, at Echo Lake Resort.) You walk west on the highway, now in El Dorado National Forest, to a **parking lot (8500 – 0.3),** where the permanent PCT takes off westward, being now back on the Tahoe-Yosemite Trail. Your rocky trail curves north around the nose of a ridge, crosses a runoff stream and switchbacks up an open slope to join a now-closed road that goes straight up the hill to a saddle (8800 – 1.2) on the divide between the Truckee River and the American River. From here you descend gently down the long, green, tree-dotted valley of the Upper Truckee River, fording a number of small streams that spring from the porous volcanic rocks all around. You pass the Round Lake Trail (8400 – 1.6), ford the infant river once more, and continue northwest on the two-track closed road. An ascent up a hillside in red-fir forest and over a little saddle brings you to

**Showers Lake (8630 – 1.9),** where camping and fishing are usually good, now that vehicles are not allowed to come here. The trail north from the lake crosses a stream and ascends gently, then steeply onto a high plateau, passing a trail to Schneider Camp
**84** (8980 – 1.5) and then one to Sayles Canyon (8650 – 1.8). From a
**85** summit that provides views of the Crystal Range ahead, you descend to Bryan Meadow (8520 – 0.3) with water for camping except in late season. The PCT veers right to climb awhile and then descend in several forested stages, separated by willowy meadows, to Benwood Meadow (7500 – 2.5), where the wildflowers alone are "worth the trip": mountain aster, corn lily, snow plant, alpine lily, both yellow and red monkey flowers, penstemon, False Solomon's seal, yampa, pennyroyal, senecio, columbine, larkspur and mountain bluebell, plus an assortment of grasses, ferns and sedges. Past this meadow the route dips and climbs through a bushy ground cover shaded by a few conifers to the end of a Summer Home Tract Road (7450 – 0.7). You follow this road to

**State Highway 50 (7370 – 0.4),** walk 100 yards west and turn right (north) at the highway maintenance station. Take the little road that veers left and climbs over the hill past some summer homes. At the next intersection (7380 – 1.0) go left to the road signed *Echo Lakes* (7370 – 0.2) to the right (north). Take this road, overlooking the southern Tahoe Valley far below, past cabins and through a large parking lot and descend to

**Echo Lake Resort (7420 – 1.3)** (last supplies for 64 miles until Soda Springs). Now you begin perhaps the most-used part of the entire PCT, entering the most-used Federal Wilderness in California–Desolation Wilderness. If you don't want to walk all the way from Mexico to Canada, you can take the boat-taxi from the resort 2 miles to the head of Upper Echo Lake. The lakeside trail is generally hot and dusty in midsummer, and it lacks a passing lane. From the junction of the PCT and the lateral trail to the upper boat landing you ascend moderately, passing the Tamarack Lake Trail (7850 – 3.7) and the Triangle Lake Trail, to Haypress Meadows (8320 – 1.1), where you pass lateral trails to Lake of the Woods and Lake Lucille. Now you select any of several deep ruts through a tarn-dotted swale and descend almost imperceptibly to a trail junction beside

**Lake Aloha (8140 – 1.6).** This large lake with a thousand islands was a mere pond in a big glaciated basin before it was dammed for Sacramento water and power. Well, at least all that blue water sometimes provides photographable reflections of the dramatic Crystal Range to the southwest. You skirt most of the long northeast shore of Lake Aloha and then at a **junction (8120 – 1.4)** turn right, down to Heather Lake. Going straight ahead would have put you in Rockbound Valley, where you would have passed several PCT emblem signs, even though the PCT does not go there. Camping is fair at the inlet of Heather Lake
(7900 – 0.4), better than at the next lake over–Susie Lake **85**
(7780 – 1.0). On the slopes of Jacks Peak above is a clear line of
division between the medasedimentary rock of the Mt. Tallac **86**
pendant and intruding gray granite south of it. Your route turns east from Susie Lake and proceeds on the level past a short-cut trail to Glen Alpine Springs to two consecutive junctions a few yards apart, but out of sight of each other. Trails lead left to Half Moon Lake, right to Glen Alpine Springs and ahead to Dicks Pass, your immediate goal. You climb a constructed staircase and then switchback up to the

**Gilmore Lake Trail (8280 – 1.8),** which also leads to the top of Mt. Tallac. After yielding a glimpse of Gilmore through the red firs, the trail ascends steadily above Half Moon Lake through a string of pocket meadows where the wildflower show is excellent in early July of a typical year. At the saddle you thought was the pass, the pesky trail turns right, up the ridge through subalpine forest to ascend for 200 vertical feet to Dicks Pass (9400 – 2.0). The view from here extends for many miles north and south, and one may camp all night to enjoy it at sunrise when there is enough snowmelt water near the campsites east of the pass. The descent is at first a long traverse high above Dicks Lake, then a superabundance of sandy switchbacks that bring you out near the north end of the lake at a junction with the

**Middle Velma Lake** *Jeff Schaffer*

**Emerald Bay Trail (8550 – 1.4).** You veer left and pass the short lateral (8480 – 0.2) to Dicks Lake, where camping is fair, wood scarce and people probable. You continue north past Fontanillis Lake (8280 – 1.0), with fair campsites in little stands of lodgepole and hemlock, and a lavish display of red and sienna rocks to complement the usual gray granite. Beyond the outlet, the trail descends the ridgeline into red-fir forest to a **junction south of Middle Velma Lake (7960 – 0.8).** A back-country campground is just east of here, and there are fair-to-good campsites on Middle and Upper Velma lakes. Over the 8-mile stretch of trail northwest to Miller Meadows, the creeks may dry up late in the summer.

Turning west, you pass the Camper Flat Trail (7960 – 0.3) and veer north through a multi-trailed section of forest and boggy meadow. Use should establish a clear-cut groove here which will take you north to the

**General Creek Trail (8100 – 1.0),** where you leave the Tahoe-Yosemite Trail, which continues north over Phipps Pass and down to Meeks Bay roadend. You head northwest on the Miller Lakes Trail past Phipps Creek (7650 – 1.5), an adequate camping area, then along west slopes through an open forest of red fir, silver pine, lodgepole pine and mountain hemlock. You will encounter large erratic boulders from Peak 8235 (8160 – 2.0) northwest to the glacial-till-mantled ridge (7840 – 1.0). Your trail then descends to

General Creek (7470 – 0.5), crosses it to a junction with the Lake Genevieve Trail (7500 – 0.1), continues north and crosses the creek once again (7170 – 1.5). The trail then curves past the General Creek Trail (7180 – 0.2), then ascends an open slope of lupine, thistle, sagebrush and aspen to a broad saddle and a private road (7340 – 0.3). The trail beyond here is very cryptic and not maintained. Descend gently northwest through an obvious dry meadow, then north-northwest through an open forest to **Richardson Lake Road (7170 – 0.7).** Turn right (northeast) and follow it 100 yards to a junction with the private road, then north across the sometimes dry Miller Creek (and into Tahoe National Forest) to

**McKinney-Rubicon Springs Road (7130 – 0.4).** A dusty 6-mile walk east on it will take you to Tahoma, where supplies and services are available. Turn left (west) and follow the road past Lower Miller Lake (7110 – 0.3), an oversized lily pond. You should not refill your water bottles here, but you might refresh your spirit with the sighting of a few great blue herons wading among the lilies in their search for a tasty frog or garter snake. You will soon reach the **Ellis Peak Logging Road (7110 – 0.3).** If water shortage is a problem, then continue 0.1 mile further to trickling North Miller Creek. Otherwise, turn right (north) and follow this winding, rutted jeep road up to the ridge (7720 – 1.0), then
northwest to 86

**Bear Lake Road (7710 – 0.1).** Turn left (west) and immediately 87
cross North Miller Creek, where there's a good campsite, and follow the road as it diagonals up to the ridge, then descends to Bear Lake (7540 – 1.0), which provides the best camping and trout fishing since the Velma Lakes. The road now contours east of the lake to its north shore, then ascends northeast to a low saddle and plunges down into Cothrin Cove (7200 – 1.4). After descending gently southwest, it gradually turns northwest and gently ascends to an obvious road merging from the southwest (6960 – 1.0). Continue north on your same road to Barker Creek (7160 – 0.7) at the south end of Barker Meadow, a good camping area. The road crosses the creek and heads north up an east slope, then turns sharply southwest up to the ridge crest and continues north to **Blackwood Creek Road (7680 – 2.6).** Turn left (west) and follow it to the

**Big Powderhorn Trailhead (15E15) (7660 – 0.3),** the start of an enjoyable, uncrowded stretch of trail. You make a moderate ascent to a low saddle (7800 – 0.3), then a moderate descent north to Powderhorn Creek (7440 – 0.4). Soon the gradient eases off and the trail turns gradually northwest. Prominent Pliocene andesite flows cap the valley slopes, with enormous vertical hexagonal columns–easily dwarfing those of Devils Postpile National Monument–at the north end of the west slope. Glacial till mantles the valley floor. The trail has dropped from a red-fir belt to one of incense cedar, white fir and Jeffrey pine, and the temperature is noticeably warmer. Your trail now joins the

**West Meadow Trail (15E12) (6070 – 2.9),** which heads northwest across a dry meadow, then northeast across Powderhorn Creek (6040 – 0.2), past a very good campsite, to Diamond Crossing (6061 – 0.3) and the Hells Hole Trail junction. Continue north past the Bear Pen Creek Trail (6090 – 0.1), Bear Pen Creek (6090 – 0.1) and Grouse Canyon Creek (6240 – 1.6) until you reach **Shanks Cove Trail (6380 – 0.8).** Turn left (west) and head past a very good campsite at Five Lakes Creek (6325 – 0.2) to **Whisky Creek Camp Trail (6350 – 0.1).** Turn right (north) and follow it up to Whisky Creek Camp (6920 – 1.9), an excellent campsite. (If you are low on supplies, you can take the Five Lakes Trail 4 miles northeast around Squaw Peak and down into Squaw Valley Village. From there you have the option to backtrack or to head northwest on a trail that joins the route at Mountain Meadow Lake.)

Along the last few miles you have been walking over Jurassic marine sediments metamorphosed by intruding granitic plutons
87 which are exposed on the slopes of Squaw Peak, Granite Chief and Needle Peak. During the Pliocene, extensive outpourings of lava flowed down gentle-sloped stream valleys, capping and preserving the underlying bedrock. (The summits of Squaw Peak and Needle Peak are remnants of one flow.) New streams worked along the valley slopes and gradually eroded them down until finally the topography became *inverted;* that is, the old river bed is preserved today as a high ridge. Glaciation during the Pleistocene accentuated this topography.

From Whisky Creek Camp continue north on the same trail, crossing trout-inhabited Whisky Creek (6950 – 0.2), then ascending a series of short, moderately steep switchbacks up the lower, granite slopes of Squaw Peak. The trail quickly eases off and turns west past adequate campsites and through a very large (20+ acres) field of mule ears (Sunflower family), whose pungent odor permeates the valley. Your trail now climbs the forested slopes to a saddle (7940 – 1.8), then descends slightly to the **Tevis Cup Trail (16E04) (7920 – 0.1).** You can follow it west ½ mile to good campsites on the Middle Fork of the American River. Since you will soon be entering private land, you might consider these sites, for the next adequate public campsite is not until Onion Creek Campground, about 12 miles distant. Turn right (north) and follow the trail gently up to a sign:

**Granite Chief-Pacific Crest Trail 2000 (8120 – 0.4).** From here the Tevis Cup Trail heads east up to Watson Monument. Your obscure footpath strikes north immediately across the headwaters of the Middle Fork of the American River and follows ducks up an open slope to a ridge (8560 – 0.6), about 300 yards west of the saddle (8444). The panoramic view from this divide includes the trails you have been ascending, the Squaw Valley ski lifts and northern Lake Tahoe, and the impressive descent route north of you. Bejore you descend, notice how the lava flows cap all the surrounding granite ridges. You now switchback down an excellent trail to a beautiful, but frail, meadow enclosed by white granite cliffs. If you feel tempted to camp at this excellent site, please note that it is subject to rapid deterioration and treat it gently. From this site, the headwaters of Squaw Creek, the trail descends along the east side of the north ridge into private property and to the

**Painted Rock Trail (15E06) (7970 – 1.9).** Squaw Valley and supplies are 3 miles east on this trail. Turn left (northwest) and hike past photogenic Mountain Meadow Lake (7910 – 0.2), then begin a gentle descent to the North Fork of the American River. Notice in the low ridge on your right how the Jurassic metasediments have been intruded by granitic dikes. You soon reach the Tinker Knob Trail-Pacific Crest Trail 2000 junction
(7600 – 0.8). The trail at present goes only 2 miles up to Tinker 87
Knob. If you prefer a cross-country route with magnificent vistas 88
to a valley trail and a rocky road, then continue cross country from Tinker Knob, a remnant of a Pliocene andesite flow, staying near the ridge crest as it drops north-northwest to Donner Pass, and finally cross Boreal Ridge to Castle Valley. The temporary PCT continues on our same trail, heading northwest and descending several long switchbacks into the glaciated American River Canyon. The trail follows the river's east bank, crosses west over it (6500 – 2.0), and continues northwest past metamorphic Painted Rock to

**Old Soda Springs (6000 – 2.1),** today only half a dozen private summer homes. Here numerous soda springs emanate from cracks and crevices, coating the granite rocks orange and red with their iron-rich waters. Follow the road across the bridge, then west along the river past Pinehurst to a locked gate (5820 – 1.7). A long, hot, dusty trek begins here as this rocky road veers northwest up away from the river past Cedar Creek (5785 – 0.4), Onion Creek (6020 – 1.9) and Onion Creek Campground (6080 – 0.3). You might plan to camp here, for your next good campsite will be in Castle Valley, about 10 miles farther. The road now switchbacks up and along the west side of a hot, dry ridge to Ice Lakes

(6870 – 4.1) and civilization. This road from here is now paved and lined with dozens of winter cabins along it and along the numerous spur roads. Lake Van Norden is soon reached, then Old Highway 40 at

**Soda Springs (6768 – 2.2).** Supplies and services can be obtained at the west end of town. The next town will be Sierra City, 41 miles ahead. Turn right (east) and follow the paved highway just past Upper Castle Creek to the **U.S. Forest Service Central Sierra Laboratory (6840 – 0.6).** Turn left (north) and head up the private road which soon parallels Interstate 80 northwest to **Boreal Ridge (7130 – 1.6),** where a few minor supplies are available. Turn left (north) and cross under the freeway, then head east and curve gently up into Castle Valley, where the road climbs gently northwest up Andesite Ridge to a

**Parking area (7750 – 1.8).** From this point a trail and a jeep road wind north to Paradise Valley. Hike up the fairly steep trail to Castle Pass (7910 – 0.1). From here the trail starts gently north along the east side of the road, but it quickly crosses it and angles northwest down to the Sierra Club's Peter Grubb Hut in Round Valley (7830 – 0.7), now a sheep pasture. Ironically, when John Muir founded the Club to preserve the Sierra Nevada, one of his prime targets was the shepherds and their destructive flocks. Just
88 130 yards north is the Sand Ridge Trail junction; another 40 yards
and you are on the jeep road again (7830 – 0.1). Follow it north
89 across the meadow and up open slopes until the road becomes
noticeably steeper (8040 – 0.3). Here at a large **silver pine** the trail begins again, then climbs northwest, traverses an open slope with views of the distant route, descends along a small creek, and heads north to meet the jeep road again. This junction (7980 – 1.4) is 20 yards west of where the road quickly becomes steep and rocky. Go north on it 50 yards to where it turns west through a **cluster of large red firs,** then strike north 50 yards to a large **isolated fir,** where a faint trail marked with ducks and blazes starts north down a long, narrow meadow, then curves northeast to North Creek in Paradise Valley (7530 – 0.6). Cross the creek and continue north to

**Magonigal Camp Road (7540 – 0.2),** in a small level area with red fir, ¼ mile east of this road's junction with the jeep road. The obscurity of this trail section protects it from weekend dirt-bike traffic. Cross country begins here, but if you have the time, you might walk east 0.8 mile up the road to Paradise Lake, an outstanding campsite when bikers are absent. At this picturesque, island-dotted lake you can fish, swim and dive, as well as practice your climbing skills on the cracks of the surrounding granite cliffs. An impressive view of the glaciated terrain, enriched by a well diversified flora, around here may be had from just over the east saddle. In addition to the red fir, silver pine and lodgepole pine which you have commonly encountered, you may also find mountain hemlock, Sierra juniper and water birch. Shrubs include manzanita, chinquapin, mountain spiraea, ceanothus, willow and red mountain heather. Wildflowers are abundant, and a succession of species blossoms as the summer progresses. Looking west from Paradise Lake you can identify the best cross-country route to take.

From the trail-road junction mentioned earlier, strike north through the lodgepole-pine forest to the open slopes above, then diagonal west up to the andesite-capped granite ridge (8100 – 1.0), traverse northeast, drop quite steeply down to White Rock Creek (7820 – 0.9) and pass very good campsites to

**White Rock Lake Jeep Road (7880 – 0.3)** near the northwest lake shore. The next 26 miles will be along dirt roads, generally mosquito-infested through midsummer. Follow the road southwest as it descends past a spur road to White Rock Creek (7700 – 1.1), then ascends moderately north to a broad ridge (7900 – 2.0) and goes gently down to open Bear Valley (7685 – 1.3), an adequate, mosquito-free camping area. You go to the Meadow Lake road (19N11) (7585 – 1.0) and turn left (southwest) to follow the road west past a spring (7540 – 1.5) to
Meadow Lake (7290 – 1.7), a large, shallow reservoir. Continue **89**
west along its north shore to the

**Summit City site (7330 – 1.4),** indicated only by a descriptive **90**
sign. Turn right (northwest) and follow the road as it climbs over a gentle saddle, then winds down past Tollhouse Lake (7050 – 2.5) to a junction (7100 – 0.4). Your road has essentially followed the contact between Pliocene volcanics on your right and granite on your left. Continue on the same road as it gradually turns north and descends along a tributary of French Creek which flows along a contact between granite slopes and Jura-Trias metavolcanic cliffs. The road crosses French Creek (6425 – 1.4), continues past Churchs Camp (6250 – 1.2), climbs gently past Catfish Lake (6470 – 0.7)–no camping–then reaches the

**Bowman Lake Road (19N14) (6574 – 0.7).** Turn right and follow this road as it curves northeast down into the Jackson Meadow Recreation Area (6360 – 0.4) and past a Forest Service station to Woodcamp Campground (6250 – 0.4). The road now heads north, drops to the reservoir, and then climbs up to a **junction (6120 – 1.5).** Here your road turns right (northeast), immediately climbs a low saddle, then descends gently to the dam (6032 – 0.6) and crosses it to the

**Henness Pass Road (19N03) (6035 – 0.3).** From here the Sierra Buttes are visible on the northwest horizon. Turn left (north) and

follow the road as it descends into a Jeffrey pine–white fir forest to Milton Reservoir, (5690 – 1.9), a shallow reservoir, which, like Meadow Lake and Jackson Meadow Reservoir, is teeming with weekend fishermen and car-campers. Continue west past the dam (5690 – 0.5), the Milton-Bowman Tunnel Road (5710 – 0.4), and the Ahart Sheep Camp Road (5840 – 0.3) to **Road 12E08 (6200 – 0.9).** Turn right (north) and go gently up, then around the ridge to

**Hilda Mine Trail (6100 – 2.1),** well marked. It starts as a jeep road heading north down to Hilda Mine (5880 – 0.6), then continues as a trail that cuts southeast to a creek and descends along it to **Haypress Creek Trail (4750 – 1.3).** Turn left (west) and follow it through an open forest of incense cedar, white fir and black oak, obtaining impressive views of the looming Sierra Buttes as you approach **Wild Plum Campground (4450 – 0.6).** Hike west on the road through the campground, across Milton Creek (4390 – 0.3) and the North Yuba River (4240 – 0.7) to

**State Highway 49 (4315 – 0.6).** Sierra City, ½ mile west on 49, is
the last major supply center until Bucks Lake, 88 miles distant.
Turn right (northeast) and follow this paved road up past a
spring-fed cascade (5000 – 2.5) and over Salmon Creek
(5140 – 0.6) to where it levels off at the **Old Gold Lake Road**
**(5285 – 0.5).** Last-minute items might be obtained at Bassetts
Store, 0.9 mile northeast up 49. Otherwise, turn left (north) and 90
ascend this steep, sunny grade to the paved **Gold Lake Road** 91
**(5680 – 0.8).** Turn left (northwest) and follow it to

**Sardine Lakes Road (5700 – 0.2).** Turn left (west) and cross Salmon Creek to Packer Lake Road. In another 70 yards you will reach an old **jeep road (5750 – 0.3),** now used as a trail. Before starting up it, you might obtain a meal at the Sardine Lake Resort, which lies at the end of the paved road just past Sardine Lake Campground and Sand Pond Picnic Ground. The jeep road heads southwest up through dense manzanita, then switchbacks north to forested slopes and a **trail (6010 – 0.6).** Turn left (south) and follow the trail as it climbs up the exposed slope of this lateral moraine and provides you with spectacular views of the alpine scenery. The Jura-Trias metavolcanics along this trail give way to exceedingly colorful Paleozoic Sierra Buttes metavolcanics, which were transported east by glaciers. The trail soon switchbacks up to the ridge (7030 – 1.9), then down and west to

**Lower Tamarack Lake (6700 – 1.2).** If you have the time and the energy, you might attempt the two-mile hike south up the Sierra Buttes Fire Lookout (8587) for a magnificent panorama in all directions. If you do, note how the glaciated northeast slopes contrast strongly with the unglaciated old erosion surface to the

---

**Left: White Rock Lake** *Jeff Schaffer*

west and south which has been deeply incised by canyons carved during the Pleistocene. From Lower Tamarack Lake head north down the jeep road to

**Butcher Ranch Meadows Road (6250 – 0.8).** Turn right (north) and follow it to an immediate junction (6235 – 0.1). Here you are only 30 yards south of Packer Lake Road and Picnic Area. It is well worth your effort to follow the road west around the lake past the *No Trespassing* sign to Packer Lake Lodge, where you will find genuine hospitality and delicious home-cooked meals. Emergency services are also available. Packer Lake (6218) is one of the warmest lakes in this region, and although it is shallow, it is still
**91** suitable for some good swimming. From the last junction, turn right (northeast) and walk down this blocked-off road to its junction with the Packer Lake Road, then continue down 80 yards farther to the

**Deer Lake Trail (6130 – 0.2).** Turn left (north) and follow it across several creeks, then up a long switchback into Grass Lake Valley. The lake is not seen unless you climb a low ridge (6560 – 1.1) a few yards west of the trail and 0.2 mile north of where the trail had crossed Grass Lake Creek. Continue up to a broad ridge (6970 – 0.7), where an obscure trail follows a small creek northwest up to Deer Lake (7110), an excellent campsite with good swimming and fishing (rainbow and brook trout). This

obscure trail is the preferred route. The PCT route, however, continues north across Sawmill Creek (6990 – 0.3) to a saddle, then goes 15 yards north down the Salmon Lakes Trail to a **trail (7180 – 0.3),** hardly more than a footpath up a shallow gully. Turn left (west) and follow it through a verdant, moist meadow to a **jeep road (7250 – 0.4)** at a small, open, level area overlooking Deer Lake. Turn right (north) and ascend it west to **Road 12E04 (7440 – 0.2).** Turn right (north) and follow it along the ridge to the grassy Summit Lake (7025), Plumas National Forest boundary, and the

**Gold Lake Road (21N34) (7030 – 1.1).** Turn right (east) and walk 100 yards to the continuation of road 12E04, which you take north up the ridge, then northwest gently down to Oakland Pond (7220 – 1.5), an adequate campsite. Just north of this lake you reach a **trail (7230 – 0.1),** where the road starts a moderate descent west. This adequately marked footpath climbs moderately at times up the west side of the ridge through acres of wildflowers and into an open red-fir forest, which becomes predominantly lodgepole pine as the trail crosses over to the east side. Taking a few steps right to the east escarpment rewards you with a sweeping panorama of the Lakes Basin. You might also note that this ridge, like its counterpart to the south, is essentially on the contact where granite intrudes Paleozoic metavolcanics.

The trail continues northwest down the ridge, then northeast 91
down a shallow gully to a small spring-fed **creek (7210 – 1.7),** a 92
good campsite with a view. From here a road starts northeast and immediately passes 2 trails (7210 – 0.1) which descend into the Lakes Basin. It then angles west and descends gently past ponds and small creeks to a saddle (7100 – 0.6), and west to **Spencer Lakes Road (7030 – 0.5).** Your road now turns right (north) and ascends the ridge to a broad summit, then descends past the Wades Lake Trail (7230 – 1.0) to the signed site of the *A-Tree* (6520 – 1.9), from where it continues north up the gentle grade to a saddle (6740 – 0.7), then drops down to the

**Johnsville-Gibsonville Road (6200 – 1.5)**–no supplies or services at either settlement. Emergency aid can be obtained at Plumas-Eureka State Park, 5 miles east down the road. In this next stretch the Paleozoic rocks are metamorphosed marine sediments, often capped with Pliocene volcanics. Turn left (north) and follow the road past good campsites to McRae Meadow (6300 – 1.1), cross it, then head north up and around McRae Ridge, then southwest down past small creeks to the West Branch of Nelson Creek (5680 – 6.6), an adequate campsite. From this location west to the Hartman Bar Trail, water becomes increasingly scarce as the summer progresses, and you should be prepared to hike up to 10 miles between flowing creeks. Ascend the road to a saddle (6065 – 1.0), then continue west as the road winds past interesting andesitic volcanic cones, dikes, and flows, then goes down to Whiskey Creek (5700 – 5.7), another potential campsite. Continue west along the north side of the silty Delahunty Lake (5750 – 0.4) to the

**Quincy-LaPorte Road (5720 – 1.3).** Consider: you are still 48 miles from supplies at Bucks Lake. If yours are running low, it would be best for you to walk 7 miles southwest down the road to La Porte, restock at the market, then head 7 miles north to the Little Grass Valley Reservoir dam. Cross it and continue for ½ mile just past Black Rock Picnic Ground to where a road switchbacks up 2 miles to a saddle (5700) and back onto the temporary route. Otherwise, your route turns right (northwest) and gently ascends the Gibsonville Ridge (6170 – 1.0), then contours northeast past springs (6280 – 2.1) to the headwaters of the South Fork of the Feather River (6340 – 0.6). It now heads west to a saddle, a dry campsite, and the

**Chimney Rock Jeep Road (6474 – 0.3).** Turn left (southwest) and follow the road as it contours west, then (6521 – 1.5) descends moderately to an open white fir-Jeffrey pine-incense cedar forest interspersed with manzanita (6000 –0.6). The road now winds its
92 way gently to Chimney Rock (6020 – 2.5), a fifteen-foot high
pyroclastic block, whose summit provides a fairly good view
93 northwest of the type of country you will be hiking through. From
94 here the road descends west to the **Black Rock Creek Road**
**(5460 – 1.9),** straight ahead. Water can be obtained within ½ mile down this road, which parallels a spring-fed creek. Our route continues at the start of a wide lumber road 15 yards to the right (northwest). Follow this southeast to a saddle and the

**Feather Falls Road (5700 – 4.8),** where the alternate route rejoins the temporary PCT. The next stretch of road to the Hartman Bar Trail has many junctions, and it is important that you make the right decision at each, since the terrain is well-forested and it lacks prominent landmarks. Turn right (west) and go down the road to **Camel Peak Lookout Road (5692 – 0.1).** Turn right (northwest), and continue to the

**Hartman Bar Ridge Road (5730 – 1.1).** Turn right (northwest) and follow this narrower road down and west to Tamarack Flat (5580 – 0.6). The road now descends gently northwest to several tributaries of the Feather River (5470 – 0.5), climbs to a broad saddle (5590 – 0.6), and ascends past a small, spring-fed creek (5620 –0.1) to a **junction (5710 – 0.3)** and a spring. Your road turns right (northwest) and continues north to another **junction (5780 – 0.4).** Turn left (west-northwest) and walk to another

---

**Right: Hartman Bar** *Jeff Schaffer*

**junction (5800 – 0.1).** Turn left and follow the road as it descends first southeast, then west-southwest along the northwest slopes of a ridge to a **junction (5580 – 0.6).** Turn right (north) and head down into a canyon, cross a creek (5520 – 0.2) and ascend west, then north to another creek (5560 – 0.7). Now head southwest up to a ridge, then northwest to the

**Franklin Hill Road junction (5580 – 0.4).** Your road turns left (west) and contours the south slopes of a ridge, then descends west past a spring (5430 – 2.0) to the ridge crest, which it follows southwest down to a spur road (5220 – 0.7). The road now heads west-northwest for 0.1 mile, then contours southwest to a ridge and the tempting **Pinchard Creek Road (5185 – 0.6),** which heads south down toward the Middle Fork of the Feather River. **Don't take it.** Your road turns west, heads north, then weaves its way west to a flat, dry meadow with a spur road south (5225 – 1.4). Continue west to a junction with the **ridge road (5210 – 0.2),** which parallels the canyon's south wall. Turn left (southwest) and follow this rocky granite road as it descends to a flat and the

**Hartman Bar Trailhead (4780 – 1.3)** with a campsite. A small spring lies 70 yards west of the campsite among dogwood, ferns and white fir. This section of the CRHT starts 30 yards north of the campsite by a stately, solitary ponderosa pine, and it heads down the east side of the gully. Incense cedar, black oak and white fir
94 line the trail as it descends gently north on granite slopes past 2
95 pipe springs and several seasonal creeks with broad-leaf maples and thimbleberries. You will soon reach the start of many switchbacks (3850 – 1.6), gutted by dirt bikes, which take you down through Douglas fir, sugar pine, and ponderosa pine to Dan Beebe Campground (2300 – 2.6) and Hartman Bar suspension bridge (2300 – 0.1). The 300-yard-long, cascade-fed, granite-lined pool here, a classic swimming hole, could perhaps be the best of its kind in California were it not for the cyclists' trail damage, trash, and noise brought to this National Wild River region, going unchecked by the Forest Service. There is good fishing here in addition to excellent swimming and diving.

Cross the bridge and switchback up a fly-infested, hot, dry north slope mantled with live oak, manzanita, California nutmeg and poison oak, which grades into a Douglas fir forest as the trail heads up to Catrell Creek (3500 – 2.0), a welcome sight. Farther up the trail (4200 – 1.0) is an abandoned shack (beware of rattlesnakes), a pea garden, and more water. Continue up the switchbacks over Mesozoic ultramafic intrusive rocks, then past a pipe spring (4650 – 0.8) to a parking area (5080 – 0.7). The trail stays right of it and heads west up the south-facing slope to **Gravel Range Road**

**(5400 – 0.3).** The giant, near-vertical hexagonal columns you see to the south on Peak 5495 are remnants of a Pliocene andesite flow.

* * * *

The temporary route essentially follows the CRHT, which stays high, and in late summer may not have water (except for the south Haskins Valley drainage) until the Mount Pleasant area, about 23 miles farther. Since you are probably low on supplies, and may welcome water plus a refreshing swim in Bucks Lake, you can take an **alternate route** which will now be described. Water is immediately available from the small creek in the gully, 40 yards west of the trailhead. Now head back east on the road, leaving the shade of the Jeffrey pines and white firs behind as you follow the road which now contours north past giant hexagonal columns along the canyon's north rim and into China Gulch (5370 – 1.5). From China Creek the road ascends east, goes south to the rim again, and then gradually curves north as it descends to Willow Creek (5040 – 1.7 – 3.2). It crosses the creek and heads up through a narrow roadcut, then winds northeast past creeks to upper Willow Creek, an adequate campsite, and a junction with the

**Lookout Rock Road (5290 – 2.2 – 5.4).** Turn left (northwest)
and follow it up past several creeks to the **Highlands Road** 95
**(5670 – 3.4 – 8.8).** Turn right (northeast) and go gently up, then 96
moderately down, crossing the PCT temporary route (5670 – 0.2 – 9.0), and dropping into Haskins Valley to the **Haskins Valley Road (5270 – 0.6 – 9.6).** Turn left (northwest) and follow it gently down to an east spur road (5230 – 0.1), where your road now heads west to the

**Oro-Quincy Road (5165 – 0.5 – 10.2).** Turn right (north) and proceed along this paved road to Haskins Valley Resort (5170 – 0.1), where some meager supplies can be obtained. Just past it on your left is Haskins Valley Campground (5180 – 0.1) with (sometimes) hot showers. If you are particularly famished, stop at Bucks Lake Lodge (5237 – 0.3), which serves enormous meals at affordable prices. Head northeast to Lakeshore Market (5180 – 0.7) where you can restock your supplies to last until Belden, about 22 miles ahead. Continue past Bucks Creek (5180 – 1.0) to Whitehorse Campground (5220 – 0.5), a good place to stop before the next long ascent. Farther up the road (5410 – 1.4 – 14.3) the temporary PCT route comes in from the east.

* * * *

At the Hartman Bar trailhead, the PCT temporary route starts in the gully, 40 yards west, and ascends the east slope, then crosses west over the creek and up to **Road 23N15 (5690 – 0.9),** marked with CRHT signs. Turn right (north) and follow this obvious ridge route over Jura-Trias metavolcanic rocks past numerous junctions to the **Cedar Flat Road (5850 – 3.1).**Turn right (north) and follow it down to Cedar Flat (5470 – 1.5), then northeast up to the **Lookout Rock Road (5720 – 1.0).** Turn left (north) and follow the road past a lateral road that goes down to the Oro-Quincy Road (5720 – 0.1), then east gently down to the Highlands Road (5670 – 0.3)—the alternate route, mile 9.0. Your road continues northeast, then winds east past several creeks to a junction with the Haskins Valley Road (5510 – 2.4). Continue east down to a broad saddle and a junction with the **Meadow Valley-Lookout Rock Road (5450 – 0.6),** heading east. Turn left (north) and follow the dry, dusty road that tortuously winds through an open forest to the paved

**Oro-Quincy Road (5410 – 3.9),** the junction with the alternate route. Turn right (northeast) and head up to Bucks Summit, with its good view east, and the **Spanish Peak Lookout Road (5531 – 0.2).** Turn left (north) and follow this new road as it switchbacks up the granite slopes, reaching the

**Spanish Peak Trail (6550 – 2.6),** well marked, just before the
95 ridge. Turn right (north) and follow it past wet meadows, then
96 along the east slopes through an open red-fir forest up to Spanish
Peak Lookout Road (6900 – 1.5). A ½ mile walk east to the
97 lookout (7017) will provide you with a very good panorama of the
country, including Lassen Peak (10,457) on the distant northwest horizon. Cross the road and follow the trail northwest along the rim's edge to a **temporary trail (6920 – 0.6).** Turn left (west) and go 100 yards to the **jeep road (6920 – 0.1).** Turn right (northwest) and follow it through red fir and dry meadows to its end at the

**Three Lakes Trail (6850 – 1.6),** part of the CRHT route. Turn left (northwest) and follow it down into a small valley, then go west around the north side of the valley. The trail now heads northwest toward Mt. Pleasant, then west along its south slopes to its west ridge (6730 – 2.0). You now drop down to the verdant Clear Creek drainage and try to follow the trail as this unmaintained section deteriorates westward. Cross the creek where it angles north (6200 – 1.2) and increases its gradient down through a prominent gap. The trail then climbs gently northwest up to a shallow lake (6270 – 0.5) and becomes increasingly obvious as it passes 2 more grassy lakes, then descends southwest to the **Three Lakes Road (6130 – 1.3).** Turn right (west) and walk 100 yards, then head south another 100 yards to a spur road (6110 – 0.1) by the west lake. The descent to Belden is dry and this is your last source of water. Turn right (north) and go 100 yards, then start your descent west to the

**Belden Trail (6080 – 0.2),** an abandoned jeep road, marked farther up with CRHT signs. Turn right (northwest) and follow this trail as it climbs northeast through manzanita and chinquapin back into the red-fir forest, then descends gradually to the north ridge (6000 – 2.1) with good vistas. From here the trail drops straight down the ridge, then eases its gradient. Originally it switchbacked down, but hikers preferred to shortcut, thereby destroying the trail. You soon curve north and quickly begin to switchback (4960 – 1.0) down to the river. This trail began in red fir, then descended past white fir, black oak, sugar pine, Douglas fir, live oak, poison oak and California laurel. Dogwood, broadleaf maple, thimbleberry and bracken fern are found in the moist spots. Granite has given way to Paleozoic marine sediments, and except for minor outcrops on the Chips Creek Trail it will be the last you will see until Castle Crags, about 200 miles ahead.

Our trail now heads east, then drops down a small gully past a house to the railroad tracks (2300 – 3.8). Cross these and follow a road east past Belden Campground (2300 – 0.3) to Belden Town (2330 – 0.3), where you can restock your supplies. These will have to last until Fire Mountain Resort, 39 miles distant. Follow the
road across the North Fork of the Feather River (excellent swim- **97**
ming) to **State Highway 70 (2330 – 0.1).** Turn left (west) and **98**
follow it past the Indian Creek Roadside Rest (2320 – 0.1) and a Shell station (2250 – 0.7) to the

**Chips Creek-Ben Lomond Trail (2240 – 0.1).** Turn right (west) and ascend it north, contour southwest to a saddle, then descend northwest to the Ben Lomond Trail cutoff (2480 – 0.9). After 0.2 mile the Chips Creek Trail makes a few switchbacks, then climbs steadily northwest into Lassen National Forest, over Paleozoic marine sediments metamorphosed by an intruding granitic pluton, which is exposed in several places along this trail. The sequence of vegetation you encounter is the reverse of that found along the descent of the Belden Trail from the Three Lakes Basin. Water can be obtained where the trail curves west (3600 – 3.2), and soon you reach a small cabin on a forested flat (3760 – 0.6), a lovely campsite only 100 yards from roaring Chips Creek. This site is inhabited by rattlesnakes, but if you will respect them, they will respect you. If you would rather not have their company, then continue your ascent past numerous creeks until you are well into the white-fir forest. Near the head of Chips Creek Canyon, the trail switchbacks up and across the creek, then continues up switchbacks to the trailhead at a **jeep road (5920 – 4.7).** Follow this through a meadow and up to a

**Saddle (6240 – 0.7)** mantled with red firs and silver pines. From this point northward, your route will be only along volcanic rocks of Miocene age or younger until you reach the ridge northwest of Lake Britton in Shasta National Forest. Turn right (north) on another jeep road and ascend it through a well-logged area to a wide lumber road (6920 – 1.6) leading west down to Snag Lake. Cross it and ascend a trail northeast to a ridge (7000 – 0.1), then go east along it, with views of Lassen Peak, to switchbacks (7110 – 0.5). Descend these east to a spring (6900 – 0.4), your last permanent water until Willow Creek, 10 miles ahead. Now hike
98 north across a saddle to a **jeep road (6600 – 1.0).** Continue north on it past the Sunflower Flat spur road (6600 – 0.7) and down to **Road 26N02 (6380 – 1.2).** Turn left (west) and follow it to a cattle guard and the **Humbug Ridge Road (6380 – 0.2).** Turn right (north) and follow this narrow, forested road to Humbug Summit and the

**Humbug Road (27N01) (6714 – 1.9).** Turn right (northeast) and descend it to the **Lost Lake Trail Road (26N03) (6550 – 1.0)** along Sawmill Tom Creek. Turn left (west) and ascend it to the headwaters (6770 – 0.7), then east to **Lost Lake Jeep Trail (6790 – 0.1).**

Turn left (west) and follow it up a ridge to a meadow with a spur road south (7110 – 0.5). Continue northwest along the rim, then north to a saddle that provides you with a view of the Sacramento Valley off to the distant west. Just north of this saddle the road forks (7010 – 0.8), and you take the right branch, which starts to descend the east slope. It quickly deteriorates, but stay with it past a viewpoint of Lost Lake, then switchback south down a connecting road that leads past Lost Lake (6440 – 1.4)–a grassy pond–then terminates a few yards south of the

**Yellow Creek Road (6400 – 0.1).** Turn left (west) and follow it down to a junction with a spur road east (6140 – 0.7), then continue west past springs to Yellow Creek (6080 – 0.4). Your water-shortage problems are now over, but you are faced witn finding the unmarked **Eagle Rocks Trail (5E10) (6400 – 0.1).** It has an obscure beginning about 100 yards east of Yellow Creek. Head northwest up the gentle slopes until you find it, then follow it curving north up to a saddle (6470 – 0.7). It now switchbacks down to Butt Creek (5460 – 1.3) and follows blue blazes, ending at a large log with blue paint, beside the **Humboldt Road (5480 – 0.1).** Turn left (west) and follow it past Ruffa Ranch (5570 – 0.9) to

**Carter Meadow Trail (5E06) (5585 – 0.2),** by a small creek bed.
Turn right (north) and follow the road 170 yards to an open area.
The trail starts just west of it near the creek bed. Follow it north up **98**
to the saddle (6600 – 1.6), where you obtain a good view back at **99**
Eagle Rocks. You now have a delightful descent through a red-fir forest interspersed with grassy meadows and good campsites along Carter Creek. The trail soon reaches Carter Meadow and proceeds along its west edge to a **logging road (6490 – 2.3).** Follow it immediately over a low saddle, then north gently down west slopes. It is best to avoid lumbermen in this next section if you can. You soon pass several logging-road junctions, then eventually (5210 – 2.0) head east and wind down almost to Deer Creek Meadows (4800 – 1.2). Your road now contours west-northwest to a three-way junction (4770 – 1.4), then heads west and descends to

**State Highway 32 (4510 – 1.0)** at a bridge over Deer Creek. Turn right (north) and follow this paved road past Alder Creek (4520 – 0.1) and a free public campsite on private land, then northeast across Deer Creek Meadows to **State Highway 36 (4660 – 1.9).** Turn left (northwest) and follow this paved road north across Gurnsey Creek (4630 – 0.9) to **Fire Mountain Resort (4720 – 0.9),** where supplies can be obtained. Your next supplies will be at Old Station, north of Lassen Park, 52 miles distant. Continue northwest on 36 past Gurnsey Creek Campground (4710 – 0.6) to

**Paynes Creek Road (4859 – 3.6).** Turn right (east) and follow it up along a spring-fed creek with adequate campsites to Wilson Lake (5267 – 2.4), an oversized lily pond. It is very evident that people camp here although no running water is available. Continue up to Wilson Pass (5444 – 0.6), and descend into hostile territory, abundantly marked with "No Trespassing" signs, to the North Fork of the Feather River (5370 – 0.8). Your road now climbs north, then drops gradually east to a junction with **Rice Creek Road (5170 – 4.1).** If you continue east 0.6 mile on the same road, you will reach Domingo Springs Campground with excellent water. Otherwise, turn left (west) and essentially backtrack on Rice Creek Road to **Stump Ranch Road (29N16) (5150 – 0.7).** Turn right (north) and ascend this to its end at

**Little Willow Lake Trail (6080 – 4.7).** The trail climbs a low saddle then drops into Lassen Volcanic National Park and to Little Willow Lake (6060 – 0.2), essentially a wet, grassy meadow. Walk northeast to its outlet (6060 – 0.1), then descend the narrow trail that parallels the creek east until you reach an **unused road (5720 – 0.4)** which heads north to Terminal Geyser. Turn left (north) and follow it as it goes gently up, then gently down to a small gully, where the road turns slightly northeast. In 70 yards you will reach the poorly marked **Terminal Geyser Trail**
100 **(5800 – 0.6);** 100 yards farther on the road is the gurgling Terminal Geyser–worth investigating. At 203°F, it will definitely hard-boil any eggs you've brought along. Turn left (northwest) and ascend the trail past the Terminal Geyser Overlook (5880 – 0.1) to a trail fork (6100 – 0.3). The east branch is a more open and little-used footpath, but it takes you to the north end of Boiling Springs Lake, which is colored a milky green due to the hot-water algae. Your route follows the west branch, a horse trail, that takes you northwest to the south end of the 125°F lake and the

**Boiling Springs Lake Nature Loop Trail (5930 – 1.2).** Your route follows the east half of the loop to its junction with the east branch of the Terminal Geyser Trail (5890 – 0.2). It then continues northwest past the nature loop trail cutoff (5870 – 0.1) and descends to the Drakesbad Trail (5740 – 0.3), which drops north to a private resort. The trail now descends northeast past hot springs to Hot Springs Creek and a **parking area (5640 – 0.3).** Here you might take a refreshing dip in this creek, slightly warmed by the hot springs feeding it. Go north to the Drakesbad Road and follow it east to the very pleasant Warner Valley Campground and the

**Corral Meadow Trail (5640 – 0.2).** A ranger station lies about one mile down the road from here. This trail starts northeast, but quickly switchbacks west up a long grade through a Pliocene andesite flow to the Sifford Lakes Trail (6200 – 1.2). Your trail then climbs northeast over Flatiron Ridge (6370 – 0.4) and descends to the Kings Creek Trail (5985 – 0.8), which heads southeast down to Warner Valley. Continue northwest to Corral Meadow, an excellent campsite, and the **Grassy Swale Trail (5985 – 0.2).** From this campsite the Summit Creek Trail ascends northwest to Summit Lake and Lassen Park Road. Your trail crosses a well-constructed footbridge over Kings Creek, then ascends gently northeast to Grassy Swale and the

**Swan Lake Trail (6460 – 2.5).** Turn left (north), cross the creek, and follow this trail north past the Horseshoe Lake Trail (6730 – 1.5), which heads southeast past Crater Butte (7267) to the lake and a ranger station. Continue north past Swan Lake on your right (6628 – 0.3) and down to Lower Twin Lake (6537 – 0.4). Here the Upper Twin Lake Trail climbs southwest to Summit Lake and the Lassen Park Road. Your trail contours the east side of Lower Twin Lake to the Rainbow Lake Trail (6540 – 0.6). Over the next stretch to Badger Flat, the PCT takes the least desirable of 3 possibilities.

* * * *

**One alternate route** is to ascend east to Rainbow Lake (6550 – 0.9), a very good camp spot, then northeast to the **Cinder Cone Trail (6240 – 2.6 – 3.5).** If you climb up to the summit of the
Cinder Cone (6907 – 0.7), which last erupted in 1851, you obtain **100**
an excellent panorama of the terrain. The earlier basalt flows from **101-A**
this cone formed the Fantastic Lava Beds, which blocked stream drainage and created Snag Lake to the south and Butte Lake to the northeast. A fault along the east side of this lake has given rise to the Sunrise Peak escarpment. Prospect Peak (8338), to your northwest, is a Pleistocene basalt cone capped with a small, recent cincer cone. Lassen Peak (10,457) protrudes above the southeast horizon. Now descend north to the **Emigrant Trail (6370 –0.6),** turn left (southwest), and follow it to the junction with the PCT route (6354 – 3.0 – 7.8).

* * * *

The PCT route continues north from the Rainbow Lake Trail junction and passes the West Shore Trail (6540-— 0.1) to the poorly marked **Cluster Lakes Trail (6540 – 0.4), the second alternate route.**

* * * *

This alternate trail heads west down to Lower Twin Lake Creek, crosses it, then contours northwest past Feather Lake (6580 – 1.2) and Silver Lake (6575 – 0.6) to the Big Bear Lake Trail junction (6580 – 0.2), then past 2 more lakes and down to Badger Flat

(6260 – 4.6). This scenic section,. like the Twin Lakes area, is populated with both hikers and mosquitoes.

* * * *

From the Cluster Lakes Trail junction the PCT route heads north over level country through an open red fir and lodgepole pine forest to the **"Emigrant Trail" Road (6354 – 2.5).** The Cinder Cone alternate route rejoins here. Turn left (northwest) and follow this old road to a gate and Badger Flat (6260 – 2.5), where the Cluster Lakes alternate route rejoins your trail. Follow the Badger Flat Road west to the

**Emigrant Trail (6260 – 2.2),** a well-hidden footpath. The trailhead is in a small, level area just after the road has started its descent, but just before it turns west-southwest and drops again. There is a row of 3 large **Jeffrey pines** near the road. The trail starts at them and soon becomes obvious as it leaves the forest and descends a gully into a thick stand of manzanita to **Road 32N60 (5470 – 2.2),** a forest-plantation loop road. Turn left (northwest) and descend this road north, then west over to Hat Creek, which it parallels north to **Road 32N12 (4845 – 3.0).** State Highway 89 is 0.7 mile northwest on this road. Turn left (northwest) and follow it
70 yards to **Road 39N92 (4840 – 0.1)** near Twin Bridges
101-A Campground. No water will be available over the next 8.8 miles.
101-B Turn right (north) and follow this road past several junctions, then
northeast to a faulted escarpment (4680 – 1.4). The road ascends
102 this slope, then heads east to a fork. Take **Sheep Camp Loop Road**
104 **(4500 – 1.2),** which heads northeast and down along the base of
this recent basalt flow. It angles north (4355 – 2.5), then northwest (4350 – 1.7) across the flow to a junction near State Highway 89 (4315 – 1.9). You can walk ½ mile southwest on this highway to Old Station to obtain supplies. Your next opportunity for limited supplies, if you follow the temporary PCT route, will be at Cassel, 25 miles ahead. Head northeast past the Lassen National Forest Visitor Information Center to

**State Highway 44 (4365 – 0.1),** where you have 2 choices. The temporary PCT route is hot, dusty and shadeless, and it lacks fresh water. Your only satisfaction will be a 360° panorama from the Hat Creek Rim Fire Lookout–provided the fire observer is not too busy pinpointing lightning-initiated fires. This panorama includes Lassen Peak and Mt. Shasta, unfortunately both too distant for good photographs. The alternative is to go 0.1 mile west to State Highway 89 and follow this paved road 22 miles north to the State Highway 299 junction. For much of this distance the road parallels verdant Hat Creek. Fresh water, shade, good campgrounds and a store are the advantages of this route.

---

**Right: Lassen Peak** *Jeff Schaffer*

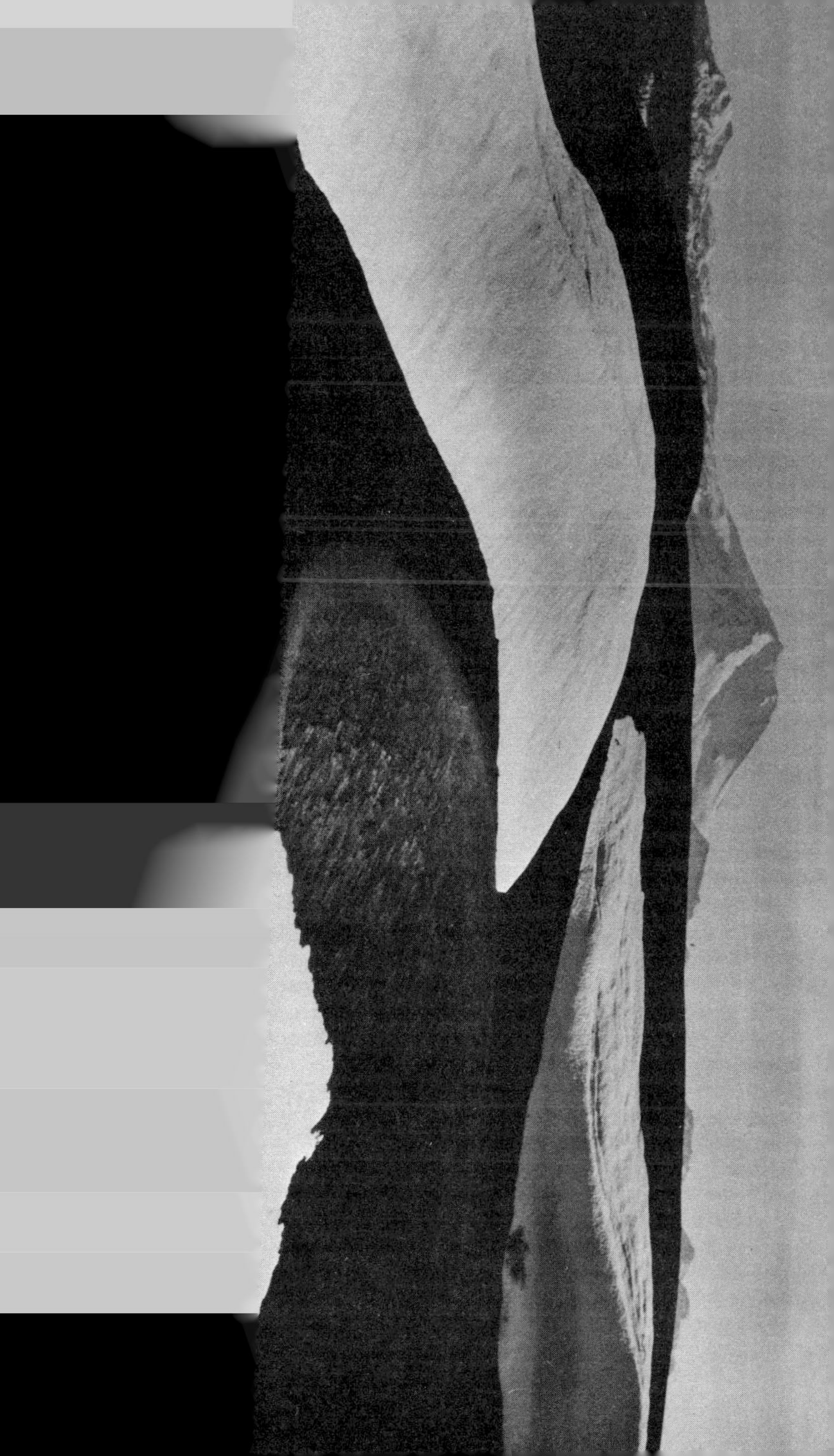

The temporary PCT route turns right on State Highway 44, then follows this paved road east to the Hat Creek Rim escarpment (4350 – 1.1). You ascend this north to **Road 33N21 (4860 – 1.8).** Turn left (north) and follow it for 6 hot miles to the Government Well turnoff northeast. Your road heads northwest, is now numbered 34N36. Continue along it to **Road 35N14 (4980 – 7.3).** Turn left (west) and follow it northwest up to Hat Creek Rim Fire Lookout (5122 – 1.9), your only reward along this section. Hat Creek Rim is a faulted escarpment of Pleistocene basalt flows. Down in Hat Creek Valley to the west are very recent, largely unvegetated basalt flows with numerous cinder cones. Mt. Shasta (14,162), a Quaternary composite cone, is the dominating peak to the northwest. Lassen Peak (10,457), a geologically more complex composite cone with dacite domes, is to the south. There were 298 outbursts, most of them minor, when Lassen erupted between 1914 and 1921. Burney Mountain (7863), another composite cone, is due west.

From the lookout continue north along rim Road 35N14 to **Road GR201 (4625 – 2.1),** ascending from Hat Creek Valley. Turn right (southeast) and walk over to **Road 36N18 (4615 – 0.2).** Turn left (north) and descend slowly along Hat Creek Rim to a fork (3970 – 6.3). The right branch heads north to Fall River
Mills; the left branch turns west to Cassel. Keep left and descend
**102** to the **Cassel-Fall River Mills Road (GR201) (3800 – 0.4).** Turn
**103** left (west) and follow this paved road past several dissected cinder
cones, then down to Cassel (3200 – 5.7), a one-store settlement.
**104** Continue west (3220 – 0.8), then north, entering Shasta National
**105** Forest, to

**State Highway 299 (3103 – 3.0).** Turn left (southwest) and follow this paved road to a junction with **State Highway 89 (3203 – 2.2),** with a small store at the intersection. (The best place for supplies, however, is the town of Burney, 5 miles southwest on 299.) Turn right (north) and follow 89 across railroad tracks (3089 – 2.3) to the

**Lake Britton Road (37N05) (2980 – 2.1),** which angles away from 89. Turn left (northwest) and follow it past a store, then continue to a long, straight, west-northwest stretch. Just after this stretch, where the road curves north, there is a parking spot on the right (2960 – 1.7). From here a short unmarked path leads east and crosses a bridge over Burney Creek to McArthur-Burney Falls Memorial State Park. Last-minute supplies are available here; they will have to last 74 miles until you reach Interstate 5 near Castle Crags State Park. The nature-trail booklet will acquaint you with the fauna and flora of this rustic volcanic woodland. After your visit, continue northwest to Lake Britton Dam (2732 – 1.5), cross it, then contour northeast to a gully and up to

**Road 37N30 (2796 – 0.6).** Turn left (northwest) and ascend it up the west side of the gully, then contour west through chaparral to Rock Creek Canyon and the Rock Creek Campground (3040 – 2.7). Your road now follows this creek northwest past several tributaries and numerous spur roads, then (4000 – 4.5) slowly curves west to a southwest ridge (4560 – 1.9). It now turns northwest and continues up to a crossing of Rock Creek (4670 – 0.5). This is your last permanent water until Bartle Gap Meadow, 15.4 miles farther. Beyond the creek, the road continues up the canyon, then (5040 – 0.7) cuts back south up its west slope to a flat ridge at the powerlines (5320 – 0.6). The road follows these west to

**Summit Lake Road (38N10) (5330 – 0.2),** which you will follow for 24 miles in a large arc west to Stouts Meadow. In this country the north and east slopes are forested, while the south and west slopes are mantled with chaparral. Turn right (north) and ascend this road to the shoulder of Red Mountain (5400 – 1.0), then curve around it on east slopes and back to the ridge at a saddle (5140 – 2.0). The road quickly leaves the ridge and heads northeast past Deadman Flat Road (5070 – 1.2) and Harlow Flat Road (5240 – 1.2), both of which descend east to Bosworth
Meadow, then go northeast to Highway 89. As you continue north, 105
you may encounter many deer or perhaps a bear and her cub 106
feeding on the gooseberries growing under the thick pine-and-fir
forest cover. Your road reaches the ridge again and descends it to 107
a saddle (5000 – 1.9). As you gaze west toward Grizzly Peak Fire Lookout 11 miles distant, you are looking across increasingly older rocks. The rocks you stand on are Mio-Pliocene basalts; the basin immediately below you is carved out of Eocene continental sediments; and farther west in Bull Canyon and Devils Canyon there are folded Triassic marine sediments which you can observe close up at Grizzly Peak.

The road now ascends northeast through chaparral, then switchbacks north up to an east ridge (5320 – 1.2) and contours northwest back along the ridge again (5340 – 1.2). Then it leaves the ridge and circles a broad summit past a spur road, then descends south to the ridge and contours west to a saddle and a wide logging road (5152 – 3.2), which descends 6 miles north to Highway 89. Cross it, contour northwest, then descend to Bartle Gap Road (4940 – 1.0) and Bartle Gap Meadow, a good campsite. Your next good campsite with water will be along Stouts Meadow, about 10 miles ahead. Your road turns left (southwest), climbs to Bartle Gap (5140 – 0.6), then ascends the dry ridge to the broad summit of Mushroom Rock (6160 – 2.9), which has snow patches until midsummer. Continue west along the ridge to another broad summit (6213 – 1.7), then descend first northwest, then southwest, back to the ridge and a logging road (5600 – 1.7). Follow the ridge southwest as your road gently descends to another road in upper Stouts Meadow (5420 – 1.9). Continue west across the meadow, then northwest through an extensively logged area and down to the west corner of Stouts Meadow and

**Grizzly Peak Road (5260 – 1.4),** just past a snow surveyor's hut. Your next permanent water will be at the McCloud-Big Bend Road junction, 9.5 miles ahead. Turn left (west) and follow the road southwest through a red-fir forest up to Pigeon Hill (5520 – 1.4), then along alternating manzanita- and fir-covered slopes up to the west slope of Grizzly Peak and a

**Jeep trail (6160 – 2.1).** It is well worth your effort to climb 0.2 mile up the road to the Grizzly Peak Fire Lookout (6252), where Triassic marine rocks are well exposed. This is also perhaps your best view of Mt. Shasta (14,162) along the temporary PCT. You can easily trace out your past 27-mile trek, whose overall shape wasn't obvious while you were on it. Descend to the jeep trail and follow it west to **Road 1W06 (6000 – 0.1).** Turn left (south) and descend through red fir, white fir, then Douglas fir to the
**McCloud-Big Bend Road (3600 – 5.9).** Water is available in the
107 gully just east of this junction. Turn right (west) and follow this
108 very winding road to Deer Creek (3100 – 1.9), then down past
smaller creeks to McCloud Reservoir Dam (2660 – 4.3). Cross the
109 dam and follow the road as it contours the west bank of the
reservoir to

**Ah-Di-Na Road (38N53) (2680 – 1.9)** at Battle Creek, an adequate campsite. Turn left (west) and follow the road west up Battle Creek, then cross it (2850 – 0.6) and ascend north slopes to a saddle and **Bald Mountain Road (38N36) (3300 – 2.0).** As your route progresses west toward the Sacramento River, you will pass over increasingly older rocks. You are now in the upper Paleozoic Era, as Permian metavolcanics compose this ridge. Turn right (west) and contour along forested but dry south slopes to **Road 4D-KT (3450 – 1.9).** Turn right (north) and ascend it to a saddle and a view overlooking Battle Creek, and **Road 4.1-KT (3640 – 0.5).** Turn left (southwest) and head up this unmaintained road, which soon becomes quite vegetated as it curves west and leads up a gully past a short, vegetated spur road, then finally goes north to a saddle (3970 – 0.9). The road now heads west along the ridge, then curves north as it descends to Water Trough Springs (3700 – 2.0), a welcome refreshment. Continue west to where the road turns northwest and starts a short, gentle descent. You can see

Mt. Shasta from here. Your road (3820 – 0.9), now numbered 2W02, curves north and passes 2 jeep roads along this flat area, then (3600 – 1.0) it begins to drop sharply down the west slopes of a north ridge to a logging road (3200 – 0.5). Cross it and continue down to a saddle and another **logging road (3000 – 0.3).** Turn left (west) and descend this wide road to

**Squaw Valley Road (2720 – 0.5).** The town of McCloud is 8 miles north of here. Turn left (southwest) and follow this road along the east side of Squaw Valley Creek, then cross it (2640 – 1.1) and ascend west to Cabin Creek (2680 – 0.5), an adequate campsite and your last water until the Sacramento River, 10.5 miles farther. Ascend the road south to its end at a broad saddle and the start of your

**Cross country (3059 – 0.6).** An old jeep road, now completely vegetated and visible on the edge of a fresh roadcut, once ascended this ridge. Your best route is to start from the top of the roadcut and climb west directly up the spine of the ridge through a relatively open Douglas-fir forest to a low summit (4042 – 0.9). You are now in Carboniferous marine sediments–but are probably too exhausted to care. With luck you might pick up a footpath–little more than a deer trail–that leads west, usually on the north side within 20 yards of the actual crest. Follow this up to

**Summit Trail (3W21) (4320 – 0.9),** a jeep road just west of a low **109**
summit. (If you are heading south down the PCT, you can easily
miss this junction. When the jeep road turns abruptly south at the **110**
small, broad, open summit, the footpath will be about 30 yards north and slightly downslope from the large fallen log at this point.) Turn right (west) and drop about 100 feet over the next 0.2 mile, then ascend the road northwest to **Girard Ridge Road (39N13) (4697 – 1.3).** Turn left (southwest) and follow it on northwest slopes to a saddle (4600 – 0.6), from where it continues on southwest slopes to another saddle and the

**Castle Crag Trail (3W04) (4790 – 1.8).** Turn right (northeast) and follow a jeep road up the ridge to a small level area (4930 – 0.4). The partly hidden trail starts here and traverses north along slopes to a junction on the west ridge (4600 – 0.9). A short outcrop of Devonian marine sediments here gives way to pre-Devonian metavolcanics a short way down. Turn left (west) and descend the obvious trail moderately down the ridge crest and across 2 fire roads just before its trailhead on the **Old County Road (2200 – 3.0).** If you need a lot of supplies, it is best to follow this road 0.1 mile west to Soda Creek Road. Take this road west another 0.1 mile across the Sacramento River to the railroad tracks, which you can then follow north 4 miles to central Dunsmuir, the last settlement until Sawyers Bar, about 105 miles ahead.

If you like a challenge, continue west on Soda Creek Road to its end just west of Interstate 5 (Bridge 6-119). Hop the gate into Castle Crags State Park, then follow a road north, then northwest, to a set of powerlines. A spectacular 17.5-mile cross-country route begins at the ridge here and ascends it to the very crest of the Castle Crags. This route is essentially the same as the proposed PCT route.

The temporary PCT route turns left (south) at the Old County Road and follows it south, then west, through verdant streamside forest. You might stop at one of the Castle Crags State Park picnic
110 areas and take a refreshing swim or try your luck at river fishing. Otherwise, follow the road across the bridge to the paved
111 **Frontage Road (2000 – 2.2)** and a small store. Turn left (southwest) and follow this road to a junction with a road that heads west under Interstate 5 Bridge 6-117 to a post office and a slightly larger store (2000 – 0.5). Continue south on the Frontage Road until it crosses the railroad tracks (1950 – 0.5), then follow these south to an obvious road (1900 – 0.6), which parallels the tracks a short distance to the **Sweetbriar Road (1900 – 0.1).** Turn right (west) and follow it across the tracks, then south to the Interstate 5 overpass, which you cross to a

**Sacramento River near Castle Crags** *Jeff Schaffer*

**Road (2000 – 0.6)** on the west side. Check your water supply. A stream, your last permanent water for the next 10.6 miles, flows from the west and under the road here. Follow the narrow paved road, which turns in a northerly direction and parallels the freeway. In 0.3 mile the paved road veers right and you keep left (north) on an eroded paved road, continuing above the freeway until you reach a view of the serrated granite cliffs of Castle Crags (2480 – 1.5), due north. The road, now dirt, makes a sharp turn west past new-growth fir and oak. Continue west, climbing gradually, past two logging roads that drop off to the right, then turn (2779 – 1.5) southeast. As you climb, second-growth Douglas firs begin to take over. You come to the

**Flume Creek Ridge Trail (4W03) (3100 – 1.0),** once a trail, but now a jeep road through to Whalan Station Road. Ascend the trail west up the ridge composed of Mesozoic ultramafics, the predominant rock type until you reach Eagle Peak many miles farther. You climb past Douglas fir, then continue along the crest, where chaparral takes over, with scattered Jeffrey and knobcone pines. High on the crest you cross a spring-fed streamlet (5880 – 6.6), which in late summer can be your first water since the Highway 5 overpass. Continue through open country up to a junction with the

**Mears Ridge Trail (5W11) (5970 – 0.9).** Here your jeep road
turns right (west) and you continue your hike through a white-fir **110**
forest past the Grey Rock Lake Trail (5880 – 0.5), which descends **111**
steeply north, its junction obscured by the relocation of your road, which was altered to protect a meadow from 4-wheel drives. The relatively isolated lake at the end of this half-mile descent provides you with a good campsite if you wish to avoid crowds. You continue west on the road past a junction with the Sacramento River Trail (6160 – 1.3), then over a saddle (6190 – 0.3) and down into the Trinity River basin to **Anderson Lode Claim (5840 – 0.5),** with water and level ground, but undesirable camping due to the mining operations. Your route follows the dirt road, which bears north, then swings southwest down to

**Tamarack Lake Road (5330 – 1.1).** The lake, with a Forest Service campground, is one mile south. Your route bears right (northwest) and shortly brings you to Twin Lakes junction (5200 – 0.5). Twin Lakes Meadow Campground is 2 miles south. Keep right (northwest) on Forest Service Road 38N17, passing Logging Spur A (5100 – 0.8), then go east down past Logging Spur B (5020 – 0.4) to Twin Lakes Creek (4980 – 0.2). Your road now descends north to the **East Fork Road (38N47) (5190 – 2.0).** Turn right (north) toward Whalan Guard Station to **Road CO 133 (5330 – 0.7),** intersecting our road at an acute angle. Turn left and follow it west a short distance to where it curves southwest and meets the

**Panther Rock Road (5323 – 0.3).** Turn right (northwest) and begin a 1500′ climb of 5 miles through a maze of logging roads and logged forest patches. Be very alert for route signs, such as yellow license plates nailed high on trees—these mark the old trail along the ridge. Boulder Peak (6968), to the northeast, is constantly visible and makes an excellent orientation landmark. Its easily accessible, broad summit rewards you with one of the better views of Mt. Shasta and Castle Crags. Climbing toward Panther Rock, which is never visible, you pass into Kimberly Clark property (5600 – 0.5) with signs clearly stating this fact. After a short climb you reach a **junction (5910 – 0.6).** Turn left (northwest) and go 200 yards to another **junction (5930 – 0.1).** Go left (west-northwest) on an old, grassy road that leads to Panther Rock. Almost at once you will spot a blaze. Should you miss this junction, you can follow a network of other roads which will take you up to the six-way junction as long as you keep bearing left at intersections and don't get lured to the prominent road traversing northwest part way up Boulder Peak. Continue up the grassy road to a

**Six-way junction (6640 – 1.3).** Once there you may want to detour 0.5 mile southeast down to where water is available from springs in a meadow. Late in the season the next running water
111 may not be until a small creek, 8.1 miles ahead. Continue straight ahead (north) at this junction, passing a sign, *Seven Lakes Basin and Echo Lake.* Almost at once you leave the jeep road and take the **Lake Helen Trail (6650 – 0.1),** where you turn left and start northwest. A logged area soon obscures the trail, so look for ducks. If these are missing, check for blazes past the logged section on the uphill side. Once these are located, the trail is very easy to follow over a ridge and down to a

**Saddle (6820 – 1.0)** above Lake Helen. A heavily used camping area lies 0.3 mile east, on the shore of this lake. Unfortunately, four-wheel drives go right to its shore. From the saddle take the jeep road left (northwest). After 200 yards you pass a spur road that takes off sharply to the right, then, as your road turns sharply westward, look for a **blaze (6800 – 0.2),** about 100 yards north of the road, where the logging ends and the trees begin. Here you pick up a trail that heads north to an obvious **lodgepole pine (6560 – 0.3)** with an old *Helen Lake* sign on it. Turn right (northeast) and follow a very obscure trail north up to a

**Jeep road (6600 – 0.2)** under Seven Lakes saddle. On this stretch watch for another trail traversing through the talus just below the crest of the north-south ridge—this is your goal. Follow the jeep road left (north) 100 yards to a point where it curves west, then leave it and continue north through a logged area. After 80 yards you reach the first blaze and the trail becomes very evident. If you've taken the challenging but rewarding Castle Crags cross-country segment, you'll come out here. Unfortunately, much of the beauty of this virgin route will be marred if the permanent trail is built along it.

Your trail soon leaves the scree footing and enters a forest of white fir and western white pine. Continue the high ridge traverse northwest, crossing roads at Gumboot saddle (6440 – 2.4) and Picayune saddle (6540 – 0.7), then passing a trail going east (6800 – 2.0) to the headwaters of the Sacramento River. Contour a short distance to a saddle and junction (6760 – 0.3), where the Little Picayune Trail begins a northwest descent. Continue your trek north, crossing a spring-fed creek in a lodgepole-pine forest (6960 – 1.9) as you gently ascend slopes to a ridge (7120 – 0.4), then head north to a junction (7200 – 0.6), where a spur trail heads 0.2 mile west to Porcupine Lake, where there's better camping than at Toad Lake. You quickly reach a saddle (7310 – 0.2), then descend the steep trail north down mafic intrusive rocks to the northwest shore of **Toad Lake (6920 – 0.6),** which has numerous campsites with tables, toilets, and car campers arriving from the east road. When you reach the *Bear Creek* sign, pointing northwest, head cross country in that direction up the slopes to the
well-defined 111

**Bear Creek Trail (7200 – 0.3).** Head north, then switchback up 112
bare slopes to a saddle (7820 – 0.6), which presents you with a 113
sweeping view of Scott Mountain (6829) to the west, China Mountain (8542) to the northwest, and Mt. Shasta (14,162) to the northeast. Starting down, you enter a forest of mountain hemlock, then western white pine, as your trail descends moderately to Bear Creek (6880 – 1.0), with good campsites. From here to Bear Camp, the trail becomes vague in places due to marshy meadows and recent logging. Just keep on a northwest course with Bear Creek on your left. You'll find yourself shunted–by fencing and the lay of the land–toward a **cattle chute (6300 – 1.4)** at Bear Camp, and the only practical way out is up the chute. After you've picked yourself off the road, cross it (northwest) and head past a number of buildings on your right. Because the owners of Bear Camp have fenced in their land, the Forest Service has relocated the trail along the left side of the barbed wire for the next 0.4 mile stretch.

Although the trail has not yet been constructed, the route is easy to follow due to numerous blazes. After descending a short distance from Bear Camp, you pass the Deadfall Lakes Trail (5865 – 1.1), which climbs northeast. You continue straight ahead on the same footpath, now called the Sisson-Callahan Trail (6W06). You quickly cross Deadfall Creek and then pass the High Camp Trail (5650 – 0.6), which contours northwest. Your trail curves west and descends across a road–graded with blue serpentine rock–then reaches the Trinity River and the old Trinity River Trail (5360 – 0.6), along the west bank. Continue along Trail 6W06 as it contours southwest to the Trinity River Road (42N17) (5370 – 0.5), which you follow for 30 yards, then begin an earnest climb up a well-graded trail to Bull Lake (6860 – 2.1), where you'll find pleasant camping. A final effort west up the slope of a glacial cirque brings you to a saddle (7060 – 0.3), from which you descend moderately into another cirque, passing three glacial tarns as you progress northwest to Robbers Meadow (6560 – 1.2), where there is water and good camping. From here your trail climbs west to yet another saddle (6770 – 0.3), then contours northwest to the

**Little Trinity River Trail (7W01) (6510 – 0.9).** Turn left (southwest) and descend along this trail through a forest of lodgepole and Jeffrey pine until you reach the **7W01 Spur Trail (5800 – 1.0).** Turn right (southwest) and climb gradually toward the saddle, but reach a junction with the

113 **Scott Mountains Ridge Trail (6080 – 0.6)** at a contact with
granitic rocks. Turn left (southeast) and switchback up the dark,
114 ultramafic intrusive rocks, then traverse southwest around Peak
115 6434 and pass a good spring as you descend to a broad saddle
(6030 – 0.8), then contour along west-facing slopes to another saddle (6120 – 1.7). Here your trail descends south, passing east of granitic Scott Mountain (6829) as it reaches Masterson Meadow (5480 –1.1). Head southwest through the meadow, cross Masterson Meadow Creek, then follow the trail southwest up to a **saddle (5660 – 0.5).** The trail now becomes a rough jeep road, starting in chaparral and descending into a pine forest as it goes down the east side of Dan Rice Creek. After two fordings of the creek, you meet the

**Whiskeytown-Callahan Road (4515 – 1.5).** Turn left on this paved road and follow it southeast down to **Tangle Blue Road (3760 – 1.6).** Turn right (southwest) and follow this road as it parallels Tangle Blue Creek up toward the Salmon-Trinity Alps Primitive Area, with its numerous trails through glaciated alpine scenery. Many campsites can be found close to the creek, which your road crosses (4520 – 3.6) just before reaching the Horse Creek Trail. Here it turns westward again and curves up to a junction with the Grand National Mine Trail (5120 – 1.7), where you'll find additional streamside campsites. Continue southwest on your road along the creek, enter the Salmon-Trinity Alps

Primitive Area (5240 – 0.3) and soon reach Messner Cabin (5350 – 0.4). Pass this cabin and the Tangle Blue Lake Trail, both on your left, then Trail 8W01 (5390 – 0.1), on your right, and follow your road to its end, where it becomes the

**Tangle Blue Trail (5520 – 0.2),** and steepens. Take this trail north up around a ridge to the Marshy Lakes Road (5900 – 0.4), which you follow west for 100 yards to where the trail commences again, climbing southwest up a ridge. Follow it to the ridge crest (6690 – 1.1), then contour southwest across sparsely wooded slopes, paralleling the Trinity River Fault below you, which separates the light Eagle Creek granitic rocks from the ultramafics you're hiking on. You touched the northeast end of this fault when you crossed the Trinity River while on the Sisson-Callahan Trail. As you reach a thick forest, predominantly of western white pine, you encounter the West Boulder Creek Trail (6720 – 1.8), on your right. Continue southwest and soon reach the

**Eagle Creek Trail (6640 – 0.4).** Head right (southwest) up this trail to a saddle and an intersection with the Middle Boulder Lake–Doe Lake Trail (7130 – 0.7) and descend past the Granite Lake Loop trail to Wolford Cabin, now used as a snow-survey shelter, and the **Granite Creek Trail (6120 – 1.6).** You will find good camping along the creek. Turn left (southwest) and follow
the creekside trail past the west end of the Granite Lake Loop
Trail (5660 – 0.8), then curve gradually along the slopes as your 115
trail descends to the 116

**North Coffee Creek Trail (4800 – 2.4).** Turn right (don't cross 117
the steel bridge) and head northwest along the stream. En route you encounter first the Milk Ranch Creek Trail (4890 – 0.5), climbing south from North Fork Creek, then the Saloon Creek Trail (5050 – 0.5), ascending north. After passing pleasant streamside campsites, you reach the gutted remains of mile-high Schlomberg Cabin (5280 – 0.8). Your trail now climbs chaparral-mantled slopes up into a new-growth pine forest, where it reaches a meadow and North Fork Creek at the base of a four-foot-high waterfall (6320 – 1.8). Continue 130 yards up the trail to an ancient sign: *Trail Gulch* (6400 – 0.1), propped on a small pile of stones. No trail is visible through the scrub. Head uphill cross country 100 yards to a blaze, then follow a poor trail west up to a saddle (7400 – 0.9) above Trail Gulch Lake. (If you've mistakenly reached the Long Gulch Lake saddle instead, you can continue north down Long Gulch to the East Fork of the South Fork of the Salmon River and take the road west back to the PCT route.). Your trail now enters the Klamath National Forest and drops sharply to Trail Gulch Lake (6440 – 0.8), a popular fishing and camping site, then reaches a junction with the South Fork Coffee Creek Trail and becomes a

**Jeep road (9W14) (6400 – 0.5),** descending north through the glaciated valley to **Road 39N08 (5280 – 2.5).** Go left on this road and head northwest past private Carter Meadow Campground, then west to Trail Creek Campground, 0.1 mile beyond which you reach a junction with the paved

**Cecilville-Callahan Road (4820 – 3.1).** Turn right (east) on this highway and go a short distance up to **Road 10W19 (4850 – 0.1).** Turn left (north) and ascend this jeep road over Paleozoic metamorphic rocks along Trail Creek to a **trailhead (6100 – 1.6).** Take the trail east across the stream, then ascend it northeast to **Foster Mine Road (6720 – 0.6).** Here the map shows two buildings, but one has burned down. Turn right (northeast) and follow the road east to a

**Five-way junction (7000 – 0.5)** on a saddle. Take the road to the extreme left, west up the slopes to Siphon Lake (7240 – 1.1), where there is limited camping. A short distance farther, the road
117 ends at another **Trailhead (7300 – 0.6).** Descend the trail through
119 chaparral until you reach a **Trail junction (7040 – 0.7),** where you
turn right (north) and cross a low ridge to Waterdog Lake (7000 – 0.2), a small tarn set in a shallow bowl high on the mountain ridge. The level ground along its western shore provides you with spacious campsites under a lodgepole canopy. Leaving Waterdog, pick up the trail at its northeast end and descend a newly constructed stretch to South Russian Creek (5860 – 1.3), with a campsite. Continue northwest along a gentle descent, crossing several tributaries before you reach a **roadend (4700 – 3.3).** The road makes an open descent through chaparral to **Road 40N54 (4200 – 1.0).** Turn left (west) and follow it along south slopes above the creek down to the

**Sawyers Bar-Etna Road (Forest Highway 93) (2600 – 4.3).** Turn left (northwest) and almost immediately reach Idlewild Campground, with all facilities. You can obtain supplies at Sawyers Bar, 5.3 miles southwest, which has a post office and

**Fishing on the Salmon River** *Andy Husari*

stores. The next settlement en route is Seiad Valley, 75 miles distant. Just west of the campground's entrance is **Road 41N37 (2600 – 0.1),** which you follow north along the Salmon River past a summer-cabin tract and the Mule Bridge Campground to the

**North Fork Salmon River Trail (11W26) (2820 – 2.4).** The trail begins at a green steel bridge and crosses the river to its east bank, then begins a long, gentle rise. One-half mile north of The Cedars (3050 – 2.1), which consists of several buildings and a mining claim in pre-Cretaceous metavolcanics, you enter the Marble Mountain Wilderness. Farther north you bridge the river near Abbot Ranch (3210 – 2.2), then pass many streamside campsites before you reach a junction with the

**Right Hand Fork Trail (10W09) (3360 – 1.9),** one of the most popular camping areas in the Marbles. Turn right (northeast), cross the bridge and ascend this steeper trail up the weathered metasediments of this V-shaped canyon forested with Douglas fir, ponderosa, sugar, and western white pine, and scattered oak, madrone and incense cedar. Campsites and water are available at

**Bug Gulch Junction (4640 – 5.3),** appropriately named, where you'll be plagued by insects during the first half of the summer and cattle during the second. Overgrazing is a problem here and throughout the Marbles and adjacent areas because of the number of livestock that are wintered in the lush Scott Valley just to the
east. You now have an arduous climb largely through chaparral **119**
and new-growth fir. Turn right (east) and ascend this steep, wind- **120**
ing trail north up Timothy Gulch (5080 – 1.0), east past a lateral to Shelly Meadows (6200 – 1.7), then through an extensive stand of knobcone pines up to Shelly Saddle (6350 – 0.3). Construction has begun on the permanent Pacific Crest Trail, which crosses your path, and will allow future backpackers to avoid the logging area ahead. Switchback northeast down the steep, rocky, eroded trail to Shelly Pond (5300 – 1.0), now a marsh with a stream running through it, but in Gold Rush days an artificial lake for the storage of water for late-season mining. Continue down the trail, which becomes a logging road just outside the wilderness area (4680 – 1.2) and descends northeast to the

**Kidder Creek Parallel Road (4400 – 0.5).** Here you have several choices. You can take a long route east down this road to an obvious crossing, then ascend west on the north-slope road until you reach the trailhead (3.1 miles). If you prefer a shorter route with cross country, turn left (west) and follow the road for 80 yards, then angle right on a logging spur which ends 15 yards from Kidder Creek. Wade the creek, then pick up a spur that comes to within 30 yards of the creek on the other side. Ascend this east to the Kidder Creek Road on the north slope, then west up it to the

**Marble Trail (11W23) (4600 – 1.0).** During high-water runoff, neither route is advisable, and you'll have to look upstream for a suitable log to ford over to the north slope. Contour west along the trail, re-enter the Marble Mountain Wilderness (4640 – 1.3), and continue up to the *Hayes Cabin* trail sign, where this trail forks left. Stay right on the

**Kidder Lake Trail (11W38) (4600 – 1.0)** even though the other one looks better. Your trail switchbacks up steep, rocky terrain and brings you to marshy Kidder Lake (5900 – 1.5), with limited camping. Continue your strenuous climb up treeless, flower-painted slopes, the playground of hundreds of hummingbirds, and switchback up to the east ridge, where you rejoin the dangerous Hayes Cabin route (6800 – 1.2). Your trail now switchbacks up to the northeast ridge of Peak 7550 (7220 – 0.6), then traverses northwest across a steep 100-yard-wide perennial snowfield. After a cautious traverse, continue northwest along a ridge route which drops to the Shackleford Creek Trail (6620 – 2.5), going right, then descends steadily to a saddle and the Cold Spring Trail (6290 – 1.9), which leads south 0.3 mile to the spring. Also at this saddle, the Red Rock Valley Trail descends north. Water can be obtained farther west on your trail at Soft Water Spring (6510 – 1.5), which flows just below the trail. Your next junction is
**120** with the Sky High Trail (6300 – 1.4), which curves northeast on an
arete, then drops east into a cirque. Continue northwest down the
**121** ridge to a saddle and a junction with the

**Marble Rim Trail (6232 – 0.4).** Turn right (north) and descend the trail into Little Marble Valley, then contour north to Marble Guard Station (5881 – 1.1), where a ranger station, plentiful campsites, and a stream make this a logical stop. From this point too, a trail descends to Lovers Camp and the Scott River. Your trail now climbs northwest up to a junction (6120 – 0.6), from where an obscure trail switchbacks west up and over Marble Mountain. You keep right and climb around the east flank of Black Mountain (7050), contour northwest to Big Rock Camp (6640 – 2.2), then curve northeast to a saddle and the

**Box Camp Trail (6680 – 0.4).** Turn left and continue your traverse northwest down to Paradise Lake (6120 – 2.6), a beautiful gem with good but limited campsites. Your trail curves northwest past the north shore, then enters a lush meadow with a good stream, which may be your last source of water until Buckhorn Springs, 5.6 miles ahead. This site is a possible camping area if the lakeshore is crowded. If you find this short stretch up from Paradise Lake hard to follow, just head for two tall fir and pick up the trail as it climbs northwest up the slopes past Kings Castle (7405). You reach the crest, then descend slightly to a saddle and a junction with the Kelsey Trail (6600 – 1.6). This is one of the main east-west Marble Mountain trails. Continue straight ahead on the Big Ridge Trail, which traverses the ridge through alternating chaparral and open forest, with continuous sweeping views west. Your trail descends to a saddle and a junction with the Cliff Valley Trail (6640 – 3.5), which, despite the sign, goes to nowhere. Traversing west across Buckhorn Mountain (6908), your trail passes through a stand of young pines, then comes to a large hillside meadow in which Buckhorn Spring (6580 – 0.7) can be located 100 yards northwest. To find it, diagonal downslope toward a standing dead tree. Late in the season this may be your only water until Cold Spring, 6.7 miles ahead. Continue your gentle descent north, pass the trail (6400 – 0.4) descending west to Elk Creek Road, then traverse the west slope of the ridge to the end of the Big Ridge route just southeast of Huckleberry Mountain (6000 – 1.1). Climb the slight rise northeast across the grassy meadow, then make a steep descent to a

**Road (5420 – 0.7)** on the east-facing slope, where you start 9 miles of hot, dusty, open-road trudging. Turn left (northwest) and follow this road as it winds its way north, then switchbacks southeast down to a creek and north to a road **junction (4800 – 2.9).** Turn left and continue your protracted descent northwest, passing another road (4500 – 1.4) which descends east
to a pool on Cliff Valley Creek. Your road passes just below Cold **121**
Water Spring, then quickly reaches a **junction (4370 – 0.3)** on the **122**
ridge. Keep right (north) and contour the ridge crest to your next **junction (4300 – 1.3).** Turn right and descend this tortuous road east down to the

**Grider Creek Trail (12W08) (3040 – 3.5).** This trail down Grider Creek is best remembered for its 14 crossings, some of which could be troublesome during high water. Along this verdant path you pass a number of delightful, solitary campsites. The canyon's metamorphic rocks give way to granite and you soon reach the **trailhead (1680 – 7.7).** Follow a dirt road north up to a **junction (1750 – 0.2)** with a road graded with blue serpentine. Turn right (north) and follow it down to a bridge (1560 – 1.1) which crosses Grider Creek, west to east. Continue north on the road, now paved, as it reaches the Klamath River and then parallels the river's meandering course east to

**State Highway 96 (1430 – 4.3),** where you face a dilemma: the California temporary PCT route ends at the state border in the middle of nowhere and 30 miles west of where the Oregon route begins. If you wish to hike the entire Oregon PCT route, you'll have to walk east 42 miles along this paved highway, paralleling the river and passing several settlements, then finally reaching

Interstate 5 (Highway 99). Volume Two of this trail guide describes the roads you must take in order to reach the start of the Oregon PCT at the border. Considering your location, however, a more logical choice is to continue along the temporary PCT route by turning left and ambling west across the bridge (1430 – 0.5) and over to the settlement of Seiad Valley (1375 – 0.7), with a post office, grocery store, cafe, and tavern. The store, like some others along the way, has a Pacific Crest Register for hikers to sign. The next settlement you'll encounter will be Ashland, Oregon, 57 miles farther. Continue northwest along the highway past Seiad Valley Road (1370 – 0.4), where around the bend from the last inhabited structure–the Idlewood Tavern–you'll see a

**Trailhead (1400 – 0.4)** on the right (north) side of the road. This is a logical place to tank up for the long climb ahead. Your trail starts north through chaparral, climbs west to Fern Spring (2010 – 0.8), then switchbacks up the ridge, first through oak and then through ponderosa pine. As this beautifully designed trail climbs high on the ridge of Paleozoic metavolcanic rocks, it provides you with panoramas of the surrounding country. A final half mile of switchbacks up a steep slope brings you to the crest (5040 – 5.0) just north of the Lower Devils Peak Fire Lookout, which is no longer permanently maintained. Head north up the
crest where, just under the east side of Middle Devils Peak, you
122 reach a junction with the

123 **Darkey Creek Trail (5170 – 0.7),** ascending from Seiad Valley.
124 Turn left (northwest) and hike up along the western slopes of
Upper Devils Peak to a spur trail (5540 – 1.1), that leads west 0.1 mile down to Jackass Spring, with welcome water and acceptable camping. Continue north up the ridge, passing the Portuguese Creek Trail (5760 – 1.2) on your left, then go up to the southeast slopes of Kangaroo Mountain (6694), where you reach a spring and a good campsite (5750 – 0.8). The final section of the temporary PCT in California will now head east-northeast along a ridge that separates the Klamath National Forest to the south from the Rogue River National Forest to the north. Contour east a short distance to a saddle, then north to a **road (5900 – 1.0)** above Lily Pad Lake, which is a foot-deep tangle of Indian pond lilies where one is serenaded at night by a resounding chorus of frogs. Turn right (northeast) on the jeep road and follow it gradually down to

**Cook and Green Pass (4750 – 4.1).** At this intersection you return to a trail, which proceeds east up the ridge of ultrabasic rocks and through an open knobcone-pine forest to the summit of Peak 5845 (1.2), then climbs to Copper Butte (6194 – 0.8). From here east to Donomore Meadows just south of the border, you hike along highly metamorphosed rocks—predominantly mica schist. Your trail now descends northeast along the north slope, traverses a bare area above a logged section, then joins a

**Logging road (5700 – 0.7).** Turn right and follow this road east 100 yards until you see a large stump with a duck, above you and to your right. Here you turn right and climb southeast up a steep slope to a trail. You regain the ridge and pass near the summits of two peaks, then drop slightly to a junction with the Lowdens Cabin Trail (6000 – 1.4), which descends north. Bear right (southeast) and curve south down the slopes through heavy fern growth and across several cattle trails. In your descent, keep left (east) of the gully, and you will pick up the trail as it heads into the brush. Now you'll see a flat, bare area below you known as **Johnsons Dairy (5720 – 0.5),** which you descend to, and encounter the Horse Creek Trail switchbacking down to the Klamath River. Turn left and walk east, and you'll soon come upon a recognizable trail through the trees, and shortly thereafter reach a tributary of Horse Creek (5520 – 0.5). Contouring east through a forested area, you pass a trail on your right which descends to Selby Cabin. You soon enter an open area, where your trail climbs the ridge and heads east, then curves southeast down to a saddle and a road

**Junction (6300 – 4.2).** The road to the right heads south 0.5 mile
to Reeves Ranch Springs, where the water is good, but the camping leaves something to be desired due to overgrazing and the 124
effects of a 1971 fire. From this junction east to the Mt. Ashland 125
Ski Area, 32 miles ahead, you follow a series of dirt roads along the Siskiyou Ridge. It's a very pleasant hike in spite of the road: many deer roam the slopes, the camping areas are good, and you'll probably have the area pretty much to yourself. Starting out southeast on the left road, follow it gently up, then east to a saddle, where you pass an entrance to Buckhorn Campground (6634 – 3.2) south of you, then one to Alex Hole Campground (6670 – 0.2) north of you. Both campgrounds are 0.3 mile from your road. At the junction with the **Dry Lake Lookout Road (40S01) (6740 – 0.3),** turn sharply left (north), then hike through a thick forest of mountain hemlock to a

**Figure 8 junction (6143 – 4.0)** in a grassy, open area. Here you first go right (northeast), then left (north). If you first turn left, however, you'll go north 0.3 mile on Dog Fork Road to Miller Glade Campground, which features good water, wood and campsites, plus a Swiss-chalet-styled outhouse. Similarly, if at the second half of the junction you go right, you'll reach Bearground Spring Campground in 0.5 mile. Overgrazing by cattle makes this campground less desirable than Miller Glade. Here, as at many places elsewhere, ranchers have put salt blocks next to the springs in the meadows—a violation of Forest Service regulations—and the cattle become camp-meadow squatters. Continue northeast on your road, which winds its way down to a

**Six-way junction (5317 – 1.9).** Here you have two route choices. The longer but easier-to-follow route starts on a road almost directly across from you as you enter the intersection. It heads east-northeast, then east to a ridge (5300 – 1.6), where it switchbacks northwest up to a junction (5839 – 0.8). The more direct route is to follow either of the two logging roads northeast up to **Donomore Meadows junction (5839 – 0.9).** If Pacific Fruit Growers and Southern Pacific have finished their logging, then this "cross country" route will be quite obvious. From this junction head northeast on the paved road and arrive at an obscure **dirt road junction (6080 – 0.9),** where the paved road curves west. Take the dirt road northeast across a saddle and up to the California-Oregon State Line (6500 – 0.6). Your road curves east, then contours a ridge southeast to the border again (6720 – 0.7), from where it continues northeast to a saddle and a **junction (6670 – 1.2).** Here your road turns sharply left (west) toward the crest, then parallels it north to a junction with the

**Dutchman's Peak Lookout Road (7061 – 2.7)** at Jackson Gap.
Turn right and follow a road curving northeast to Sheep Camp
125 Spring (6920 – 0.5), where good camping and water are available
0.3 mile down the spur road. Continue along your ridge route, first
126 contouring and then descending gradually to the Wrangle
127 Campground spur road (6496 – 2.3), on your left, which leads one
mile west down to the campground. Your road continues east past Wymer Glade, a large hillside meadow identified by a sign, then descends through a forest of young pines to a road junction at Siskiyou Gap (5879 – 3.2). Tread straight ahead on your ridge route and follow the road as it snakes northwest through second-growth forest, passing numerous junctions, then reaches the Mt. Ashland Day Camp (6240 – 6.9), operated by the Forest Service. Your dirt road soon ends at the

**Mt. Ashland Ski Area (6600 – 0.6),** with a ski lodge. Here you have a choice of two paved roads. If you are low on supplies, you will have to follow the Ashland Loop Road north down to **Ashland (1850 – 13.0).** This ridge route can be entirely dry during late summer, so tank up on water before you start your descent. The other route, on the Mount Ashland Ski Road, winds down dry Siskiyou Ridge to three restaurants at the **Interstate 5-Ashland Mountain Ski Area Interchange (4320 – 9.1).** This is the shorter and more scenic route east to the Oregon section of the Pacific Crest Trail. You may take either route, since both will be continued in Volume Two of this trail guide.

# Index

Acorn Canyon Trail 61, 62
Acton 16, 17, 65
Agnew Meadows 94
Agua Caliente Creek 48
Alder Creek 125
Alder Saddle 64
Alex Hole Campground 145
Aloha, Lake 107
American River 106, 110, 111
Andesite Ridge 112
Angeles National Forest 18, 62
Angelus Oaks 54
Antelope Valley 67, 68, 69
Anza 17, 49
Applewhite Campground 60
Arc Pass 81
Army Pass Trail 80
Arrastre Creek 56
Asa Lake 102
Ashland 16, 17, 146

backpacking basics 7
Baden-Powell, Mt. 62
Baden-Powell Summit Trail 62
Badger Flat 127, 128
Baldy Notch 61
Banner Peak 93
Barker Creek 109
Barker Meadow 109
Bartle Gap 131
Bartle Gap Meadow 131
Bartolas Country Trail 75
Battle Creek 132
Baxter Pass Trail 86
Beach Creek 76
Beach Meadows 76
Beach Meadows Guard Station 76
Beach Meadows Trail 76
Bear Campground 68
Bear Creek 55, 90, 137
Bear Creek Trail 137
Bear Lake 109
Bear Pen Creek 110
Bear Pen Creek Trail 110
Bear Ridge 90
Bear Valley 113
Bearground Spring Campground 145
Beer Keg Trail 78, 79
Belden 16, 17, 122
Belden Campground 123
Belden Trail 123
Ben Lomond Trail 123
Bench Lake Trail 86
Benson Pass 97
Benwood Meadow 106
Big Bear City 17, 57
Big Bear Lake 17
Big Bear Lake Trail 127
Big Dry Meadows 79
Big Meadow 75
Big Pete Meadow 88
Big Pine 17
Big Pine Flat 57
Big Powderhorn Trail 109
Big Ridge Trail 143
Big Rock Camp 142
Big Whitney Meadow 80
Bighorn Plateau 83
biology 28-38
Bishop 16, 17
Bishop Pass Trail 88
Black Mountain Group Campground 52
Blue Lake Campground 105
Blue Lakes 105
Blue Ridge 61, 62
Blue Ridge Campground 62
Boggy Meadow 51
Boiling Springs Lake 126
Bond Pass Trail 98
Bonita Creek Trail 76
Bonita Meadows 76
Bonnie Lake 98
Boreal Ridge 111, 112
Bouquet Reservoir 66
Box Camp Trail 142
Bright Star Creek 74
Bright Star Trail 72
Britton, Lake 131
Bryan Meadow 106
Bubbs Creek 85
Bubbs Creek Canyon 85
Buckeye Pass Trail 97
Buckhorn Campground 145
Buckhorn Mountain 143
Bucks Creek 121
Bucks Lake Lodge 121
Bug Gulch 141
Bull Creek 103
Bull Creek Canyon 103
Bull Lake 138
Bull Lake Trail 103
Bullfrog Lake 85
Burkhart Trail 63
Burney 17, 128
Burney Creek 130
Burnt Rancheria Campground 46
Burro Pass Trail 97
Butt Creek 125

Cabazon 16, 17, 52
Cabin Creek 133
Cahuilla Indian Reservation 49
Cajon Pass 60
Cameron Ranger Station 45
Camper Flat Trail 108
Campo 17, 45
Cannell Creek 73
Cannell Meadow 73
Cannell Meadow Trail 73, 75
Cannell Trail 73
Cantil 17, 70
Caples Resort 106
Carson Pass 106
Carson River 101
Carter Creek 125
Carter Meadow 92, 125
Carter Meadow Campground 140
Carter Meadow Trail 125
Casa Vieja Meadows Guard Station 78
Cascade Creek 98
Cascade Valley 92
Cascade Valley Trail 92
Cassel 17, 128
Castella 17
Castle Crag Trail 133
Castle Crags State Park 134, 137
Castle Pass 112
Castle Valley 111, 112
Catfish Lake 113
Catrell Creek 120
Cedar Creek 111
Cedar Grove 17, 85
Center Basin Creek 85
Center Basin Trail 85
Chain of Lakes Trail 98
Charlotte Lake 85
Charlotte Lake Trail 85
Charlton Peak 54
Chihuahua Valley 49
Chimney Rock 118
China Creek 121
Chips Creek Trail 123
Cienaga Seca Creek 56
Cinco 70
Cinder Cone 127
Cinko Lake 98
Cinko Lake Trail 98
Clarke, Clinton 1-2
Clear Creek 122
Cleveland Natl. Forest 18, 45, 46
Cliff Valley Creek 143
Cliff Valley Trail 143
clothing 7
Cloudburst Summit 63
Cluster Lakes Trail 127, 128
Cold Spring Trail 142
Comanche Trail Camp 61
Consultation Lake 82
Cook and Green Pass 144
Coon Creek 56
Cooper Canyon 49, 63
Cooper Canyon Trail 63
Cooper Canyon Trail Camp 63
Copper Butte 144
Corral Meadow 127
Corral Meadow Trail 126
Cothrin Cove 109
Cottonwood Creek 69, 72
Cottonwood Pass Trail 80
courtesy 12-13
Cox Creek Trail 57
Crab Flats Campground 56
Crab Flats Trail 57
Crabtree Ranger Station 82, 83
cross-country 9
Crowder Canyon Trail 60
Crystal Range 106, 107
Cucamonga Wilderness 18, 60, 61
Curliss Meadows Guard Station 76
Cuyamaca Rancho State Park 47
Cuyamaca Mountains 48
Cuyamaca Reservoir 48

Dan Beebe Campground 120
Dan Rice Creek 138
Darkey Creek Trail 144
Dawson Peak 61
Deadfall Lakes Trail 137
Deadmans Lake 56
Deadwood Meadow 76
Deep Creek 56, 57
deer 34-35
Deer Creek 92, 125, 132
Deer Creek Meadows 125
Deer Lake 116, 117
Deer Lake Trail 116
Deer Meadow 88
Deer Springs Trail 51
Deer Springs Trail Camp 51
Delahunty Lake 118
Desert View Picnic Area 46
Desolation Wilderness 18
Devil's Backbone 61
Devils Peak 144
Devils Postpile Natl. Mon. 92
Diamond Crossing 110
Dicks Lake 107, 108
Dicks Pass 107
Domingo Springs Campground 126
Donner Pass 111

Donohue Pass 94
Donomore Meadows 146
Dorothy Lake 98
Dragon Lake Trail 86
Dry Lake-North Fork Meadows Trail 54
Dry Meadows Trail 74
Duck Lake Trail 92
Dunsmuir 16, 17, 133
Durasna Valley 49
Durrwood Meadows 76
Dusy Creek 88

Eagle Creek Trail 139
Eagle Rocks Trail 125
Eagles Roost Picnic Area 63
Echo Lake 17, 106, 136
Echo Lakes 106, 107
Ediza Lake Trail 93
Eldorado Natl. Forest 18, 106
Elephants Back 105
Emerald Bay Trail 108
emergencies 10-12
Emigrant Basin Primitive Area 100
Emigrant Trail 127, 128
environmental influences 31-34
equipment 9-10
Etna 17
Evelyn Lake Trail 94
Evolution Creek 88, 90
Evolution Lake 88
Evolution Valley 90

Fallen Leaf 17
fauna 34-37
Fay Creek 75
Feather Lake 127
Feather River 118, 120, 123, 126
Filaree Flat Trail 54
fire 11-12
Fire Mountain Resort 125
Fish Creek 53, 92
Fish Creek Meadows 53
Fish Creek Trail Camp 53
Five Lakes Creek 110
Five Lakes Trail 110
flora 29-34
Florence Lake Trail 90
Flume Creek Ridge 135
Fontanillis Lake 108
food 8
footgear 8
Forestdale Creek 105
Forester Pass 85
French Creek 113
French Meadow 72
Fuller Ridge 52
Fuller Ridge Trail 51

Garnet Lake 93
General Creek 109
General Creek Trail 108, 109
geography, plant 30
geology 19-27
Giant Forest 83
Gilmore Lake Trail 107
Glacier Creek 88
Gleason, Mt. 64
Glen Aulin 97
Glen Pass 86
Golden Canyon 101
Golden Trout Creek 80
Golden Trout Creek Trail 80
Goodale Pass Trail 92
Gorman 16, 69

Grace Meadow 98
Grand National Mine Trail 138
Granite Chief 110
Granite Chief Trail 111
Granite Creek Trail 139
Granite Lake Loop Trail 139
Grass Valley Creek 59
Grassy Hollow Campground 62
Grassy Swale 127
Grassy Swale Trail 127
Green Valley 47, 56, 66
Green Valley Lake 56
Green Valley Trail 47, 55
Grey Rock Lake Trail 135
Grider Creek Trail 143
Grinnell Mountain 53
Grizzly Peak 132
Grouse Canyon Creek 110
Grouse Meadows 88
Guffy Campground 62
Gurnsey Creek Campground 125
Guyot Creek 83

Harper Creek 47
Harriet Lake 98
Hartman Bar Trail 120, 122
Harvey Moore Trail 47
Harwood, Mt. 61
Haskins Valley Campground 121
Haskins Valley Resort 121
Hat Creek 17, 128
Hat Creek Rim 130
Hat Creek Valley 130
Hawkins, Mt. 62
Haypress Creek Trail 115
Heart Bar Creek 56
Heart Lake 90
Heather Lake 107
Helen Lake 88, 92
Helen, Lake 136
Hells Hole Trail 110
Herkey Creek Camp 50
Hetch Hetchy Trail 97
High Camp Trail 138
highways 16
hiking 8, 40-41
Hilda Mine Trail 115
Hilgard Creek 90
history, geologic 25-27
history, PCT 1-4
Hitchcock Lakes 82
Holcomb Creek 57
Holcomb Creek Trail 57
Holcomb Trail Camp 57
Holcomb Valley 57
Holcomb Valley Campground 57
Horse Creek Trail 138, 145
Horse Heaven Group Campground 46
Horseshoe Lake Trail 127
Horsethief Canyon 60
Hot Springs Creek 126
Humbug Summit 124
Hurley Flat 52
Hurley Flat Trail 52

Ice Lakes 111
Icehouse Saddle 61
Idlewild Campground 140
Independence 16, 17
Indian Creek 47
Inyo National Forest 78
Iridescent Lake 81
Iron Spring Canyon 49
Isabella, Lake 73
Island Pass 94

Islip Saddle 63

Jack Main Canyon Trail 97
Jackson Gap 146
Jackson Meadow Recreation Area 113
Jackson Meadow Reservoir 115
Jawbone Canyon 70
Jepson Peak 54
John Muir Trail 82, 83-94
John Muir Wilderness 18
Johnston Meadow 93
Jordan Hot Springs Trail 78
June Lake 17

Kangaroo Mountain 144
Kearsarge Pass Trail 85
Kelsey Trail 143
Kelso Valley 72
Kennedy Canyon 100
Kern Plateau 75, 76
Kern River 80, 83, 85
Kernville 17, 73
Kidder Creek 141
Kidder Lake 142
Kidder Lake Trail 142
Kings Canyon Natl. Park 18, 85-90
Kings Castle 142
Kings Creek 127
Kings Creek Trail 127
Kings River 85, 86, 88
Kitchen Creek 46
Kitchen Creek Camp 45
Klamath Natl. Forest 18, 139, 144
Klamath River 143

Laguna Mountains 46, 47
Laguna Rim Trail 47
Lake Alpine 17
Lake Arrowhead 17, 59
Lake Genevieve Trail 109
Lake Helen Trail 136
Lake Hughes 17
Lake Isabella 17, 23
Lake Italy Trail 90
Lake South America Trail 85
Lakes Basin 117
La Porte 17, 118
Lassen Natl. Forest 18, 123, 128
Lassen Volcanic Natl. Park 18, 126-128
Lassen Peak 127, 130
Leavitt Lake 100
Leavitt Meadows 98
Leavitt Meadows Resort 100
Lee Vining 16
Lembert Dome 94
Leona Valley 67
Liebre Mountain 68
Lily Pad Lake 144
Limber Pine Trail Camp 54
Little Bear Creek 59
Little Buck Meadow 75
Little Cannell Meadow 75
Little Grass Valley Reservoir 118
Little Green Valley 55
Little Horse Meadows 78
Little Horse Meadows Trail 78
Little Horsethief Canyon 60
Little Horsethief Junction 60
Little Jimmy Trail Camp 62
Little Norway 17
Little Pete Meadow 88
Little Picayune Trail 137

Little Rock Creek 63
Little Round Valley Trail Camp 51
Little Trinity River Trail 138
Little Willow Lake 126
Little Willow Lake Trail 126
Lone Pine 16, 17, 83
Long Canyon Creek 78
Long Lakes Trail 98
Long Meadow 75
Los Angeles Aqueduct 69, 70
Lost Lake 60, 125
Lost Trout Creek 78
Lowdens Cabin Trail 145
Lower Sunset Lake 105
Lytle Creek 60, 61

Macomb Ridge 97
Main Summit Trail 75
Major General, The 81
Mammoth Lakes 16, 17
Mammoth Pass 92
map description 151
Marble Guard Station 142
Marble Mountain 142
Marble Mountain Wilderness 18, 141, 142
Marble Rim Trail 142
Marble Trail 142
Marjorie, Lake 86
Markleeville 17, 103
Masterson Meadow 138
Mather Pass 88
Matterhorn Canyon 97
McArthur-Burney Falls Memorial State Park 130
McCabe Creek 97
McCabe Lakes Trail 97
McCloud 133
McCloud Reservoir 132
McClure Meadow 90
McDermand, Lake 88
McGee Pass Trail 92
McRae Meadow 117
Meadow Lake 113, 115
Meadow Valley 17
Mears Ridge Trail 135
Messenger Flats Campground 64
Mexican border 45
Middle Creek Campground 105
mileage table, cumulative 42-43
Milk Ranch Creek Trail 139
Mill Creek Summit 64
Miller Canyon 59
Miller Creek 109
Miller Glade Campground 145
Miller Lake 97
Miller Lakes 109
Miller Lakes Trail 108
Milton Reservoir 115
Minaret Creek 93
Minarets 93
Minarets Wilderness 18
Mission Creek 53
Mojave 16, 17, 69
Mojave River 59
Monache Meadows 79
Mono Creek 90
Mono Creek Trail 90
Mono Hot Springs 17
Monolith 17
Mosquito Meadow 76
Mt. Ashland Day Camp 146
Mt. Ashland Ski Area 146
Mt. Laguna 17, 46
Mt. Laguna Recreation Area 46
Mt. Shasta 16
Mt. Whitney Trail 82
Mountain Meadow Lake 110, 111
Muir, John 88
Muir Pass 88
Mule Bridge Campground 141
Mulkey Meadows Trail 79
Murray Canyon Creek 101
Murray Canyon Trail 101

Nelson Creek 117
Nobel Canyon 103
Nobel Creek 103
Nobel Lake 103
North Creek 112
North Fork Creek 139
North Fork Meadow 53, 56
North Fork Salmon River Trail 141
North Shore Campground 59

Oakland Pond 117
Old Soda Springs 111
Old Station 17, 128
Onion Creek Campground 111
Onion Valley 85
Onyx Summit Trail 56
Oregon border 146
Osa Meadows 78

Pacifico Mountain 64
Packer Lake 116
Packer Lake Lodge 116
Painted Rock 111
Painted Rock Trail 111
Palisade Creek 88
Palisades 88
Palisades Basin 88
Palisades Lakes 88
Palm Springs 16
Panther Rock 136
Paradise Lake 112, 142
Paradise Valley 112
Pennsylvania Creek 104
Perspiration Point 64
Phipps Creek 108
Pinchot Pass 86
Pine Mountain 61
Pinehurst 111
Piute Creek 90, 97
Piute Mountains 72
Piute Pass Trail 90
planning and preparation 5-7
Pleasant, Mt. 122
Pleasant Valley Trail 104
Plumas-Eureka State Park 117
Plumas National Forest 18, 117
porcupine 35-36
Porcupine Lake 137
Portuguese Creek Trail 144
post offices 17
Powderhorn Creek 109, 110
Purple Lake 92

Quail Lake Fire Station 68
Quail Meadows 90
Quail Springs Meadow 46
Quincy 16, 17

Rae Lakes 86
Rafferty Creek Trail 94
Rainbow Lake Trail 127
Ramshaw Meadows 79
Rancheria Creek 97
rattlesnake 37
Rattlesnake Creek Trail 76
Rattlesnake Trail 63
Raymond Creek 104, 105
Raymond Lake 104
Raymond Meadows Creek Canyon 103
Raymond Peak 104
Red Lake 105
Red Mountain 131
Red Rock Valley Trail 142
Redrock Creek Trail 79
Reds Meadow 17, 92
regulations 13-15
Return Creek 97
Right Hand Fork Trail 141
Ritter Range 93
Robbers Meadow 138
Rock Camp Ranger Station 59
Rock Creek 16, 83, 131
Rock Creek Campground 131
Rock Creek Patrol Cabin 83
Rock Creek Trail 80
rocks 19-23
Rocky Basin Lakes 80
Rogue River Natl. Forest 18, 144
Rosemarie Meadow 90
Round Lake Trail 106
Round Valley 50, 112
Round Valley Trail Camp 50
Rush Creek 94
Ryback, Eric 3-4

Sacramento River 133, 137
Sacramento River Trail 135
Saddle Junction 50
Sally Keyes Lake 90
Salmon Creek 75, 115
Salmon Lakes Trail 117
Salmon River 139, 141
Salmon-Trinity Alps Primitive Area 18, 138
Saloon Creek Trail 139
San Antonio, Mt. 61
San Bernardino Natl. Forest 18, 49, 53
San Bernardino Peak Divide Trail 54
San Bernardino Peaks 54
San Felipe Valley 48
San Gabriel Mountains 61
San Gorgonio Mountain 54
San Gorgonio Pass 52
San Gorgonio River 52
San Gorgonio Wilderness 18, 53, 54
San Jacinto Peak 50, 51
San Jacinto Peak Trail 50
San Jacinto Wilderness 18, 50
San Joaquin River 90, 92
San Luis Rey River 49
Sand Ridge Trail 112
Santa Ana River 54
Sapphire Lake 90
Sardine Lake Campground 115
Sardine Lake Resort 115
Sardine Meadow 100
Sawmill Campground 68
Sawmill Creek 117
Sawmill Mountain 68
Sawmill Pass Trail 86
Sawmill Tom Creek 124
Sawyers Bar 17, 140
Scott Mountain 138
Scott Mountains Ridge Trail 138
Scovern Hot Springs 73
Seavey Pass 97
Seiad Valley 17, 144

Selden Pass 90
Senger Creek 90
Sequoia Natl. Forest 18, 72
Sequoia Natl. Park 18, 80-85
Seven Lakes Basin 136
Seven Pines 54
Shackleford Creek Trail 142
Shadow Lake 93
Shanks Cove Trail 110
Shasta-Trinity Natl. Forest 18, 130
Shelly Saddle 141
Shepherd Pass Trail 85
Sherman Pass 76
Showers Lake 106
Siberia Creek 55
Siberia Creek Trail 54
Siberia Creek Trail Camp 55
Siberian Pass 80
Siberian Pass Creek 82
Siberian Pass Trail 80, 82
Sierra Buttes 115
Sierra City 17, 115
Sierra National Forest 18
Sifford Lakes Trail 126
Silver Creek 104
Silver Creek Campground 103
Silver Lake 127
Silver Mountain 104
Silver Pass 92
Silverwood Reservoir 59
Siphon Lake 140
Siskiyou Gap 146
Siskiyou Ridge 145
Sisson-Callahan Trail 138
60 Lakes Trail 86
Ski Lake 100
Sky Blue Lake 81
Sky High Trail 54, 142
Smedberg Lake 97
Snow Valley 55
Soda Springs 17, 112
Soda Springs Trail 101
Soledad Canyon 65
Sonora Pass 100
Sorenson's Resort 105
South Fork Coffee Creek Trail 139
South Fork Trail 79, 86
South Lake Tahoe 16, 17
South Ridge Trail 50
South Russian Creek 140
Spanish Creek Trail 122
Spiller Creek 97
Spunky Canyon Campground 66
Squaw Valley 17, 110, 111
Squaw Valley Creek 133
Stanislaus National Forest 18
Stella Lake 98
Stonewall Creek 47
Stonewall Creek Trail 47
storms 11
Stouts Meadow 132
Strawberry Cienaga 51
Strawberry Cienaga Trail 50, 51
Strawberry Creek 79
Strawberry Meadows Trail 79
Stubblefield Canyon Creek 97
Summit Creek Trail 127
Summit Lake 117, 127
Summit Pass Trail 97
Summit Trail 133
Susie Lake 107
Swan Lake 127
Swan Lake Trail 127

Taboose Pass 86
Tahoe, Lake 16
Tahoe National Forest 18, 109
Tahoe-Yosemite Trail 94, 105, 106-108
Tahquitz Peak 50
Tallac, Mt. 107
Tamarack Flat 118
Tamarack Lake 105
Tamarack Lake Trail 107
Tamarack Lakes 115, 116
Tangle Blue Creek 138
Tangle Blue Lake Trail 139
Tangle Blue Trail 139
Tecate 17, 45
Tehachapi 16, 17
Tehachapi Mountains 69
Telegraph Peak 61
Templeton Meadows 79
Tent Rock Campground 68
Terminal Geyser 126
Terminal Geyser Trail 126
Tevis Cup Trail 110, 111
Third Canyon Trail Camp 61
Thomas Mountain 50
Thomas Mountain Camp 49
Thousand Island Lake 93
Three Lakes Trail 122
Three Points 64
Throop Peak 62
Thunder Mountain 61
Tilden Canyon Creek 97
Tilden Lake-Tiltill Valley Trail 97
Tilden Lake Trail 97
Timber Mountain 61
Timberline Lake 82
time, geologic 24
Tinker Knob Trail 111
Toad Lake 137
Toiyabe National Forest 18
Tollhouse Lake 113
Tool Box Spring Camp 49
Toowa Range 78, 79
Toowa Valley 79
Trail Creek 140
Trail Creek Campground 140
Trail Gulch Lake 139
trail symbols 40
transportation 6, 16
trees 29-30
Triangle Lake Trail 107
Trinity River 135, 138, 139
Trinity River Trail 138
Trout Creek Trail 76
Truckee 16
Truckee River 106
Tully Hole 106
Tuolumne Meadows 16, 17, 94
Tuolumne Meadows High Sierra Camp 94
Tuolumne River 94
Twin Bridges Campground 128
Twin Lakes 49, 105, 127, 135
Tyndall Creek 85

Upper Blue Lake Damsite Campground 105
Upper Castle Creek 112
Upper Rock Creek Trail 80

Velma Lakes 108
Vidette Meadow 85
Vincent Gap 62
Virginia Canyon 97
Virginia, Lake 92
Volcanic Ridge 93

Wade Lake Trail 117
Wallace Creek 83
Wanda Lake 88
Warner Springs 17, 48
Warner Valley Campground 126
Waterdog Lake 140
Weldon 17, 75
Weldon Meadow 72
Wellmans Cienaga 50
West Antelope Aqueduct Station 69
West Boulder Creek Trail 139
West Fork of the West Walker Trail 98
West Meadow Trail 110
West Shore Trail 127
West Walker River 98, 100
Wet Meadow Reservoir 105
Whiskey Creek 118
Whisky Creek Camp 110
Whisky Creek Camp Trail 110
White Canyon 101
White Rock Creek 113
White Rock Lake 113
White Water 17
Whitehorse Campground 121
Whitewater River 53
Whitney Creek 83
Whitney, Mt. 82, 83
Whitney Portal 83
Wild Plum Campground 115
wildflowers 29
Williamson, Mt. 63
Willow Creek 50, 121
Willow Creek Canyon 59
Willow Springs 67, 69
Wilma Lake 97
Wilson Creek 97
Wilson Lake 126
Windy Gap 62
Wofford Heights 17, 73
Wolf Creek 100, 101, 102
Wolf Creek Lake 101
Wolf Creek Lake Saddle 101
Wolf Creek Meadows 102
Wolf Creek Saddle 101
Woodcamp Campground 113
Woodfords 17
Woodlands 56
Woods Creek 85, 86
Woolstalf Creek 74
Woolstalf Meadow 74
Woolstalf Trail 74
Wrangle Campground 146
Wright Creek 83
Wrightwood 17, 62
Wymer Glade 146

Yellow Creek 125
Yosemite Natl. Park 18, 94-98
Yosemite Valley 16
Yuba River 115

# The Maps

# 6
# The Maps

The 127 pages of topographic maps which follow cover the entire PCT route (permanent, proposed, temporary) and our suggested alternate routes. Some maps have shaded portions since they were photographed from topographic maps available only in green overprint. All maps are oriented so that north is at the top of the page. The great majority of these maps, which are portions of U.S. Geological Survey 15′ quadrangles reduced by 40%, have a scale of about 1:104,000, or about 1.7 miles per inch. Where 15′ coverage was lacking, we used 7.5′ quadrangles, also reduced by 40% to give a scale of 1:40,000, or about 0.63 mile per inch. On these maps there is no border overlap; the next page continues exactly where the preceding page left off. The Tehachapi Mountains-Mojave Desert region, because of its special re-routing problems, is partly covered on the 1:104,000 scale, but is also covered in its entirety on a one-page map with a scale of about 1:417,000, or about 6.6 miles per inch. The graphic scale for the reduced 15′ quadrangles (1:104,000) is reproduced below. (A graphic scale is printed on each page with a map of the 1:40,000 or 1:417,000 scale.)

## LEGEND

| U.S.G.S. map symbols | Wilderness Press additions |
|---|---|
| Heavy-duty road | *All roads |
| Medium-duty road | *Trail |
| Improved light-duty road | Cross-country |
| Unimproved dirt road | Permanent PCT |
| Trail | Proposed PCT |
| Railroad: single track | Temporary PCT |
| Railroad: multiple track | Alternate routes |

(*An arrow means the route continues in that direction.)

1 ½ 0 1 2 3 4 MILES
3000 0 3000 6000 9000 12000 15000 18000 21000 FEET
1 .5 0 1 2 3 4 5 KILOMETERS

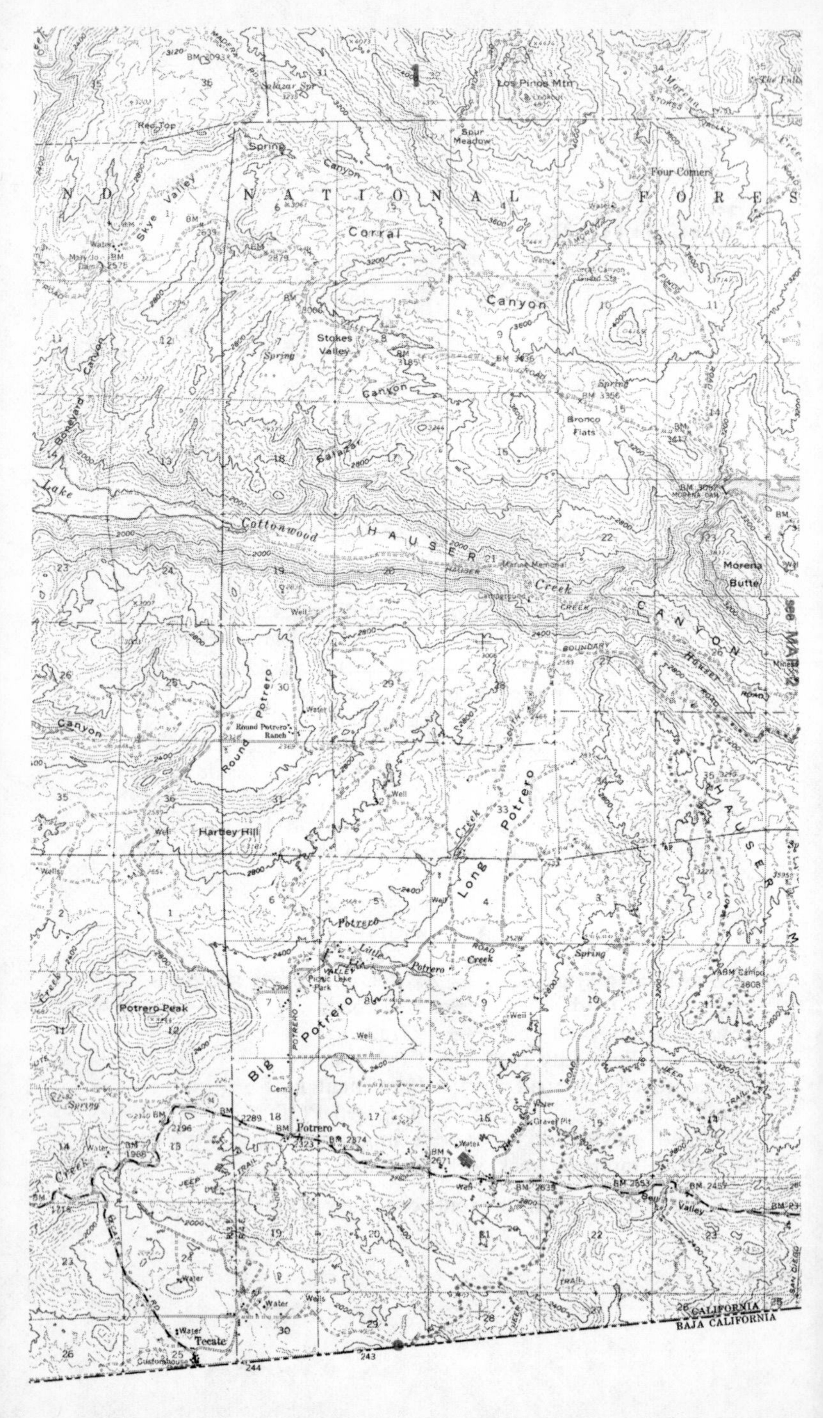

Los Pinos Mtn
Spur Meadow
Red Top
Salazar Spr
Four Corners
N D N A T I O N A L F O R E S
Skye Valley
Corral
Canyon
Stokes Valley
Spring
Boneyard Canyon
Bronco Flats
Salazar
Lake
Cottonwood
HAUSER
Creek
CANYON
Morena Butte
Round Potrero
Round Potrero Ranch
Hartley Hill
Long Potrero
Creek
Potrero
Little Potrero
Creek
Picnic Lake Park
Big Potrero
Potrero Peak
Spring
Potrero
Gravel Pit
Bell Valley
Tecate
Customhouse
CALIFORNIA
BAJA CALIFORNIA

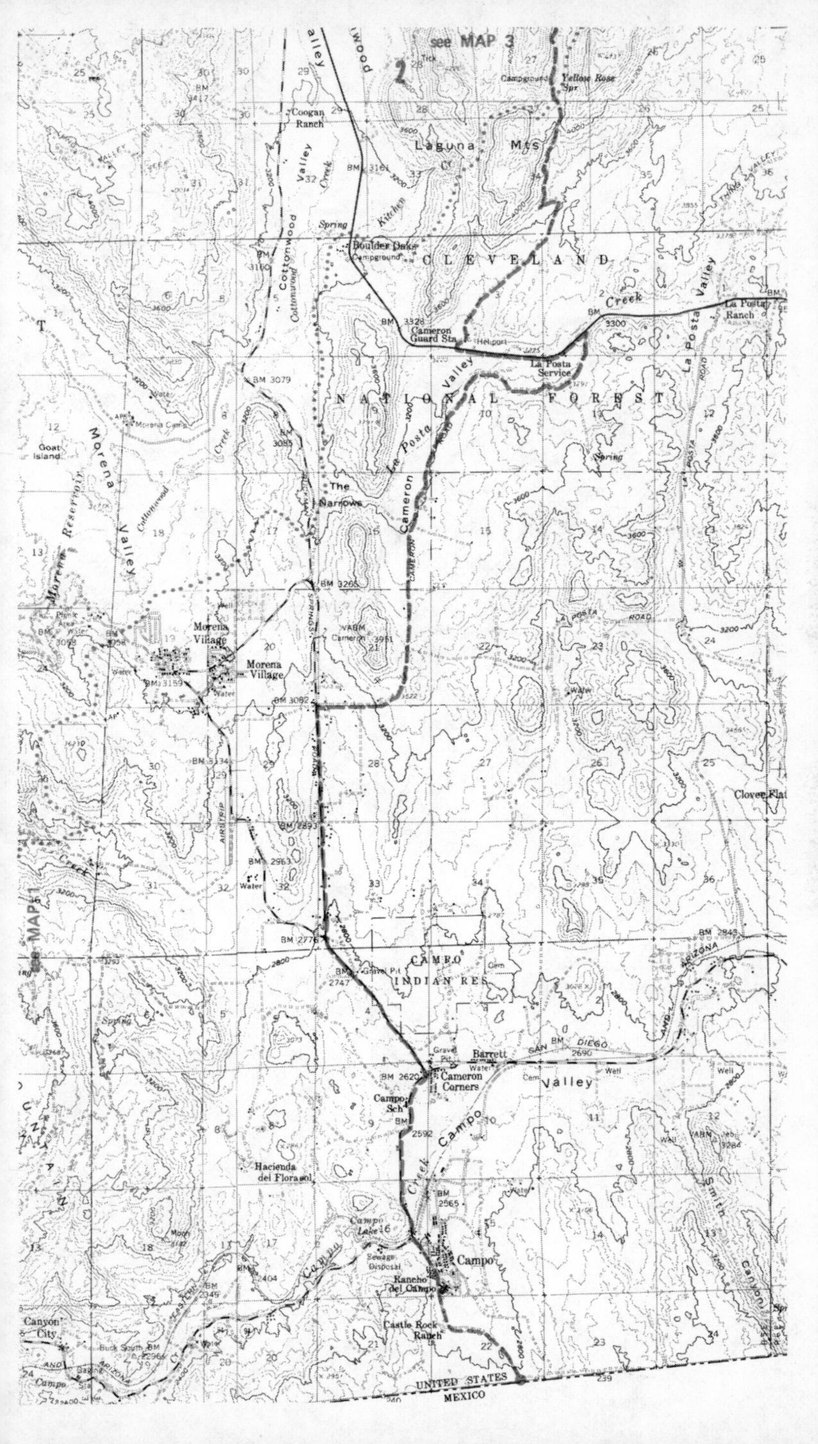

see MAP 3
Laguna Mts
CLEVELAND
NATIONAL FOREST
Coogan Ranch
Boulder Oaks Campground
Cameron Guard Sta
La Posta Service
La Posta Ranch
The Narrows
Morena Village
Morena Reservoir
Goat Island
Cameron Corners
Barrett
Campo
Rancho del Campo
Castle Rock Ranch
Hacienda del Florasol
Canyon City
Clover Flat
CAMPO INDIAN RES
UNITED STATES
MEXICO
see MAP 1

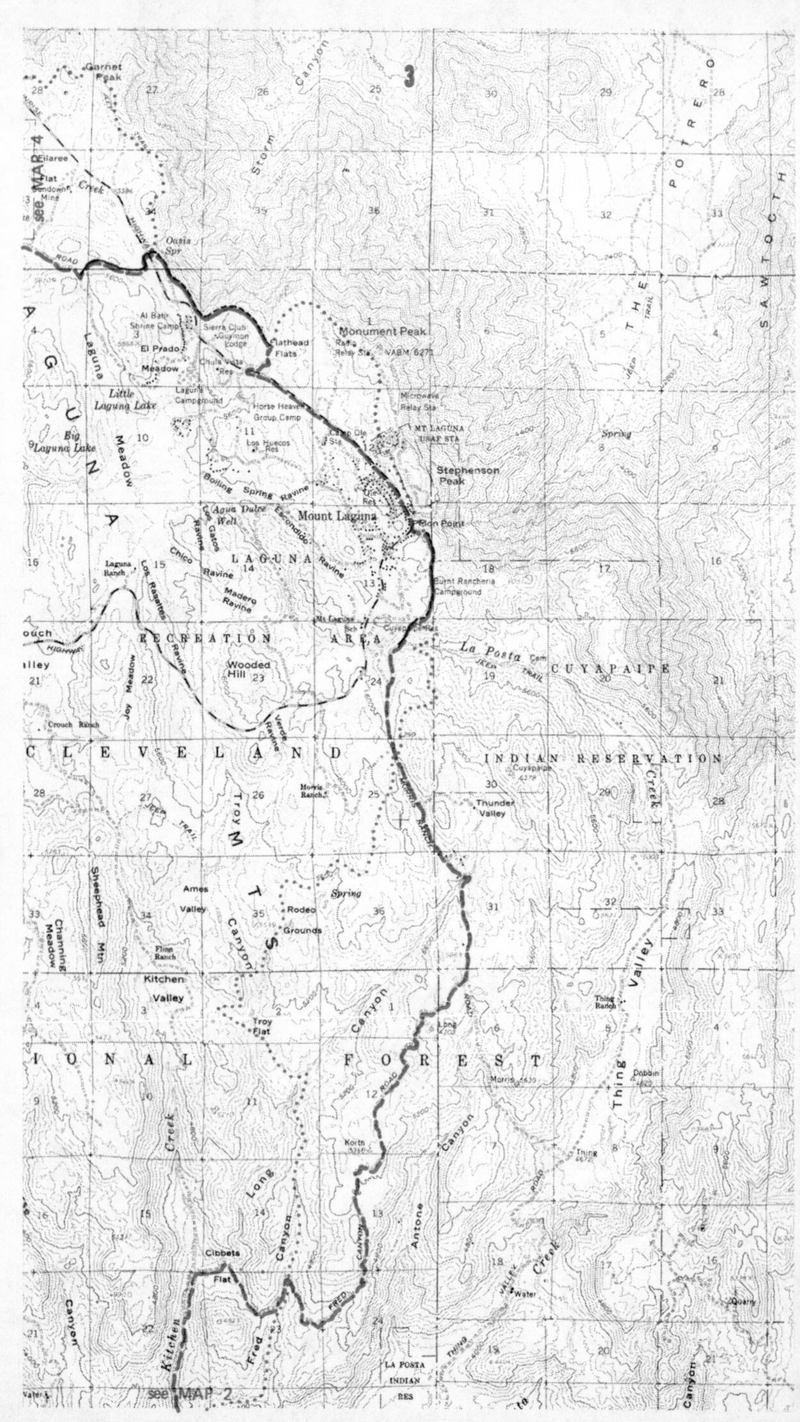

3
see MAP 4
see MAP 2
Monument Peak
Mount Laguna
Stephenson Peak
LAGUNA RECREATION AREA
CLEVELAND NATIONAL FOREST
CUYAPAIPE INDIAN RESERVATION
LA POSTA INDIAN RES

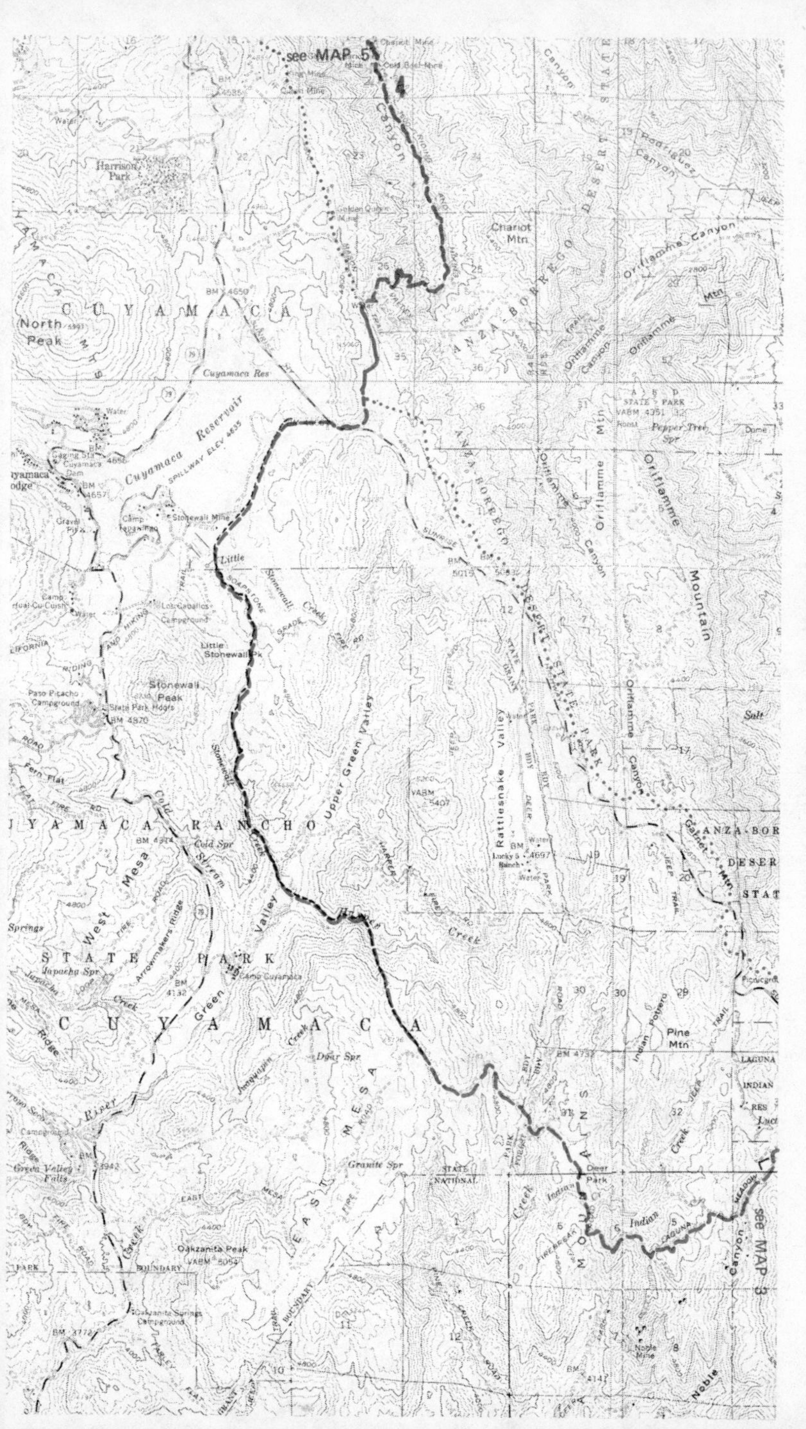

see MAP 5
Chariot Mtn
CUYAMACA
North Peak
Cuyamaca Res
Cuyamaca Reservoir
Harrison Park
ANZA BORREGO
Oriflamme Canyon
Oriflamme Mtn
Oriflamme Mountain
Rodriguez Canyon
Stonewall Mine
Little Stonewall Pk
Stonewall Peak
Stonewall Creek
Upper Green Valley
Rattlesnake Valley
CUYAMACA RANCHO
STATE PARK
West Mesa
Arrowmakers Ridge
EAST MESA
Pine Mtn
Deer Park
Oakzanita Peak
Noble Canyon
LAGUNA INDIAN RES
see MAP 3

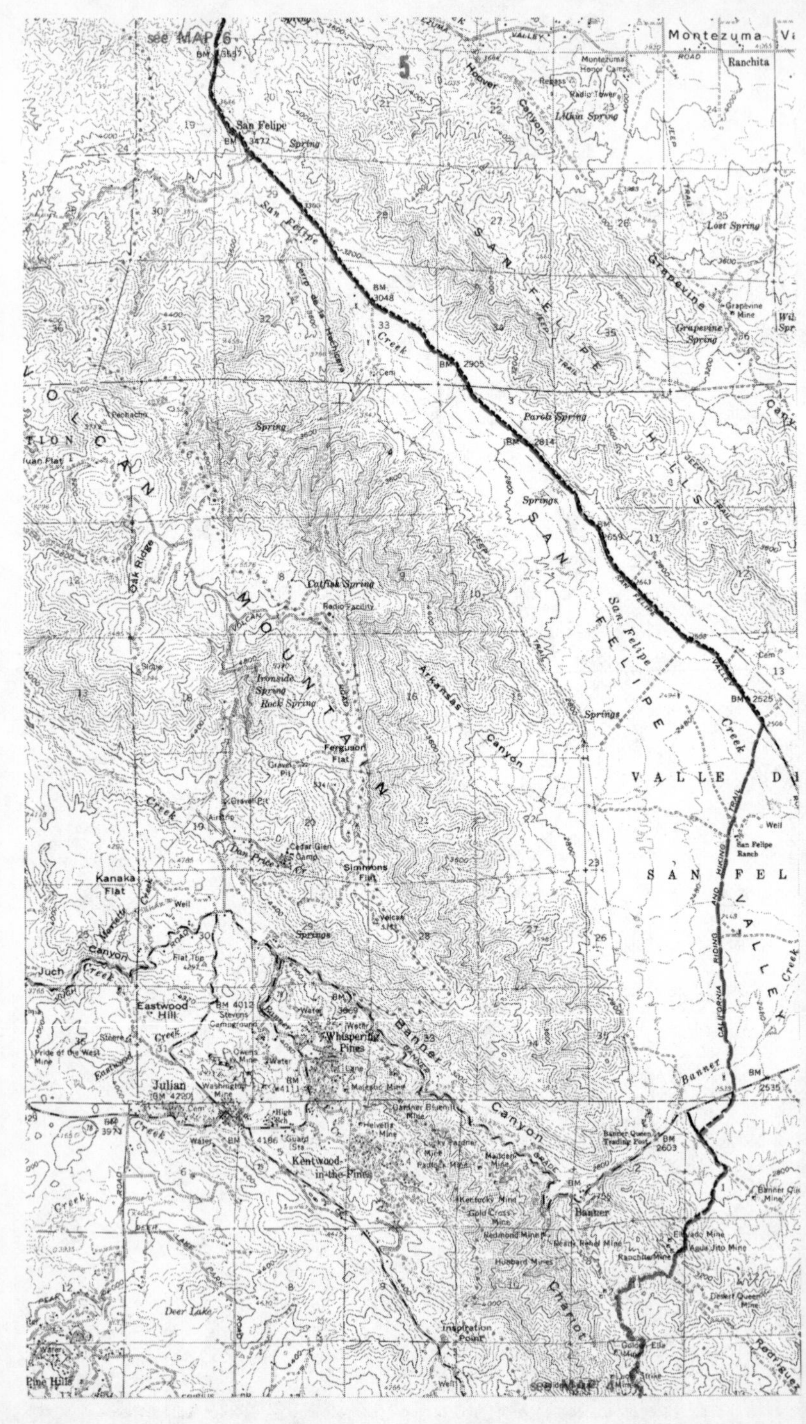

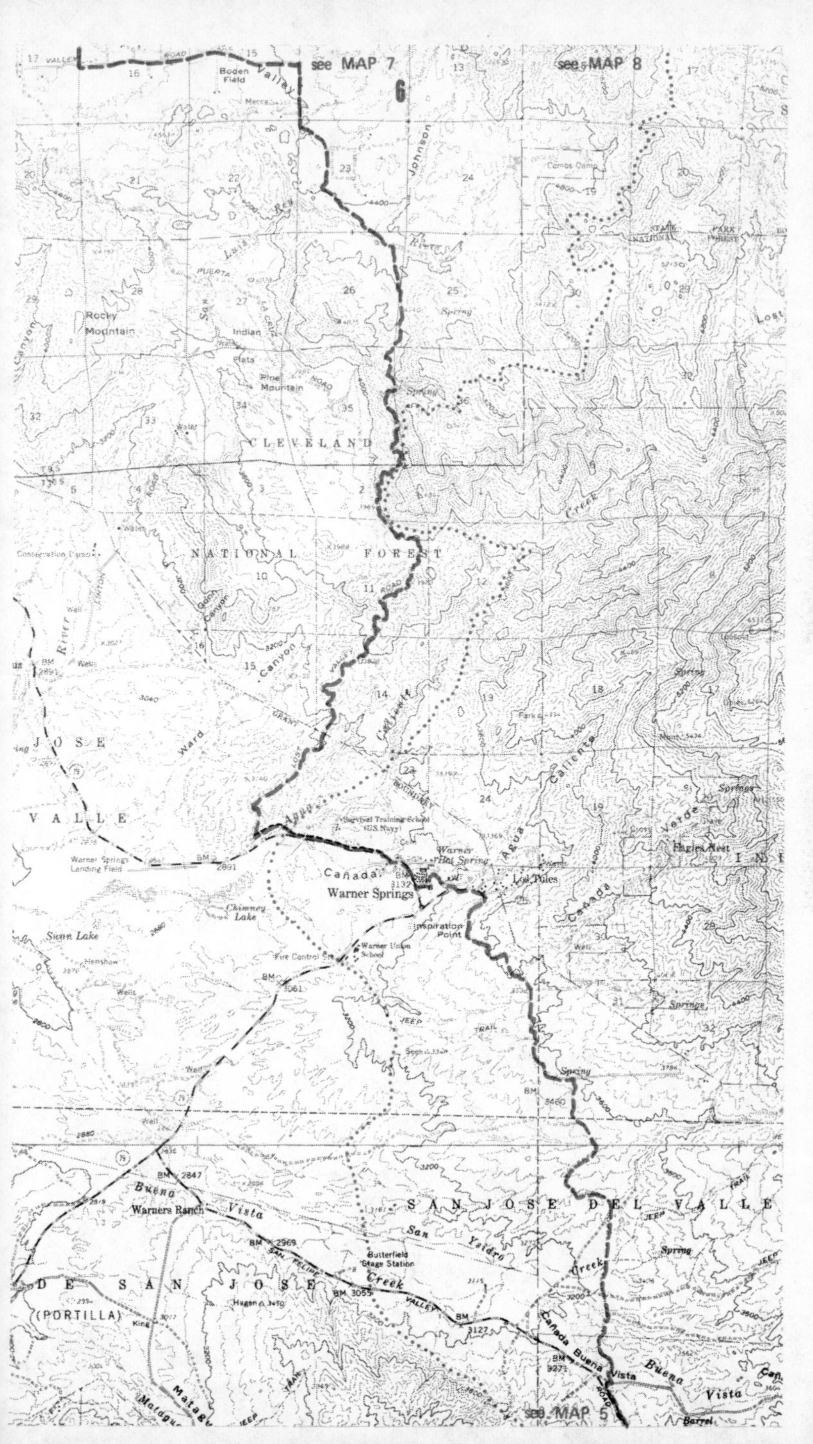

see MAP 7
see MAP 8
6
Boden Field
Johnson
Combs Camp
Rocky Mountain
Indian Flats
Pine Mountain
CLEVELAND
NATIONAL FOREST
Conservation Camp
Canyon
Ward
JOSE
VALLE
Agua
Survival Training School (U.S. Navy)
Warner Hot Spring
Agua Caliente
Canada
Warner Springs
Los Tules
Warner Springs Landing Field
Chimney Lake
Swan Lake
Henshaw
Inspiration Point
Warner Union School
Fire Control Sta
Canada Verde
Eagles Nest
JEEP TRAIL
SAN JOSE DEL VALLE
Buena Vista
Warners Ranch
San Ysidro
Creek
Butterfield Stage Station
DE SAN JOSE
(PORTILLA)
Hagen
Cañada Buena Vista
Buena Vista
see MAP 5
Barrel

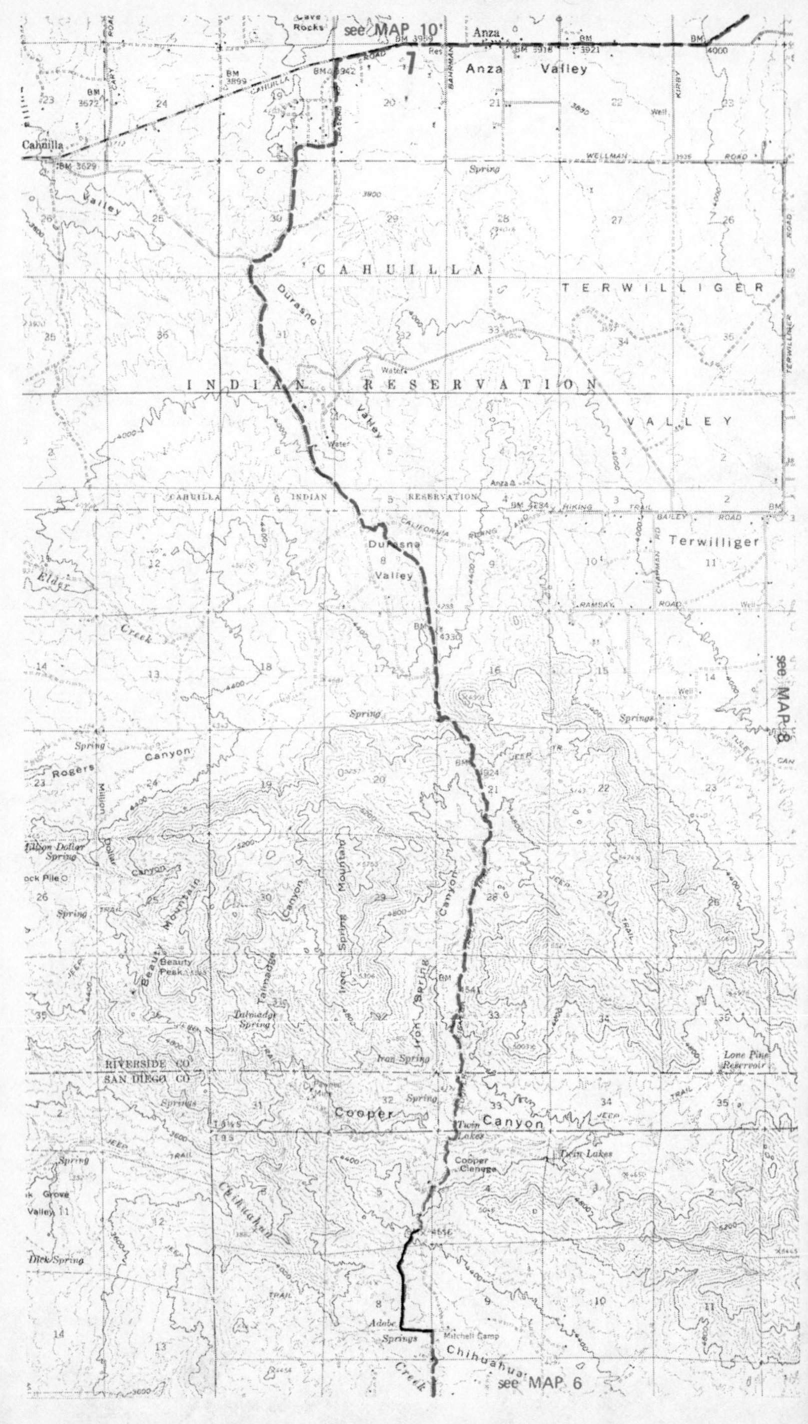
see MAP 10
7
Anza
Anza Valley
Cahuilla
CAHUILLA
INDIAN RESERVATION
TERWILLIGER
VALLEY
Durasno
Durasno Valley
Terwilliger
see MAP 8
Rogers Canyon
Million Dollar Spring
Beauty Mountain
Beauty Peak
Talmadge Canyon
Talmadge Spring
Iron Spring Mountain
Iron Spring Canyon
Iron Spring
RIVERSIDE CO
SAN DIEGO CO
Cooper Canyon
Twin Lakes
Cooper Cienega
Lone Pine Reservoir
Chihuahua
Dick Spring
Adobe Springs
Mitchell Camp
Chihuahua Creek
see MAP 6

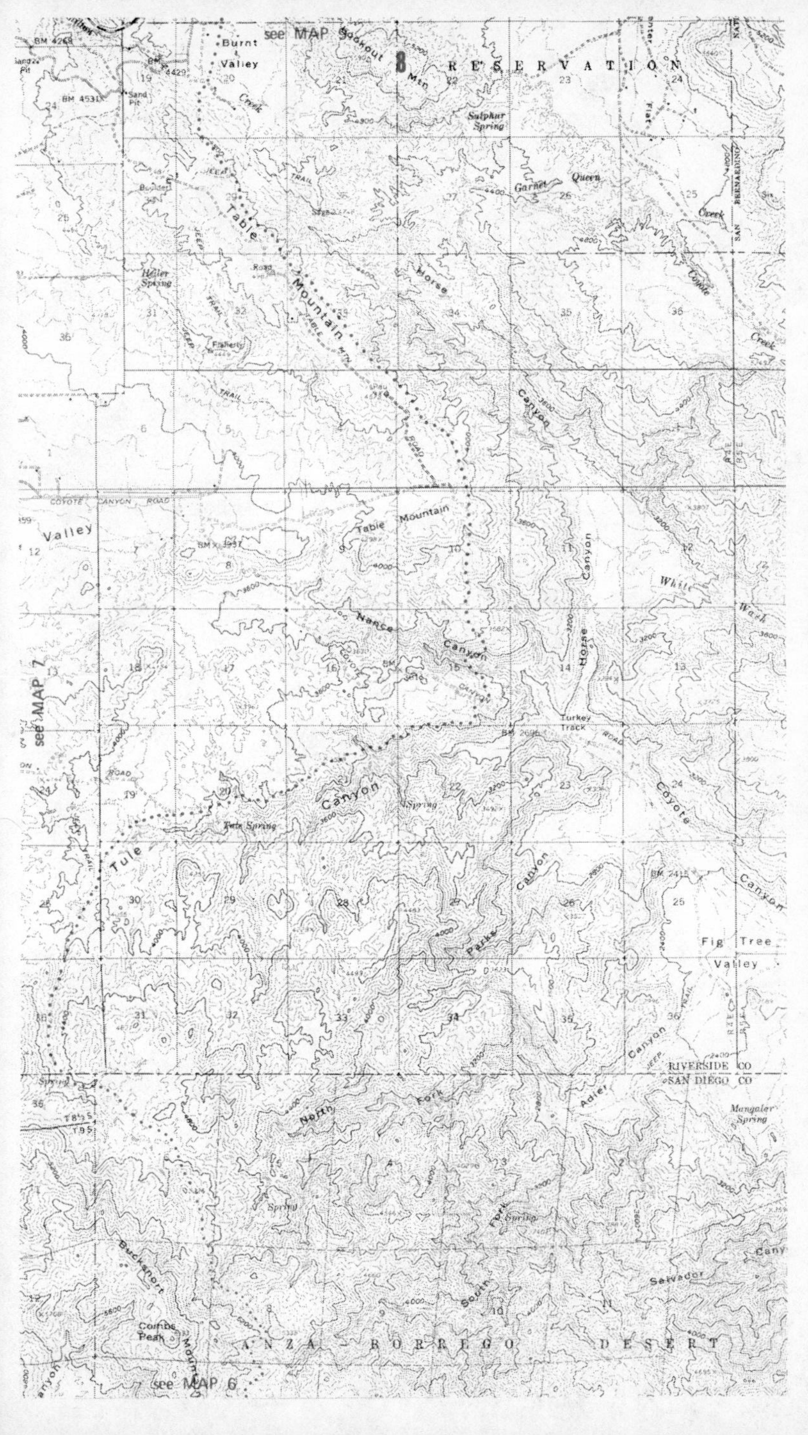

see MAP 9
8
RESERVATION
Burnt Valley
Lookout Mtn
Sulphur Spring
Garnet Queen
Coyote Creek
Table Mountain
Horse Canyon
Heller Spring
Flaherty
COYOTE CANYON ROAD
Valley
Table Mountain
Nance Canyon
White Wash
Turkey Track
Tule Canyon
Tule Spring
see MAP 7
Coyote Canyon
Parks Canyon
Fig Tree Valley
Adler Canyon
RIVERSIDE CO
SAN DIEGO CO
Mangalar Spring
North Fork
South Fork
Salvador Canyon
Bucksnort Mountain
Combs Peak
ANZA-BORREGO DESERT
see MAP 6

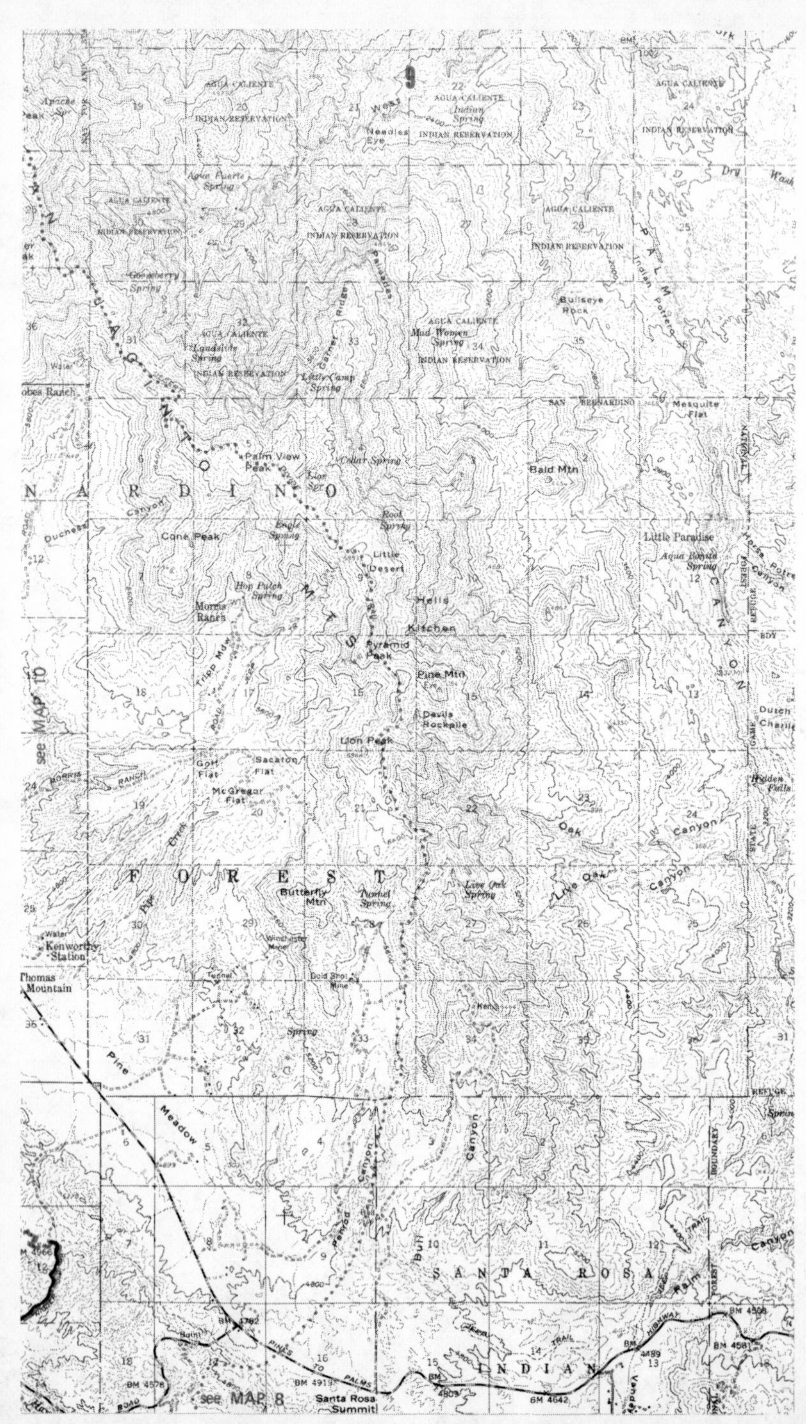

9
AGUA CALIENTE INDIAN RESERVATION
Needles Eye
Indian Spring
Agua Fuerte Spring
Gooseberry Spring
Palisades
Garner Ridge
Bullseye Rock
Indian Potrero
Mud Women Spring
Little Camp Spring
Dry Wash
PALM CANYON
SAN BERNARDINO NATIONAL FOREST
Mesquite Flat
Palm View Peak
Cellar Spring
Lion Spr
Bald Mtn
Root Spring
Cone Peak
Eagle Spring
Little Desert
Little Paradise
Agua Bonita Spring
Horse Potrero Canyon
Duchess Canyon
Hop Patch Spring
Morris Ranch
Hells Kitchen
SANTA ROSA MTS
Pyramid Peak
Pine Mtn
Tripp Mdw
Davis Rockpile
Dutch Charlie
Lion Peak
Goff Flat
Sacaton Flat
McGregor Flat
Hidden Falls
Oak Canyon
Live Oak Canyon
Live Oak Spring
Butterfly Mtn
Tunnel Spring
Pipe Creek
Kenworthy Station
Winchester Mine
Gold Shot Mine
Thomas Mountain
Pine Meadow
Spring
STATE GAME REFUGE BOUNDARY
Bull Canyon
Penrod Canyon
Canyon
SANTA ROSA INDIAN
Palm Canyon
PINES TO PALMS HIGHWAY
BM 4919
BM 4903
BM 4642
BM 4489
BM 4581
BM 4508
BM 4576
BM 4566
Santa Rosa Summit
see MAP 10
see MAP 8

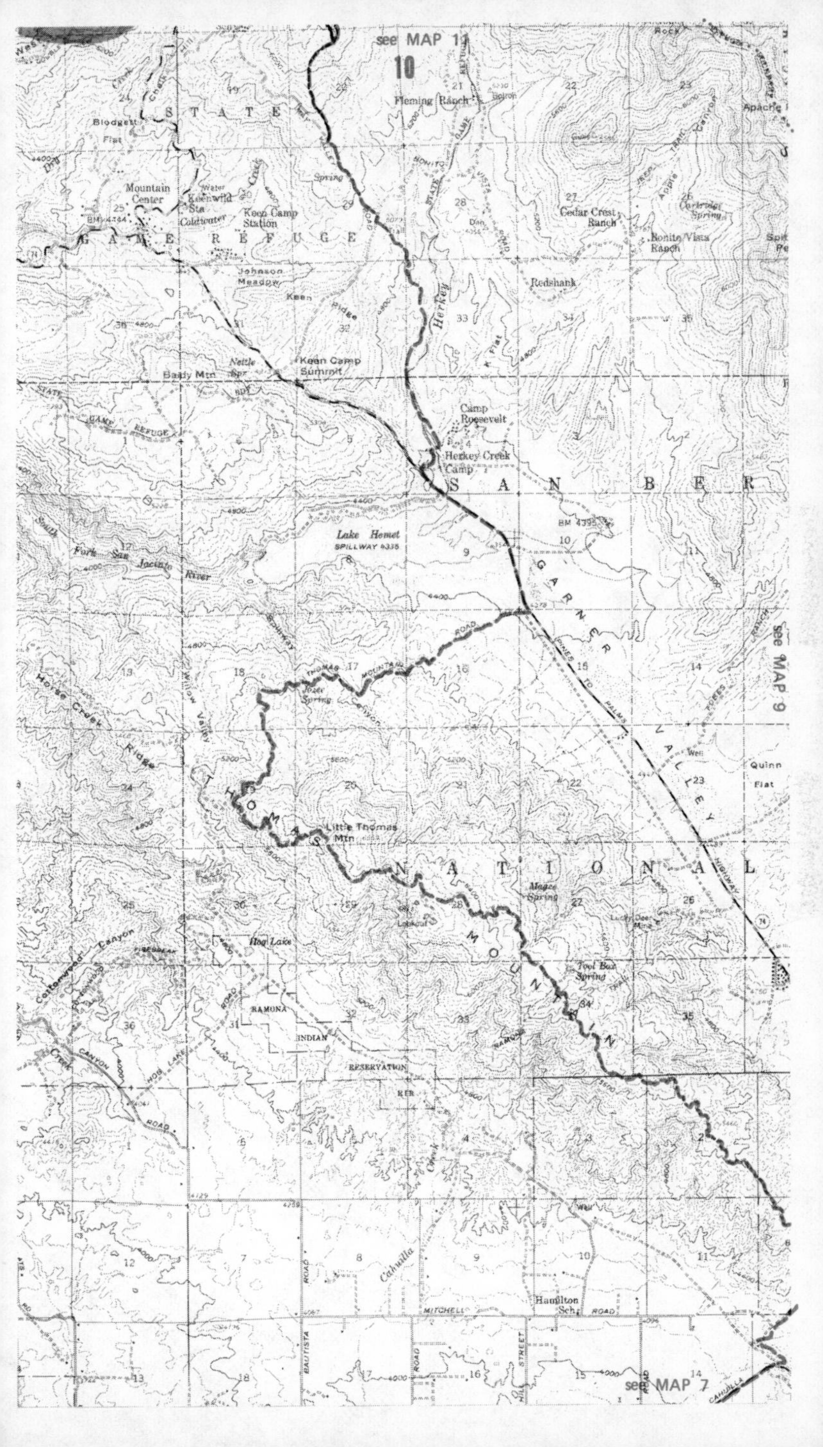

see MAP 11
10
Fleming Ranch
STATE
GAME REFUGE
Blodgett Flat
Mountain Center
Keenwild Sta
Keen Camp Station
Johnson Meadow
Keen Ridge
Cedar Crest Ranch
Bonito Vista Ranch
Redshank
Herkey
Bally Mtn
Nettle Spr
Keen Camp Summit
Camp Roosevelt
Herkey Creek Camp
SAN BER
Lake Hemet
SPILLWAY 4335
South Fork San Jacinto River
GARNER
VALLEY
see MAP 9
Thomas Mountain Road
Tool Box Spring
Horse Creek Ridge
Willow Valley
Quinn Flat
Little Thomas Mtn
THOMAS MOUNTAIN
NATIONAL
Hog Lake
Cottonwood Canyon
RAMONA INDIAN RESERVATION
Cahuilla
Hamilton Sch
MITCHELL ROAD
BAUTISTA ROAD
see MAP 7

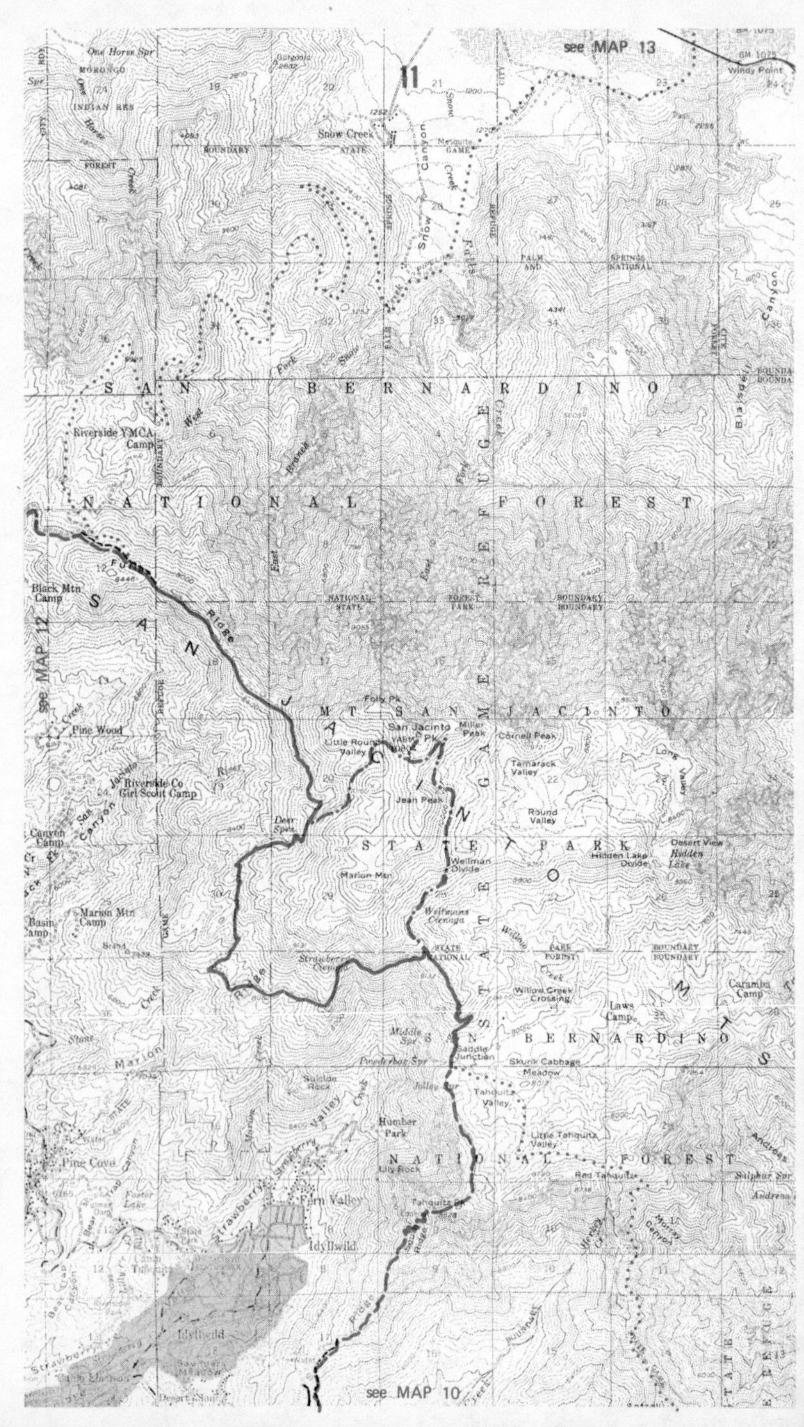
see MAP 13
11
One Horse Spr
MORONGO
INDIAN RES
Snow Creek
Windy Point
Snow Canyon
Snow Creek
Falls
PALM SPRINGS
Blaisdell Canyon
S A N B E R N A R D I N O
N A T I O N A L F O R E S T
Riverside YMCA Camp
Black Mtn Camp
Fuller Ridge
see MAP 12
S A N J A C I N T O
M T S A N J A C I N T O
Folly Pk
San Jacinto Pk
Miller Peak
Cornell Peak
Little Round Valley
Tamarack Valley
Long Valley
Jean Peak
Round Valley
Pine Wood
Riverside Co Girl Scout Camp
Deer Spgs
S T A T E P A R K
Desert View
Hidden Lake Divide
Hidden Lake
Wellman Divide
Marion Mtn
Wellmans Cienaga
Marion Mtn Camp
Strawberry Cienaga
Willow Creek
Willow Creek Crossing
Laws Camp
Caramba Camp
Middle Spr
Saddle Junction
Skunk Cabbage Meadow
Suicide Rock
Strawberry Valley
Jolley Spr
Tahquitz Valley
Humber Park
Little Tahquitz Valley
N A T I O N A L F O R E S T
Lily Rock
Red Tahquitz
Sulphur Spr
Pine Cove
Fern Valley
Tahquitz Pk
Idyllwild
Hurkey Cr
Murray Canyon
Andreas
Strawberry
Idyllwild
see MAP 10

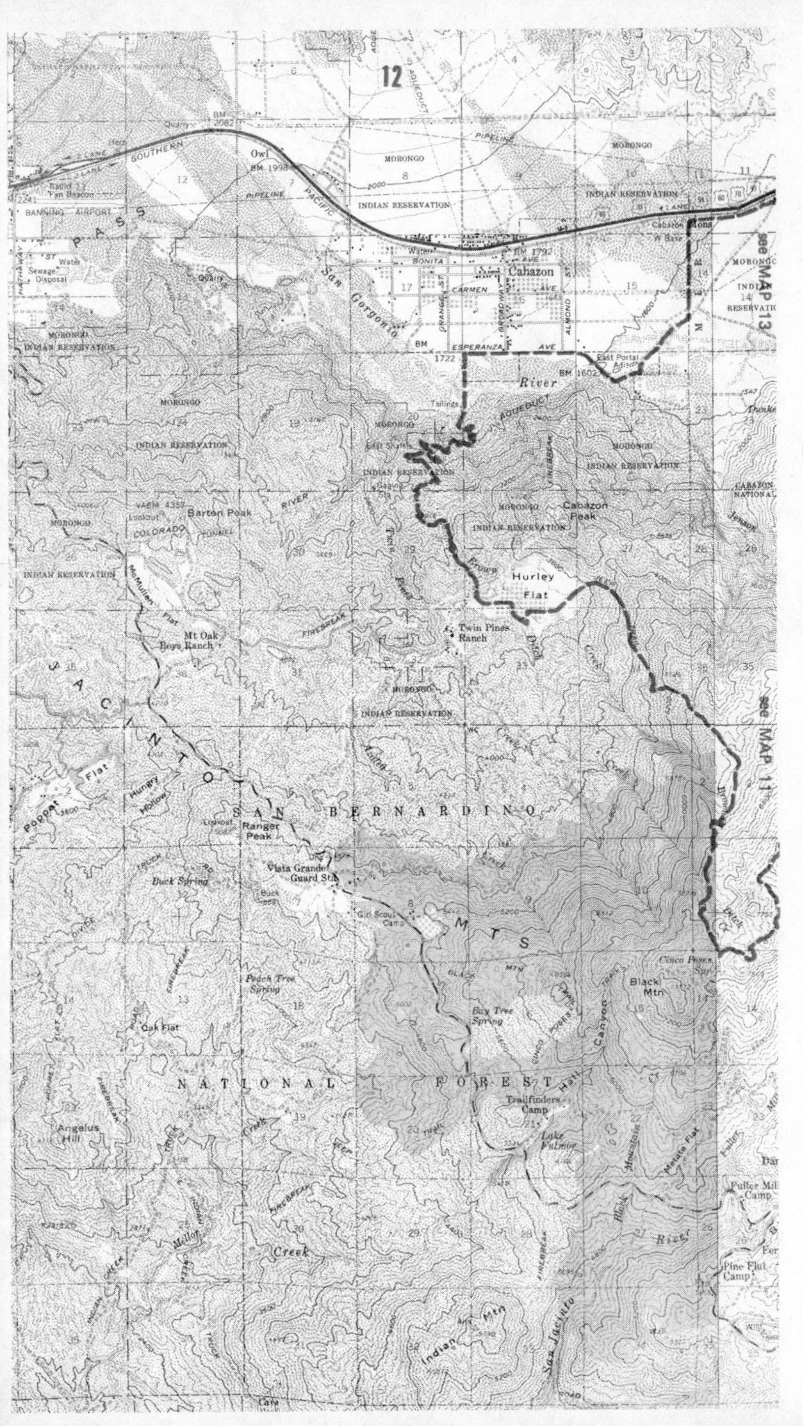
12
see MAP 13
see MAP 11
MORONGO INDIAN RESERVATION
BANNING AIRPORT
PASS
Cabazon
San Gorgonio
Barton Peak
Cabazon Peak
Hurley Flat
Twin Pines Ranch
Mt Oak Boys Ranch
Ranger Peak
Vista Grande Guard Sta
Girl Scout Camp
Buck Spring
Peach Tree Spring
Bay Tree Spring
Oak Flat
Angelus Hill
Trailfinders Camp
Lake Fulmor
Black Mtn
Fuller Mill Camp
Pine Flat Camp
Indian Mtn
SAN JACINTO
SAN BERNARDINO MTS
NATIONAL FOREST

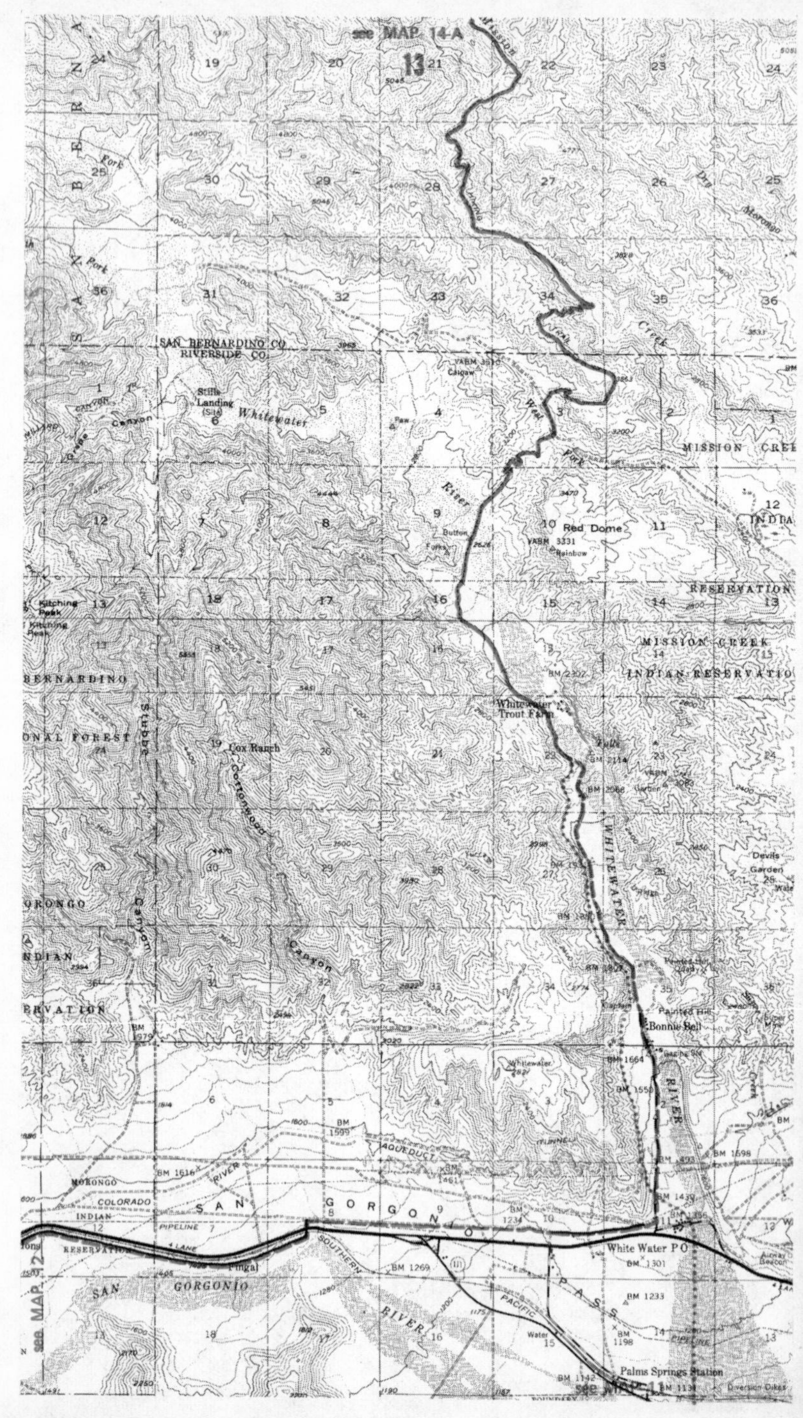

see MAP 14-A
13
SAN BERNARDINO CO.
RIVERSIDE CO.
Stills Landing (Site)
Whitewater
West Fork
River
Red Dome
MISSION CREEK
INDIAN RESERVATION
Whitewater Trout Farm
Cox Ranch
Cottonwood
Canyon
WHITEWATER
Bonnie Bell
Painted Hill
Devils Garden
AQUEDUCT
COLORADO RIVER
SAN GORGONIO
PASS
SOUTHERN PACIFIC
White Water P O
Palms Springs Station
Diversion Dikes
see MAP 12
see MAP 11

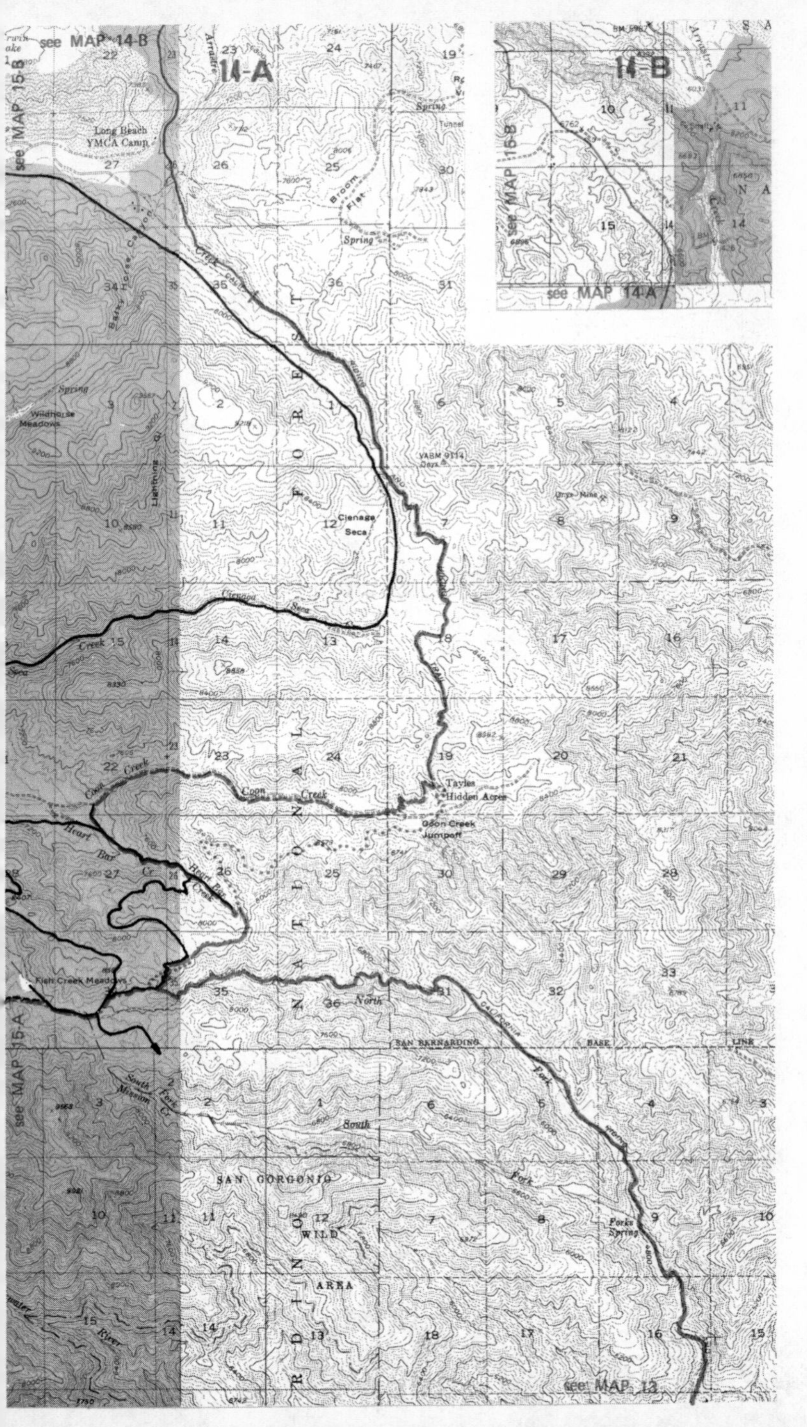

see MAP 14-B
14-A
14-B
see MAP 15-B
see MAP 14-A
Long Beach YMCA Camp
Broom Flat
Spring
Wildhorse Meadows
VABM 9114
Cienaga Seca
Tayles Hidden Acres
Coon Creek Jumpoff
Coon Creek
Heart Bar Cr
Fish Creek Meadows
SAN BERNARDINO BASE LINE
SAN GORGONIO WILD AREA
Forks Spring
see MAP 15-A
see MAP 13
NATIONAL FOREST

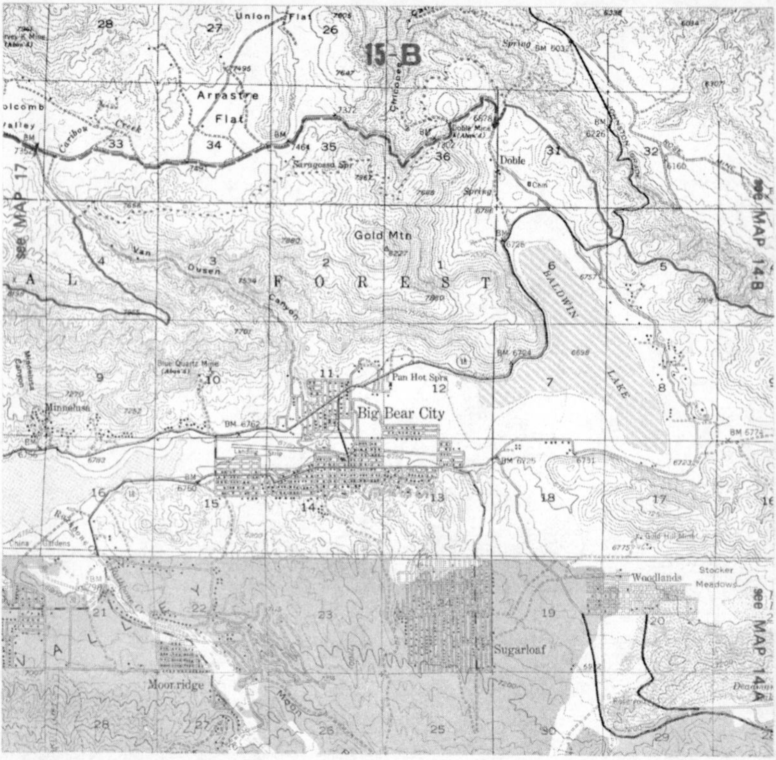

15-B

Union Flat
Arrastre Flat
Caribou Creek
Valley
Saragossa Spr
Doble
Doble Mine (Aban'd)
Gold Mtn
Van Dusen Canyon
FOREST
BALDWIN LAKE
Blue Quartz Mine (Aban'd)
Pan Hot Sprs
Minnelusa
Big Bear City
Woodlands
Stocker Meadows
Sugarloaf
Moonridge
VALLEY

see MAP 17
see MAP 14-B
see MAP 14-A

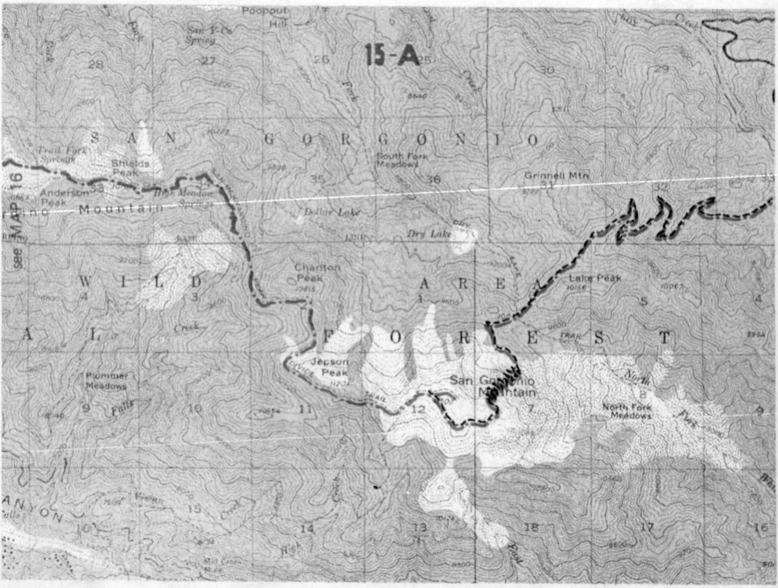

15-A

Poopout Hill
San-Y-Co Spring
SAN GORGONIO
Trail Fork Springs
Shields Peak
Anderson Peak
South Fork Meadows
Grinnell Mtn
High Meadow Springs
Dollar Lake
Dry Lake
Charlton Peak
Lake Peak
WILD AREA
FOREST
Jepson Peak
San Gorgonio Mountain
Plummer Meadows
North Fork Meadows
CANYON

see MAP 16

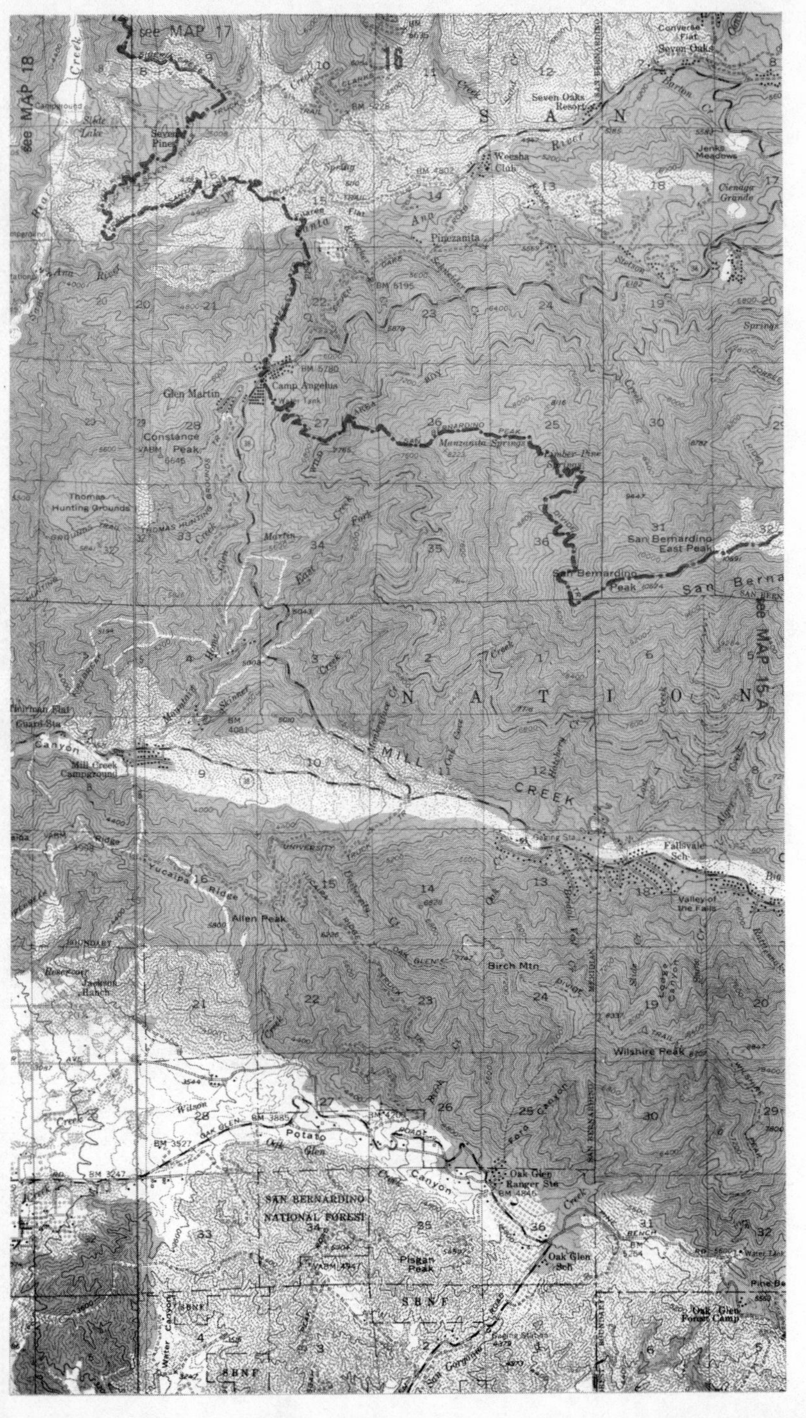

see MAP 17
see MAP 18
16
see MAP 15A
Seven Oaks
Seven Oaks Resort
Converse Flat
Jenks Meadows
Cienaga Grande
Weesha Club
Pinezanita
Slide Lake
Seven Pines
Camp Angelus
Glen Martin
Constance Peak
Thomas Hunting Grounds
Manzanita Springs
Lumber Pine Springs
San Bernardino East Peak
San Bernardino Peak
Mill Creek Campground
Fallsvale Sch.
Valley of the Falls
Allen Peak
Birch Mtn
Wilshire Peak
Jackson Ranch
Potato Glen
Oak Glen Ranger Sta
SAN BERNARDINO NATIONAL FOREST
Pisgah Peak
Oak Glen Sch
Oak Glen Forest Camp
N A T I O N
S A N
MILL CREEK
Yucaipa Ridge

see MAP 18
see MAP 15B
see MAP 16
Holcomb Valley
Delamar Mtn
Little Bear Pk
Fawnskin Valley
Fawnskin
Hanna Flat
Big Pine Flat
Campground
Ranger Sta
Greenleaf Camp
Holcomb Creek
Bertha Pk
Upper Holcomb
Butler Peak
Grout Bay
Windy Pt
BIG BEAR LAKE
Big Bear Lake
Gillner Pt
Eagle Pt
Big Bear Lake Ranger Sta
Treasure Island
Boulder Bay
Metcalf Bay
Big Bear Lake
Pine Knot Ranger Sta
Red Ant Canyon
Cedar Lake
Castle Rock
Bluff Lake
Pasadena YMCA Camp
Siberia Cr
Merriman Meadows
Grand View Point
Clarks Summit
Lookout Point
Bellyache Springs
Camp Radford
Wild Rose Canyon
Bousic Canyon
Crystal Creek
White Mtn
Liberty Mine
Wright Mine
Deep Canyon
Polique Canyon
Grout Creek
North Fork
S A N
N A T I O N
B E A R

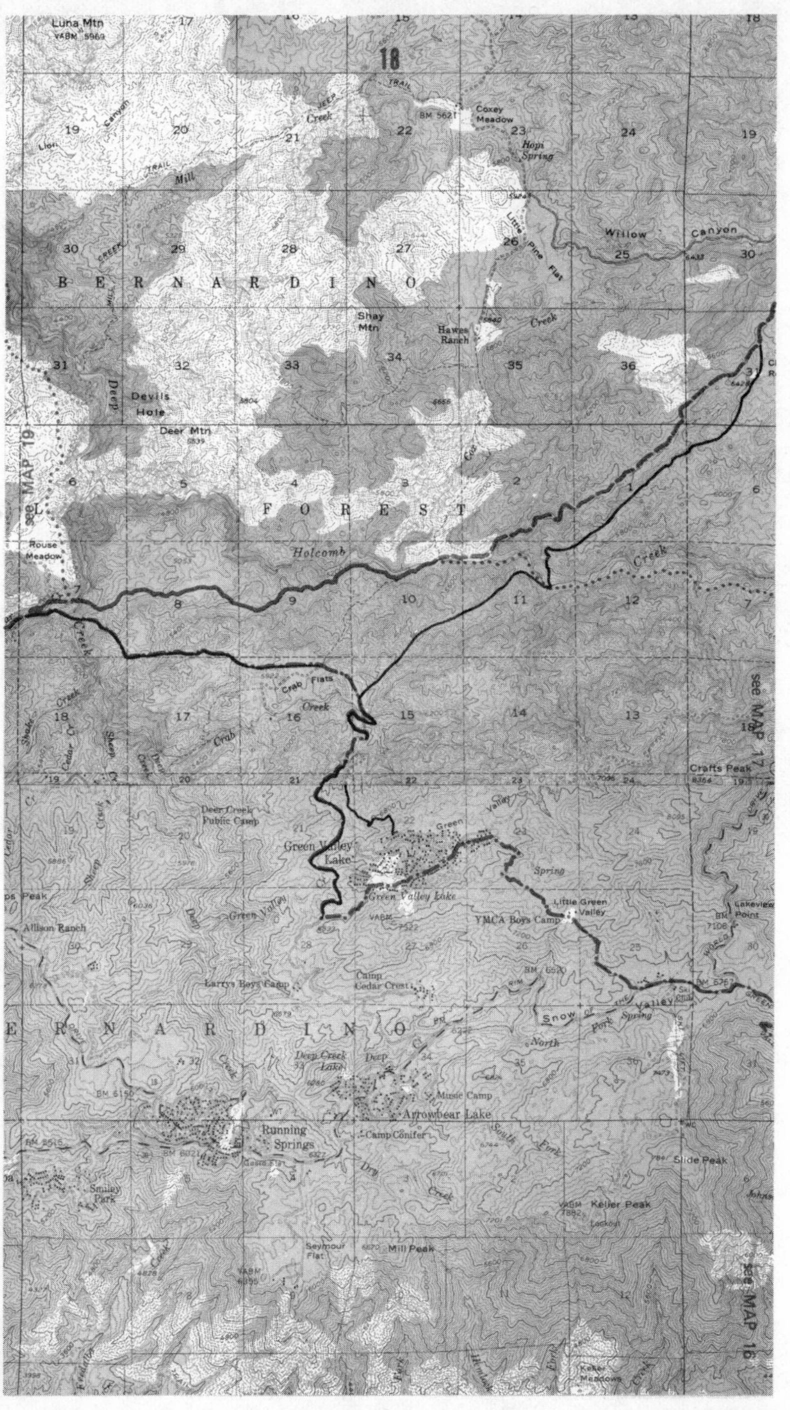

18
Luna Mtn
Coxey Meadow
Hopi Spring
Little Pine Flat
Willow Canyon
BERNARDINO
Shay Mtn
Hawes Ranch
Devils Hole
Deer Mtn
see MAP 19
Rouse Meadow
FOREST
Holcomb
Creek
Crab Flats
see MAP 17
Crafts Peak
Deer Creek Public Camp
Green Valley Lake
Little Green Valley
YMCA Boys Camp
Lakeview Point
Allison Ranch
Larrys Boys Camp
Camp Cedar Crest
Snow Valley
ERNARDINO
Deep Creek Lake
Music Camp
Arrowbear Lake
Running Springs
Camp Conifer
Slide Peak
Smiley Park
Keller Peak
Seymour Flat
Mill Peak
see MAP 16
Keller Meadows

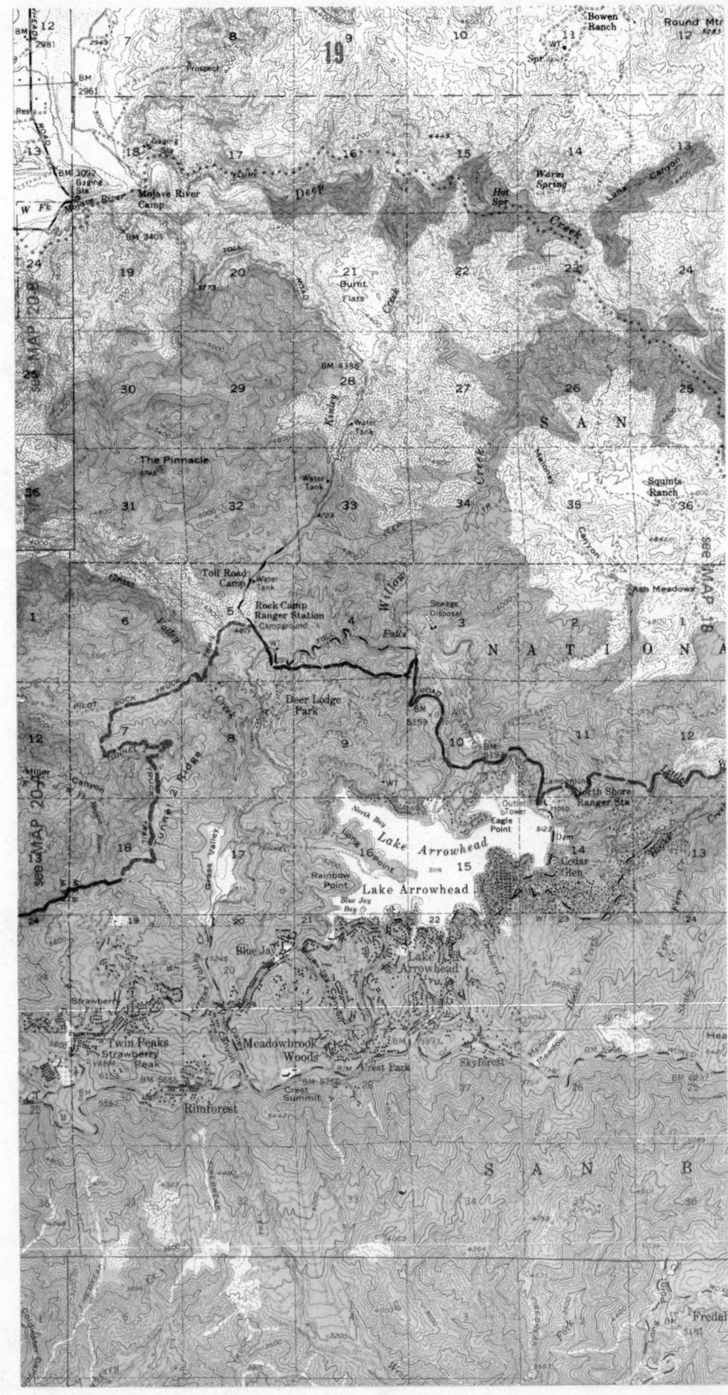
19
Bowen Ranch
Round Mtn
Mojave River Camp
Deep Creek
Warm Spring
Hot Spr
Burnt Flats
The Pinnacle
Toll Road Camp
Rock Camp Ranger Station
Deer Lodge Park
Willow
North Shore Ranger Sta
Eagle Point
Cedar Glen
Lake Arrowhead
Rainbow Point
Blue Jay
Twin Peaks
Strawberry Peak
Meadowbrook Woods
Crest Park
Skyforest
Crest Summit
Rimforest
Squints Ranch
Ash Meadows
S A N
N A T I O N A
S A N B
see MAP 20-B
see MAP 20-A
see MAP 18

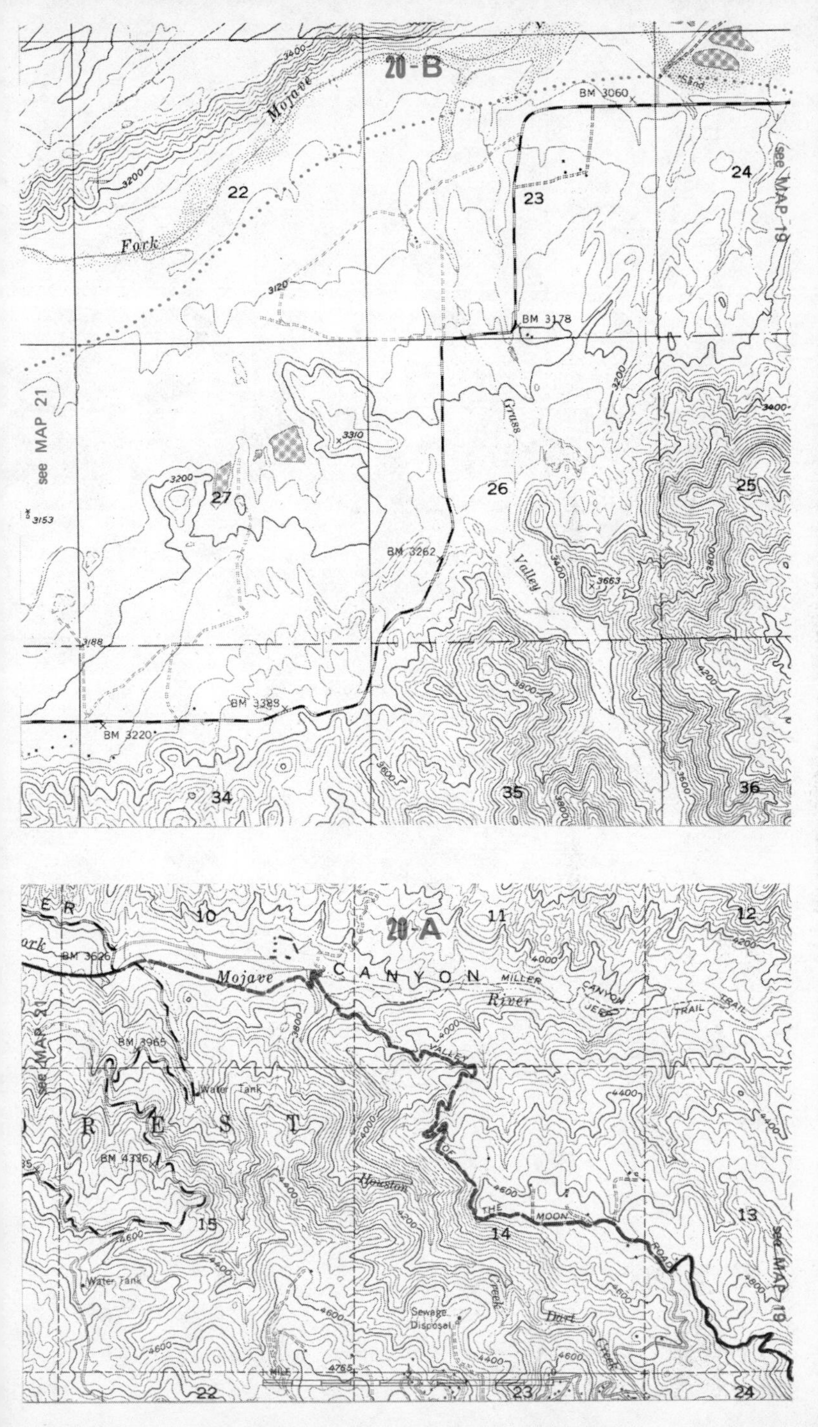

20-B
Mojave
Fork
BM 3060
see MAP 19
see MAP 21
BM 3178
Gruss
Valley
BM 3262
BM 3388
BM 3220
20-A
BM 3626
Mojave
CANYON
MILLER CANYON JEEP TRAIL
River
VALLEY
BM 3965
Water Tank
BM 4336
Houston
THE MOON ROAD
Water Tank
Creek
Dart
Creek
Sewage Disposal

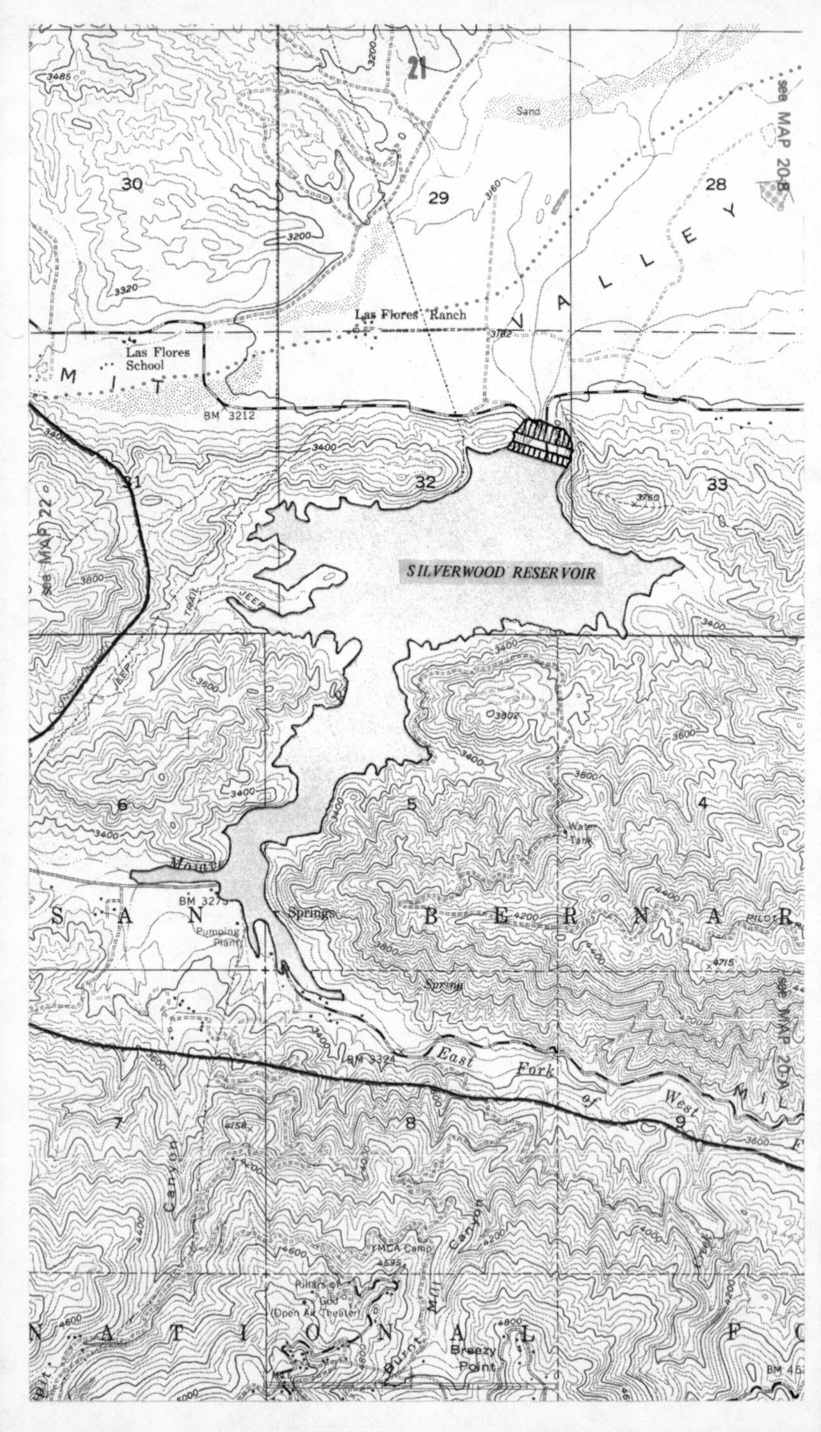

21
Sand
30
29
28
see MAP 20-B
VALLEY
Las Flores Ranch
Las Flores School
MIT
BM 3212
31
32
33
see MAP 22
SILVERWOOD RESERVOIR
JEEP TRAIL
6
5
4
Water Tank
BM 3275
Springs
SAN BERNAR
Pumping Plant
Spring
see MAP 20-A
BM 3324
East Fork of West
7
8
9
Canyon
YMCA Camp
Pillars of God (Open Air Theater)
Burnt Mill Canyon
Breezy Point
NATIONAL F

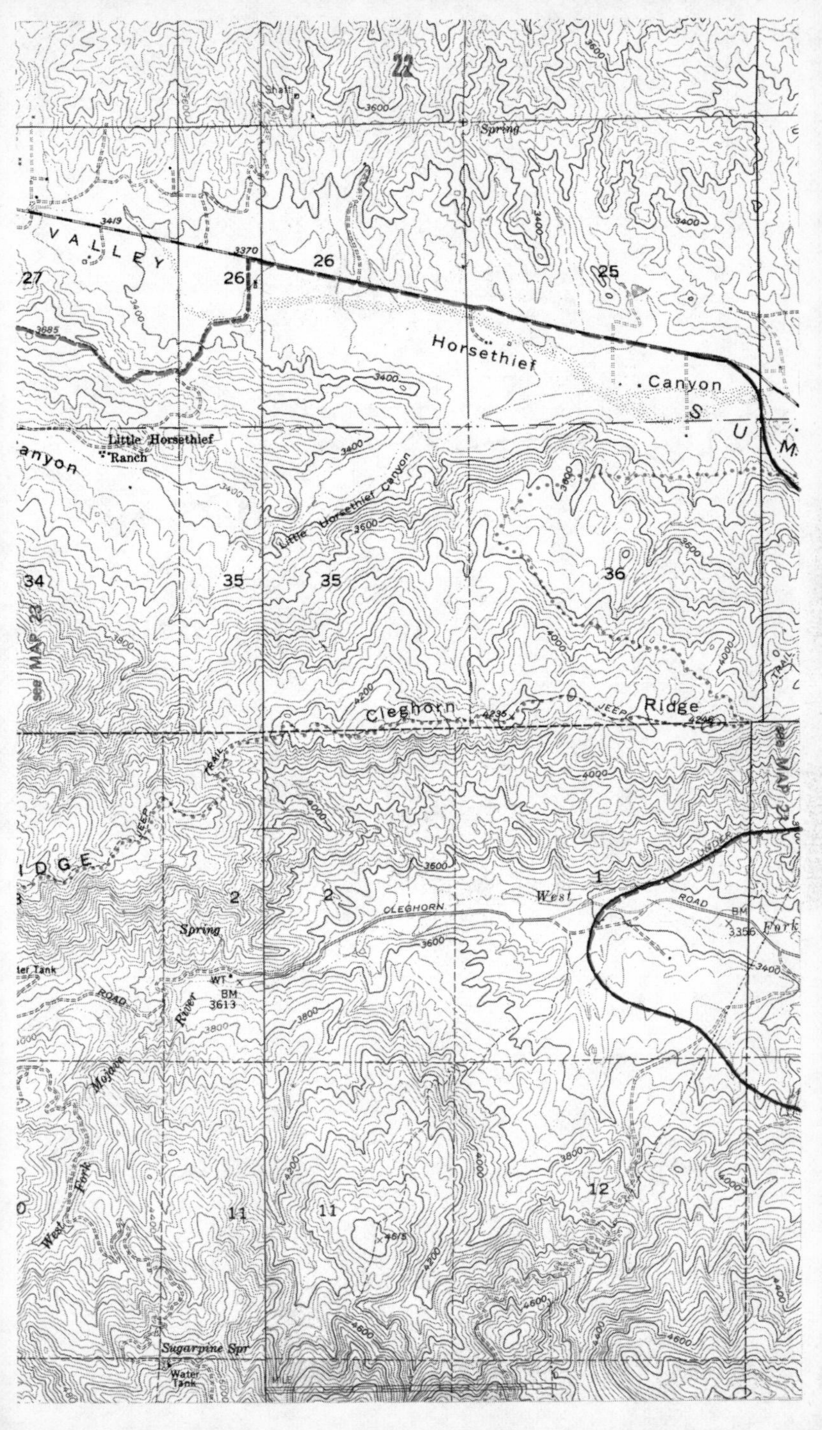

22
Shaft
Spring
VALLEY
3419
3370
26
27
26
25
3685
Horsethief
Canyon
S
U
M
Little Horsethief
Ranch
anyon
Little Horsethief Canyon
34
35
35
36
see MAP 23
Cleghorn
4235
JEEP
Ridge
4248
see MAP 27
TRAIL
JEEP
RIDGE
2
2
1
West
CLEGHORN
ROAD
BM
3356
Fork
Spring
Water Tank
WT
BM
3613
ROAD
River
Mojave
West Fork
11
11
12
4615
Sugarpine Spr
Water
Tank

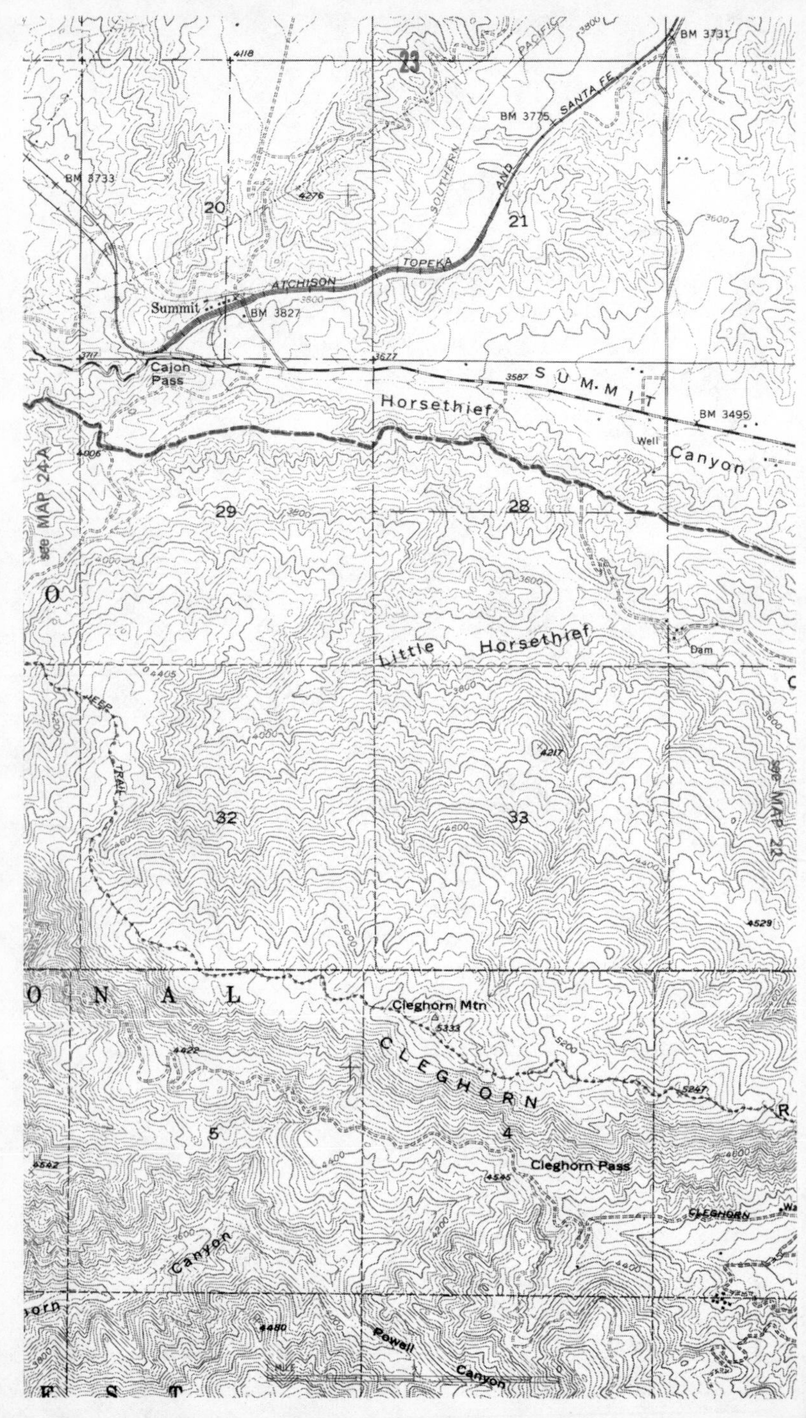

23
BM 3731
BM 3775
SANTA FE
PACIFIC
SOUTHERN
AND
BM 3733
20
21
TOPEKA
ATCHISON
Summit
BM 3827
Cajon
Pass
SUMMIT
Horsethief
BM 3495
Well
Canyon
see MAP 24-A
29
28
O
Little Horsethief
Dam
JEEP
TRAIL
32
33
see MAP 22
O N A L
Cleghorn Mtn
CLEGHORN
R
5
4
Cleghorn Pass
CLEGHORN
Canyon
Powell
Canyon
MILE
E S T

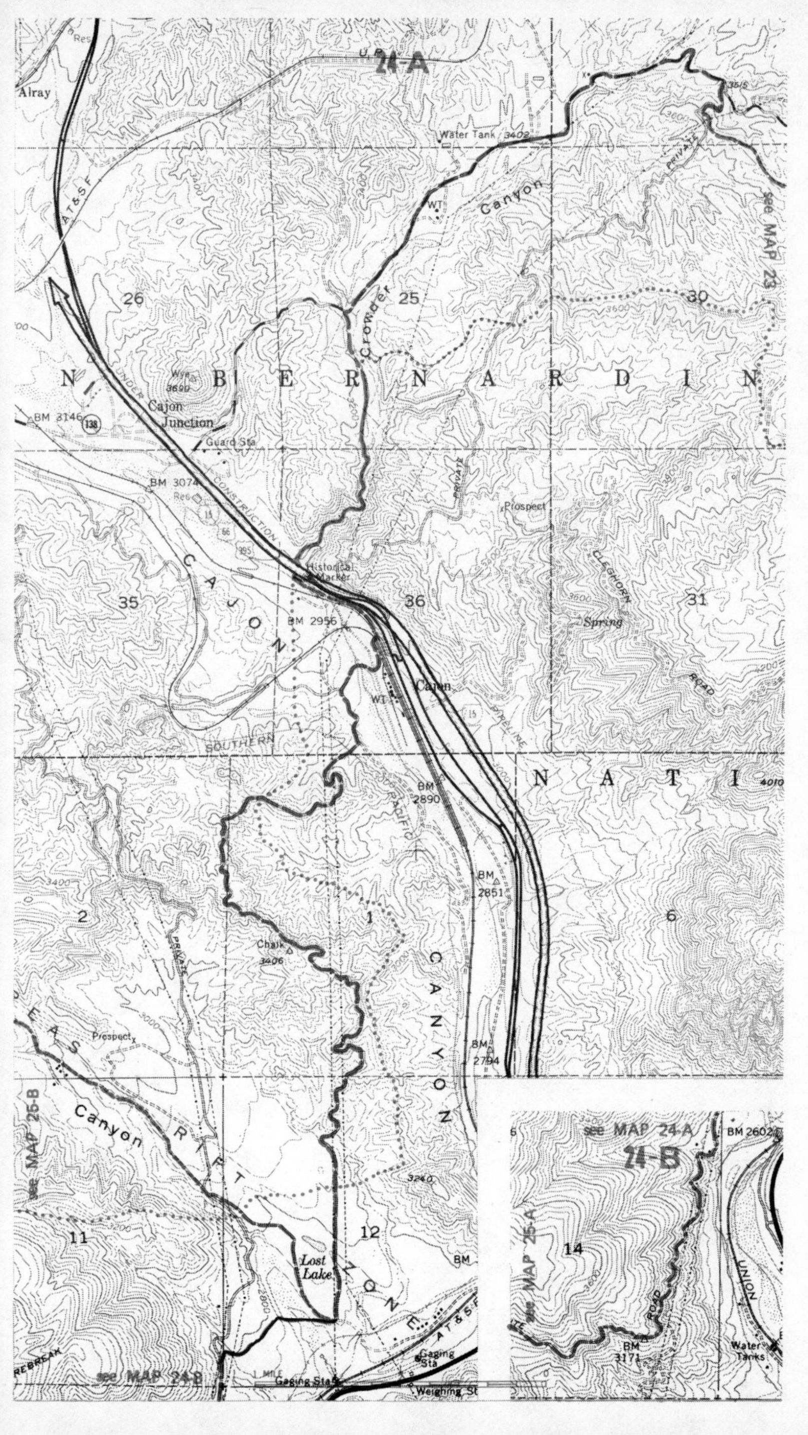

24-A
Alray
AT&SF
Water Tank 3402
Crowder Canyon
see MAP 23
Cajon Junction
Guard Sta
BM 3146
BM 3074
Historical Marker
BM 2956
Cajon
CLEGHORN ROAD
Spring
Prospect
N A T I
SOUTHERN PACIFIC
BM 2890
BM 2851
BM 2794
Chalk 3406
CANYON
Canyon
RIFT ZONE
Lost Lake
see MAP 25-B
see MAP 24-B
Gaging Sta
Weighing St
see MAP 24-A
24-B
see MAP 25-A
BM 2602
BM 3171
UNION
Water Tanks

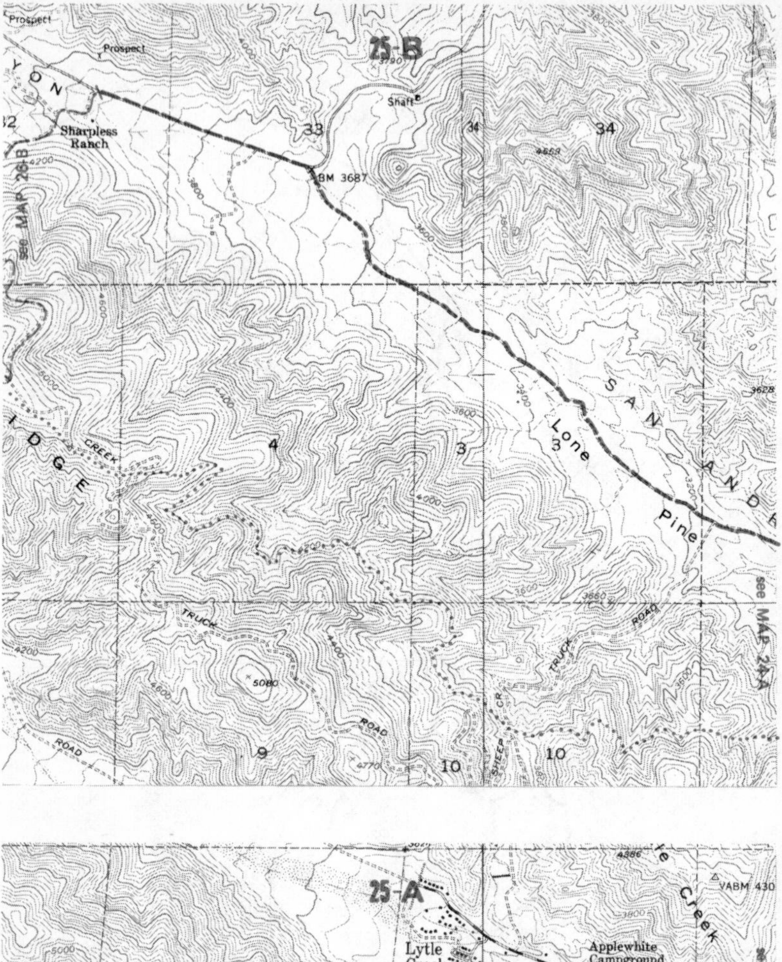

25-B

Prospect
Prospect
Y O N
Sharpless Ranch
32
33
34
34
Shaft
BM 3687
see MAP 26-B
I D G E
CREEK
4
3
3
S A N A N D
Lone Pine
TRUCK
ROAD
TRUCK ROAD
5080
9
10
10
SHEEP CR
see MAP 24-A

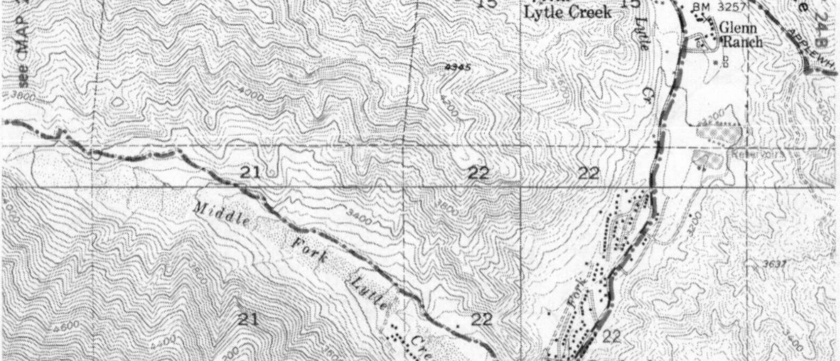

25-A

Lytle Creek
Lytle Creek
N Fk
Applewhite Campground
VABM 430
Creek Ridge
see MAP 24-B
APPLEWHI
BM 3257
Glenn Ranch
16
15
15
Lytle Cr
see MAP 26-A
Reservoirs
21
22
22
Middle Fork Lytle Creek
21
22
22
Fork
Scotland

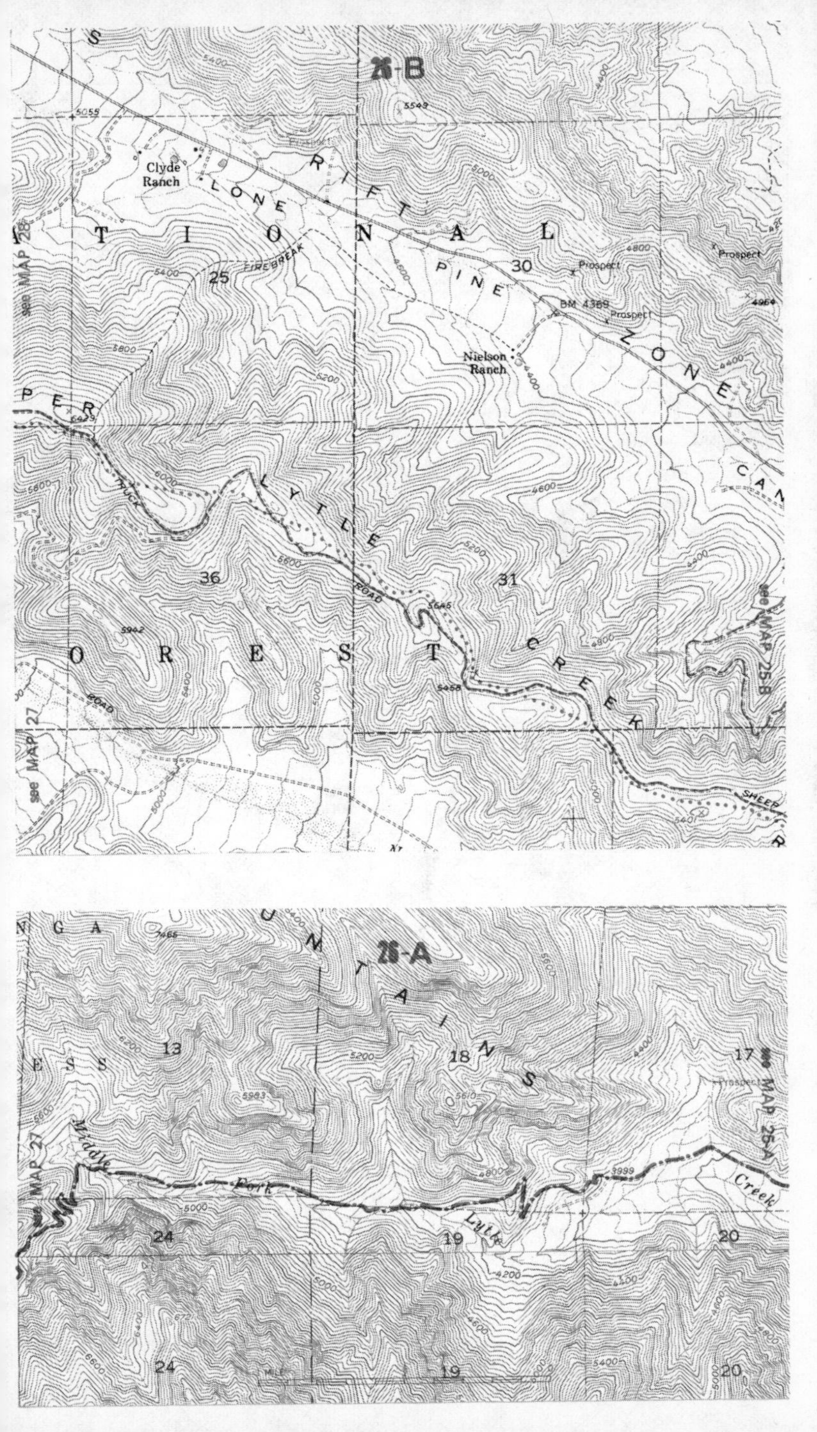

25-B
Clyde Ranch
LONE PINE
RIFT ZONE
Nielson Ranch
LYTLE CREEK
ROAD
FIREBREAK
Prospect
BM 4369
see MAP 26
see MAP 27
see MAP 25B
25-A
Middle Fork Lytle Creek
see MAP 25A
MILE

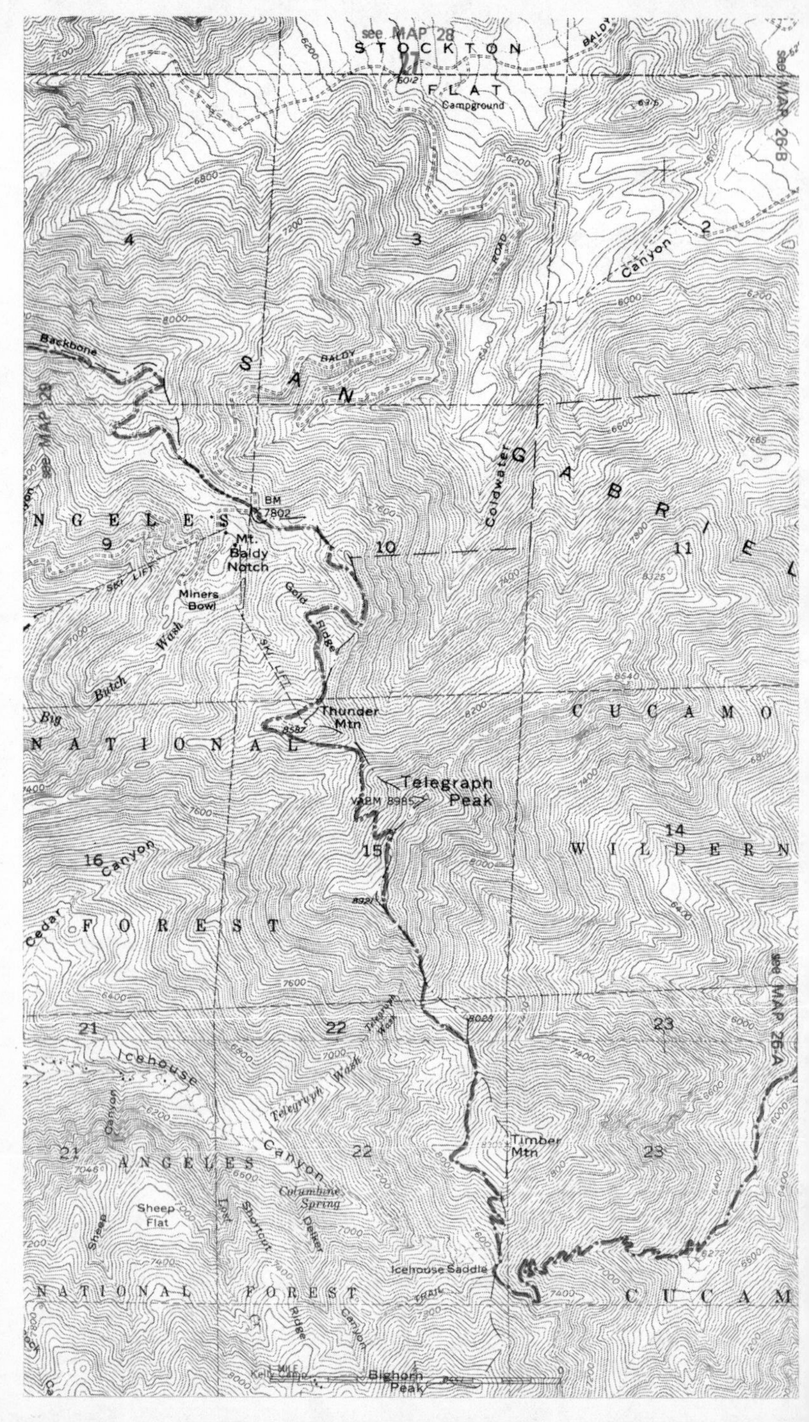

see MAP 28
STOCKTON
FLAT
Campground
see MAP 26-B
Canyon
Backbone
see MAP 29
SAN
GABRIEL
BALDY
ROAD
Coldwater
BM 7802
NGELES
Mt. Baldy Notch
SKI LIFT
Miners Bowl
Gold Ridge
Butch Wash
Big
Thunder Mtn
NATIONAL
CUCAMO
Telegraph Peak
WILDERN
Canyon
Cedar
FOREST
see MAP 26-A
Icehouse Canyon
Telegraph Wash
Timber Mtn
ANGELES
Columbine Spring
Sheep Flat
Shortcut
Lost
Delker
Icehouse Saddle
NATIONAL FOREST
TRAIL
CUCAM
Ridge
Canyon
Kelly Camp
Bighorn Peak

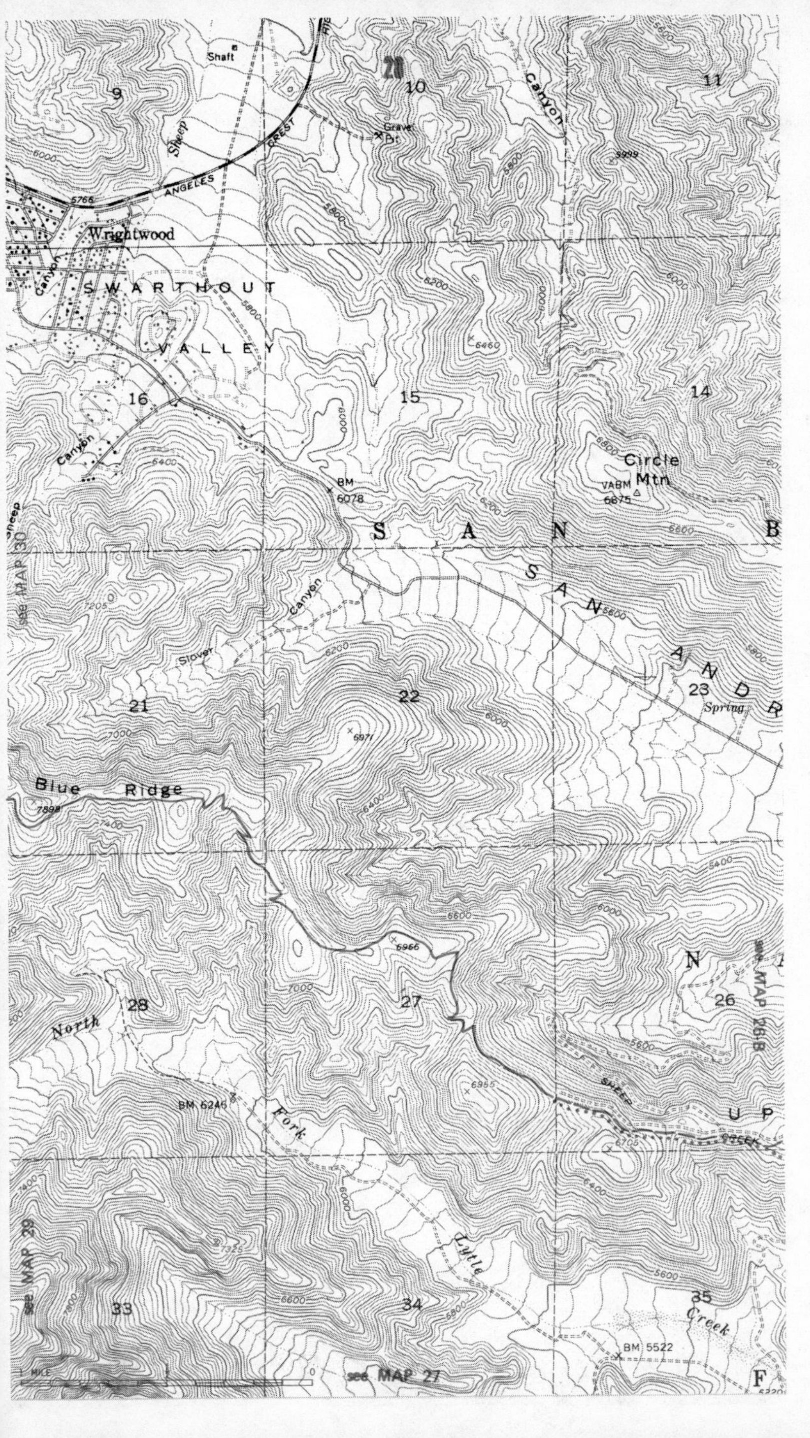
Shaft
28
9
10
11
Canyon
Sheep
Gravel Pit
ANGELES CREST
5765
Wrightwood
Canyon
SWARTHOUT
VALLEY
16
15
14
Canyon
Circle Mtn
VABM 6875
BM 6078
S A N B
S A N
A N D R
see MAP 30
Canyon
Slover
21
22
23
Spring
Blue Ridge
7898
6971
6966
N
28
27
26
see MAP 26B
North
Fork
BM 6246
6955
SHEEP
CREEK
U P
6705
Lytle
see MAP 29
7328
33
34
35
Creek
BM 5522
1 MILE
0
see MAP 27
F

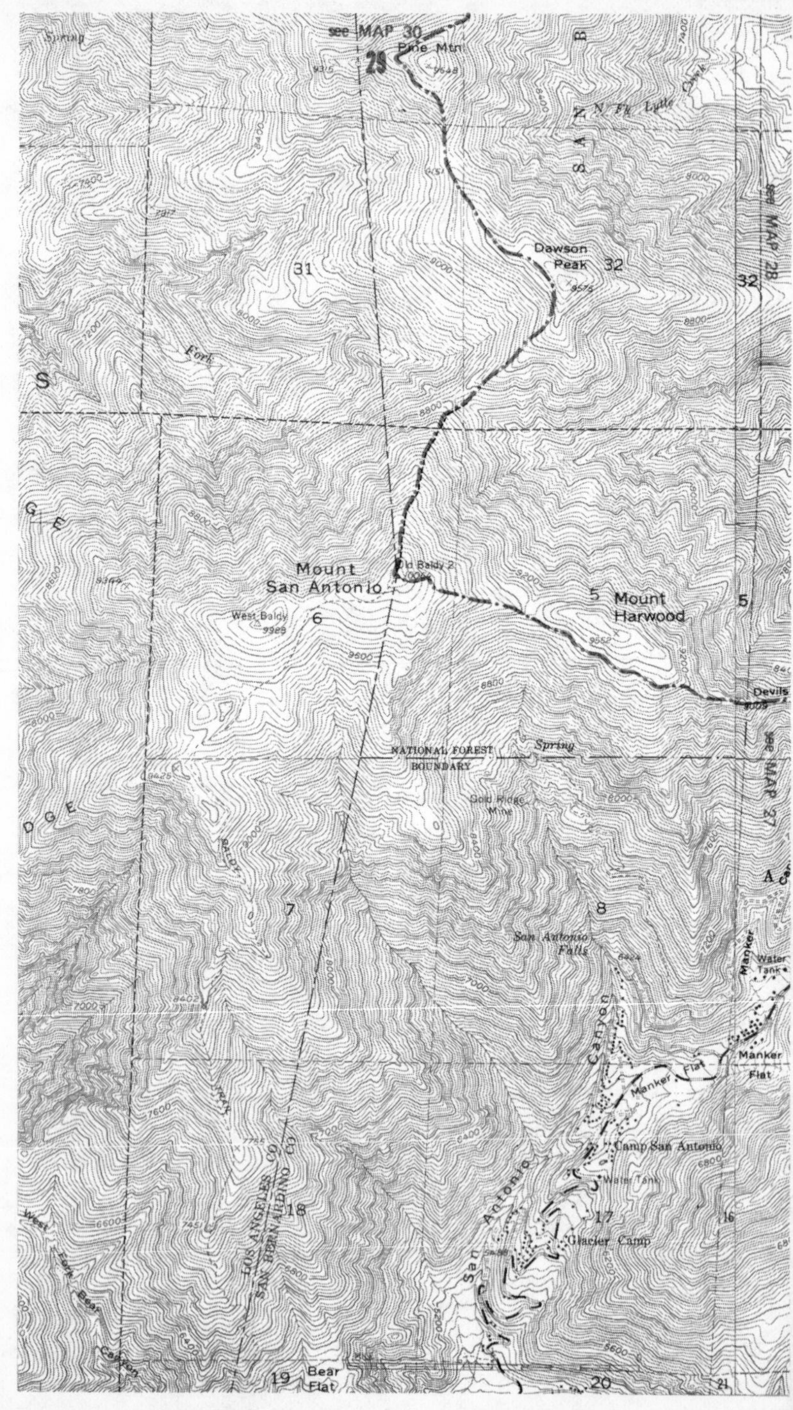

see MAP 30
29
Pine Mtn
Dawson Peak
31
32
see MAP 28
Mount San Antonio
Old Baldy 2
West Baldy
6
5
Mount Harwood
Devils
NATIONAL FOREST BOUNDARY
Spring
see MAP 27
Gold Ridge Mine
7
8
San Antonio Falls
Manker
Water Tank
Manker Flat
Camp San Antonio
Water Tank
18
17
16
Glacier Camp
LOS ANGELES CO
SAN BERNARDINO CO
San Antonio Canyon
West Fork Bear Canyon
19
Bear Flat
20
21

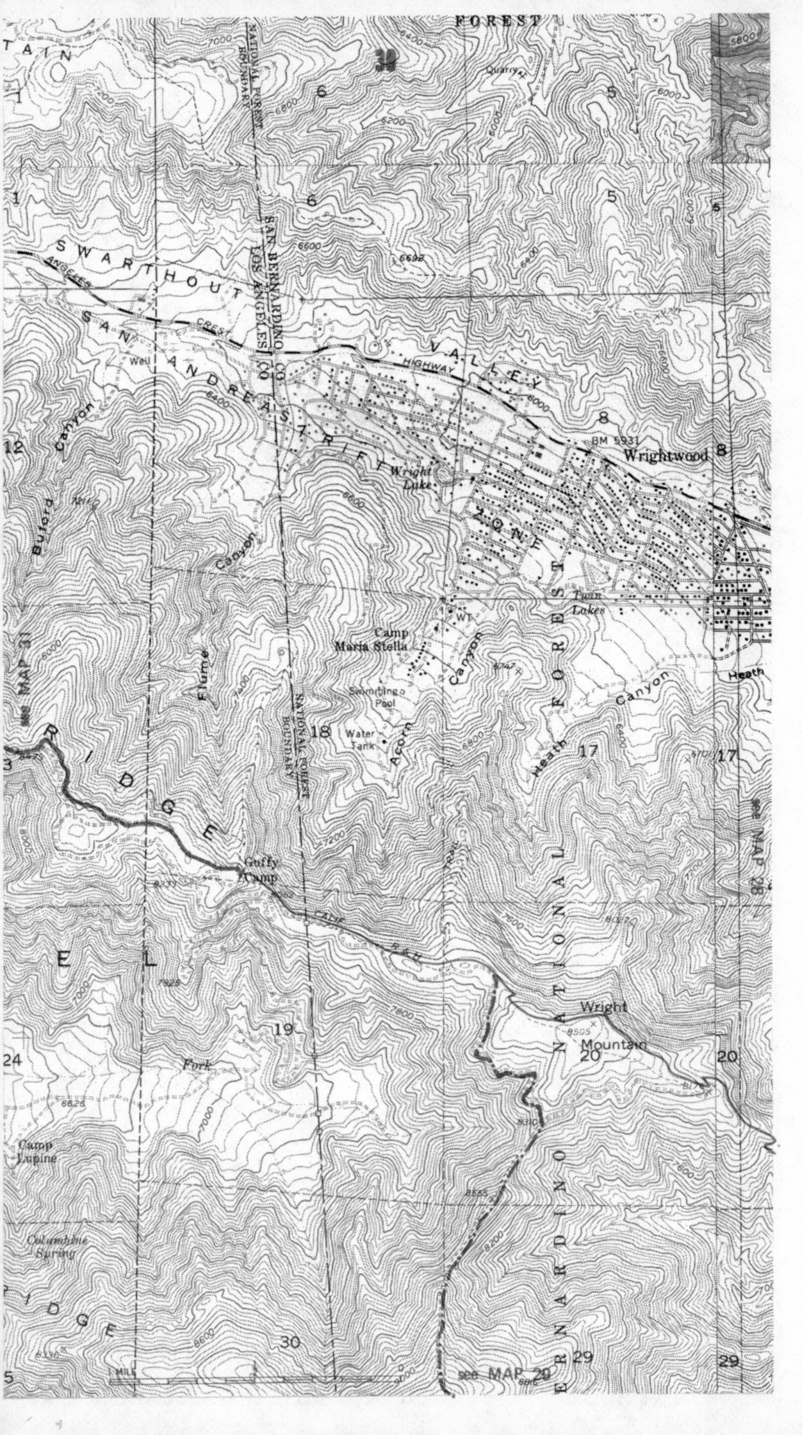
FOREST
SWARTHOUT
SAN ANDREAS RIFT
VALLEY
ANGELES CREST HIGHWAY
SAN BERNARDINO CO
LOS ANGELES CO
NATIONAL FOREST BOUNDARY
Quarry
Well
Buford
Canyon
Canyon
BM 5931
Wrightwood
Wright Lake
ZONE
Twin Lakes
WT
Camp Maria Stella
Swimming Pool
Water Tank
Acorn
Canyon
Flume
Heath
Canyon
Heath
see MAP 31
see MAP 28
RIDGE
Guffy Camp
CALIF R&H
EL
Fork
Wright Mountain
Camp Lupine
Columbine Spring
RIDGE
SAN BERNARDINO NATIONAL FOREST
see MAP 29
MILE

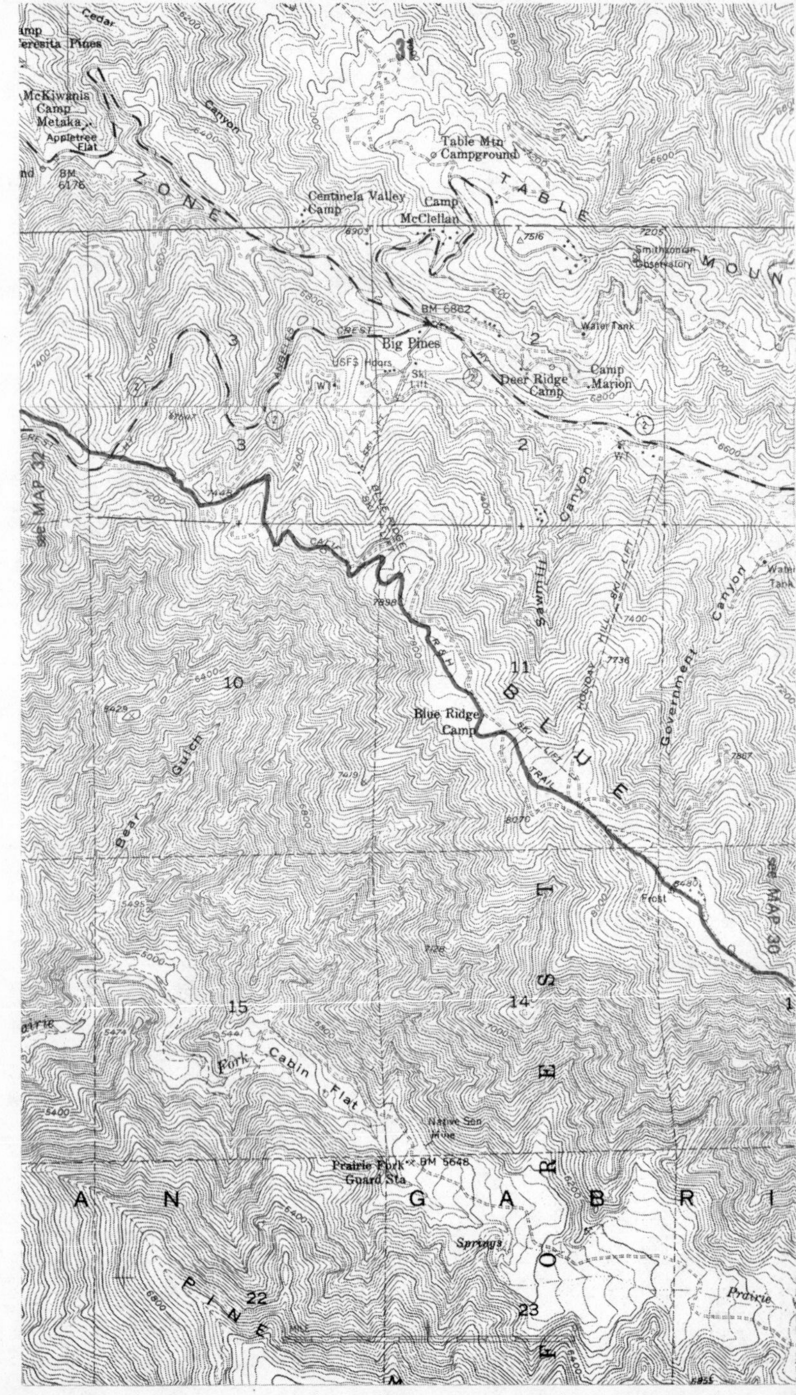

Camp Teresita Pines
McKiwanis Camp
Metaka
Appletree Flat
BM 6176
Cedar
Canyon
Z O N E
Table Mtn Campground
T A B L E
Centinela Valley Camp
Camp McClellan
Smithsonian Observatory
M O U N
BM 6862
Big Pines
USFS Hdqrs
Ski Lift
Water Tank
Deer Ridge Camp
Camp Marion
CREST
see MAP 32
Sawmill
Canyon
Blue Ridge Camp
B L U E
HOLIDAY HILL SKI LIFT
Government
Canyon
Water Tank
Bear Gulch
Frost
see MAP 30
Fork Cabin Flat
Native Son Mine
Prairie Fork Guard Sta.
BM 5648
A N G A B R I
Springs
P I N E
Prairie
T S E R O F

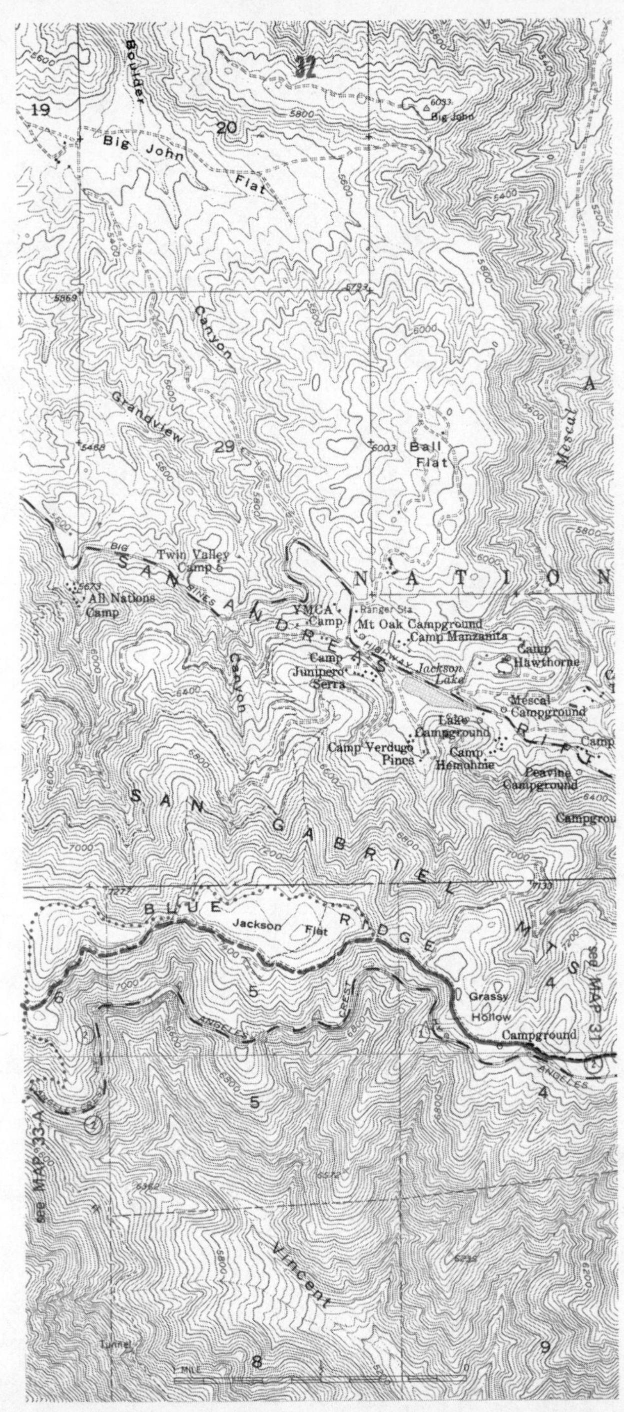

Boulder
32
19
20
Big John
Big John Flat
Canyon
Grandview
29
Ball Flat
Mescal
Twin Valley Camp
All Nations Camp
YMCA Camp
Ranger Sta
Mt Oak Campground
Camp Manzanita
Camp Hawthorne
Camp Junipero Serra
Jackson Lake
Mescal Campground
Lake Campground
Camp Verdugo Pines
Camp Hemohme
Peavine Campground
SAN ANDREAS RIFT
NATION
SAN GABRIEL MTS
BLUE RIDGE
Jackson Flat
Grassy Hollow Campground
see MAP 31
see MAP 33-A
Vincent
Tunnel
MILE

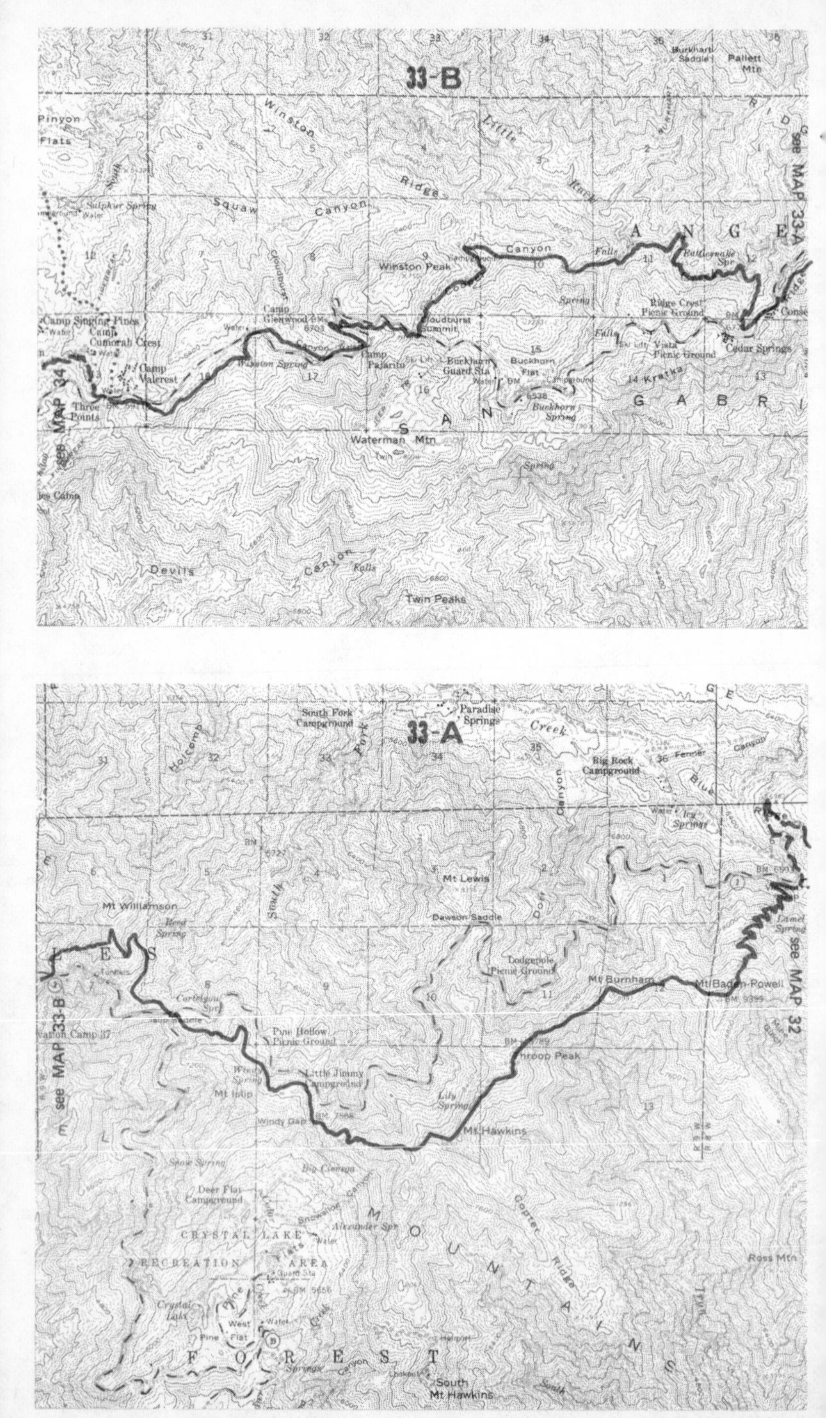

33-B
Pinyon Flats
Winston Ridge
Little Rock
Squaw Canyon
Sulphur Spring
Burkhart Saddle
Pallett Mtn
see MAP 33-A
Winston Peak
Rattlesnake Spr
Camp Singing Pines
Camp Cumorah Crest
Camp Glenwood
Cloudburst Summit
Ridge Crest Picnic Ground
Vista Picnic Ground
Cedar Springs
Camp Valerest
Winston Spring
Camp Pajarito
Buckhorn Guard Sta
Buckhorn Flat
Buckhorn Spring
Three Points
see MAP 34
Waterman Mtn
Devils Canyon
Twin Peaks
33-A
South Fork Campground
Paradise Springs
Holcomb
Big Rock Campground
Icy Springs
Mt Lewis
Mt Williamson
Dawson Saddle
Lodgepole Picnic Ground
Mt Burnham
Mt Baden-Powell
see MAP 32
see MAP 33-B
Pine Hollow Picnic Ground
Little Jimmy Campground
Throop Peak
Mt Islip
Windy Gap
Mt Hawkins
Lily Spring
Snow Spring
Deer Flat Campground
CRYSTAL LAKE RECREATION AREA
Crystal Lake
MOUNTAINS
Copter Ridge
Ross Mtn
FOREST
South Mt Hawkins

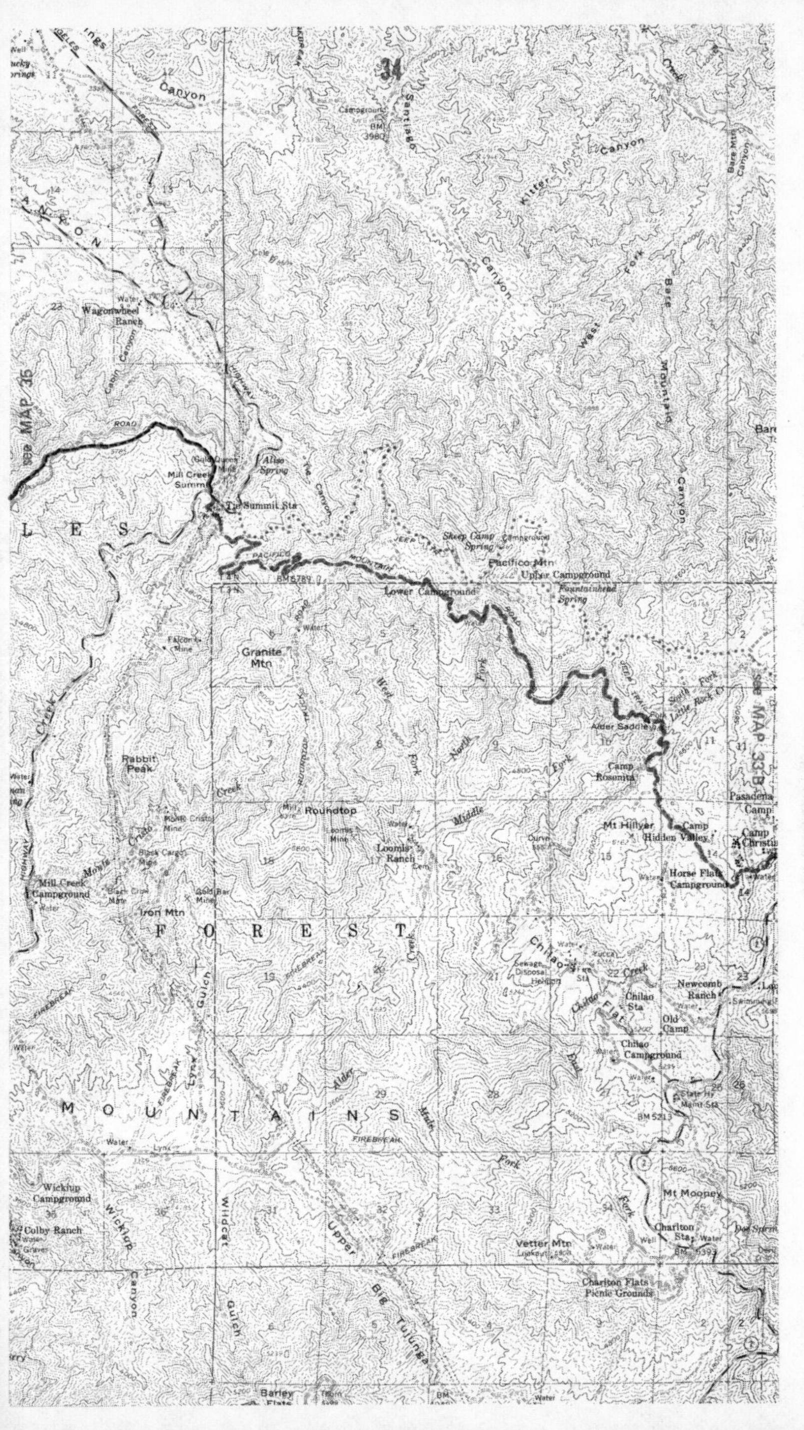

Canyon
Santiago
Campground
BM 3980
Kitter Canyon
West Fork
Bare Mountain Canyon
Wagonwheel Ranch
Cabin Canyon
see MAP 35
ROAD
HIGHWAY
Mill Creek Summit
Aliso Spring
Tie Summit Sta
L E S
Sheep Camp Spring
Campground
Pacifico Mtn
PACIFICO MOUNTAIN
JEEP
Upper Campground
Lower Campground
BM 5789
Fountainhead Spring
Falcon Mine
Granite Mtn
Alder Saddle
South Fork Little Rock Cr
see MAP 33-B
Camp Rosenita
Pasadena Camp
Rabbit Peak
Roundtop
Loomis Mine
Loomis Ranch
Middle Fork
Mt Hillyer
Camp Hidden Valley
Camp Christian
Horse Flats Campground
Monte Cristo Mine
Black Cargo Mine
Black Crow Mine
Gold Bar Mine
Mill Creek Campground
Iron Mtn
F O R E S T
Chilao
Sewage Disposal
Chilao Creek
Newcomb Ranch
Chilao Sta
Chilao Flat
Old Camp
Chilao Campground
State Hy Maint Sta
BM 5213
Lynx Gulch
FIREBREAK
Alder
M O U N T A I N S
Mule Fork
Wickiup Campground
Wickiup Canyon
Colby Ranch
Wildcat Gulch
Upper Big Tujunga
Mt Mooney
Charlton Sta
Vetter Mtn Lookout
Charlton Flats Picnic Grounds
Barley Flats

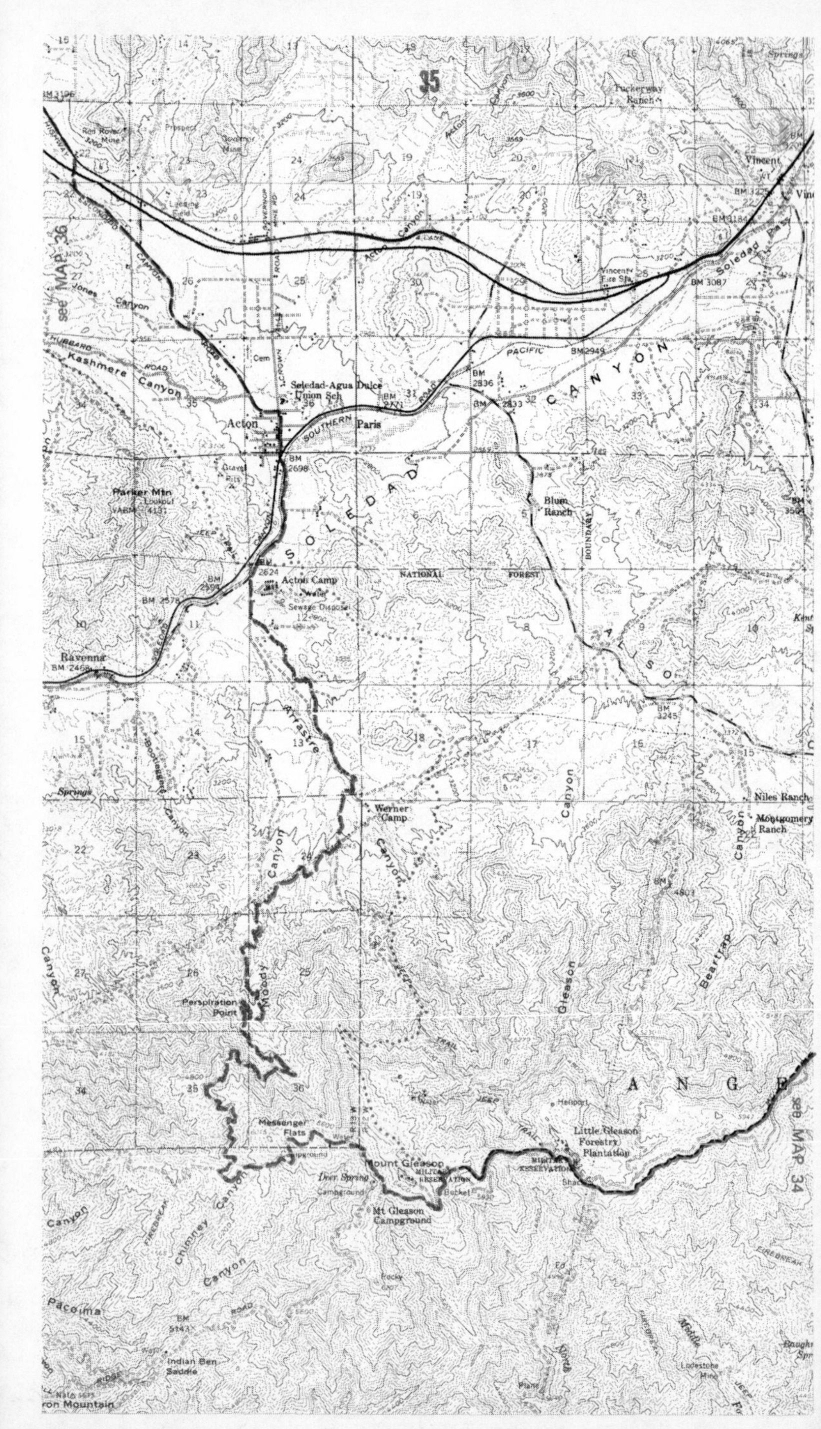

35
see MAP 36
see MAP 34
Acton
Soledad-Agua Dulce Union Sch
Paris
SOLEDAD CANYON
NATIONAL FOREST
Parker Mtn
Acton Camp
Ravenna
Kashmere Canyon
Jones Canyon
Vincent
Puckerway Ranch
Blum Ranch
ALISO
BOUNDARY
Werner Camp
Arrastre
Moody Canyon
Perspiration Point
Messenger Flats
Mount Gleason
Mt Gleason Campground
Deer Spring
Little Gleason Forestry Plantation
Gleason Canyon
Beartrap Canyon
Niles Ranch
Montgomery Ranch
Chimney Canyon
Pacoima
Indian Ben Saddle
Iron Mountain
Lodestone Mine
Bootlegger Canyon
ANGE
SOUTHERN PACIFIC
FIREBREAK
JEEP TRAIL
MILITARY RESERVATION

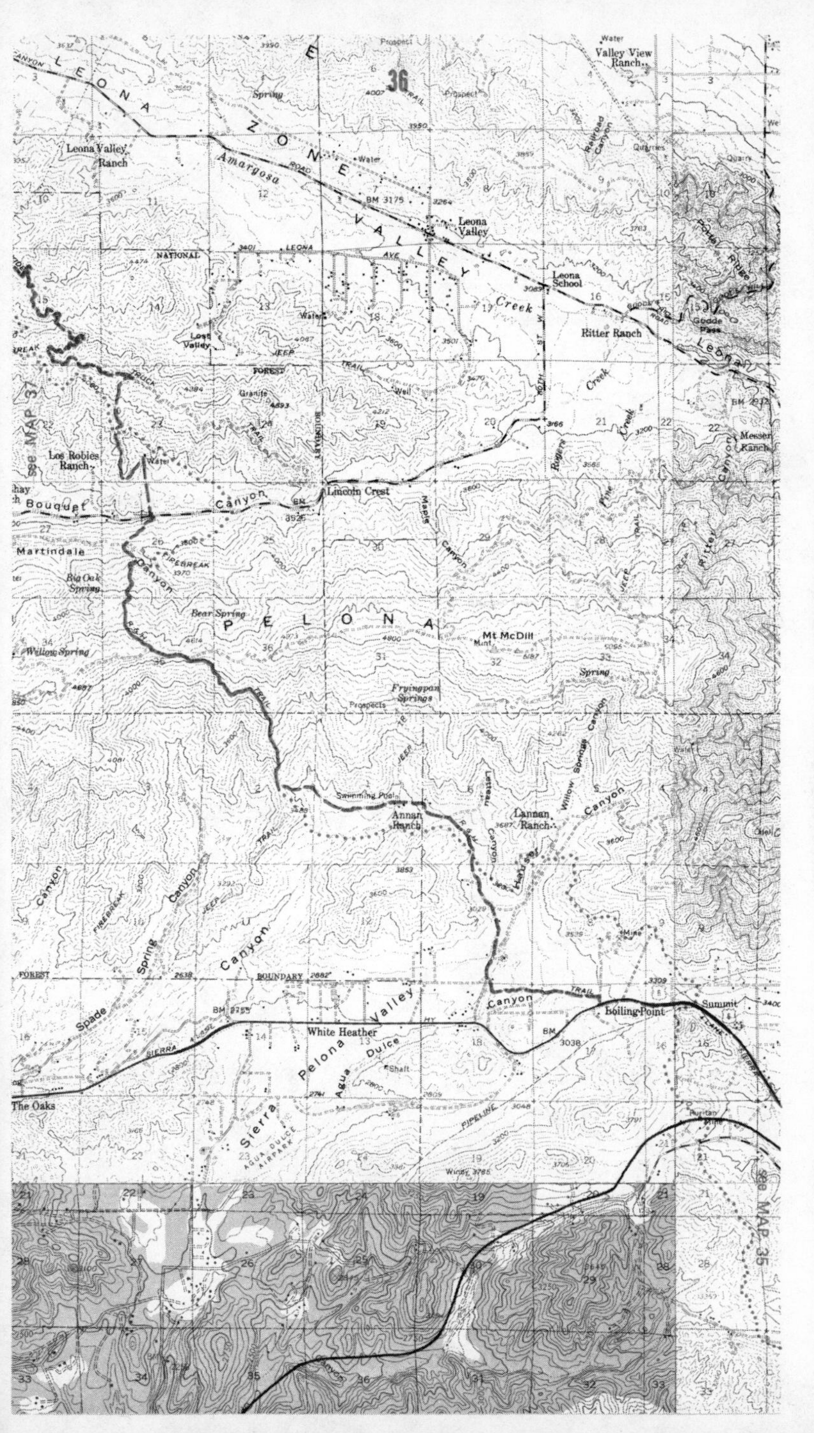

36
LEONA ZONE VALLEY
Valley View Ranch
Leona Valley Ranch
Amargosa
Leona Valley
Railroad Canyon
Quarries
Portal Ridge
LEONA AVE
NATIONAL FOREST BOUNDARY
Leona School
Creek
Ritter Ranch
Godde Pass
Leona
Lost Valley
Granite
Well
Los Robles Ranch
Rogers Creek
Pine Creek
Messer Ranch
Ritter Canyon
Bouquet Canyon
Lincoln Crest
Maple Canyon
Martindale
Big Oak Spring
Bear Spring
PELONA
Mt McDill
Willow Spring
Fryingpan Springs
Prospects
Swimming Pool
Annan Ranch
Lannan Ranch
Letteau Canyon
Willow Springs Canyon
Spade Spring Canyon
Boiling Point
Summit
Valley Canyon
White Heather
Sierra Pelona
Agua Dulce
AGUA DULCE AIRPARK
The Oaks
see MAP 37
see MAP 35

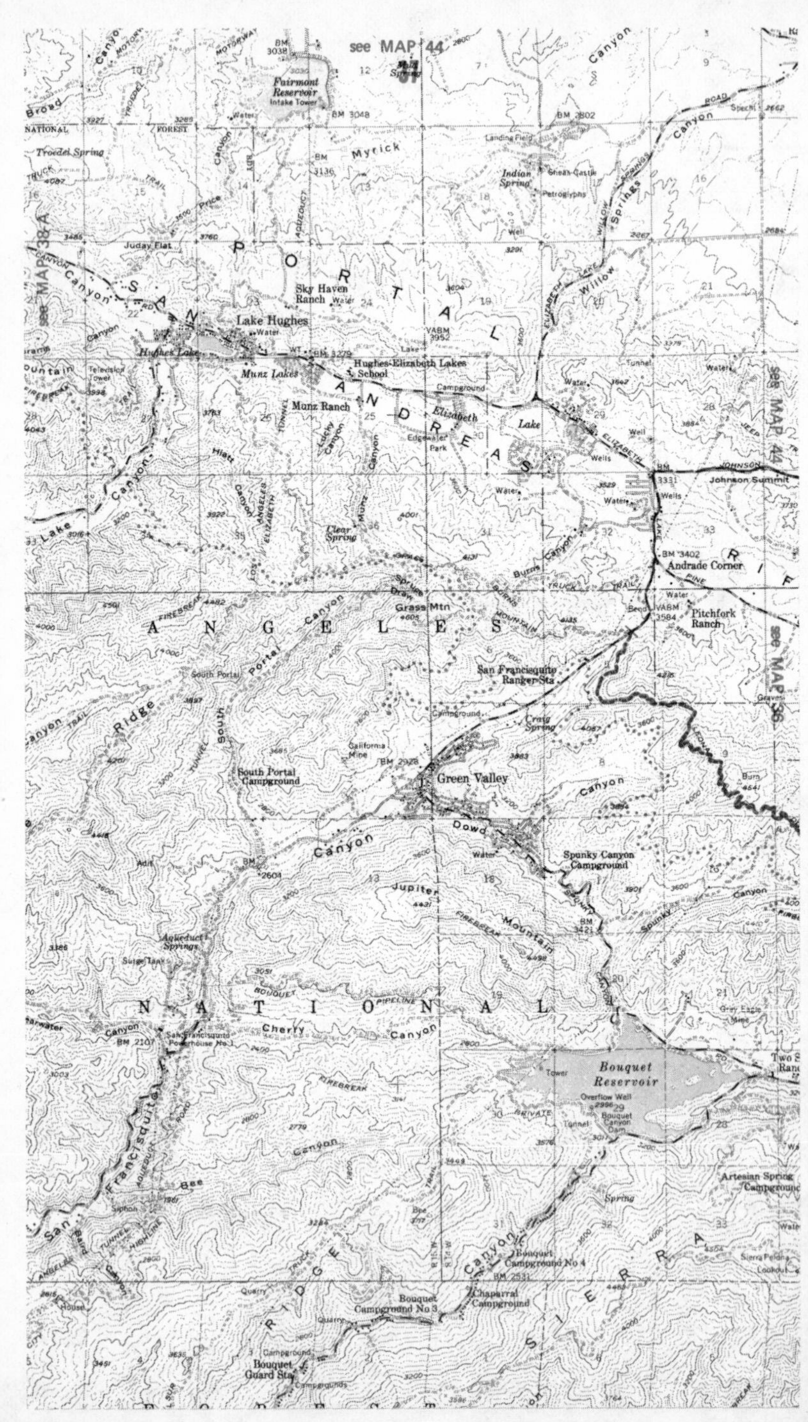

see MAP 44
see MAP 38-A
see MAP 44
see MAP 36
Fairmont Reservoir
Lake Hughes
Hughes Lake
Munz Lakes
Munz Ranch
Sky Haven Ranch
Hughes-Elizabeth Lakes School
Elizabeth Lake
Juday Flat
Troedel Spring
Indian Spring
Landing Field
Shea's Castle
Petroglyphs
Johnson Summit
Andrade Corner
Pitchfork Ranch
Grass Mtn
San Francisquito Ranger Sta
Green Valley
South Portal Campground
California Mine
Craig Spring
Spunky Canyon Campground
Jupiter Mountain
Aqueduct Springs
Surge Tank
San Francisquito Powerhouse No 1
Bouquet Reservoir
Bouquet Canyon Dam
Artesian Spring Campground
Bouquet Campground No 4
Chaparral Campground
Bouquet Campground No 3
Bouquet Guard Sta
Sierra Pelona Lookout
S A N A N D R E A S
P O R T A L
A N G E L E S
N A T I O N A L
R I D G E
S I E R R A

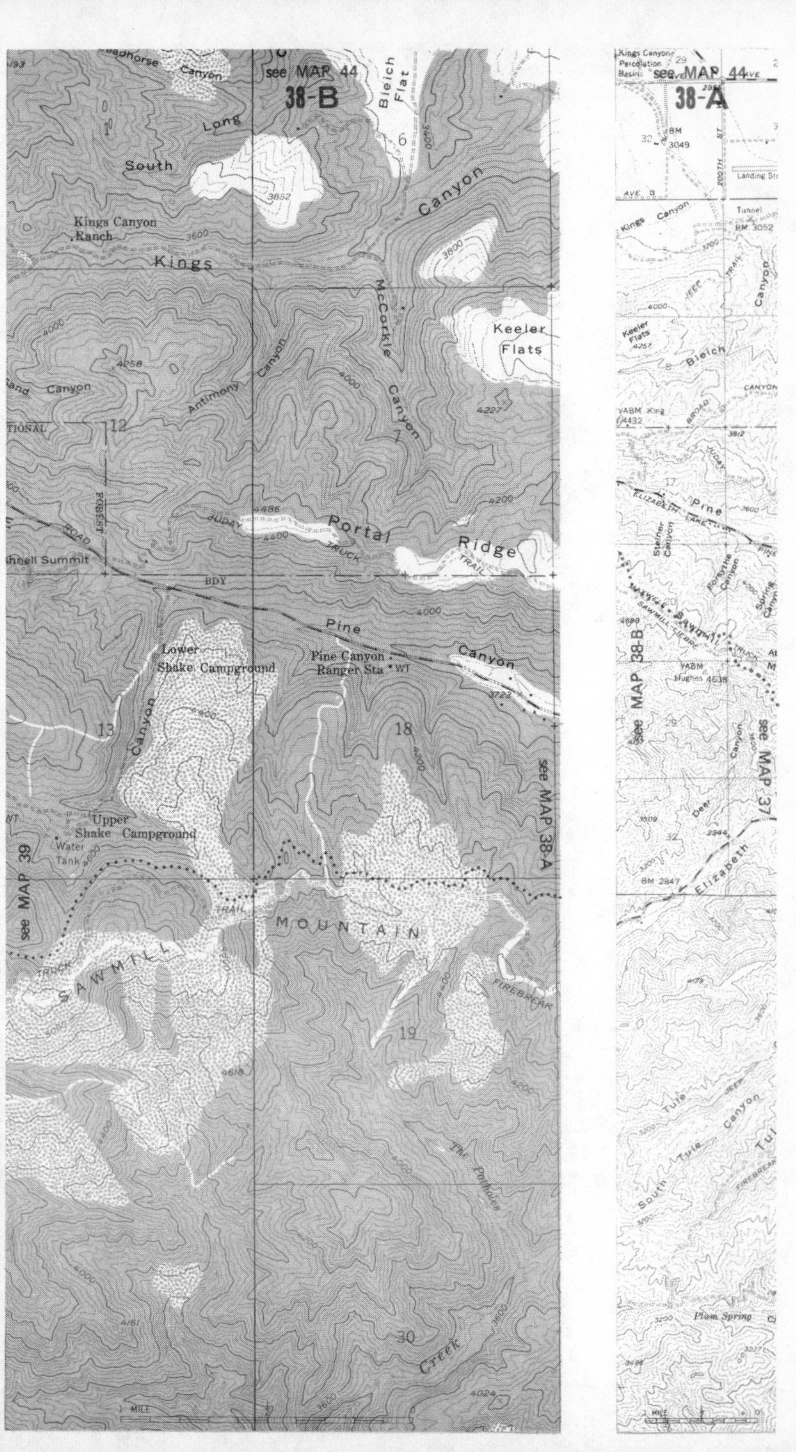

see MAP 44
38-B
Bleich Flat
Long
South
Kings Canyon Ranch
Kings
Canyon
McCorkle Canyon
Keeler Flats
Antimony Canyon
Portal Ridge
Pine Canyon
Lower Shake Campground
Pine Canyon Ranger Sta
Upper Shake Campground
see MAP 38-A
see MAP 39
MOUNTAIN
SAWMILL
FIREBREAK
Creek
see MAP 44
38-A
Kings Canyon Percolation Basin
see MAP 38-B
see MAP 37
Keeler Flats
Bleich
Pine
Steiner Canyon
Forsythe Canyon
Spring Canyon
Sawmill
Deer
Elizabeth
Tule
South Tule Canyon
Plum Spring

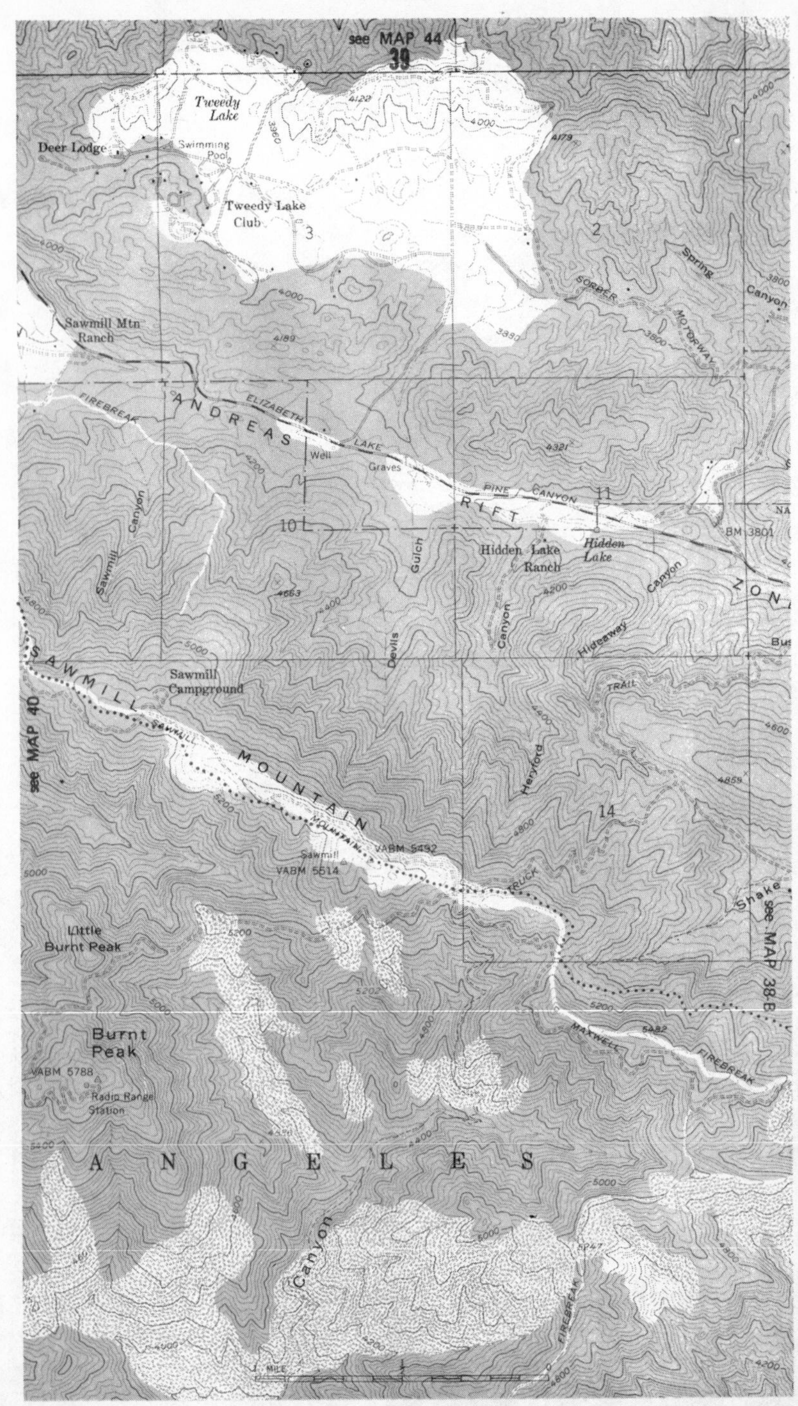

see MAP 44
39
Tweedy Lake
Deer Lodge
Swimming Pool
Tweedy Lake Club
Sawmill Mtn Ranch
SAN ANDREAS RIFT ZONE
ELIZABETH LAKE PINE CANYON
Well
Graves
Hidden Lake Ranch
Hidden Lake
BM 3801
Sawmill Canyon
Gulch
Devils
Canyon
Hideaway Canyon
Spring Canyon
SORBER MOTORWAY
FIREBREAK
Sawmill Campground
SAWMILL MOUNTAIN
TRAIL
Heryford
see MAP 40
Sawmill VABM 5614
VABM 5492
TRUCK
Shake
see MAP 38-B
Little Burnt Peak
Burnt Peak
VABM 5788
Radio Range Station
MAXWELL FIREBREAK
ANGELES
Canyon
FIREBREAK
1 MILE

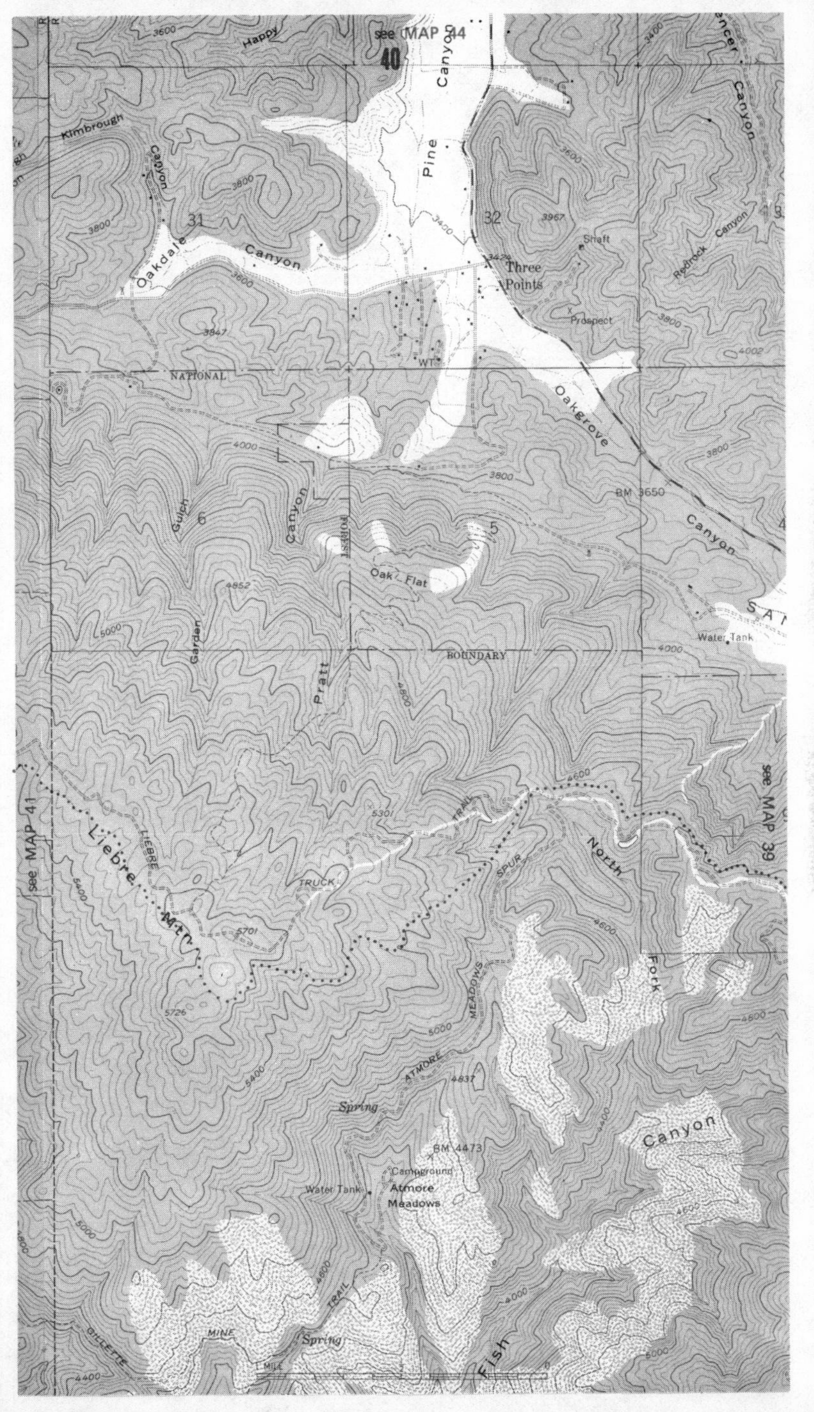

see MAP 44
40
Happy
Pine Canyon
Kimbrough
Canyon
Oakdale Canyon
31
32
Three Points
Shaft
Prospect
Redrock Canyon
Canyon
NATIONAL
BOUNDARY
Oakgrove Canyon
BM 3650
Gulch
Garden
Canyon
Pratt
6
5
Oak Flat
Water Tank
see MAP 39
see MAP 41
Liebre Mtn
LIEBRE
TRUCK TRAIL
North Fork
SPUR
MEADOWS
ATMORE TRAIL
Spring
BM 4473
Campground
Water Tank
Atmore Meadows
Canyon
GILLETTE
MINE
TRAIL
Spring
Fish
1 MILE

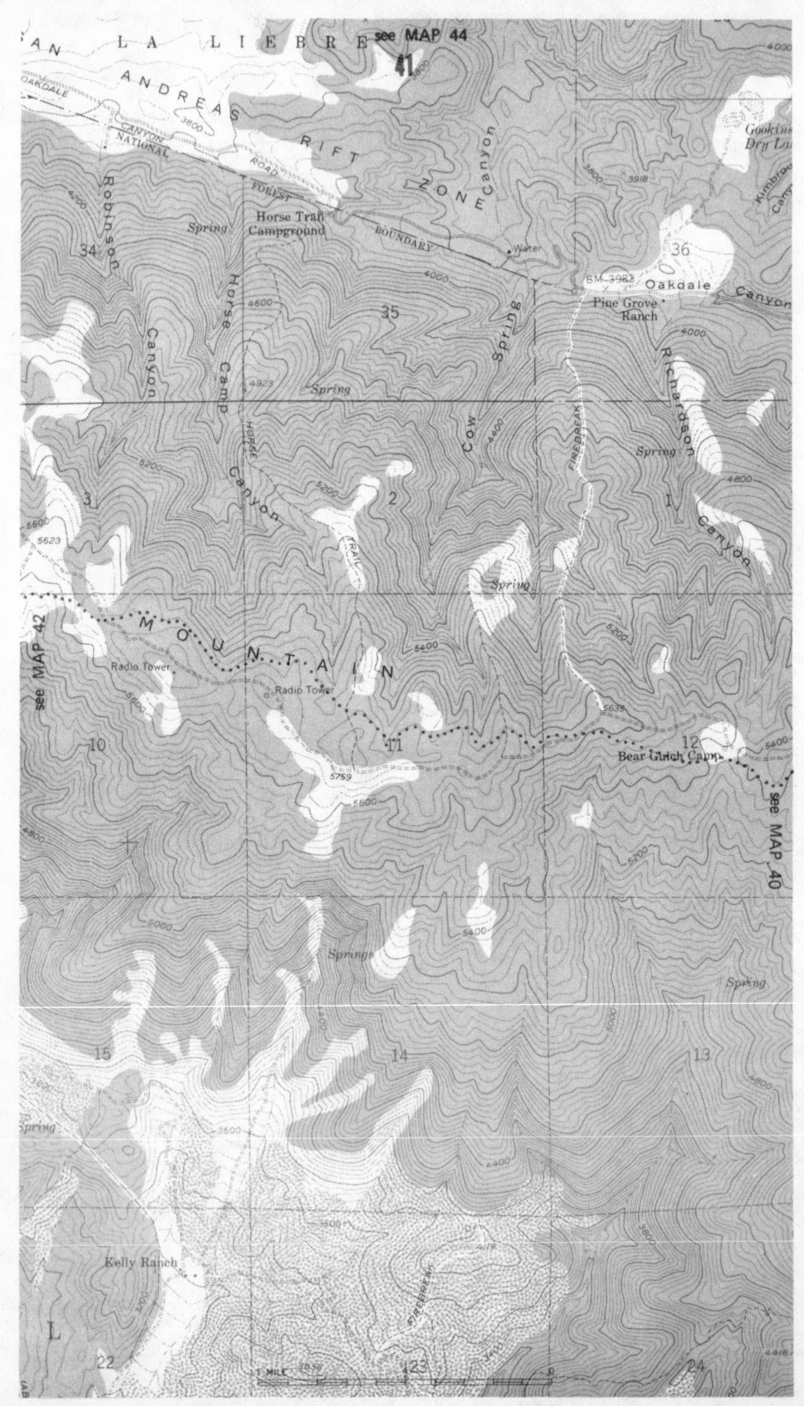
see MAP 44
41
SAN ANDREAS RIFT ZONE
LIEBRE
Robinson Canyon
Horse Camp Canyon
Horse Trail Campground
Spring
ANGELES NATIONAL FOREST BOUNDARY
Cow Spring Canyon
Oakdale
Pine Grove Ranch
Oakdale Canyon
Richardson Canyon
Gookins Dry Lake
FIREBREAK
MOUNTAIN
Radio Tower
Radio Tower
Bear Gulch Camp
see MAP 42
see MAP 40
Springs
Spring
Kelly Ranch
1 MILE

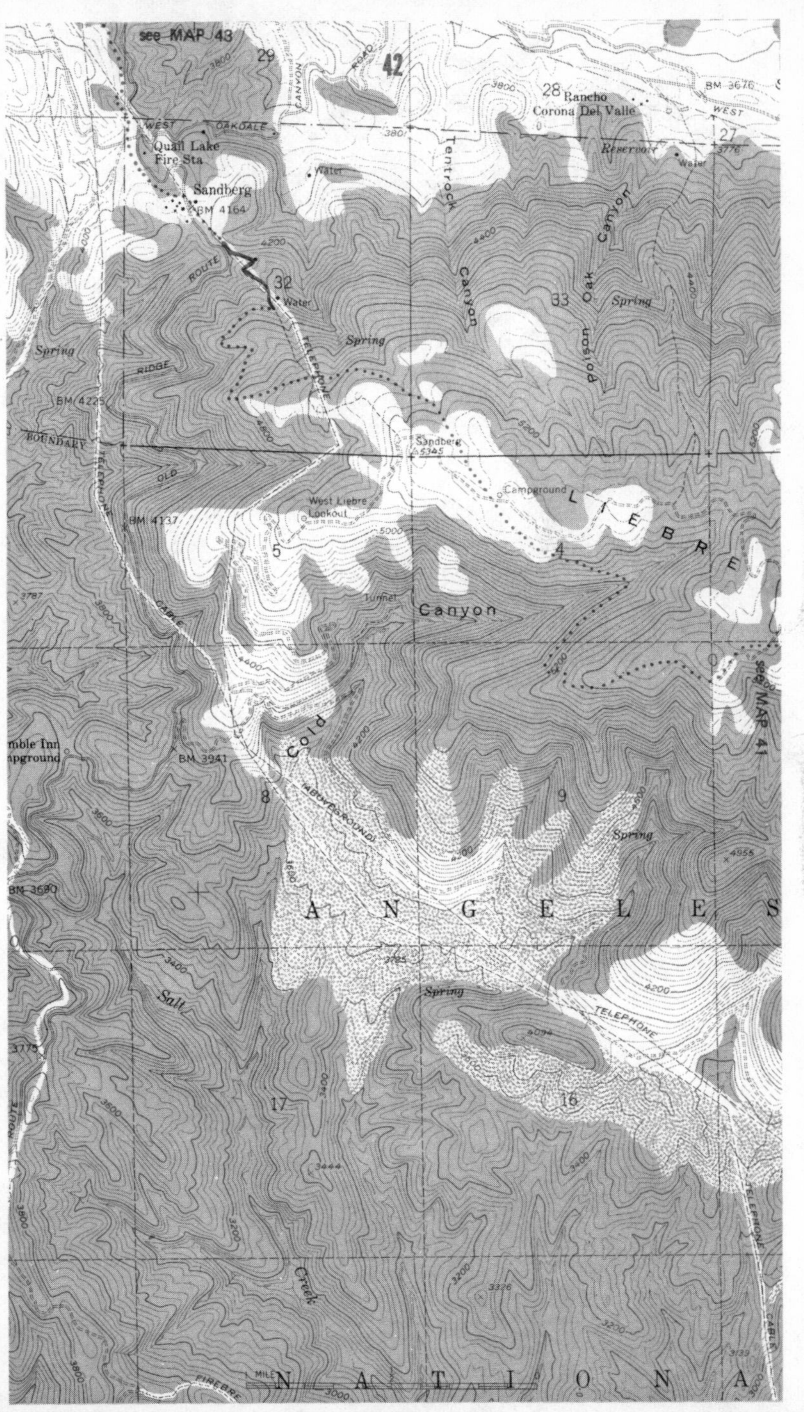

see MAP 43
42
29
28
Rancho
Corona Del Valle
BM 3676
WEST
27
Reservoir
Water
Tentrock
Canyon
Poison Oak Canyon
Spring
33
Quail Lake
Fire Sta
Sandberg
BM 4164
WEST
OAKDALE
CANYON
ROAD
Water
32
Water
ROUTE
RIDGE
Spring
Spring
TELEPHONE
BM 4225
BOUNDARY
Sandberg
5345
Campground
LIEBRE
OLD
West Liebre
Lookout
BM 4137
5
4
Tunnel
Canyon
CABLE
Cold
see MAP 41
BM 3941
8
9
Spring
(ABOVEGROUND)
BM 3680
ANGELES
3725
Spring
Salt
TELEPHONE
17
16
3444
Creek
3326
TELEPHONE
CABLE
ROUTE
FIREBRE
MILE
NATIONA

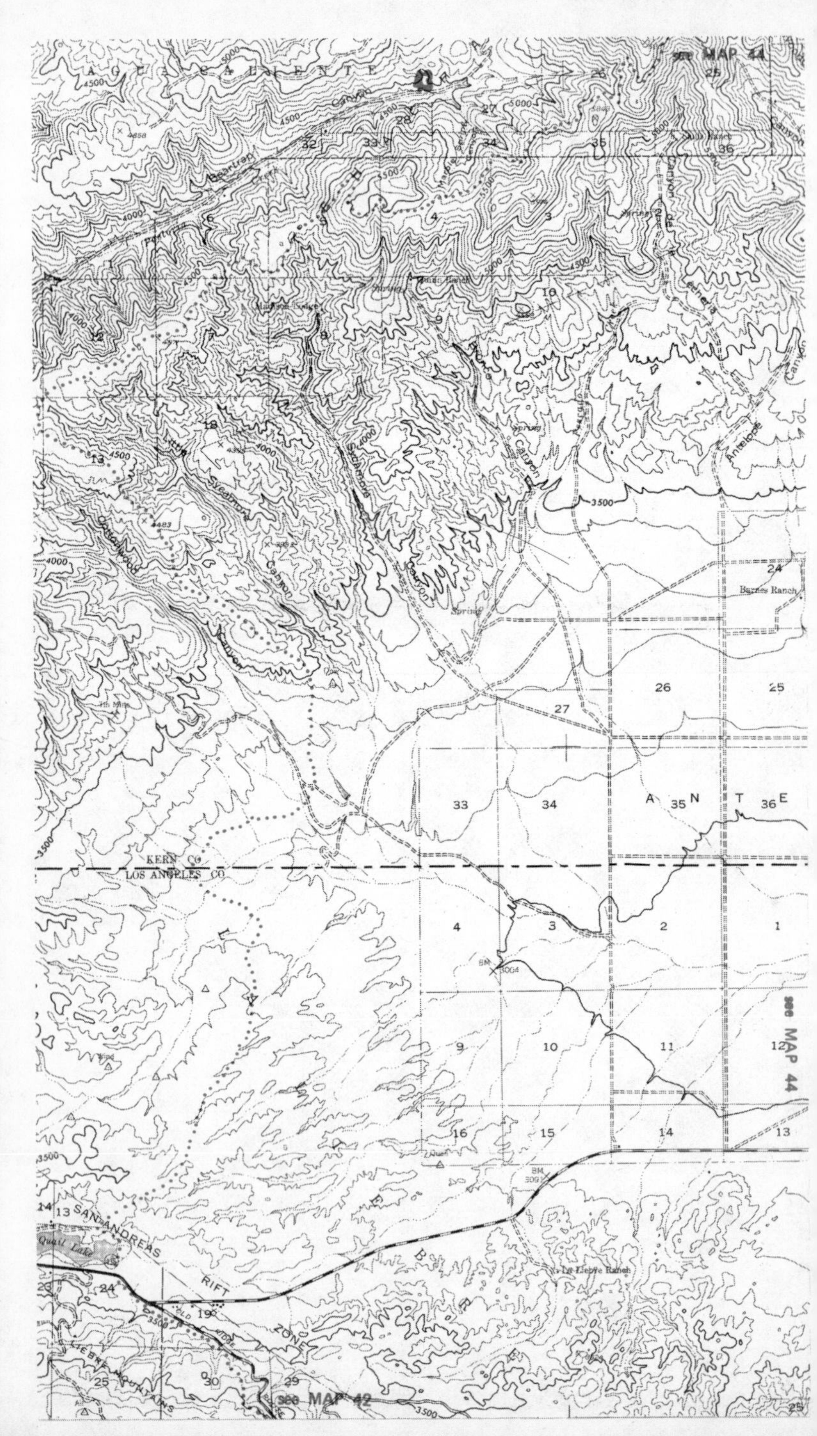

SEE MAP 44
AGUA CALIENTE
Canyon
Beartrap
Sycamore
Little Sycamore Canyon
Cottonwood Canyon
Antelope Canyon
Burnes Ranch
KERN CO
LOS ANGELES CO
SAN ANDREAS RIFT ZONE
Quail Lake
LIEBRE MOUNTAINS
Liebre Ranch
SEE MAP 42

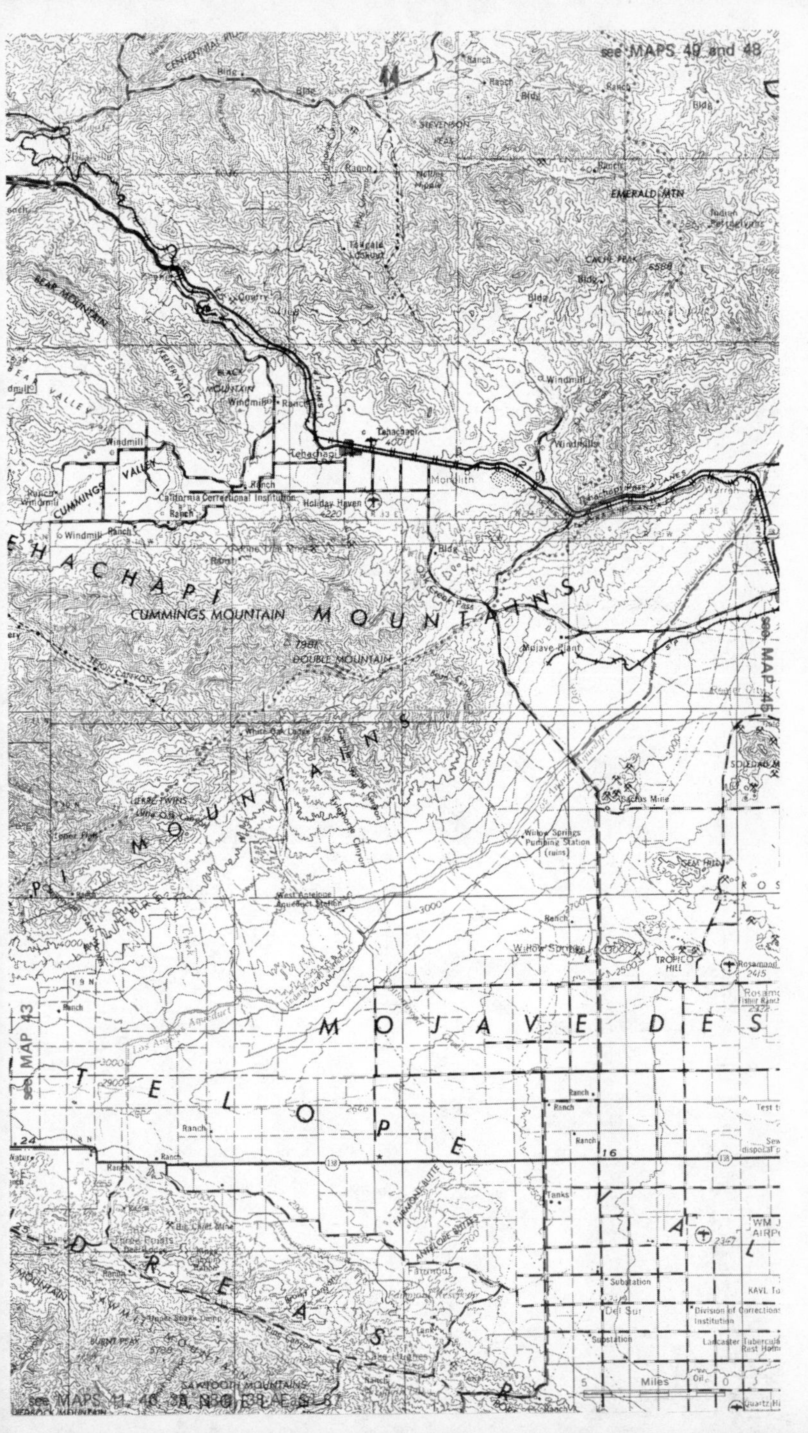

see MAPS 49 and 48
STEVENSON PEAK
EMERALD MTN
CACHE PEAK
6588
BEAR MOUNTAIN
BLACK MOUNTAIN
Tehachapi
4001
Monolith
Tehachapi Pass
CUMMINGS VALLEY
California Correctional Institution
Holiday Haven
TEHACHAPI MOUNTAINS
CUMMINGS MOUNTAIN
7981
DOUBLE MOUNTAIN
Oak Creek Pass
Mojave Plant
see MAP 45
White Oak Lodge
Willow Springs Pumping Station (ruins)
West Antelope Aqueduct Station
Willow Springs
TROPICO HILL
Rosamond
2415
MOJAVE DESERT
ANTELOPE VALLEY
see MAP 43
Ranch
16
138
FAIRMONT BUTTE
ANTELOPE BUTTES
Fairmont
Three Points
Big Chief Mine
Lake Hughes
Substation
Del Sur
Division of Corrections Institution
SAWTOOTH MOUNTAINS
BURNT PEAK
5788
Miles
see MAPS 41, 40, 38 AND 37

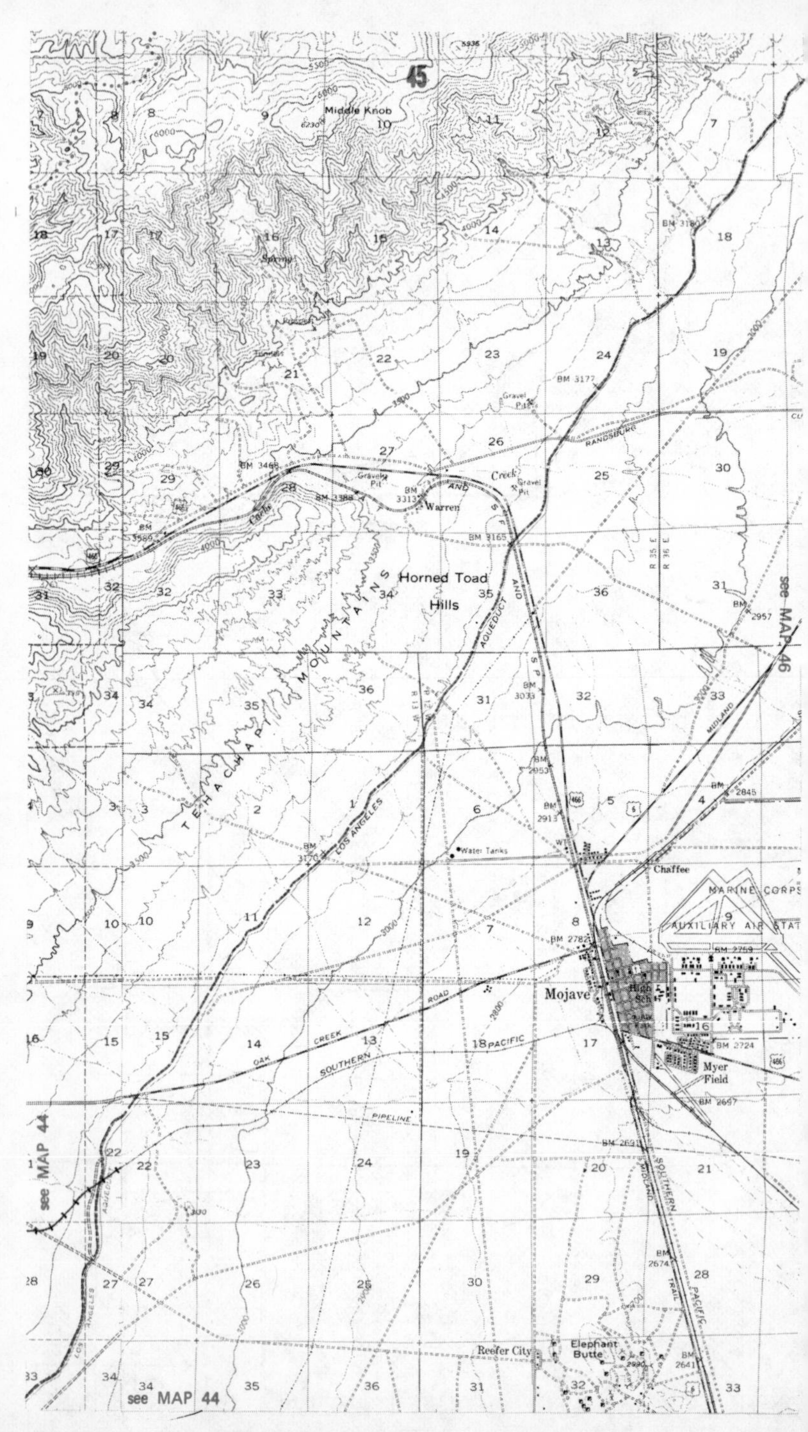
45
Middle Knob
Horned Toad
Hills
TEHACHAPI MOUNTAINS
Warren
Mojave
Chaffee
MARINE CORPS
AUXILIARY AIR STAT
Myer
Field
Reefer City
Elephant
Butte
RANDSBURG
LOS ANGELES
AQUEDUCT
SOUTHERN
PACIFIC
MIDLAND
OAK CREEK ROAD
PIPELINE
see MAP 46
see MAP 44
see MAP 44

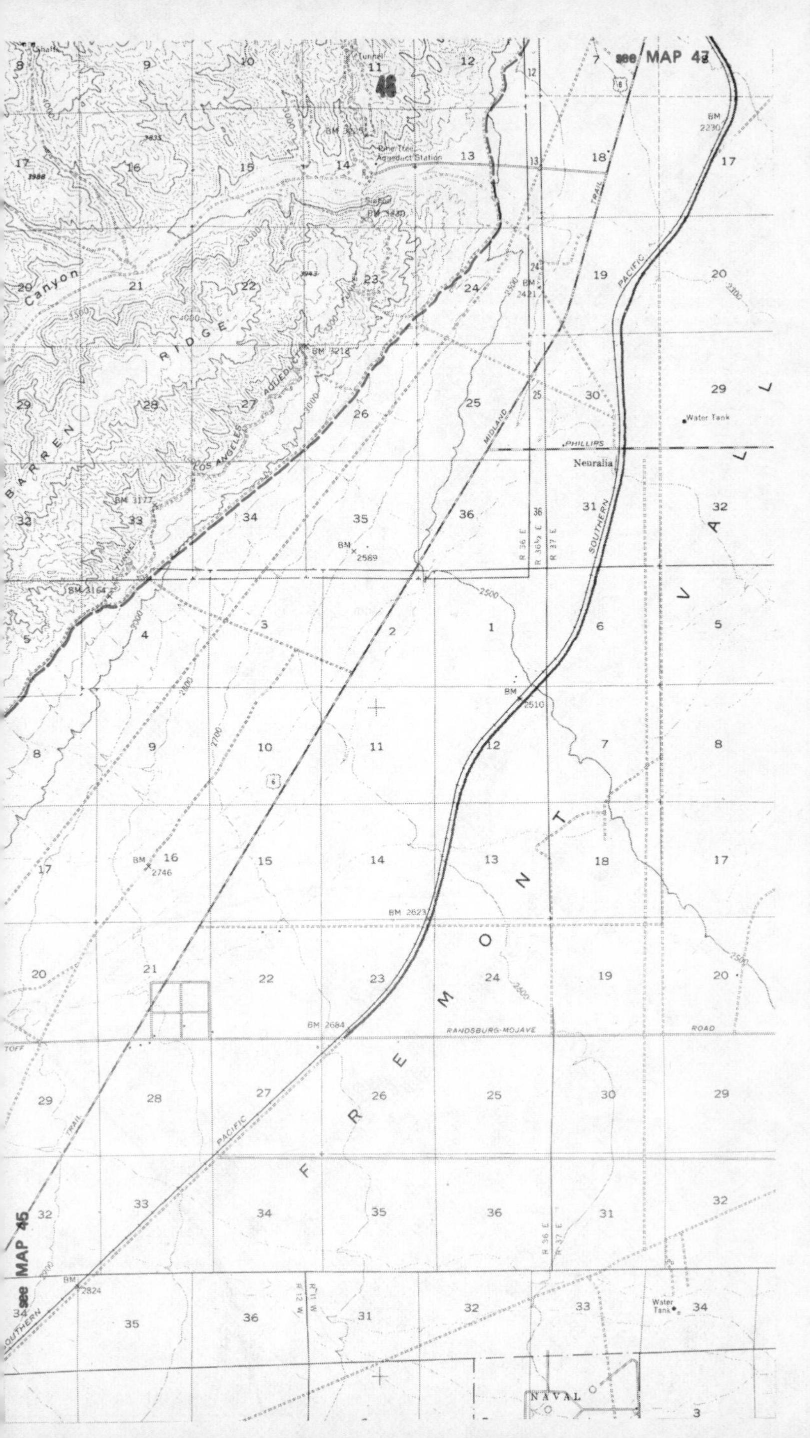

see MAP 47
46
BARREN RIDGE
Canyon
LOS ANGELES AQUEDUCT
Pine Tree Aqueduct Station
MIDLAND TRAIL
SOUTHERN PACIFIC
PHILLIPS
Neuralia
FREMONT VALLEY
RANDSBURG-MOJAVE ROAD
Water Tank
NAVAL
see MAP 45

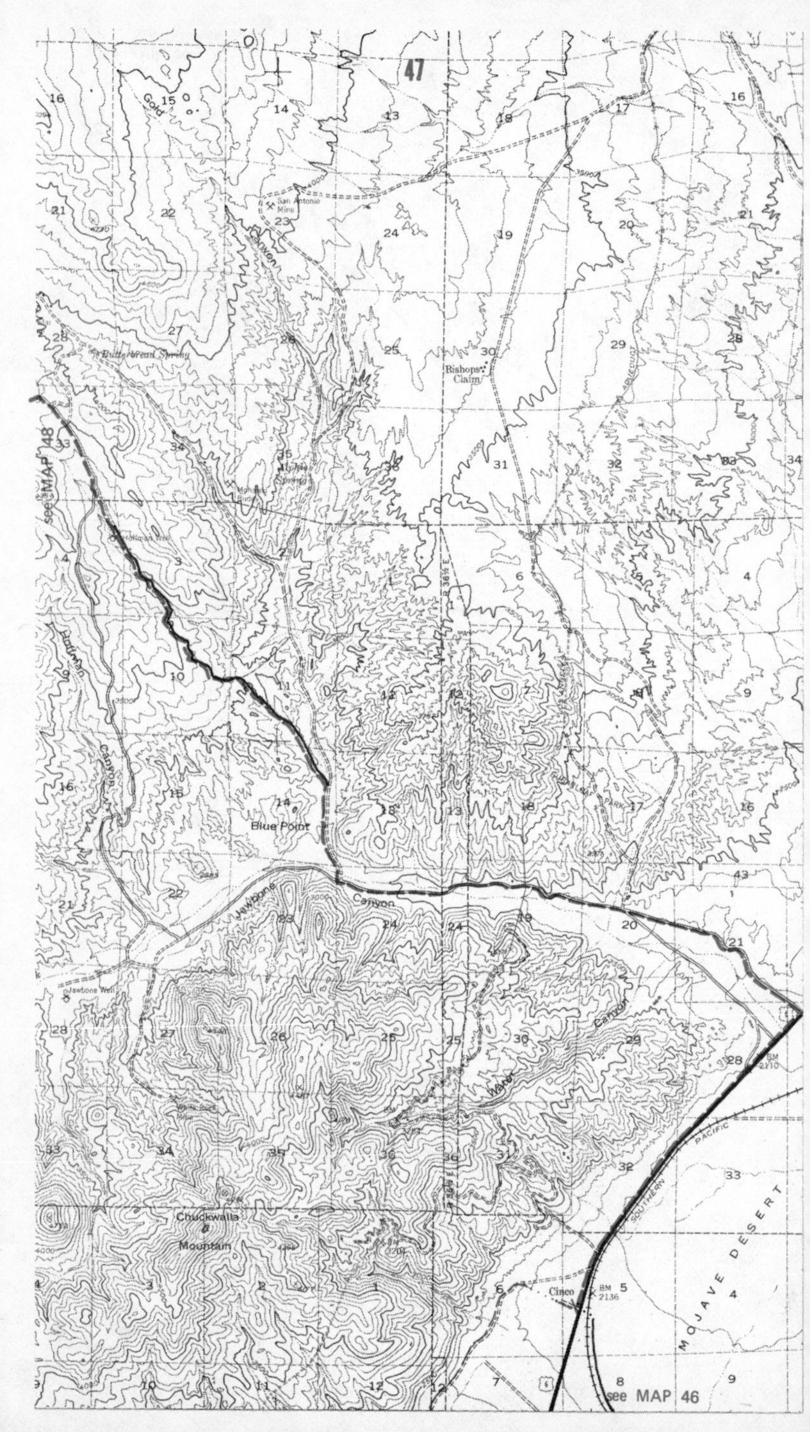
47
Gold
San Antonio Mine
Canyon
Butterbread Spring
see MAP 48
Bishops Claim
AQUEDUCT
Blue Point
Jawbone
Canyon
Jawbone Well
Water
Canyon
White Rock Mine
Chuckwalla Mountain
Cinco
SOUTHERN PACIFIC
MOJAVE DESERT
see MAP 46

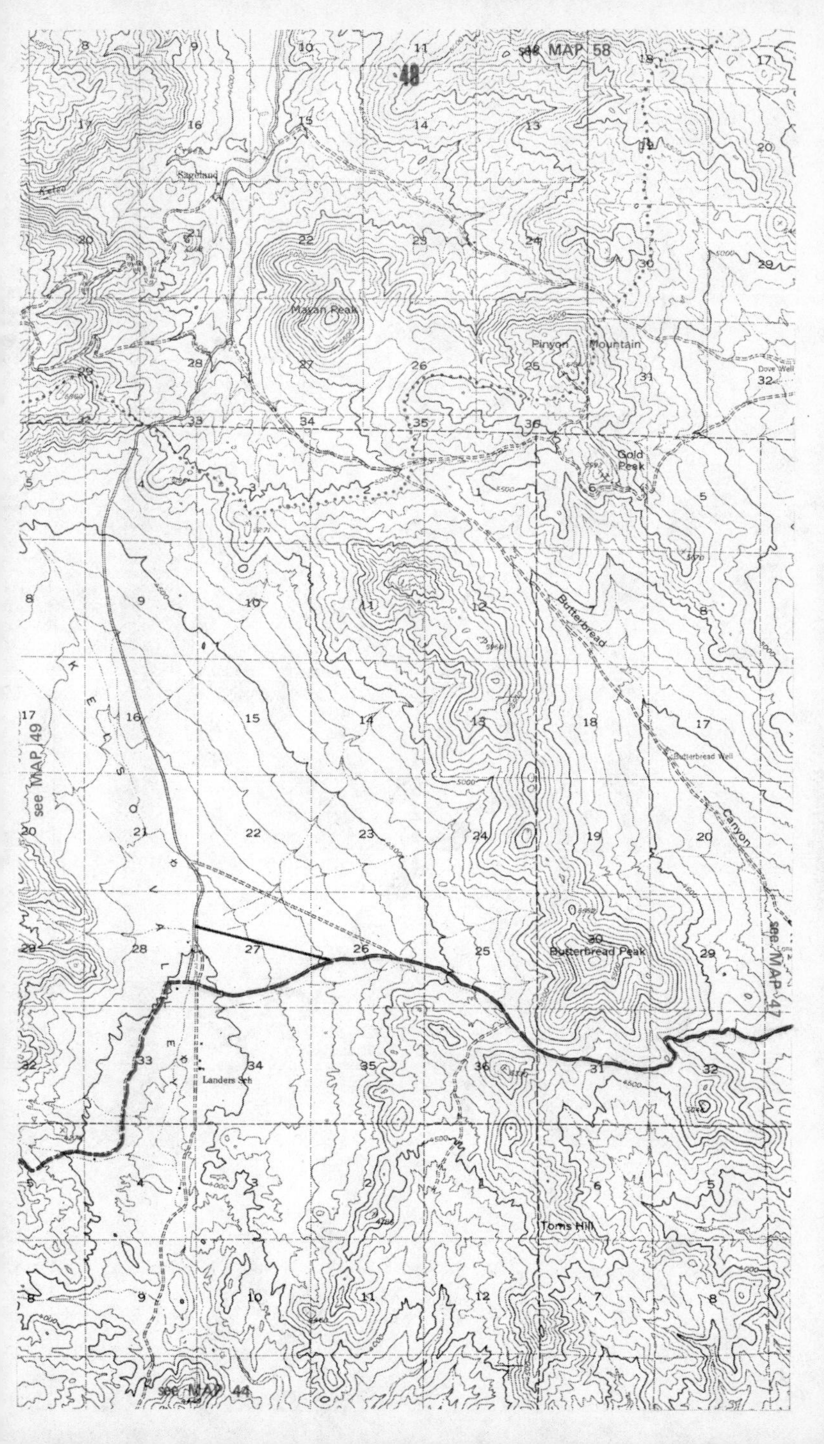

see MAP 58
48
Sagaland
Mayan Peak
Pinyon Mountain
Dove Well
Gold Peak
Butterbread
Canyon
Butterbread Well
see MAP 49
Butterbread Peak
see MAP 47
Landers Sch
Toms Hill
see MAP 44

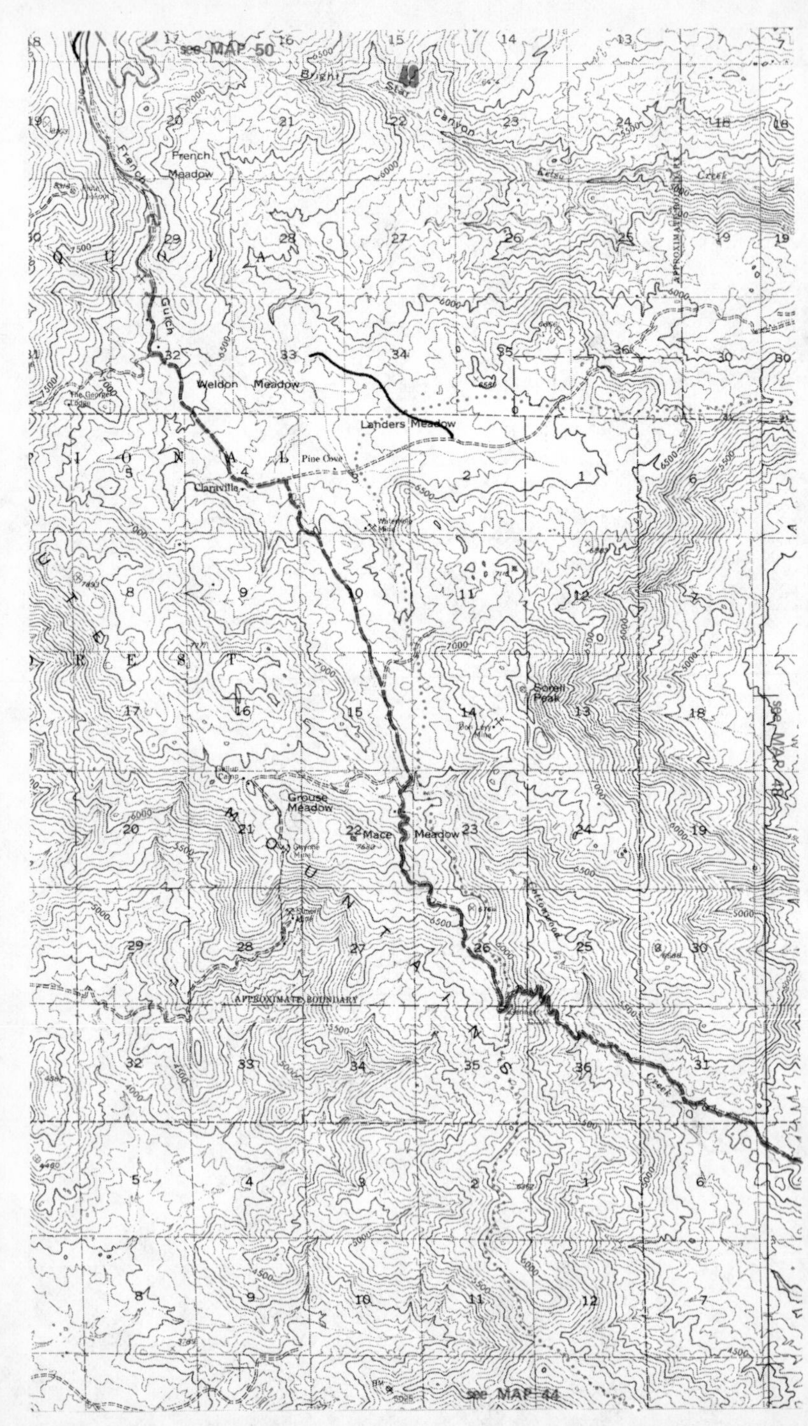

see MAP 50
Bright Star Canyon
French Meadow
French Gulch
Kelso Creek
APPROXIMATE BOUNDARY
Q U Q I A
Weldon Meadow
Landers Meadow
Pine Cove
P I O N A L
Clarraville
Sorell Peak
D R E S T
U T E
Grouse Meadow
Mace Meadow
M O U N T A I N S
Creek
see MAP 48
see MAP 44

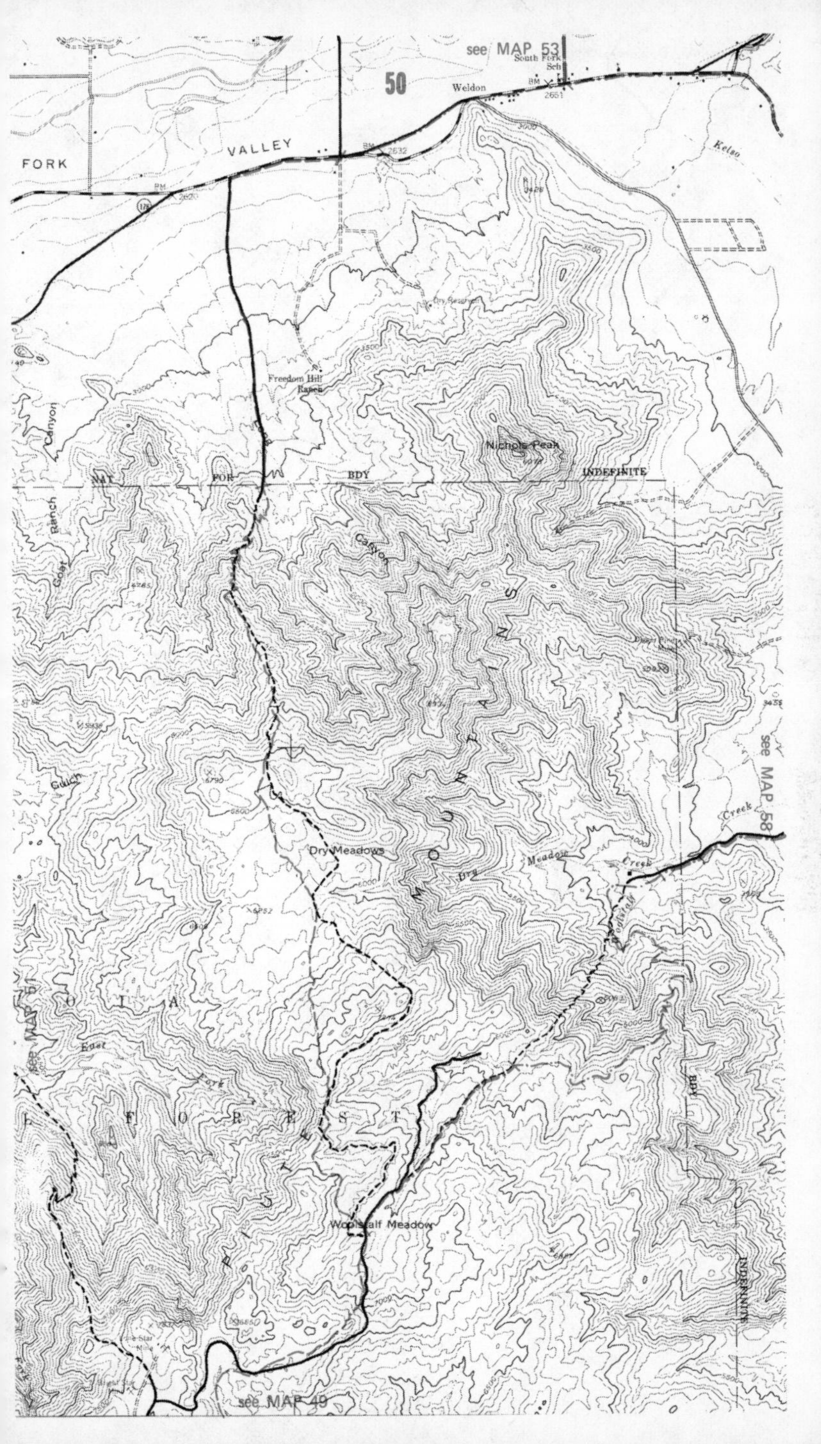
see MAP 53
South Fork Sch
50
Weldon
FORK
VALLEY
Kelso
Freedom Hill Ranch
Canyon
Nichols Peak
NAT
FOR
BDY
INDEFINITE
Ranch
Goat
Canyon
M O U N T A I N S
Gulch
see MAP 58
Creek
Dry Meadows
Meadow
Creek
see MAP 51
O T A
East
Fork
F O R E S T
BDY
Woolstalf Meadow
INDEFINITE
see MAP 49

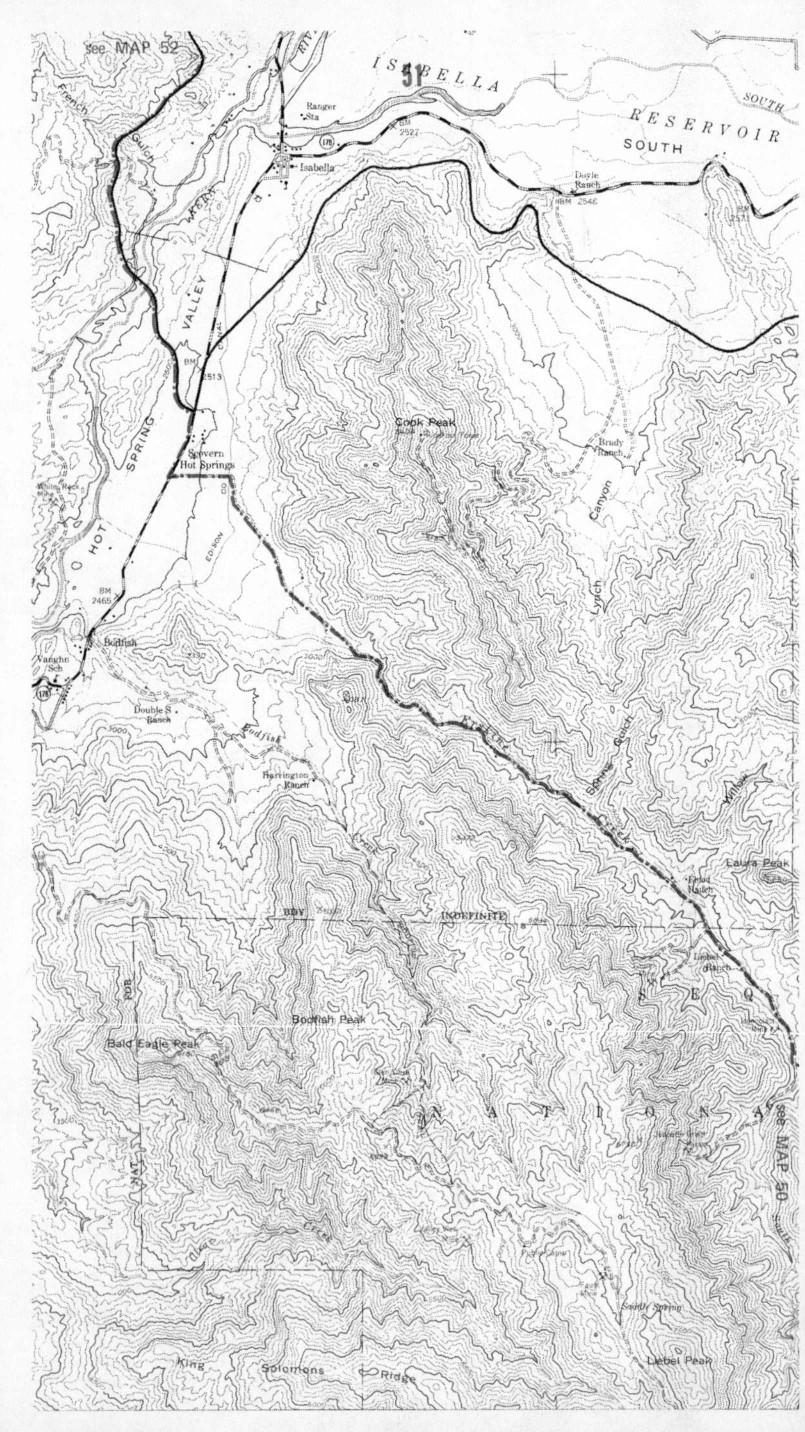

see MAP 52
51
ISABELLA
RESERVOIR
SOUTH
Ranger Sta
Isabella
BM 2527
178
Doyle Ranch
BM 2546
French
Gulch
KERN
VALLEY
CANAL
BM 2513
HOT
SPRING
Severn Hot Springs
EDISON
BM 2465
Bodfish
Vaughn Sch
Double S Ranch
Bodfish
Harrington Ranch
Cook Peak
Brady Ranch
Canyon
Lynch
Spring
Gulch
Erskine
Creek
Willow
Laura Peak
BDY
INDEFINITE
Bodfish Peak
Bald Eagle Peak
S
E
Q
N
A
T
I
O
N
A
see MAP 50
King
Solomons
Ridge
Saddle Spring
Liebel Peak

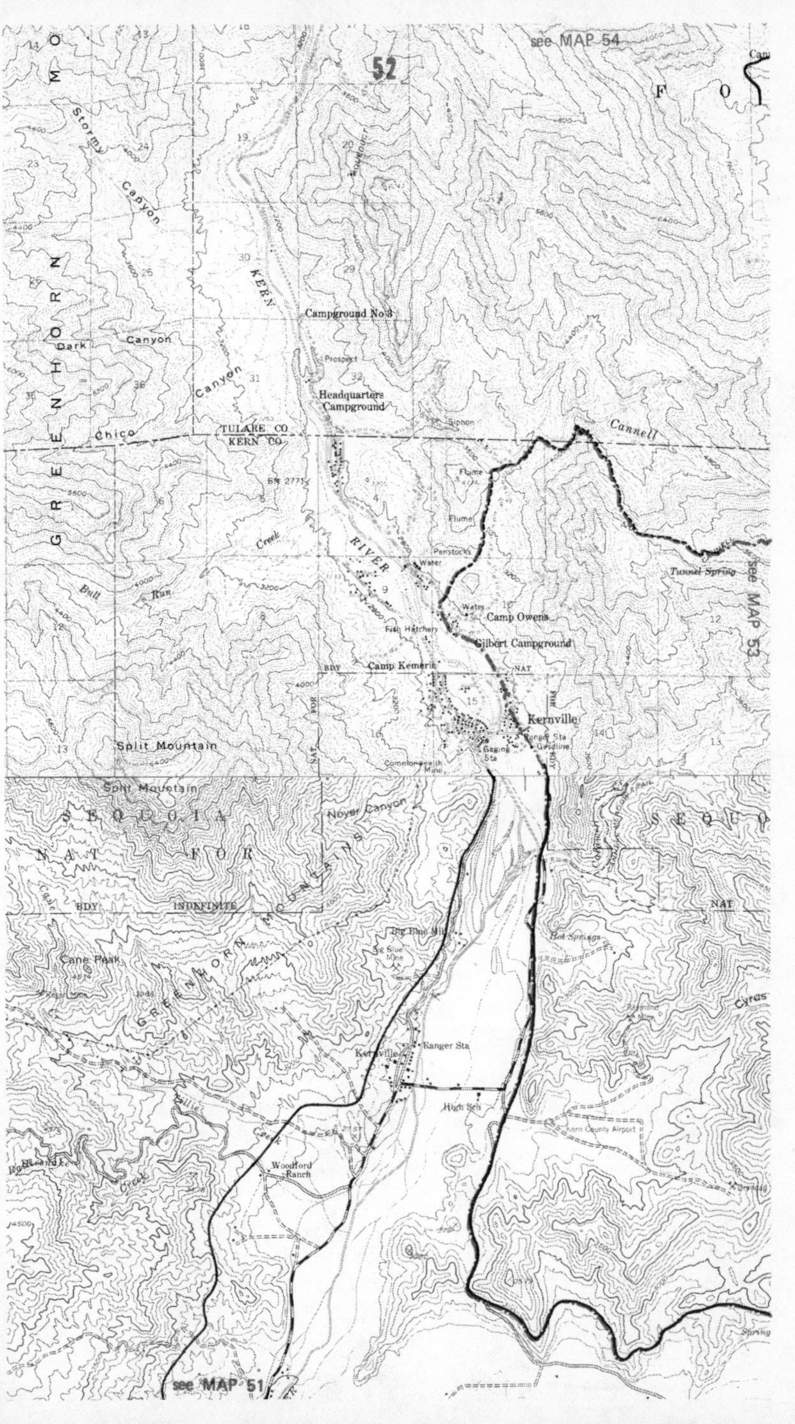

52
see MAP 54
see MAP 53
see MAP 51
GREENHORN MO
Stormy Canyon
Dark Canyon
Chico Canyon
KERN
Campground No 3
Prospect
Headquarters Campground
Siphon
TULARE CO
KERN CO
Cannell
Flume
Penstocks
Water
RIVER
Creek
Bull Run
Camp Owens
Fish Hatchery
Gilbert Campground
Camp Kemeric
Kernville
Ranger Sta
Gasoline
Gaging Sta
Split Mountain
Tunnel Spring
SEQUOIA NAT FOR
BDY INDEFINITE
Noyer Canyon
GREENHORN MOUNTAINS
Cane Peak
Big Blue Mill
Big Blue Mine
Hot Springs
Cyrus
Kernville
Ranger Sta
High Sch
Kern County Airport
Woodford Ranch
SEQUO
NAT

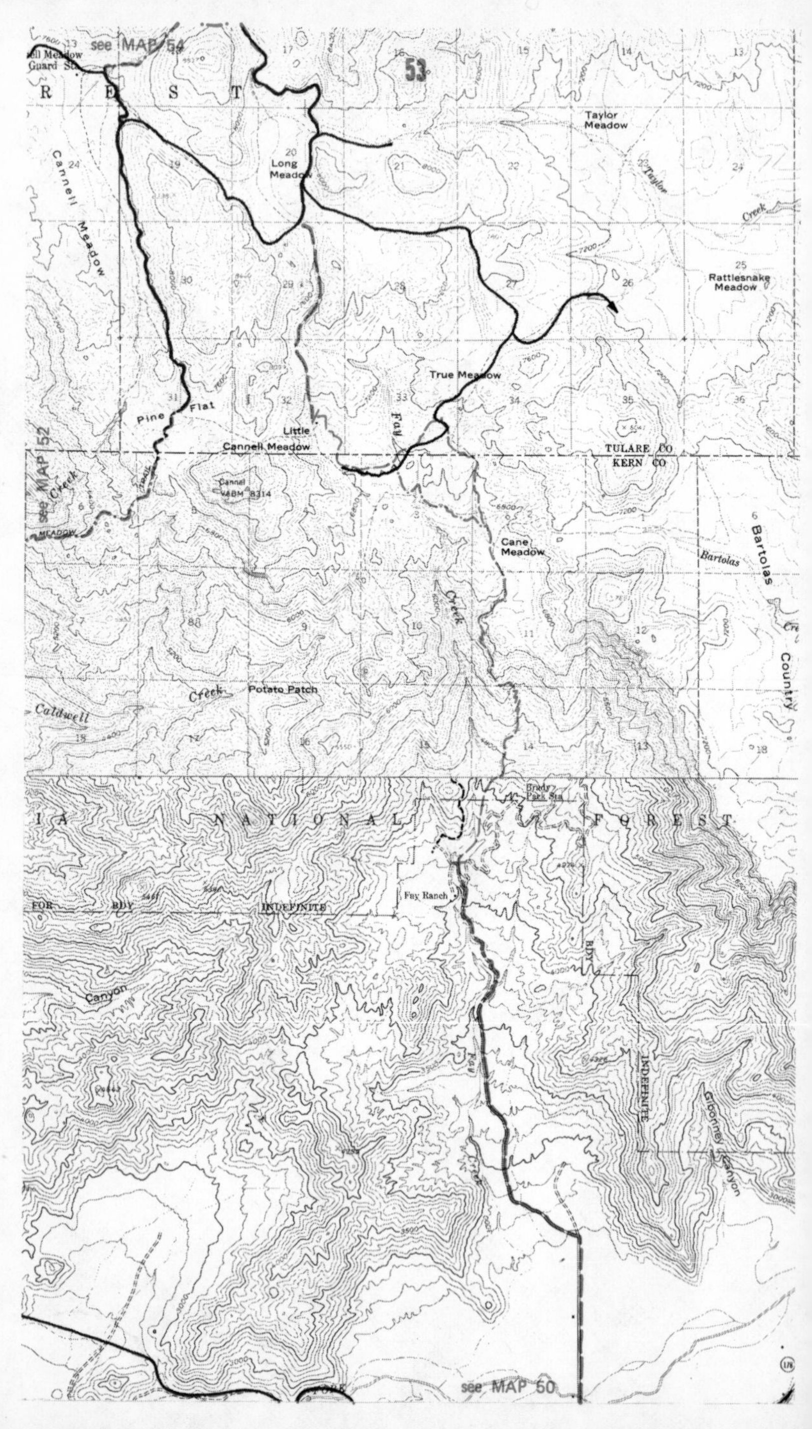

see MAP 54
53
Taylor Meadow
Long Meadow
Cannell Meadow
Rattlesnake Meadow
True Meadow
Pine Flat
Little Cannell Meadow
TULARE CO
KERN CO
see MAP 52
Cane Meadow
Bartolas Country
Potato Patch
Caldwell Creek
Brady Park Sta
NATIONAL FOREST
Fay Ranch
INDEFINITE
Fay Creek
Canyon
Gibonney Canyon
see MAP 50

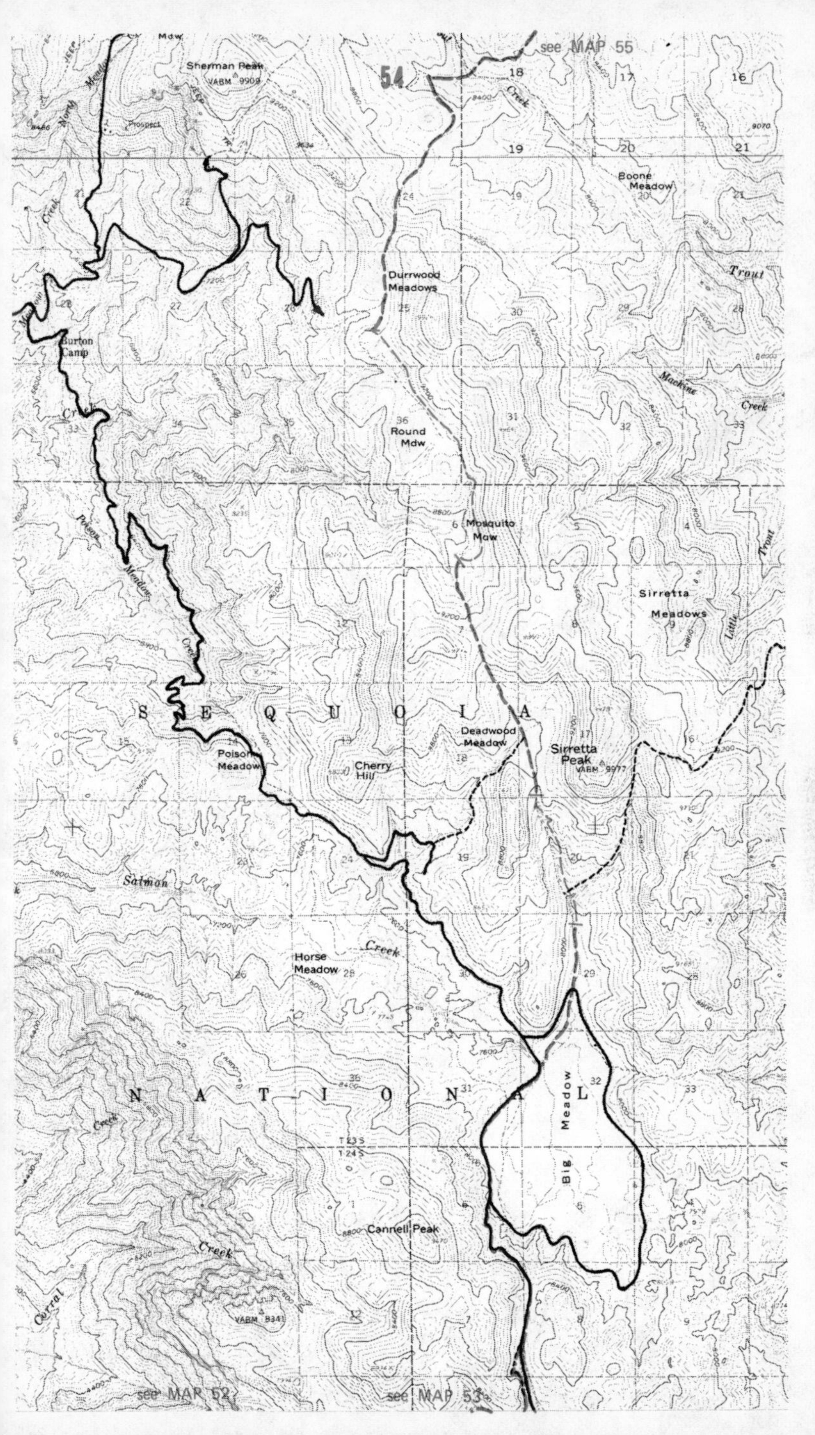

see MAP 55
54
Sherman Peak
VABM 9909
Prospect
Boone Meadow
Trout
Durrwood Meadows
Burton Camp
Round Mdw
Machine
Creek
Mosquito Mdw
Poison
Meadow
Sirretta Meadows
Little
SEQUOIA
Deadwood Meadow
Sirretta Peak
VABM 9977
Poison Meadow
Cherry Hill
Salmon
Creek
Horse Meadow
NATIONAL
Big Meadow
T23S
T24S
Cannell Peak
Corral
VABM 8341
see MAP 52
see MAP 53

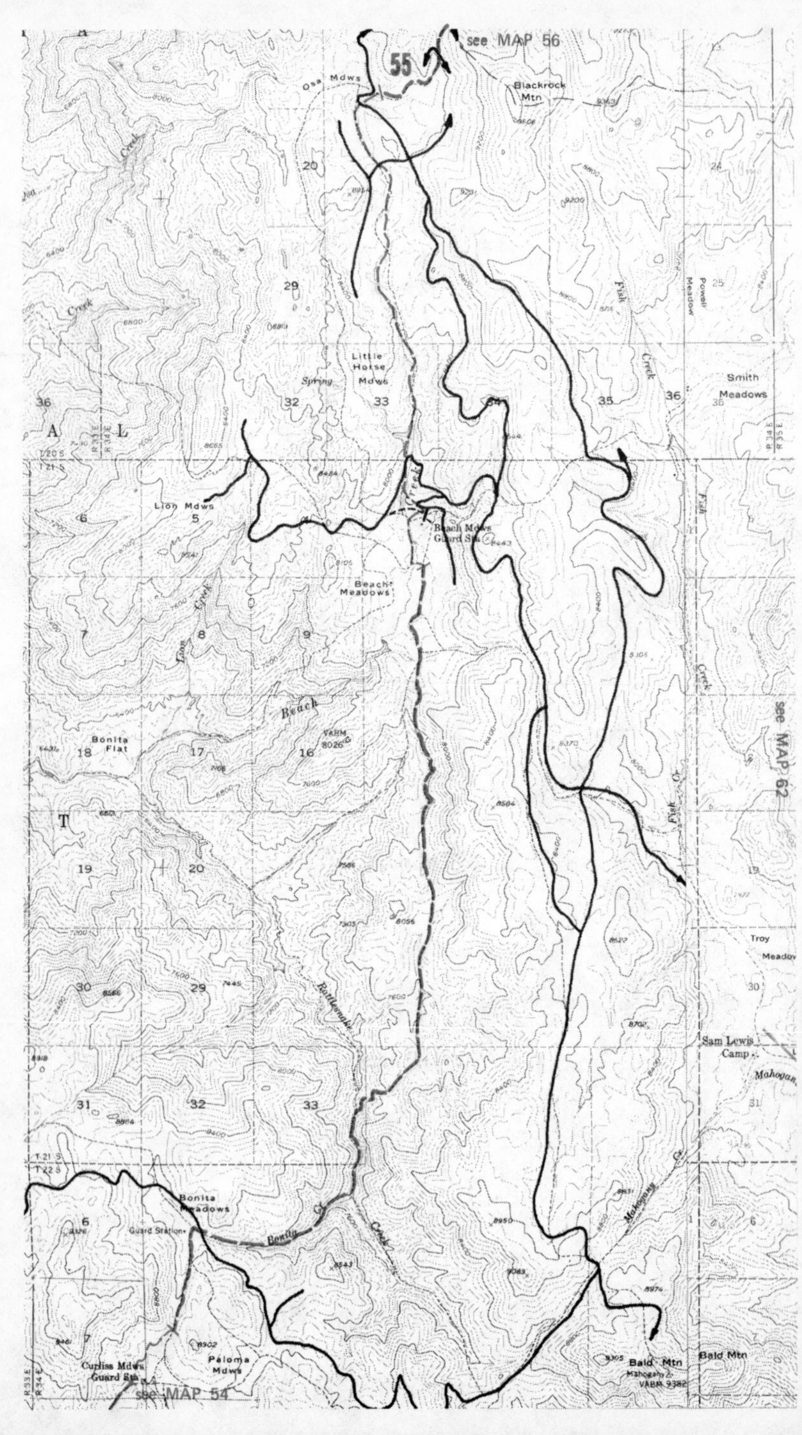

see MAP 56
55
Osa Mdws
Blackrock Mtn
Little Horse Mdws
Spring
Powell Meadow
Fish Creek
Smith Meadows
Lion Mdws
Beach Mdws Guard Sta
Beach Meadows
Lion Creek
Beach
Bonita Flat
VABM 8026
see MAP 62
Troy Meadow
Rattlesnake
Sam Lewis Camp
Mahogany Cr
Bonita Meadows
Guard Station
Bonita Cr
Creek
Paloma Mdws
Curliss Mdws Guard Sta
see MAP 54
Bald Mtn
Mahogany
VABM 9382

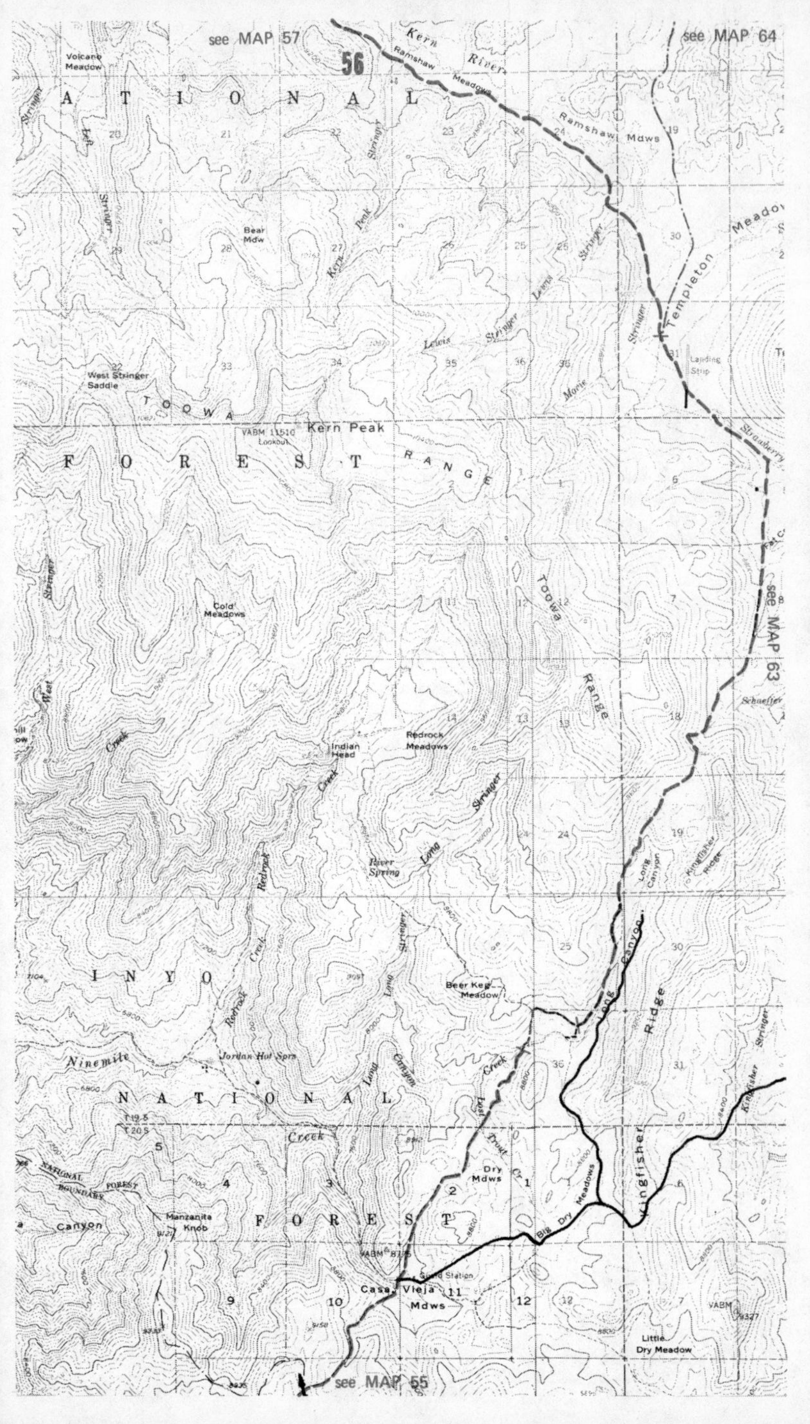
see MAP 57
see MAP 64
56
Kern River
Ramshaw Meadows
Ramshaw Mdws
Volcano Meadow
NATIONAL
Bear Mdw
Templeton Meadow
Landing Strip
West Stringer Saddle
TOOWA
VABM 11510 Lookout
Kern Peak
RANGE
FOREST
Strawberry
Cold Meadows
Toowa Range
see MAP 63
Schaeffer
Indian Head
Redrock Meadows
River Spring
Long Canyon
Kingfisher Ridge
Beer Keg Meadow
INYO
Long Canyon
Ridge
Ninemile
Jordan Hot Sprs
NATIONAL
T 19 S
T 20 S
NATIONAL FOREST BOUNDARY
Dry Mdws
Manzanita Knob
Canyon
FOREST
Big Dry Meadows
Kingfisher
Guard Station
Casa Vieja Mdws
Little Dry Meadow
see MAP 55

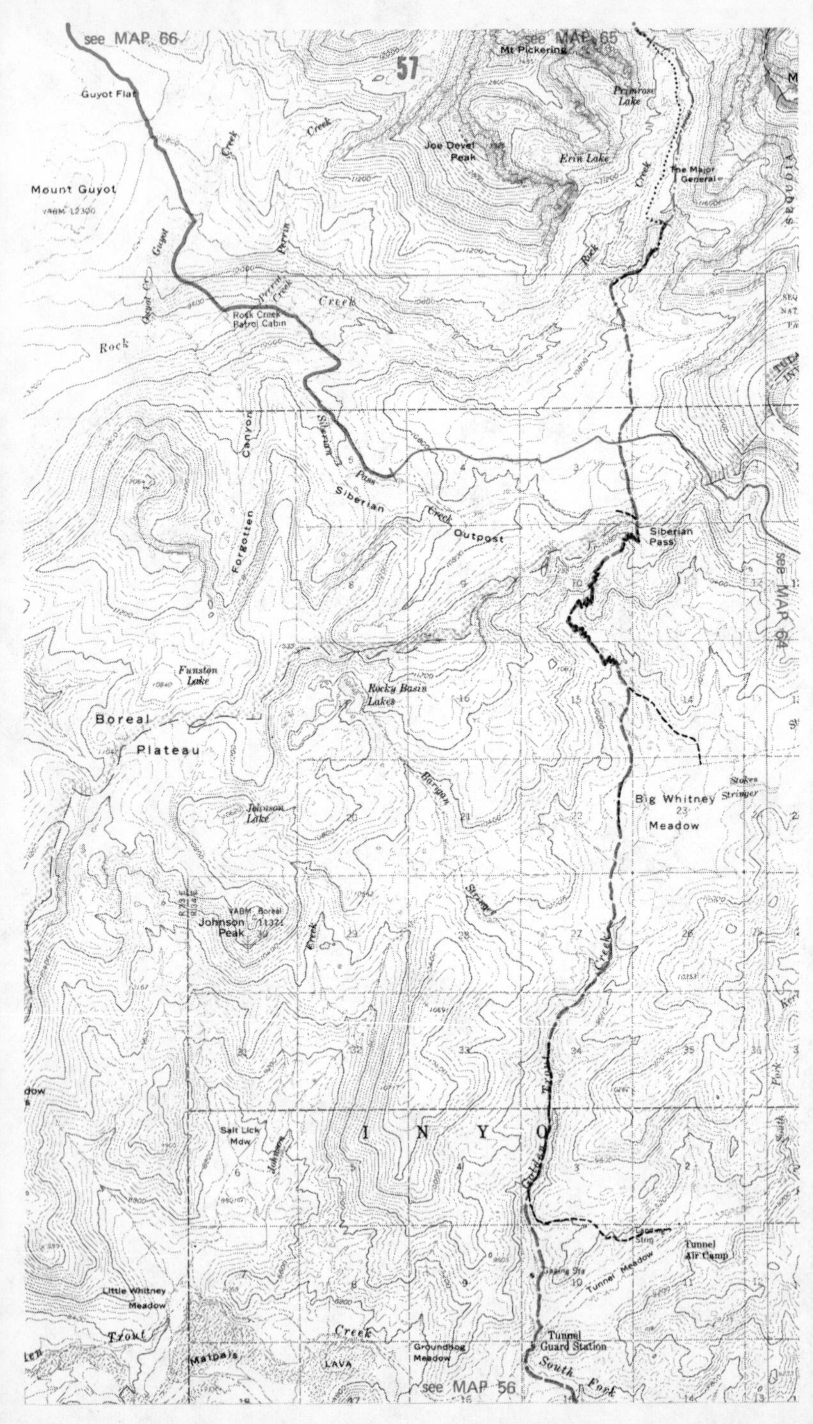

see MAP 66
see MAP 65
57
Mt Pickering
Guyot Flat
Primrose Lake
Joe Devel Peak
Erin Lake
The Major General
Mount Guyot
Rock Creek Patrol Cabin
Siberian Pass
Siberian Creek
Outpost
Siberian Pass
see MAP 64
Forgotten Canyon
Funston Lake
Boreal Plateau
Rocky Basin Lakes
Johnson Lake
Big Whitney Meadow
Stokes Stringer
Johnson Peak
Salt Lick Mdw
I N Y O
Golden Trout Creek
Tunnel Meadow
Tunnel Air Camp
Little Whitney Meadow
Trout Creek
Malpais
LAVA
Groundhog Meadow
Tunnel Guard Station
South Fork
see MAP 56

58
Onyx Peak
Short Canyon
Short Canyon Well
Chollo Well
Cane Well
Cane Canyon
Rocky Point
Skinner Peak
Pinyon Well
Kelso Peak
see MAP 59
see MAP 48

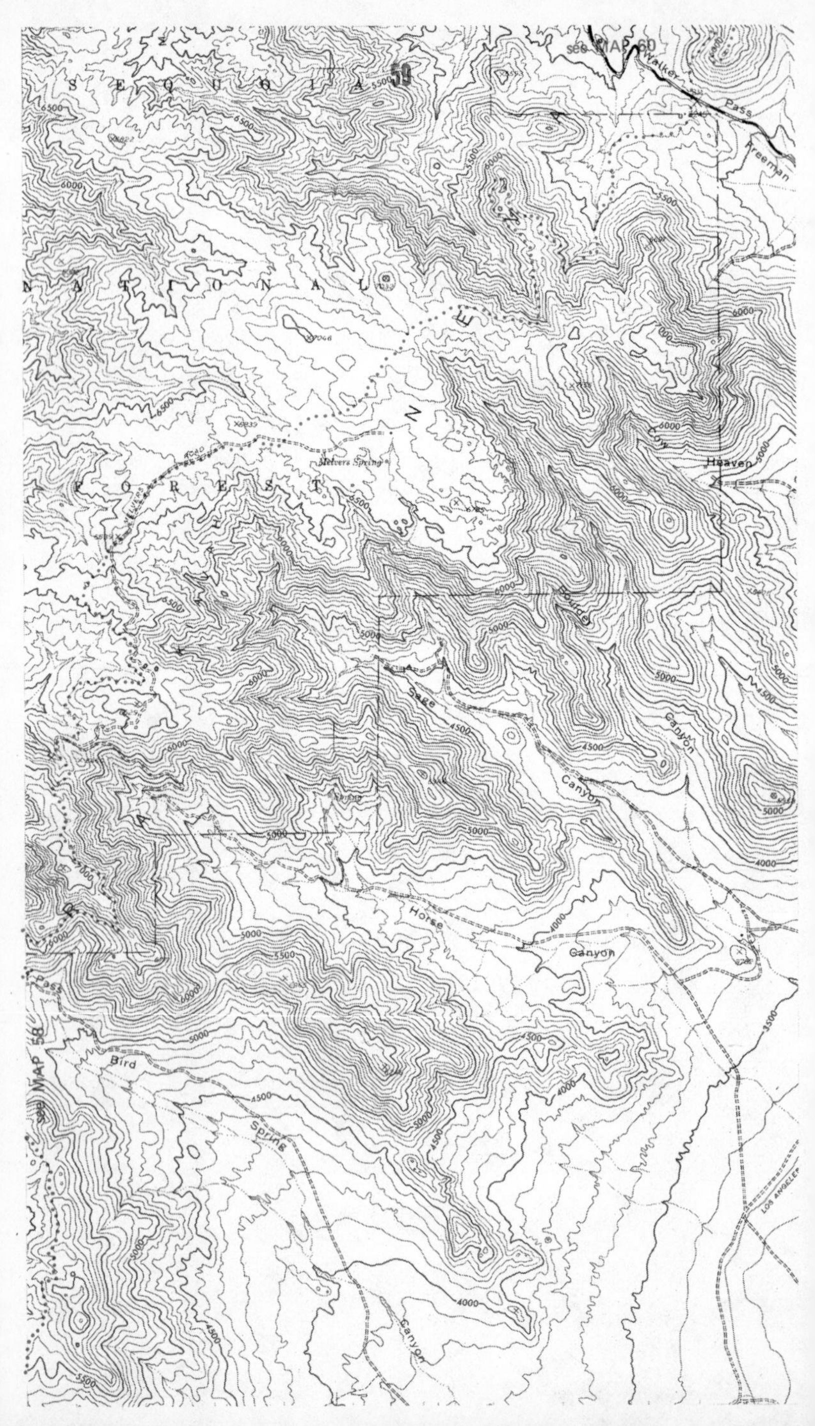
see MAP 60
59
S E Q U O I A
N A T I O N A L
F O R E S T
Walker
Pass
Freeman
Melvers Spring
Cow
Heaven
Boulder
Canyon
Sage
Canyon
Horse
Canyon
Pass
see MAP 58
Bird
Spring
Canyon

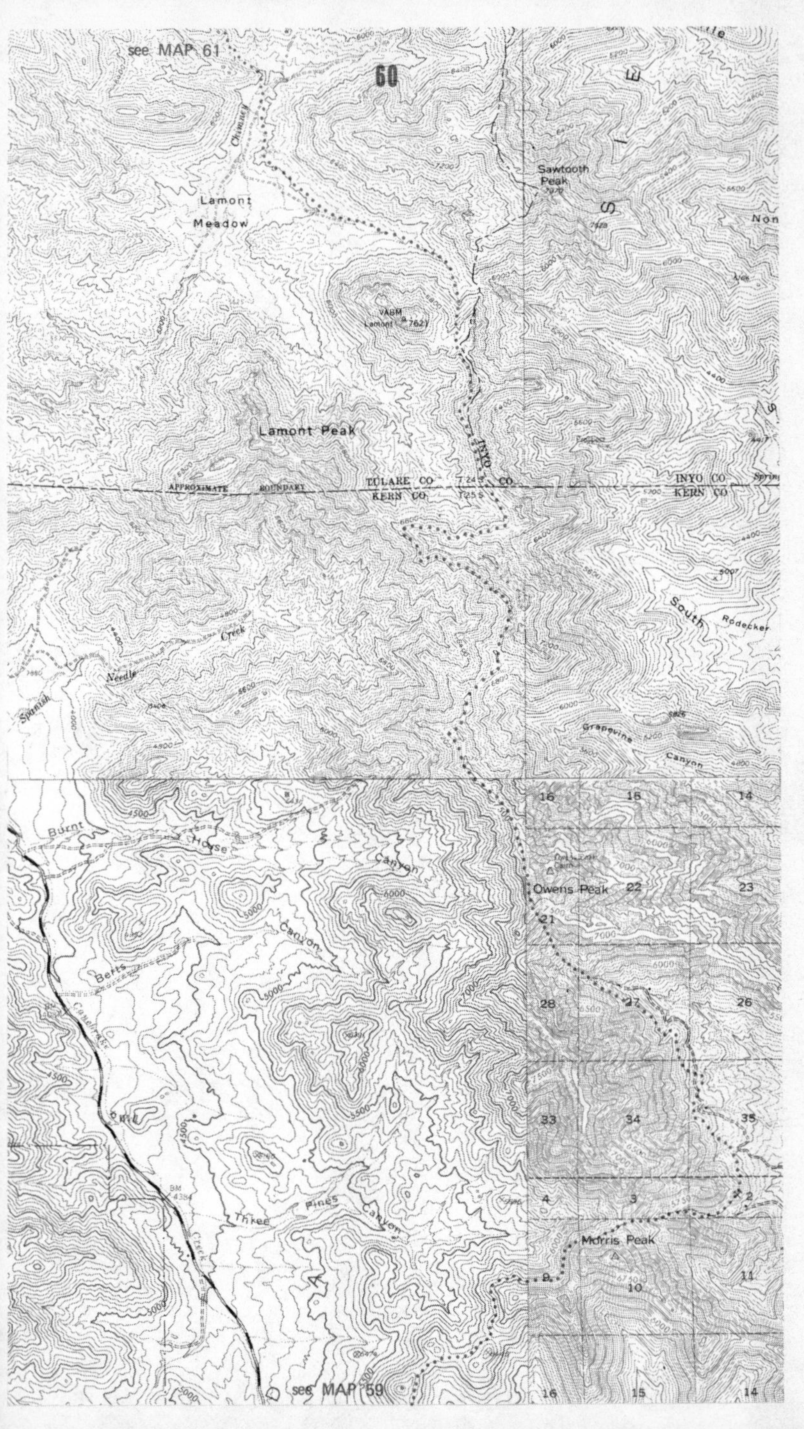

see MAP 61
60
Sawtooth Peak
Lamont Meadow
Chimney
VABM Lamont 7621
Lamont Peak
APPROXIMATE BOUNDARY
TULARE CO
KERN CO
INYO CO
KERN CO
INYO
South Rodecker
Grapevine Canyon
Spanish
Needle Creek
Burnt Horse Canyon
Canyon
Owens Peak
Betts
Three Pines Canyon
Morris Peak
Canebrake Creek
see MAP 59

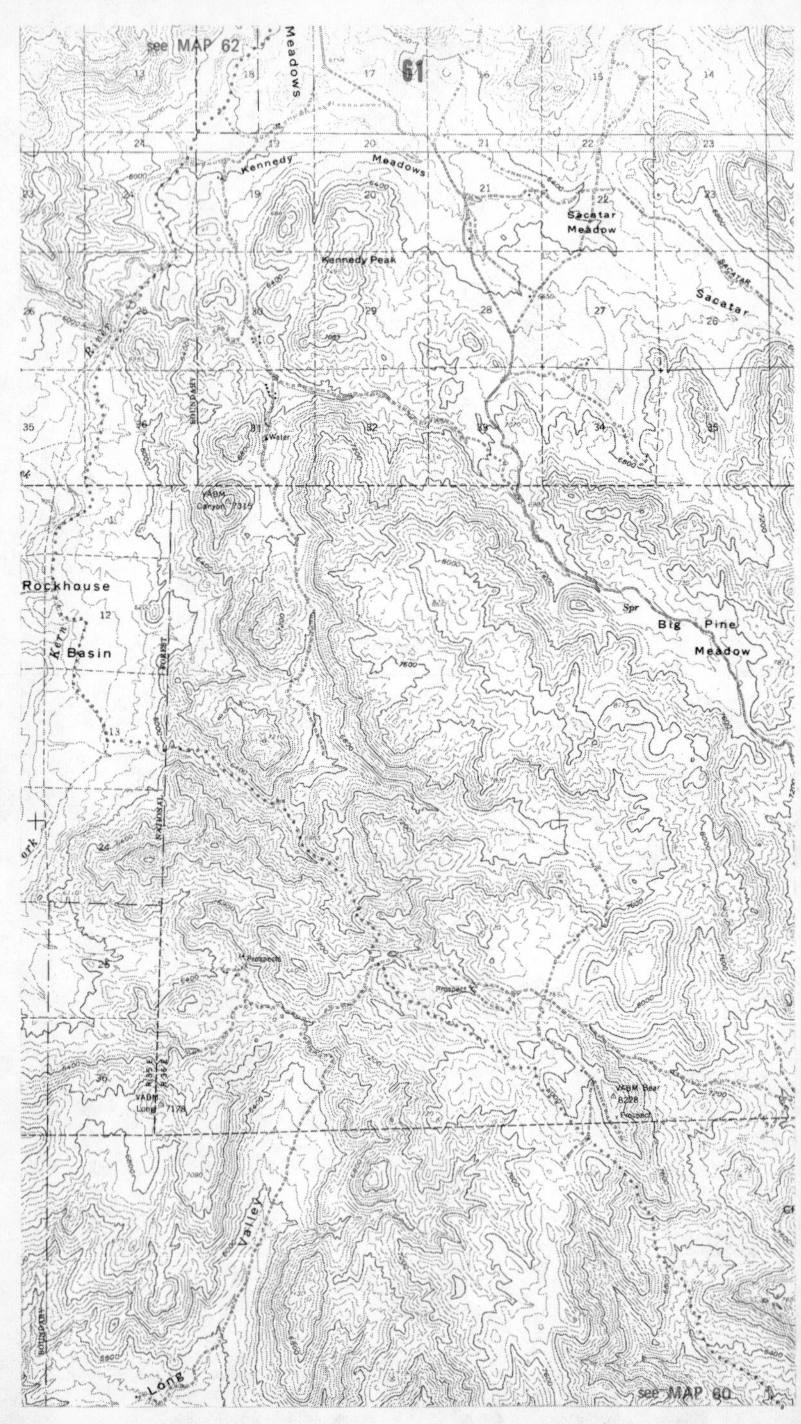

see MAP 62
61
Meadows
Kennedy
Meadows
Sacatar
Meadow
Kennedy Peak
Sacatar
River
BOUNDARY
Water
VABM
Canyon 7315
Rockhouse
Kern
Basin
Spr
Big Pine
Meadow
NATIONAL
FOREST
Prospects
Prospect
VABM Bear
8228
Prospect
VABM
Long 7178
R 35 E
R 36 E
Valley
Long
BOUNDARY
see MAP 60

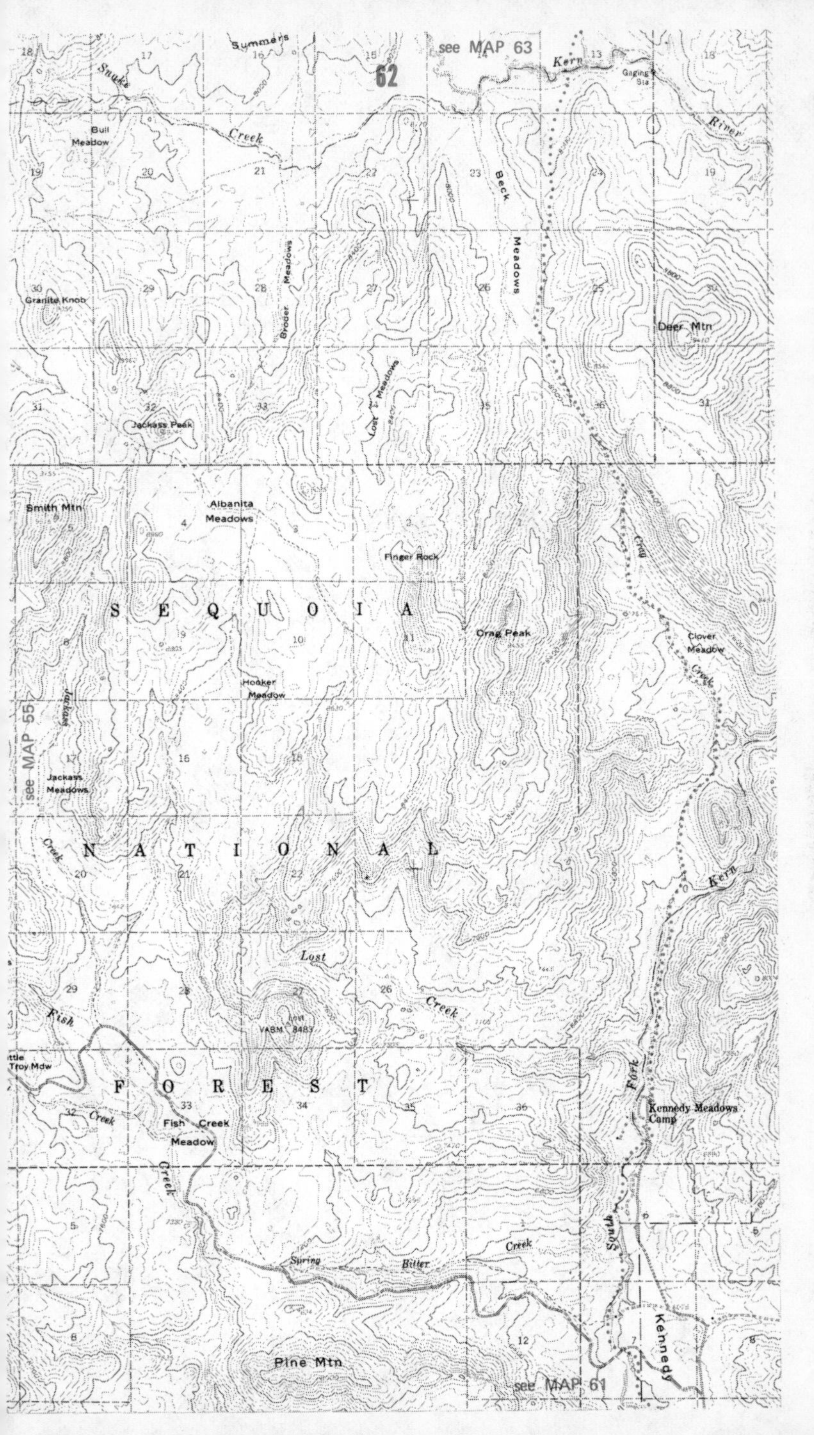

see MAP 63
62
Summers
Snake
Creek
Kern
River
Gaging Sta
Bull Meadow
Beck
Meadows
Broder
Meadows
Granite Knob
Deer Mtn
Lost Meadows
Jackass Peak
Smith Mtn
Albanita Meadows
Finger Rock
Crag
S E Q U O I A
Crag Peak
Clover Meadow
Creek
Hooker Meadow
see MAP 55
Jackass
Jackass Meadows
N A T I O N A L
Creek
Kern
Lost
Creek
Fish
VABM 8483
Troy Mdw
F O R E S T
Fork
Kennedy Meadows Camp
Creek
Fish Creek Meadow
Creek
South
Creek
Spring
Bitter
Kennedy
Pine Mtn
see MAP 61

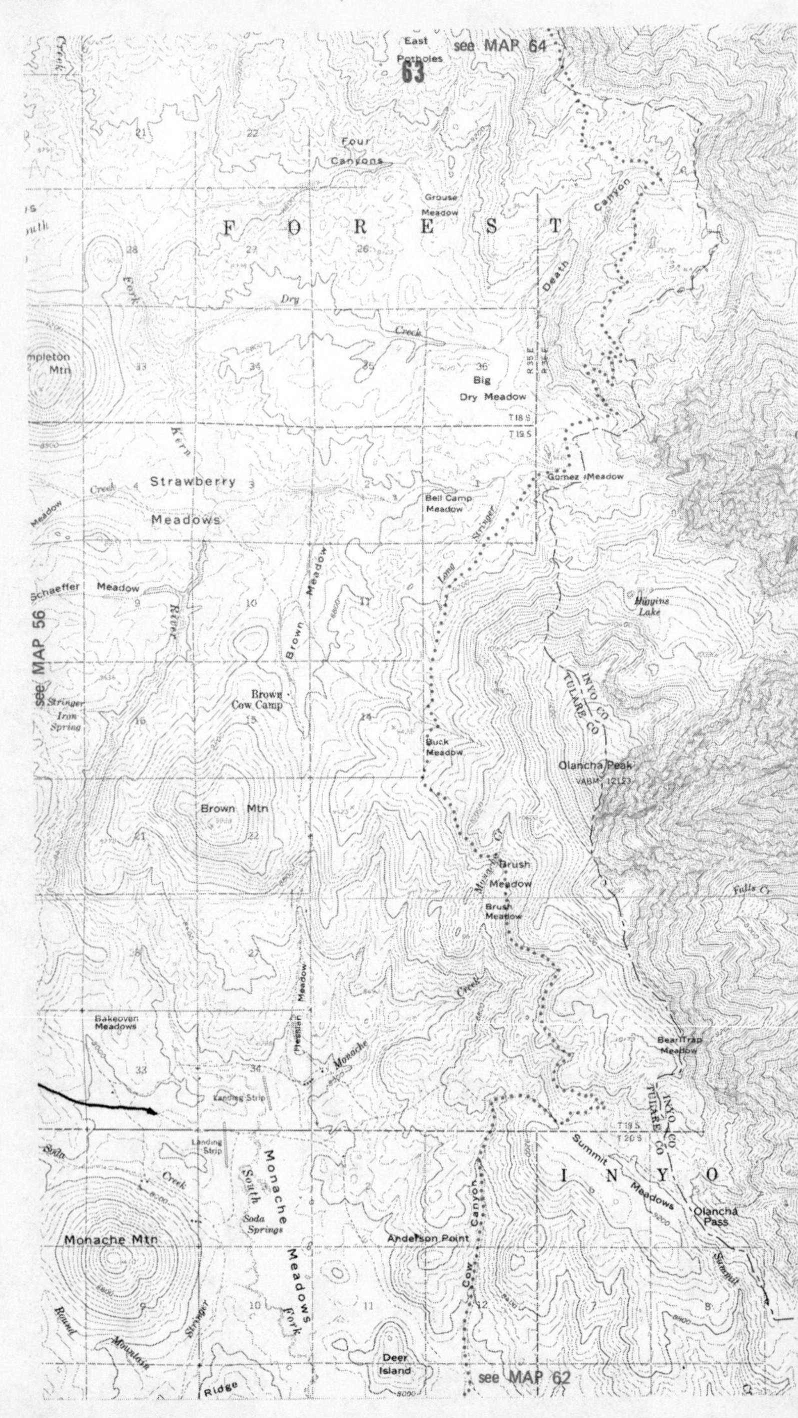

63
see MAP 64
East Potholes
Four Canyons
Grouse Meadow
F O R E S T
Death Canyon
Dry Creek
Big Dry Meadow
T 18 S
T 19 S
R 35 E
R 36 E
Gomez Meadow
Strawberry Meadows
Kern River
Bell Camp Meadow
Long Stringer
Schaeffer Meadow
Brown Meadow
Higgins Lake
see MAP 56
Stringer Iron Spring
Brown Cow Camp
INYO CO
TULARE CO
Buck Meadow
Olancha Peak
VABM 12123
Brown Mtn
Monache Cr
Brush Meadow
Falls Cr
Creek
Bakeoven Meadows
Meadow
Bear Trap Meadow
Monache
Landing Strip
T 19 S
T 20 S
Soda Creek
Monache
South
Soda Springs
Summit Meadows
I N Y O
Cow Canyon
Olancha Pass
Monache Mtn
Anderson Point
Meadows
Fork
Summit
Round
Mountain
Stringer
Deer Island
Ridge
see MAP 62

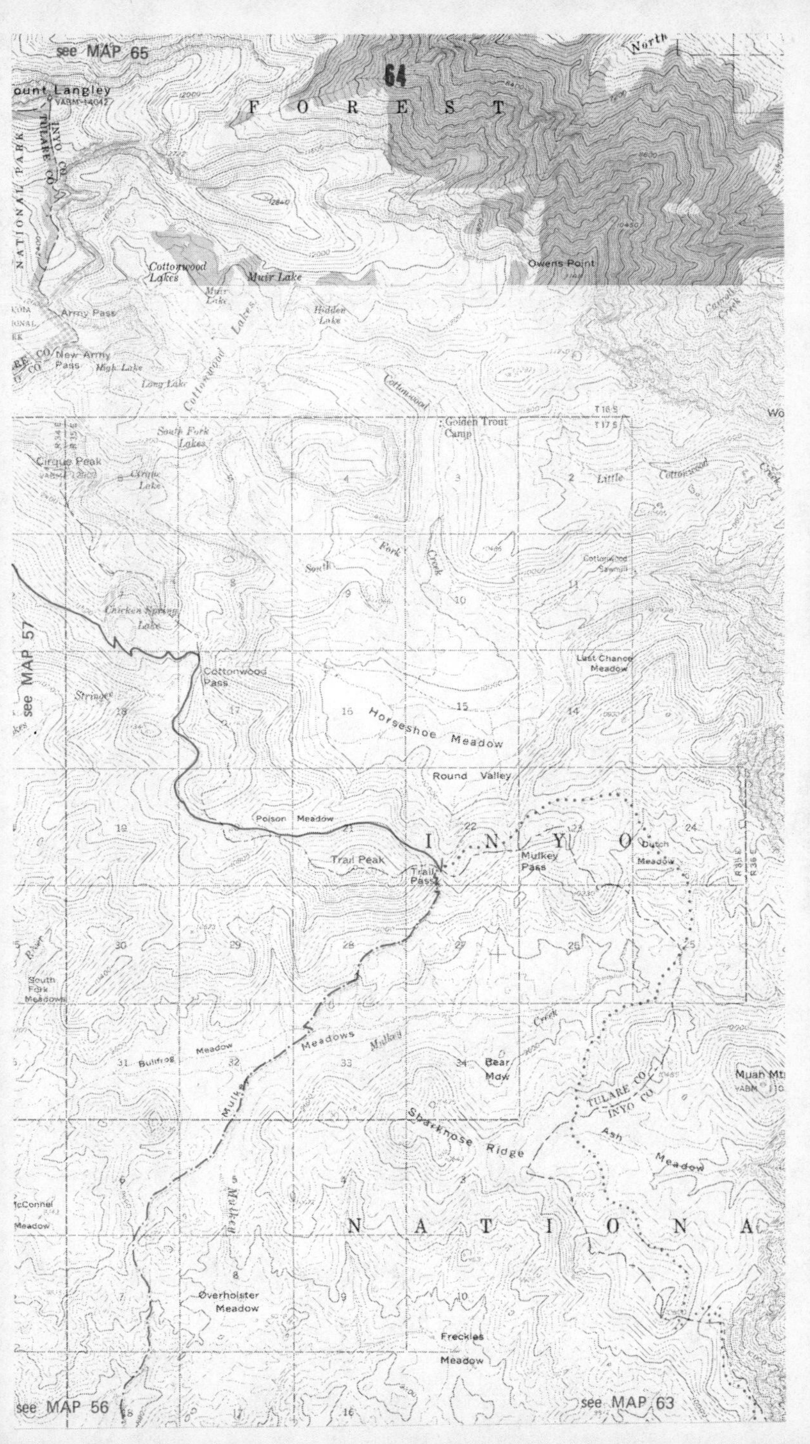

see MAP 65
64
Mount Langley
F O R E S T
North
INYO CO
TULARE CO
NATIONAL PARK
Owens Point
Cottonwood Lakes
Muir Lake
Muir Lake
Army Pass
New Army Pass
High Lake
Long Lake
Cottonwood Lakes
Hidden Lake
Cottonwood
Carroll Creek
Golden Trout Camp
T 16 S
T 17 S
South Fork Lakes
Cirque Peak
Cirque Lake
Little
Cottonwood
Creek
South Fork Creek
Cottonwood Sawmill
Chicken Spring Lake
see MAP 57
Cottonwood Pass
Stringer
Last Chance Meadow
Horseshoe Meadow
Round Valley
Poison Meadow
I N Y O
Trail Peak
Trail Pass
Mulkey Pass
Dutch Meadow
South Fork Meadows
Bullfrog Meadow
Meadows
Mulkey
Creek
Bear Mdw
Muah Mtn
Mulkey
TULARE CO
INYO CO
Sharknose Ridge
Ash Meadow
McConnel Meadow
Mulkey
N A T I O N A
Overholster Meadow
Freckles Meadow
see MAP 56
see MAP 63

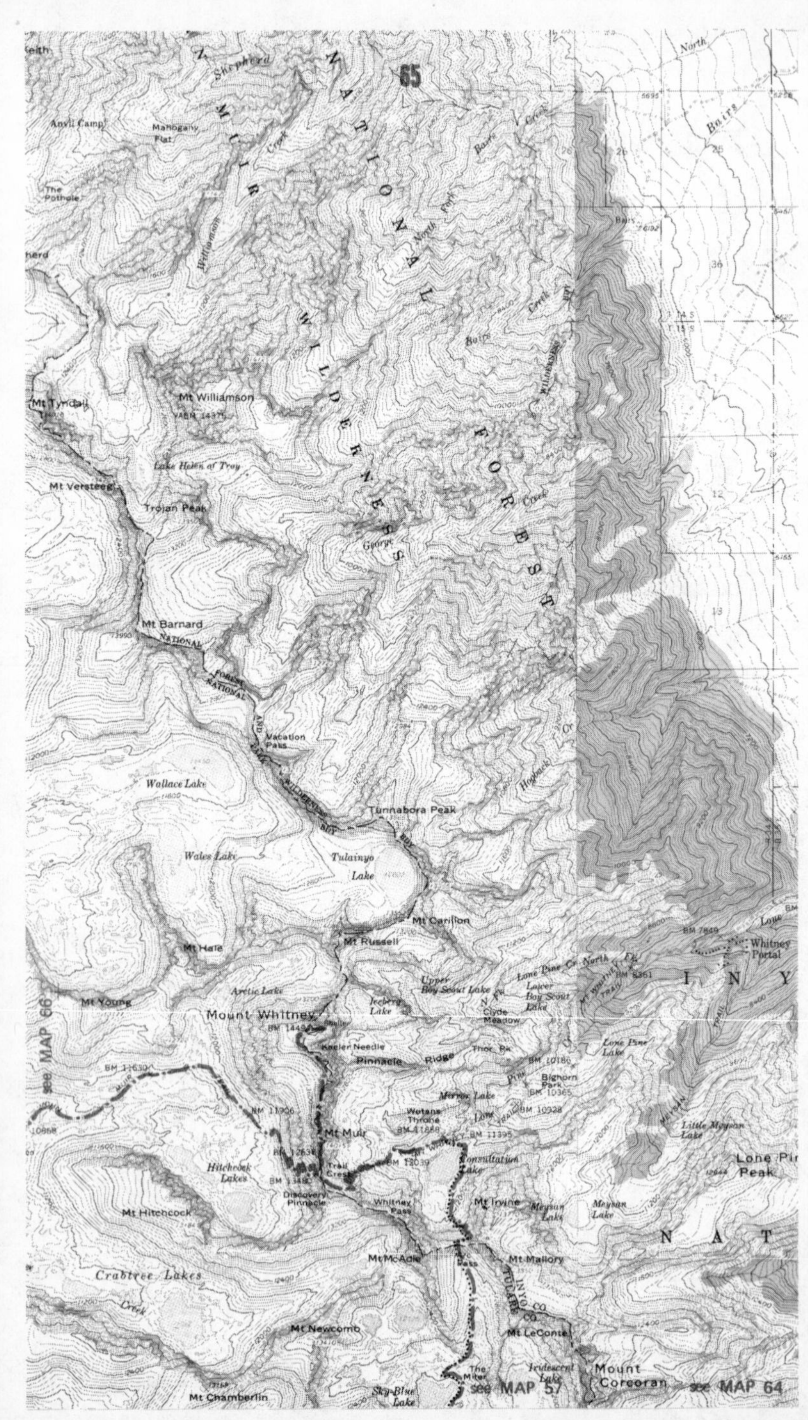

65
Anvil Camp
Mahogany Flat
The Pothole
Mt Tyndall
Mt Williamson
Lake Helen of Troy
Mt Versteeg
Trojan Peak
Mt Barnard
Vacation Pass
Wallace Lake
Tunnabora Peak
Wales Lake
Tulainyo Lake
Mt Carillon
Mt Russell
Mt Hale
Mt Young
Arctic Lake
Mount Whitney
Upper Boy Scout Lake
Iceberg Lake
Lower Boy Scout Lake
Clyde Meadow
Whitney Portal
Keeler Needle
Pinnacle Ridge
Thor Pk
Lone Pine Lake
Bighorn Park
Mirror Lake
Wotans Throne
Mt Muir
Consultation Lake
Hitchcock Lakes
Trail Crest
Discovery Pinnacle
Mt Hitchcock
Whitney Pass
Mt Irvine
Meysan Lake
Little Meysan Lake
Lone Pine Peak
Mt McAdie
Mt Mallory
Crabtree Lakes
Mt Newcomb
Mt LeConte
The Miter
Iridescent Lake
Mount Corcoran
Sky-Blue Lake
Mt Chamberlin
see MAP 66
see MAP 57
see MAP 64

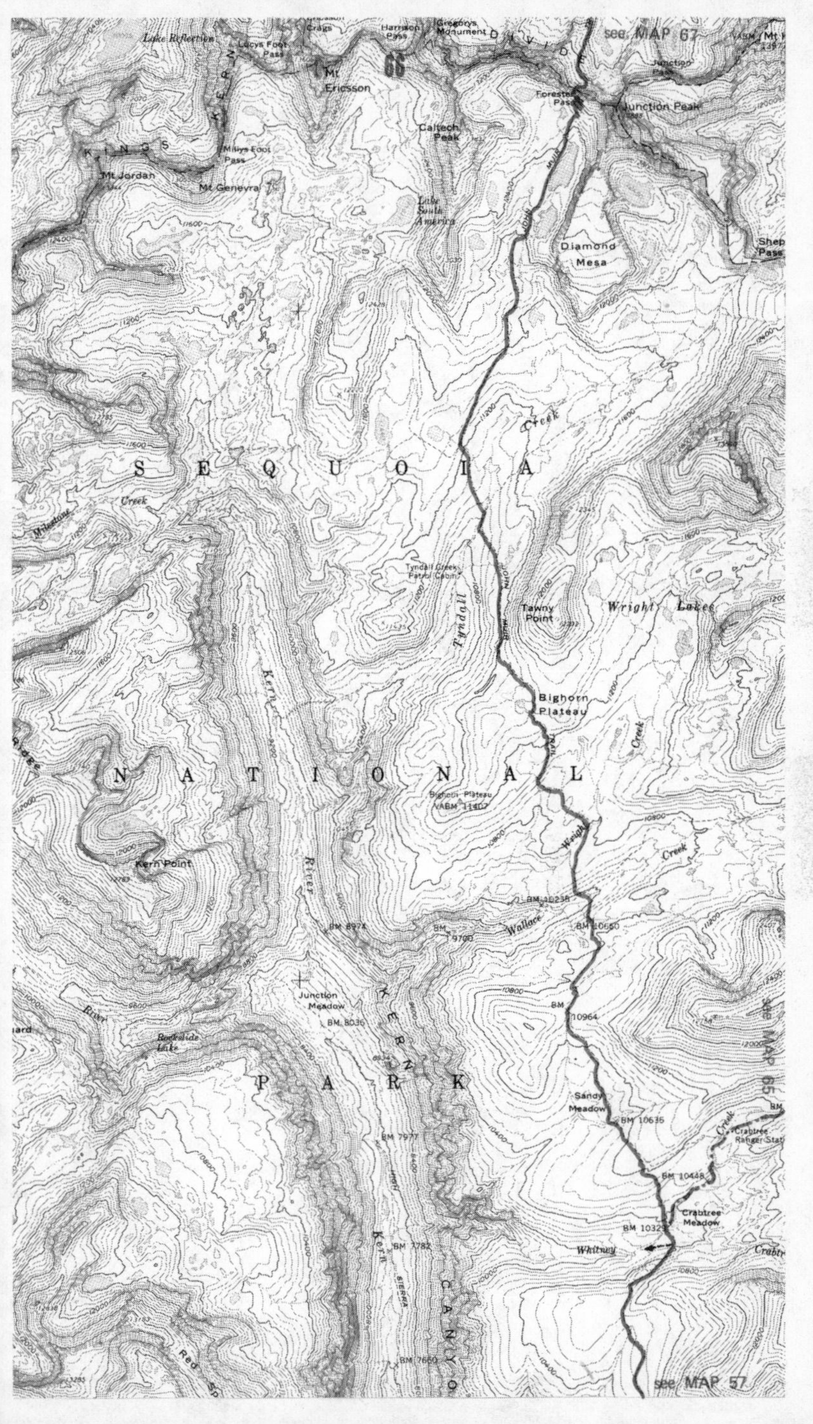

see MAP 67
Lake Reflection
Lucys Foot Pass
Harrison Pass
Gregorys Monument
Mt Ericsson
66
Junction Pass
Forester Pass
Junction Peak
Caltech Peak
KINGS
Millys Foot Pass
Mt Jordan
Mt Genevra
Lake South America
Diamond Mesa
Shep Pass
Creek
SEQUOIA
Milestone
Tyndall Creek Patrol Cabin
Tyndall
Tawny Point
Wright Lakes
Kern
Bighorn Plateau
Creek
NATIONAL
Bighorn Plateau VABM 11407
Wright
Creek
River
Kern Point
BM 10238
Wallace
BM 10650
BM 8974
BM 9700
Junction Meadow
BM 8036
BM
10964
KERN
River
Rockslide Lake
see MAP 65
PARK
Sandy Meadow
BM 10636
Creek
Crabtree Ranger Stat
BM 7977
BM 10448
Crabtree Meadow
BM 10322
Whitney
Crabtr
Kern
BM 7782
CANYON
BM 7660
Red
see MAP 57

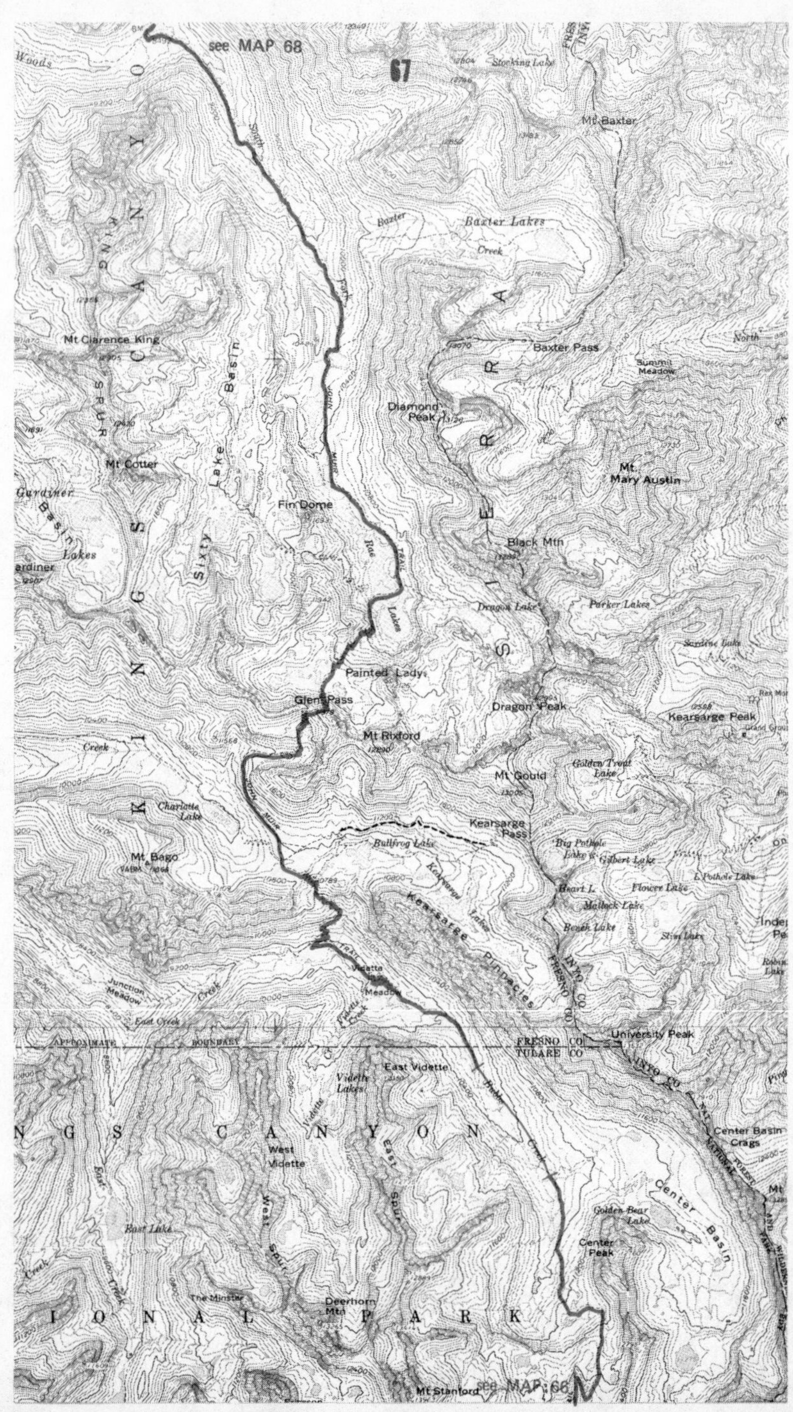

see MAP 68
67
Stocking Lake
Mt Baxter
Baxter Lakes
Baxter Creek
Baxter Pass
Summit Meadow
Mt Clarence King
Diamond Peak
Mt Cotter
Mt. Mary Austin
Gardiner Basin Lakes
Sixty Lake Basin
Fin Dome
Black Mtn
Rae Lakes
Dragon Lake
Parker Lakes
Sardine Lake
Painted Lady
Glen Pass
Dragon Peak
Kearsarge Peak
Mt Rixford
Mt Gould
Golden Trout Lake
Charlotte Lake
Kearsarge Pass
Bullfrog Lake
Big Pothole Lake
Gilbert Lake
Mt Bago
Kearsarge Lakes
Heart L.
Flower Lake
Matlock Lake
Kearsarge Pinnacles
Bench Lake
Slim Lake
Junction Meadow
Vidette Meadow
East Creek
FRESNO CO
INYO CO
TULARE CO
University Peak
APPROXIMATE BOUNDARY
East Vidette
Vidette Lakes
Center Basin Crags
KINGS CANYON NATIONAL PARK
KINGS SPUR
SIERRA
West Vidette
West Spur
East Spur
Center Basin
Golden Bear Lake
Center Peak
East Lake
The Minster
Deerhorn Mtn
Mt Stanford
see MAP 66

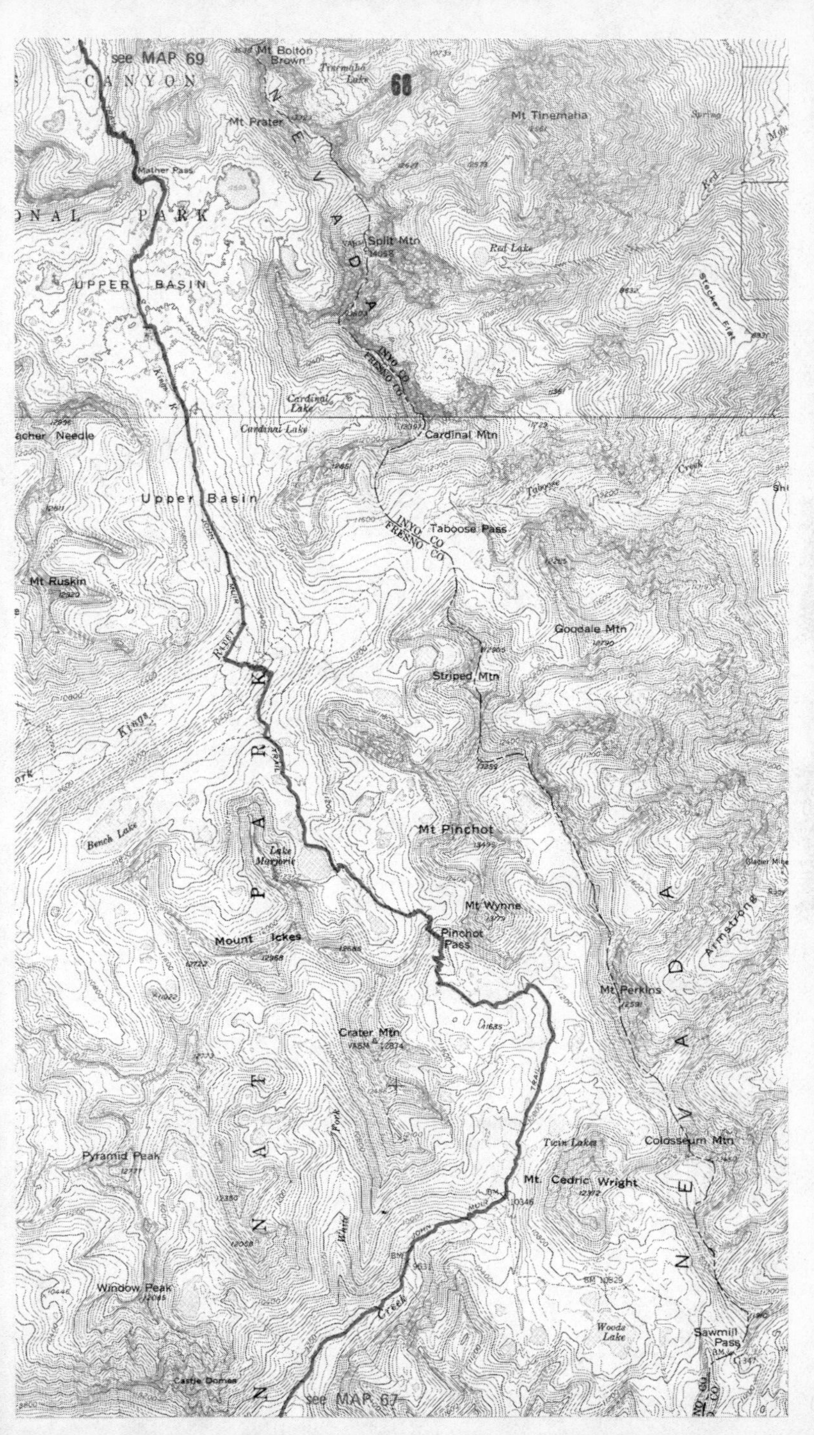

see MAP 69
Mt Bolton Brown
68
CANYON
Mt Prater
Mt Tinemaha
Mather Pass
ONAL PARK
Split Mtn
Red Lake
UPPER BASIN
Stecker Flat
INYO CO
FRESNO CO
Cardinal Lake
Cardinal Mtn
Glacier Needle
Upper Basin
Taboose Pass
Taboose Creek
Mt Ruskin
Goodale Mtn
Striped Mtn
Kings River
Bench Lake
Mt Pinchot
Lake Marjorie
Mt Wynne
Pinchot Pass
Mount Ickes
Armstrong
Mt Perkins
Crater Mtn
Twin Lakes
Colosseum Mtn
Pyramid Peak
Mt. Cedric Wright
Window Peak
Woods Lake
Sawmill Pass
Castle Domes
see MAP 67

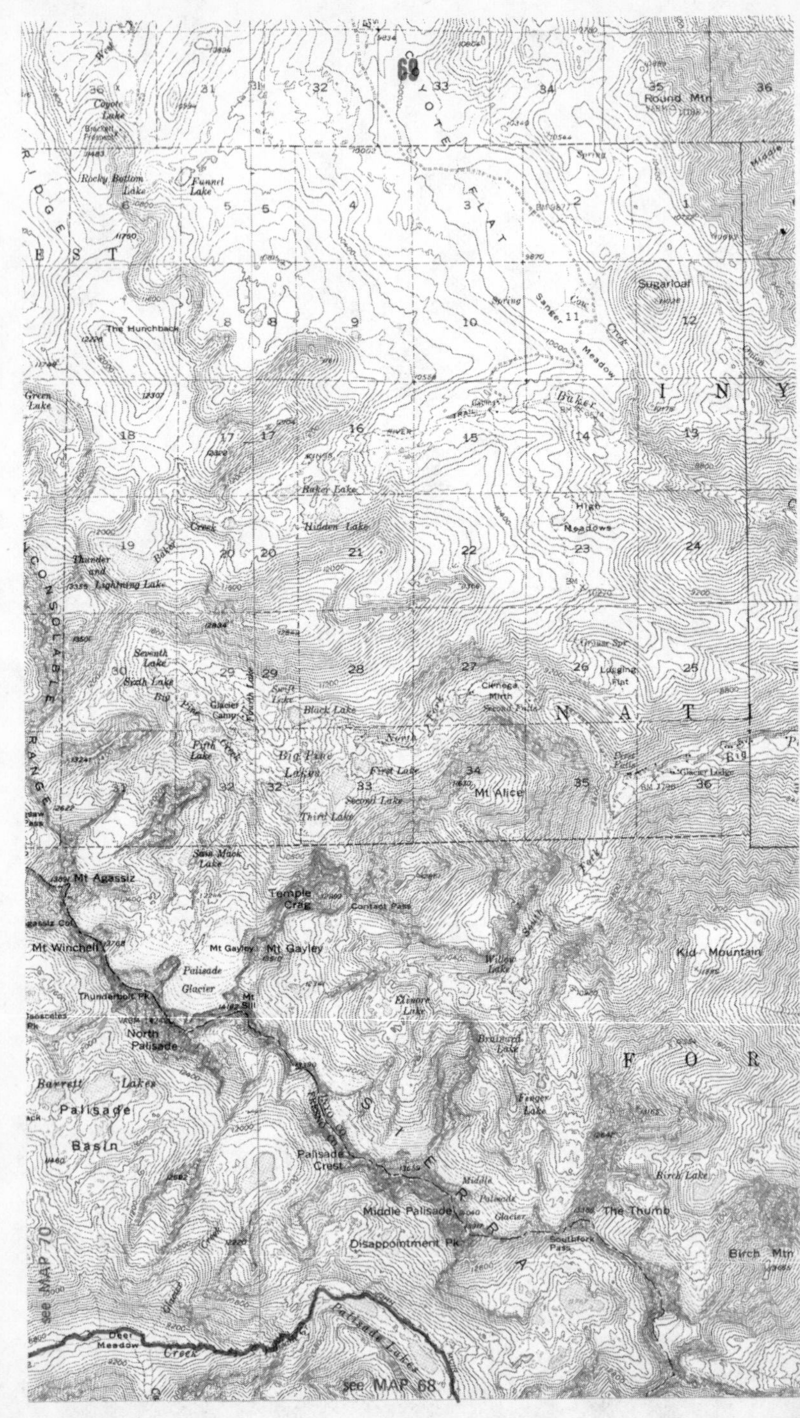

69
Coyote Lake
Rocky Bottom Lake
Funnel Lake
COYOTE FLAT
Round Mtn
Sugarloaf
The Hunchback
Green Lake
Baker Lake
Hidden Lake
High Meadows
Thunder and Lightning Lake
Seventh Lake
Sixth Lake
Glacier Camp
Fifth Lake
Black Lake
Big Pine Lakes
First Lake
Second Lake
Third Lake
Mt Alice
Logging Flat
Glacier Lodge
Sam Mack Lake
Mt Agassiz
Temple Crag
Contact Pass
Mt Winchell
Mt Gayley
Palisade Glacier
Willow Lake
Kid Mountain
Thunderbolt Pk
Mt Sill
North Palisade
Elinore Lake
Brainard Lake
Barrett Lakes
Palisade Basin
Finger Lake
Palisade Crest
Birch Lake
Middle Palisade
Middle Palisade Glacier
The Thumb
Disappointment Pk
Southfork Pass
Birch Mtn
Deer Meadow
Palisade Lakes
see MAP 70
see MAP 68

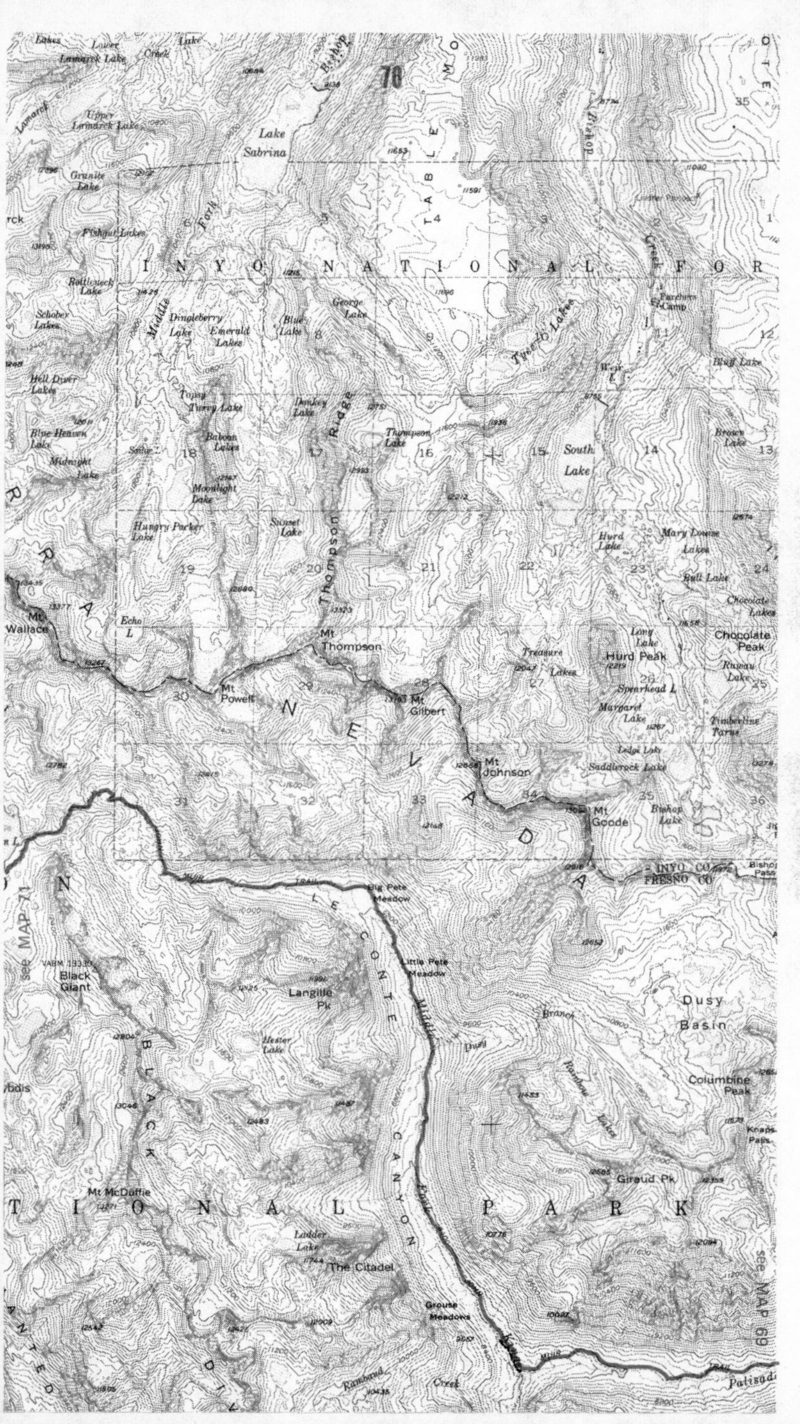

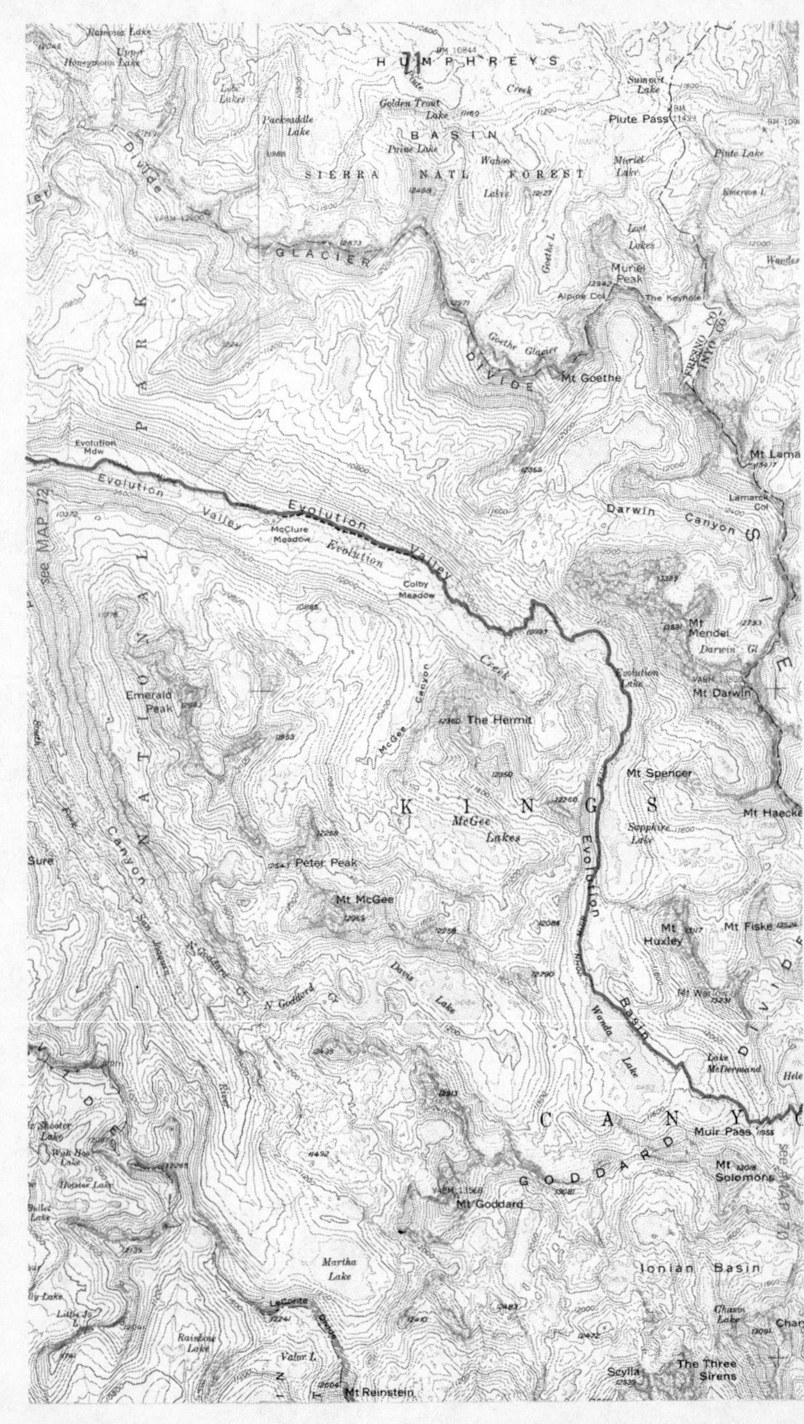
71
HUMPHREYS
BASIN
SIERRA NATL FOREST
Piute Pass
Piute Lake
Summit Lake
Golden Trout Lake
Packsaddle Lake
Paine Lake
Wahoo Lakes
Muriel Lake
Emerson L.
Lost Lakes
Muriel Peak
Alpine Col
The Keyhole
Goethe L.
Goethe Glacier
GLACIER
DIVIDE
Mt Goethe
FRESNO CO
INYO CO
Ramona Lake
Upper Honeymoon Lake
Lobe Lakes
Divide
PARK
Evolution Mdw
Evolution Valley
McClure Meadow
Evolution
Colby Meadow
Darwin Canyon
Lamarck Col
Mt Lamarck
Mt Mendel
Darwin Gl
Mt Darwin
Evolution Lake
Evolution Creek
see MAP 72
NATIONAL
Emerald Peak
McGee Canyon
The Hermit
Mt Spencer
KINGS
McGee Lakes
Sapphire Lake
Mt Haeckel
Peter Peak
Mt McGee
Canyon
San Joaquin
N Goddard Cr
Davis Lake
Mt Huxley
Mt Fiske
Mt Warlow
Wanda Lake
Evolution Basin
Lake McDermand
CANYON
Muir Pass
Mt Solomons
GODDARD
see MAP 70
Mt Goddard
Martha Lake
Ionian Basin
LeConte Divide
Rainbow Lake
Valor L.
Chasm Lake
Scylla
The Three Sirens
Mt Reinstein
River

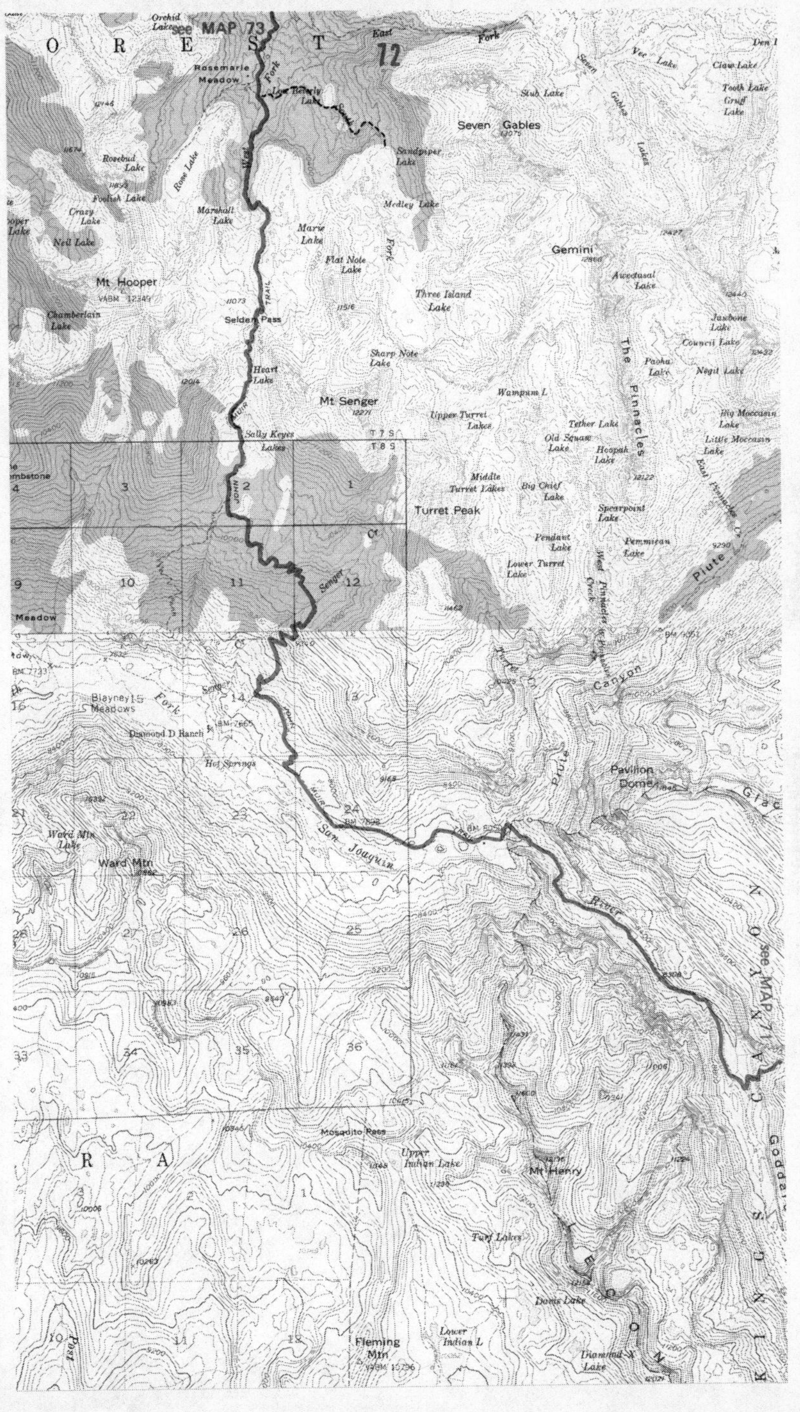
see MAP 73
72
see MAP 71
Rosemarie Meadow
Seven Gables
Sandpiper Lake
Medley Lake
Marie Lake
Flat Note Lake
Gemini
Mt Hooper
Chamberlain Lake
Selden Pass
Three Island Lake
Heart Lake
Sharp Note Lake
Mt Senger
Sally Keyes Lakes
Turret Peak
The Pinnacles
Rosebud Lake
Rose Lake
Marshall Lake
Crazy Lake
Nell Lake
Foolish Lake
Stub Lake
Vee Lake
Claw Lake
Tooth Lake
Gruff Lake
Awetasal Lake
Jawbone Lake
Council Lake
Pasha Lake
Negit Lake
Wampum L
Upper Turret Lakes
Tether Lake
Old Squaw Lake
Hoopah Lake
Big Moccasin Lake
Little Moccasin Lake
Middle Turret Lakes
Big Chief Lake
Spearpoint Lake
Pendant Lake
Pemmican Lake
Lower Turret Lake
Piute Canyon
Pavilion Dome
Blayney Meadows
Diamond D Ranch
Hot Springs
San Joaquin River
Ward Mtn Lake
Ward Mtn
Mosquito Pass
Upper Indian Lake
Mt Henry
Fury Lakes
Doris Lake
Fleming Mtn
Lower Indian L
Diamond X Lake
JOHN MUIR TRAIL

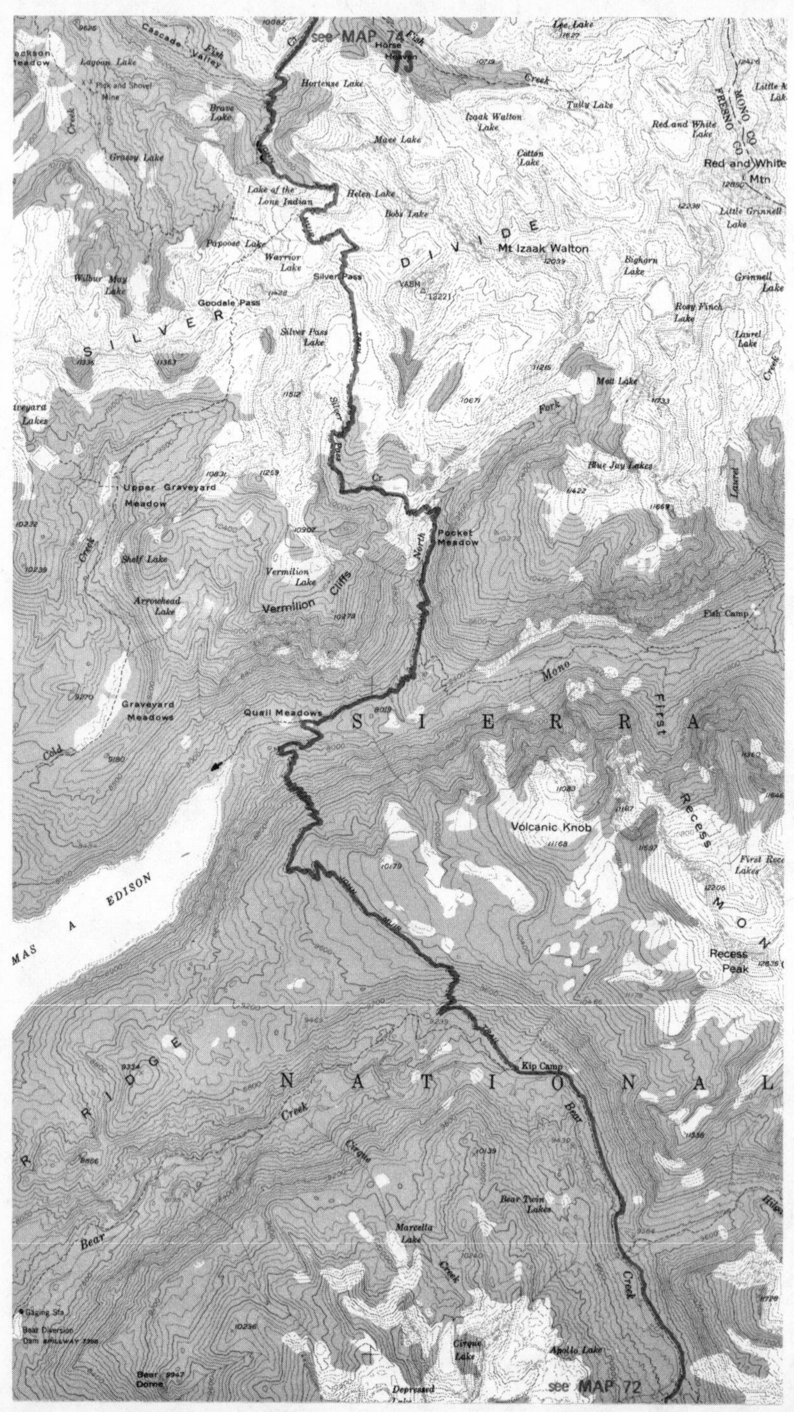

see MAP 74
73
Cascade Valley
Fish Creek
Lagoon Lake
Pick and Shovel Mine
Hortense Lake
Horse Heaven
Lee Lake
Tully Lake
Izaak Walton Lake
Red and White Lake
Little Mono Lake
FRESNO CO
MONO CO
Brave Lake
Grassy Lake
Mace Lake
Cotton Lake
Red and White Mtn
Lake of the Lone Indian
Helen Lake
Bobs Lake
Little Grinnell Lake
Papoose Lake
Warrior Lake
SILVER DIVIDE
Mt Izaak Walton
Bighorn Lake
Wilbur May Lake
Silver Pass
Goodale Pass
Grinnell Lake
Rosy Finch Lake
Silver Pass Lake
Laurel Lake
Mott Lake
Graveyard Lakes
Silver Pass Cr
Fork
Blue Jay Lakes
Upper Graveyard Meadow
Pocket Meadow
North
Shelf Lake
Vermilion Lake
Vermilion Cliffs
Arrowhead Lake
Fish Camp
Mono
Graveyard Meadows
Quail Meadows
SIERRA
First Recess
Volcanic Knob
First Recess Lakes
MONO
EDISON
LAKE THOMAS A EDISON
Recess Peak
Kip Camp
RIDGE
NATIONAL
Bear Creek
Cirque
Bear Twin Lakes
Marcella Lake
Gaging Sta
Bear Diversion Dam SPILLWAY 7350
Cirque Lake
Apollo Lake
Bear Dome
Depressed Lake
see MAP 72

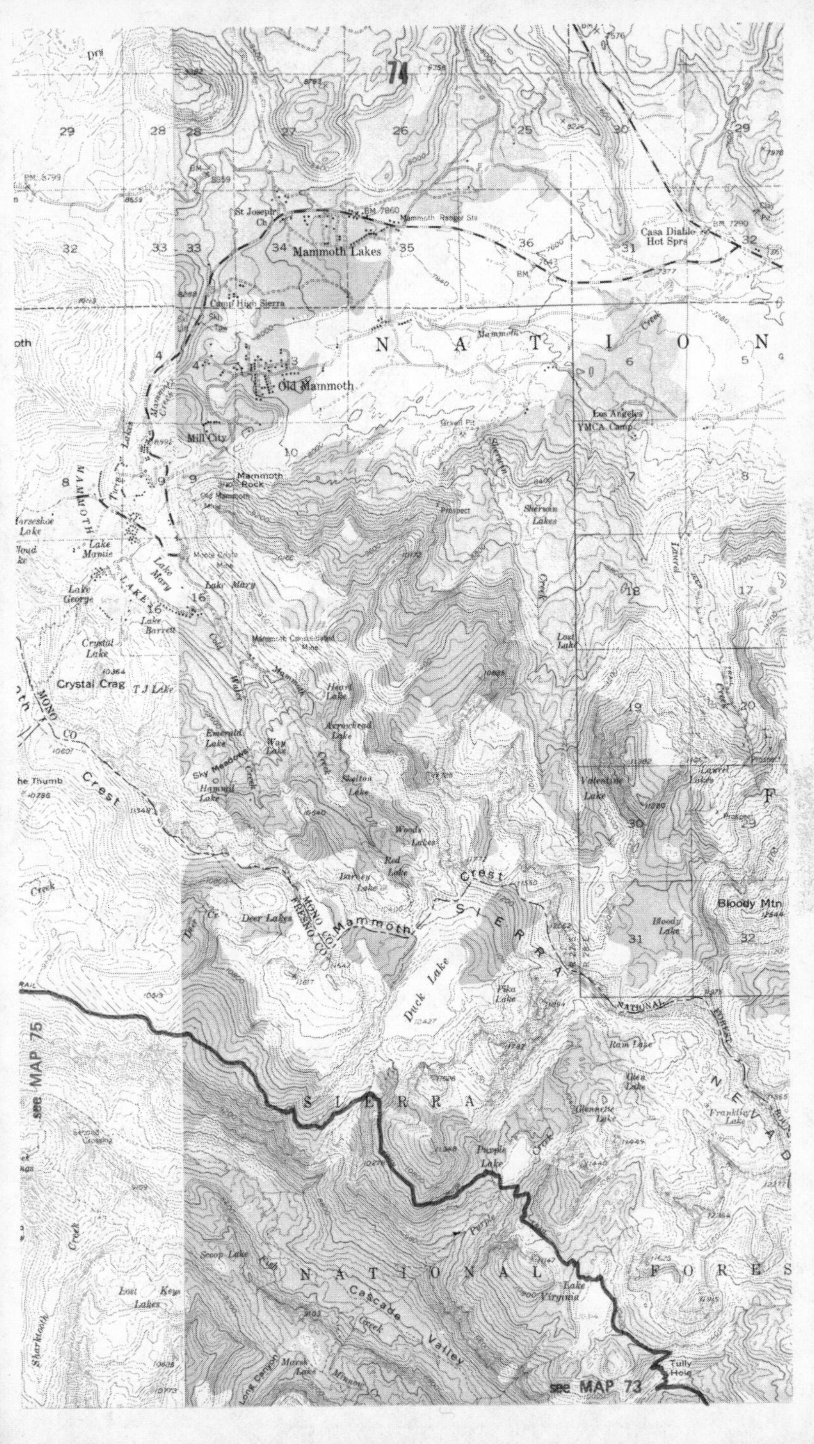

74
Mammoth Lakes
Old Mammoth
Casa Diablo Hot Sprs
Camp High Sierra
Mill City
Mammoth Rock
Lake Mary
Lake George
Lake Mamie
Horseshoe Lake
Crystal Lake
Crystal Crag
T J Lake
Lake Barrett
Emerald Lake
Sky Meadows
Hammil Lake
Way Lake
Arrowhead Lake
Heart Lake
Skelton Lake
Woods Lakes
Red Lake
Barney Lake
Deer Lakes
Duck Lake
Pika Lake
Sherwin Lakes
Lost Lake
Valentine Lake
Laurel Lakes
Bloody Mtn
Bloody Lake
Los Angeles YMCA Camp
Ram Lake
Glen Lake
Glennette Lake
Franklin Lake
Purple Lake
Lake Virginia
Tully Hole
Scoop Lake
Cascade Valley
Marsh Lake
Lost Keys Lakes
Long Canyon
The Thumb
MONO CO
FRESNO CO
Mammoth Crest
SIERRA
NATIONAL FOREST
see MAP 75
see MAP 73

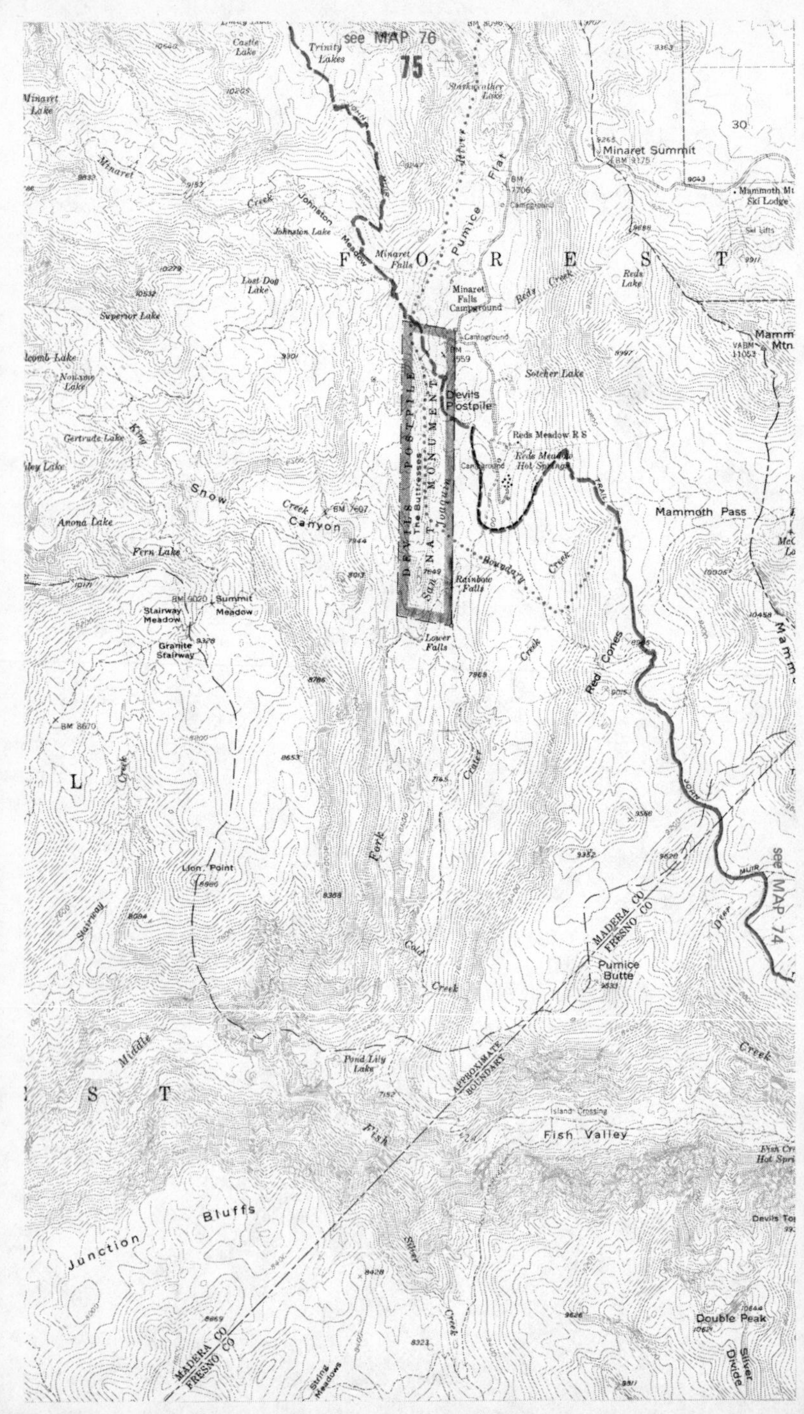

see MAP 76
75
Trinity Lakes
Castle Lake
Minaret Lake
Starkweather Lake
30
Minaret Summit
BM 9175
Mammoth Mt Ski Lodge
Ski Lifts
Minaret
Creek
Johnston
Johnston Lake
Meadow
Minaret Falls
Pumice
Flat
River
Campground
F O R E S T
Lost Dog Lake
Superior Lake
Minaret Falls Campground
Reds Creek
Reds Lake
Campground
Mammoth Mtn
Noname Lake
Sotcher Lake
Devils Postpile
DEVILS POSTPILE NAT MONUMENT
The Buttresses
San Joaquin
Reds Meadow R S
Reds Meadow Hot Springs
Gertrude Lake
King
Snow
Creek
Canyon
Anona Lake
Fern Lake
Mammoth Pass
TRAIL
Boundary
Creek
Rainbow Falls
Summit Meadow
Stairway Meadow
Granite Stairway
Lower Falls
Creek
Red Cones
BM 8670
L
Creek
Crater
Fork
JOHN
MUIR
Lion Point
Stairway
Cold
Creek
see MAP 74
MADERA CO
FRESNO CO
Pumice Butte
Deer
Middle
Pond Lily Lake
APPROXIMATE BOUNDARY
Creek
S T
Island Crossing
Fish Valley
Fish
Junction
Bluffs
Silver
Creek
Double Peak
Silver Divide
MADERA CO
FRESNO CO
String Meadows

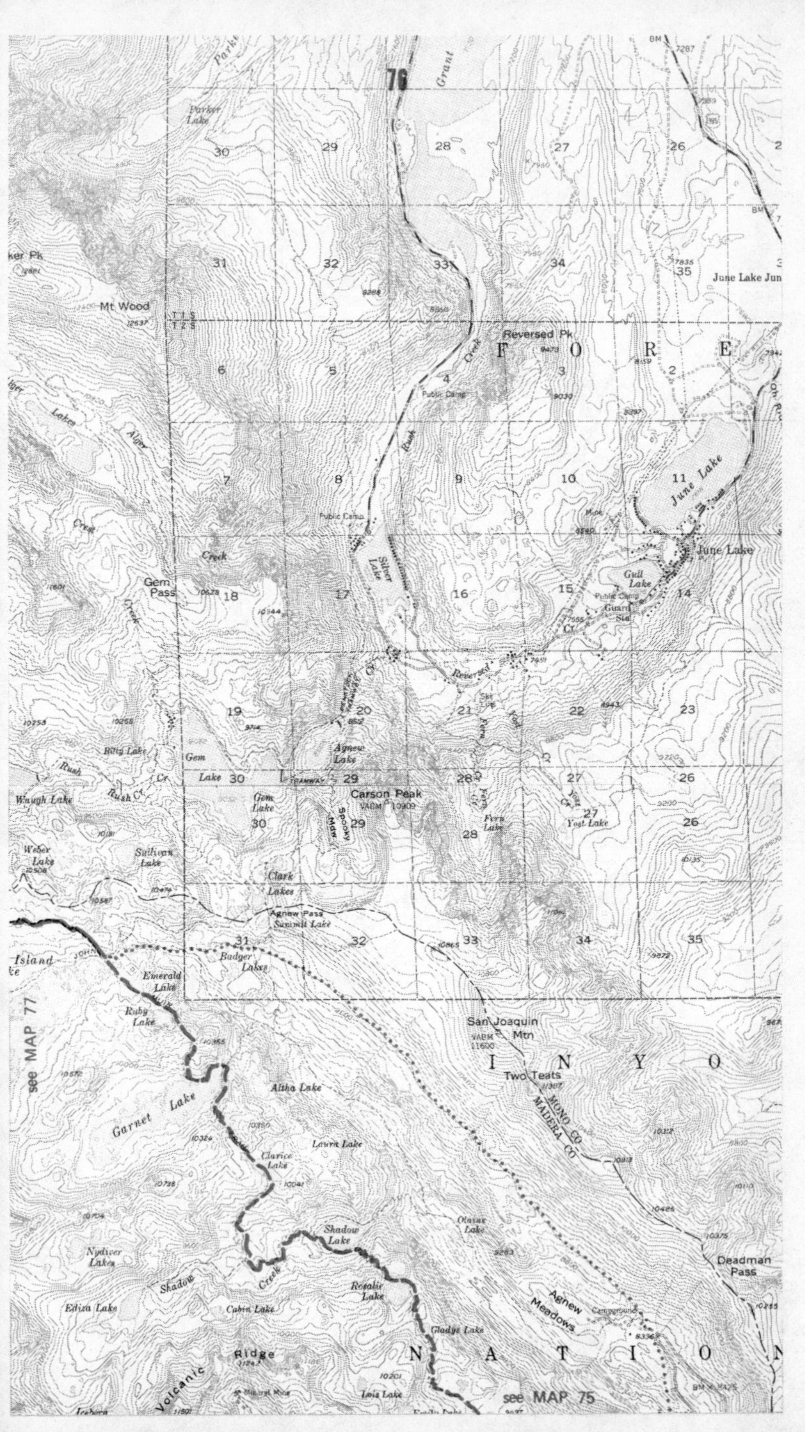

76
Parker Lake
Mt Wood
Reversed Pk
June Lake Jun
F O R E
June Lake
Silver Lake
Gull Lake
Gem Pass
Gem Lake
Agnew Lake
Carson Peak
Spooky Mdw
Fern Lake
Yost Lake
Clark Lakes
Agnew Pass
Summit Lake
Badger Lakes
Waugh Lake
Weber Lake
Sullivan Lake
Emerald Lake
Ruby Lake
Garnet Lake
Altha Lake
Laura Lake
Clarice Lake
Shadow Lake
Rosalie Lake
Gladys Lake
Olaine Lake
Nydiver Lakes
Ediza Lake
Cabin Lake
Lois Lake
Volcanic Ridge
San Joaquin Mtn
Two Teats
I N Y O
N A T I O N
MONO CO
MADERA CO
Agnew Meadows
Deadman Pass
see MAP 77
see MAP 75

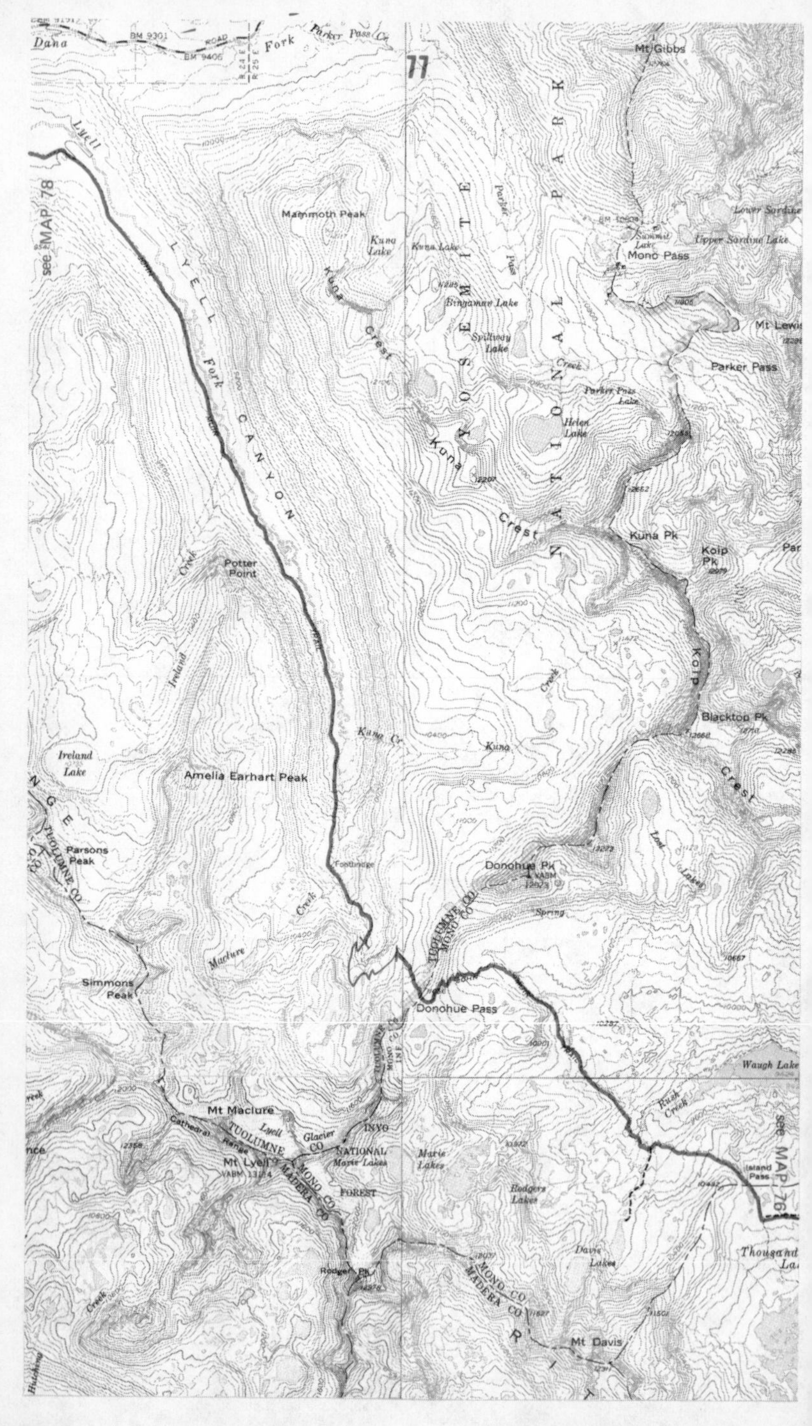

77
see MAP 78
see MAP 76
Dana
Lyell
Mammoth Peak
Kuna Lake
Kuna Crest
LYELL CANYON
Lyell Fork
Bingaman Lake
Spillway Lake
Parker Pass Lake
Helen Lake
YOSEMITE NATIONAL PARK
Mt Gibbs
Mono Pass
Summit Lake
Upper Sardine Lake
Lower Sardine
Mt Lewis
Parker Pass
Kuna Pk
Koip Pk
Koip Crest
Blacktop Pk
Potter Point
Ireland Creek
Ireland Lake
Amelia Earhart Peak
Kuna Cr
Parsons Peak
Maclure Creek
Donohue Pk
Spring
Lost Lakes
Simmons Peak
Donohue Pass
TUOLUMNE CO
MONO CO
Mt Maclure
Lyell Glacier
Cathedral Range
Mt Lyell
INYO NATIONAL FOREST
Maria Lakes
Rodgers Lakes
Rush Creek
Waugh Lake
Island Pass
Thousand
MADERA CO
Rodgers Pk
Davis Lakes
Mt Davis

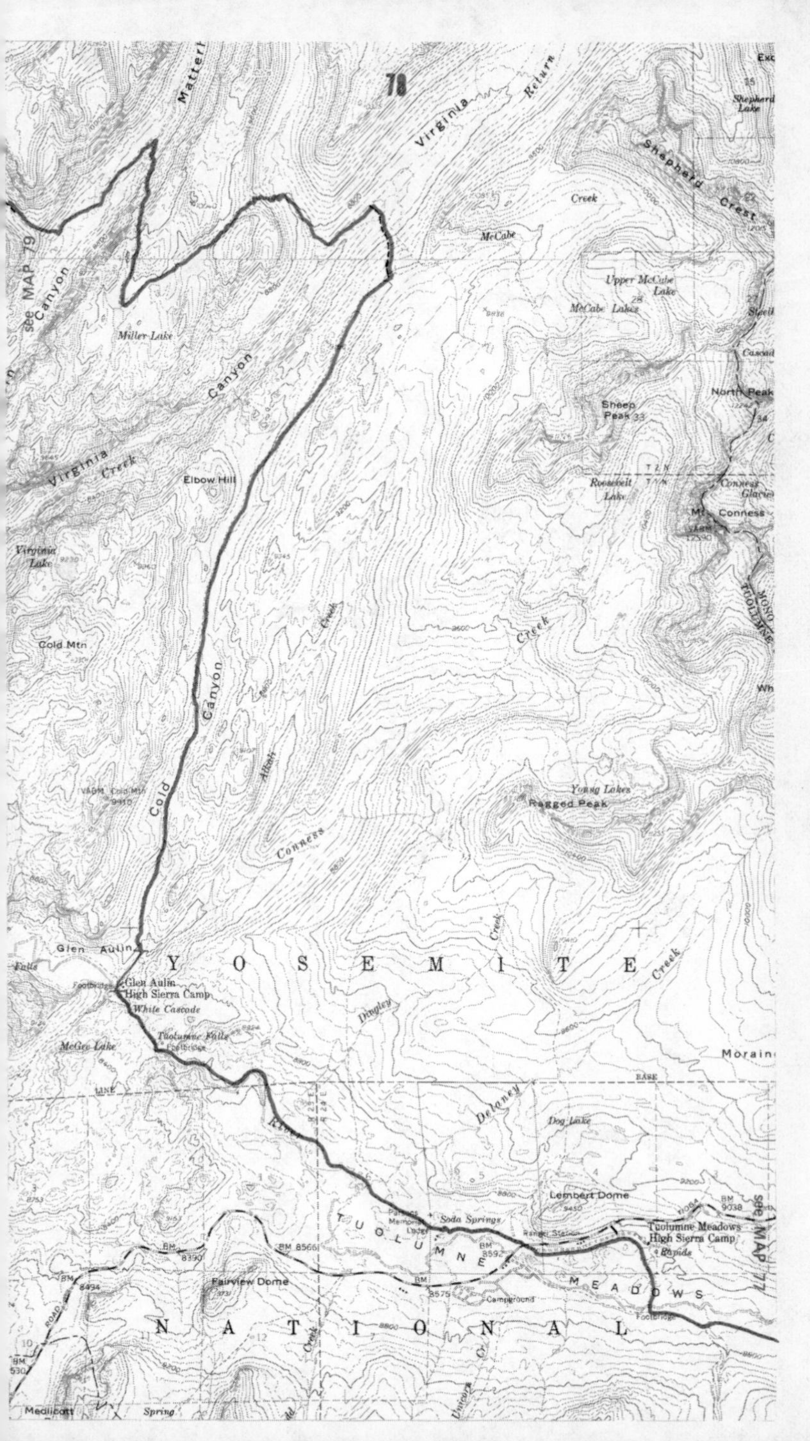

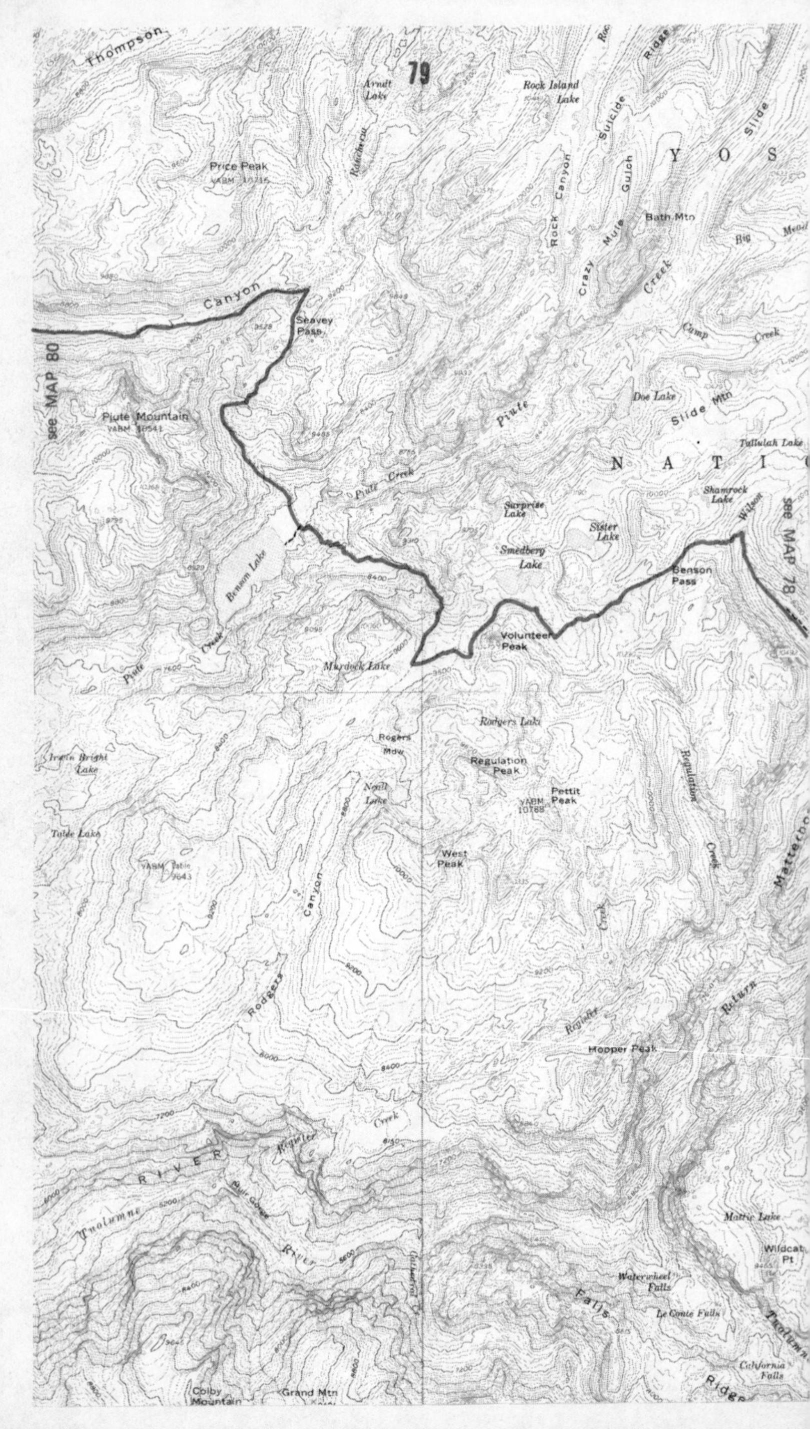
79
Thompson
Price Peak
Arndt Lake
Rock Island Lake
Suicide Ridge
Rock Canyon
Crazy Mule Gulch
Y O S
Bath Mtn
Slide
Creek
Canyon
Seavey Pass
see MAP 80
Camp Creek
Piute Mountain
Doe Lake
Slide Mtn
Piute
Tallulah Lake
N A T I
Piute Creek
Surprise Lake
Shamrock Lake
Sister Lake
Smedberg Lake
see MAP 78
Benson Lake
Benson Pass
Volunteer Peak
Murdock Lake
Piute Creek
Rodgers Lake
Rogers Mdw
Irwin Bright Lake
Regulation Peak
Neall Lake
Pettit Peak
Regulation
Table Lake
West Peak
Creek
Canyon
Creek
Rodgers
Register
Return
Hopper Peak
Creek
Register
RIVER
Muir Gorge
Tuolumne
River
Mattie Lake
Wildcat Pt
Waterwheel Falls
Falls
Le Conte Falls
Tuolumne
California Falls
Ridge
Colby Mountain
Grand Mtn

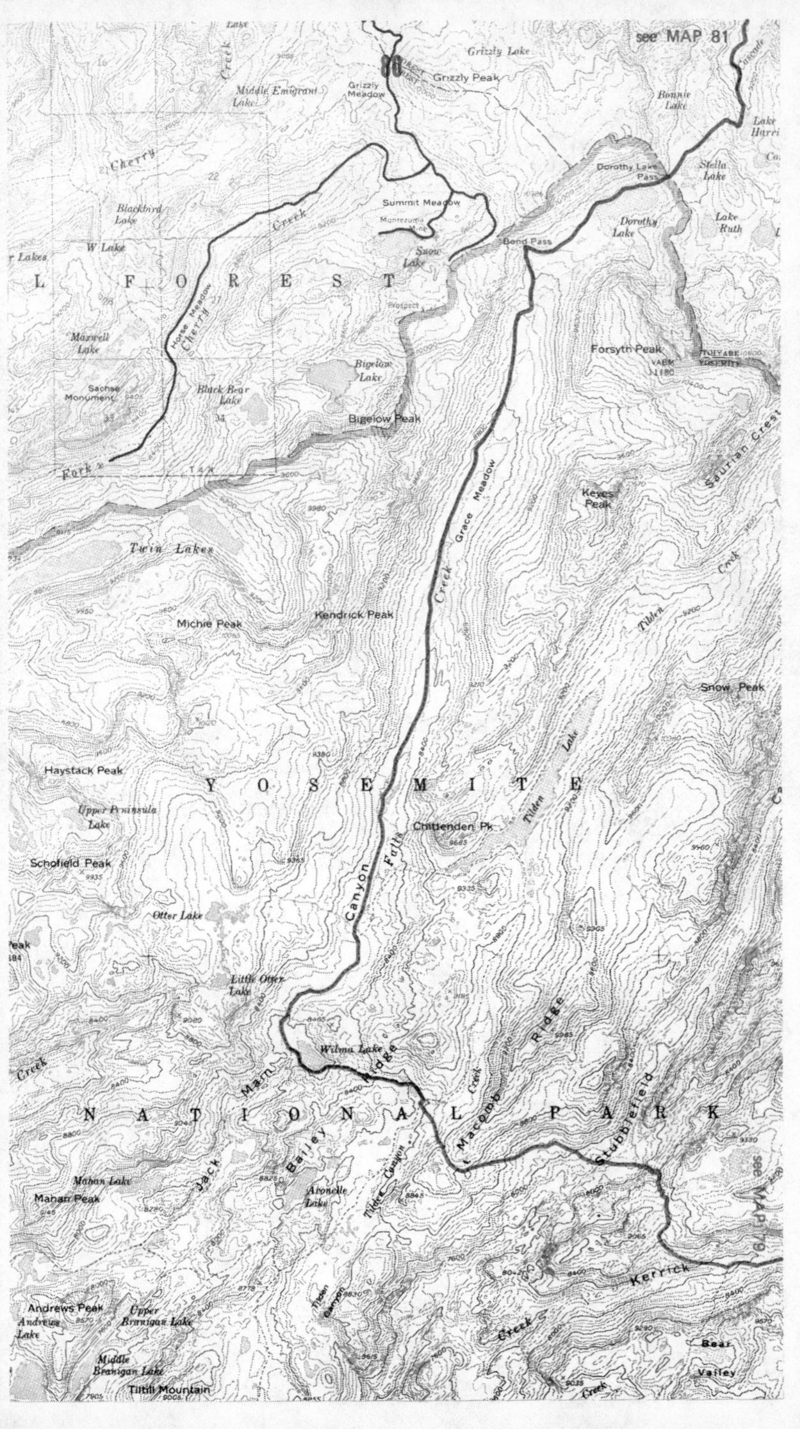

see MAP 81
Grizzly Lake
Grizzly Peak
Grizzly Meadow
Middle Emigrant Lake
Bonnie Lake
Cherry
Creek
Dorothy Lake Pass
Stella Lake
Summit Meadow
Montezuma Mine
Blackbird Lake
W Lake
Snow Lake
Bond Pass
Dorothy Lake
Lake Ruth
FOREST
Prospect
Horse Meadow
Maxwell Lake
Forsyth Peak
TOIYABE
YOSEMITE
Bigelow Lake
Sachse Monument
Black Bear Lake
Bigelow Peak
Fork
Saurian Crest
Keyes Peak
Grace Meadow
Twin Lakes
Kendrick Peak
Michie Peak
Tilden
Creek
Snow Peak
Tilden Lake
Haystack Peak
YOSEMITE
Upper Peninsula Lake
Chittenden Pk
Falls
Canyon
Schofield Peak
Otter Lake
Little Otter Lake
Wilma Lake
Ridge
Macomb
Ridge
Stubblefield
NATIONAL PARK
Jack Main
Bailey
Tilden Canyon
see MAP 79
Mahan Lake
Mahan Peak
Avonelle Lake
Kerrick
Andrews Peak
Andrews Lake
Upper Branigan Lake
Middle Branigan Lake
Tiltill Mountain
Bear Valley

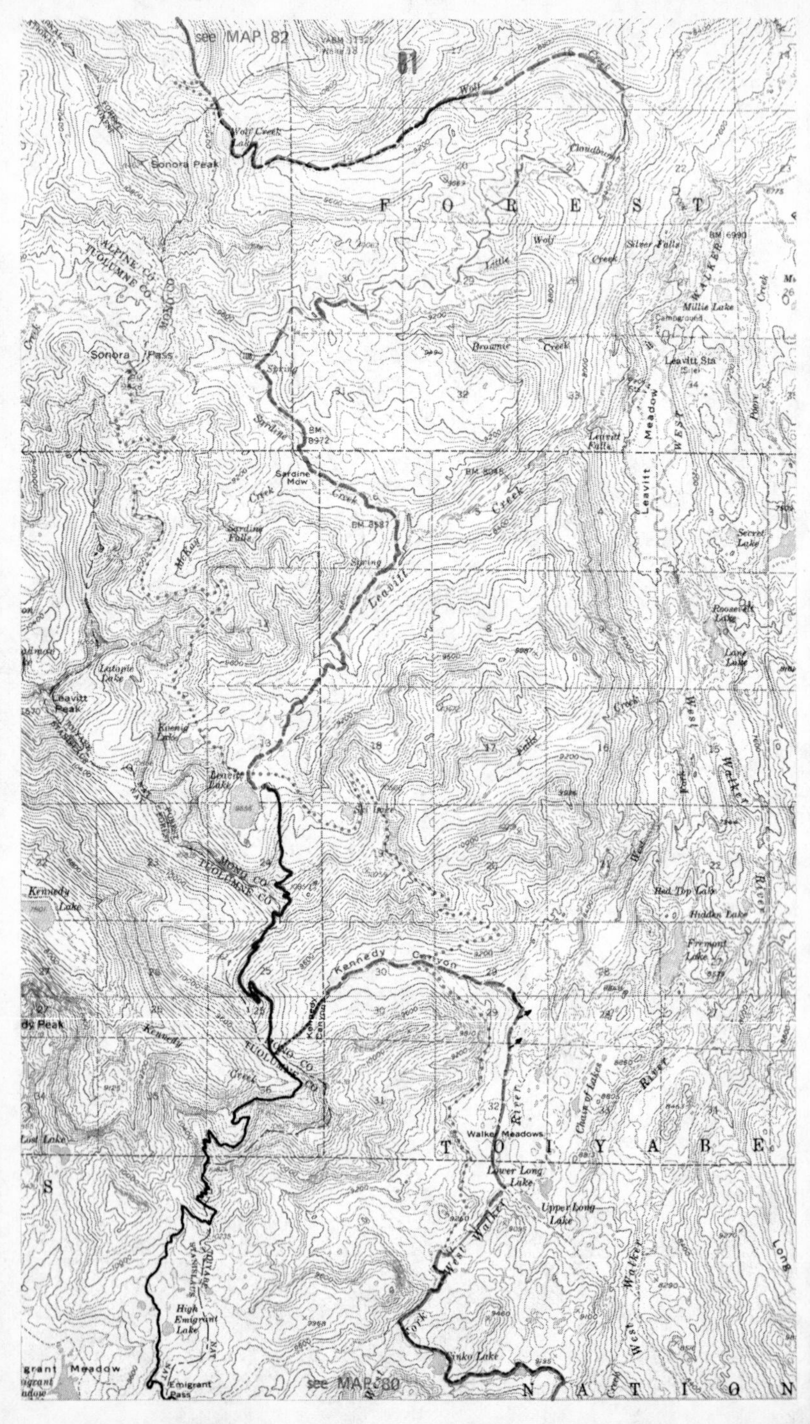

see MAP 82
Wolf Creek
Wolf Creek Lake
Sonora Peak
F O R E S T
Cloudburst
ALPINE CO
TUOLUMNE CO
MONO CO
Little Wolf Creek
Silver Falls
BM 6990
WEST WALKER
Millie Lake
Campground
Leavitt Sta
Sonora Pass
Brownie Creek
Spring
Sardine
BM 8972
Sardine Mdw
Sardine Creek
BM 8587
Sardine Falls
McKay
Leavitt Creek
Leavitt Falls
Leavitt Meadow
Secret Lake
Roosevelt Lake
Lane Lake
Latopie Lake
Leavitt Peak
Koenig Lake
Leavitt Lake
Falls Creek
West Fork Walker River
MONO CO
TUOLUMNE CO
Kennedy Lake
Red Top Lake
Hidden Lake
Fremont Lake
Kennedy Canyon
Kennedy Creek
Chain of Lakes
River
Walker Meadows
Lost Lake
T O I Y A B E
Lower Long Lake
Upper Long Lake
West Walker
High Emigrant Lake
Emigrant Meadow
Emigrant Pass
see MAP 80
N A T I O N

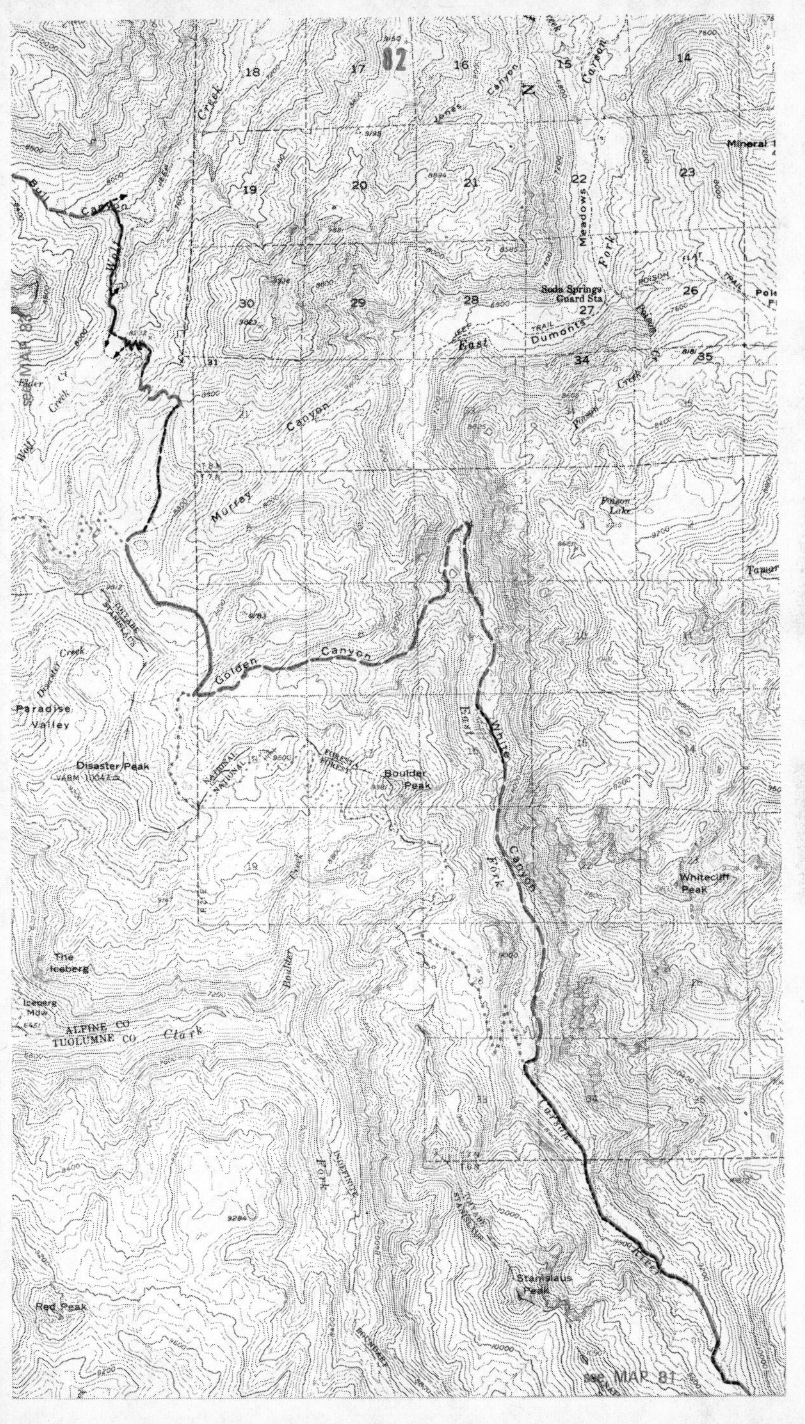
82
Mineral
Soda Springs
Guard Sta
Dumonts
Meadows
Fork
Carson
East
Jones
Canyon
Bull
Canyon
Wolf
Creek
Murray
Canyon
Golden
Canyon
Poison
Lake
Paradise
Valley
Disaster Peak
Boulder
Peak
East
White
Canyon
Fork
Whitecliff
Peak
The
Iceberg
Iceberg
Mdw
ALPINE CO
TUOLUMNE CO
Clark
Red Peak
Stanislaus
Peak
see MAP 82
see MAP 81

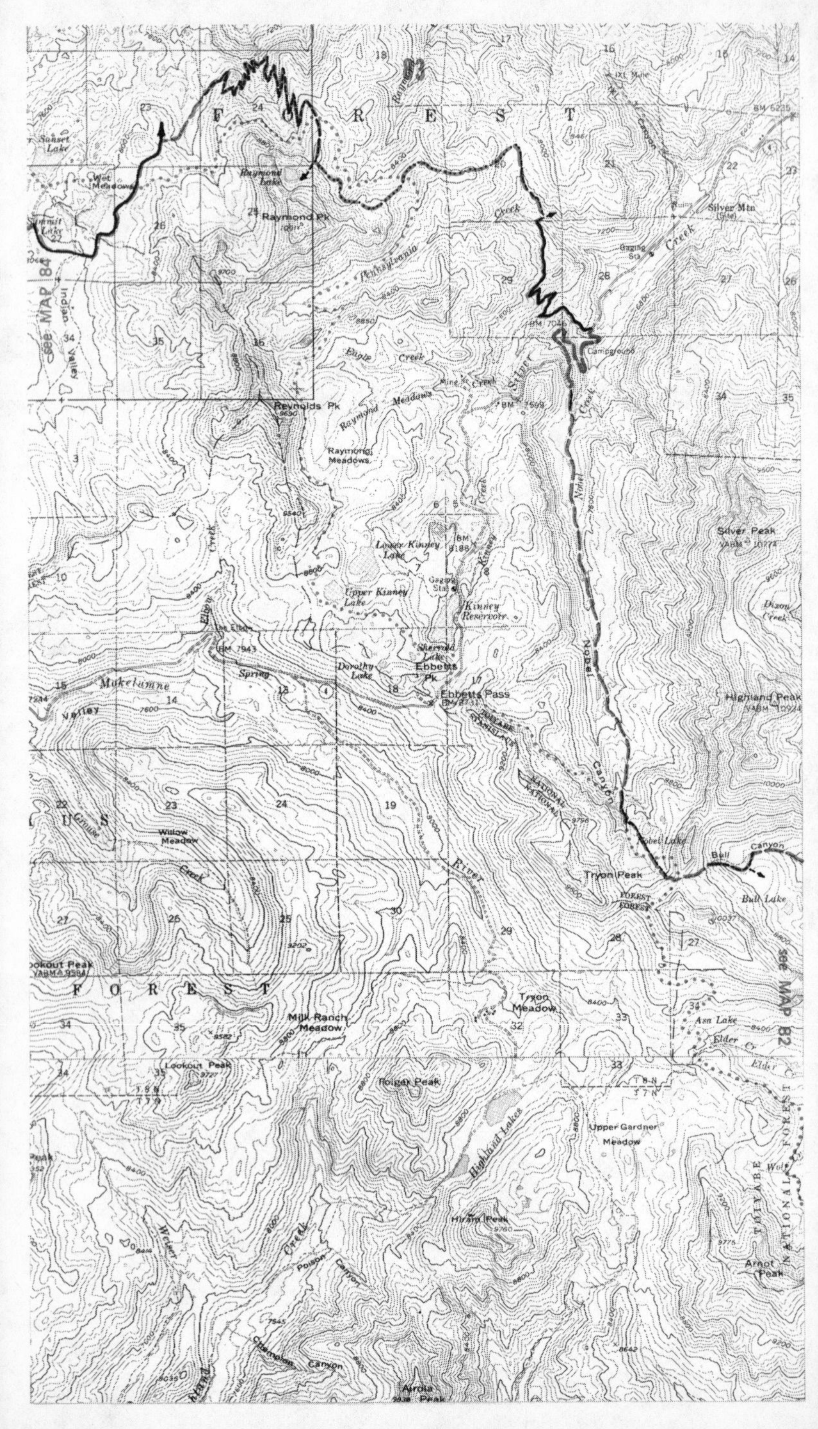

F O R E S T
Raymond Lake
Raymond Pk
Pennsylvania Creek
Silver Mtn
Silver Creek
Campground
Eagle Creek
Reynolds Pk
Raymond Meadows
Noble Creek
Silver Peak
Lower Kinney Lake
Upper Kinney Lake
Kinney Reservoir
Ebbetts Pk
Ebbetts Pass
Dorothy Lake
Mokelumne Valley
Highland Peak
Noble Canyon
Noble Lake
Tryon Peak
Bull Canyon
Bull Lake
Willow Meadow
Lookout Peak
F O R E S T
Milk Ranch Meadow
Tryon Meadow
Asa Lake
Folger Peak
Upper Gardner Meadow
Highland Lakes
Hiram Peak
Poison Canyon
Arnot Peak
Airola Peak
see MAP 84
see MAP 82
TOIYABE NATIONAL FOREST

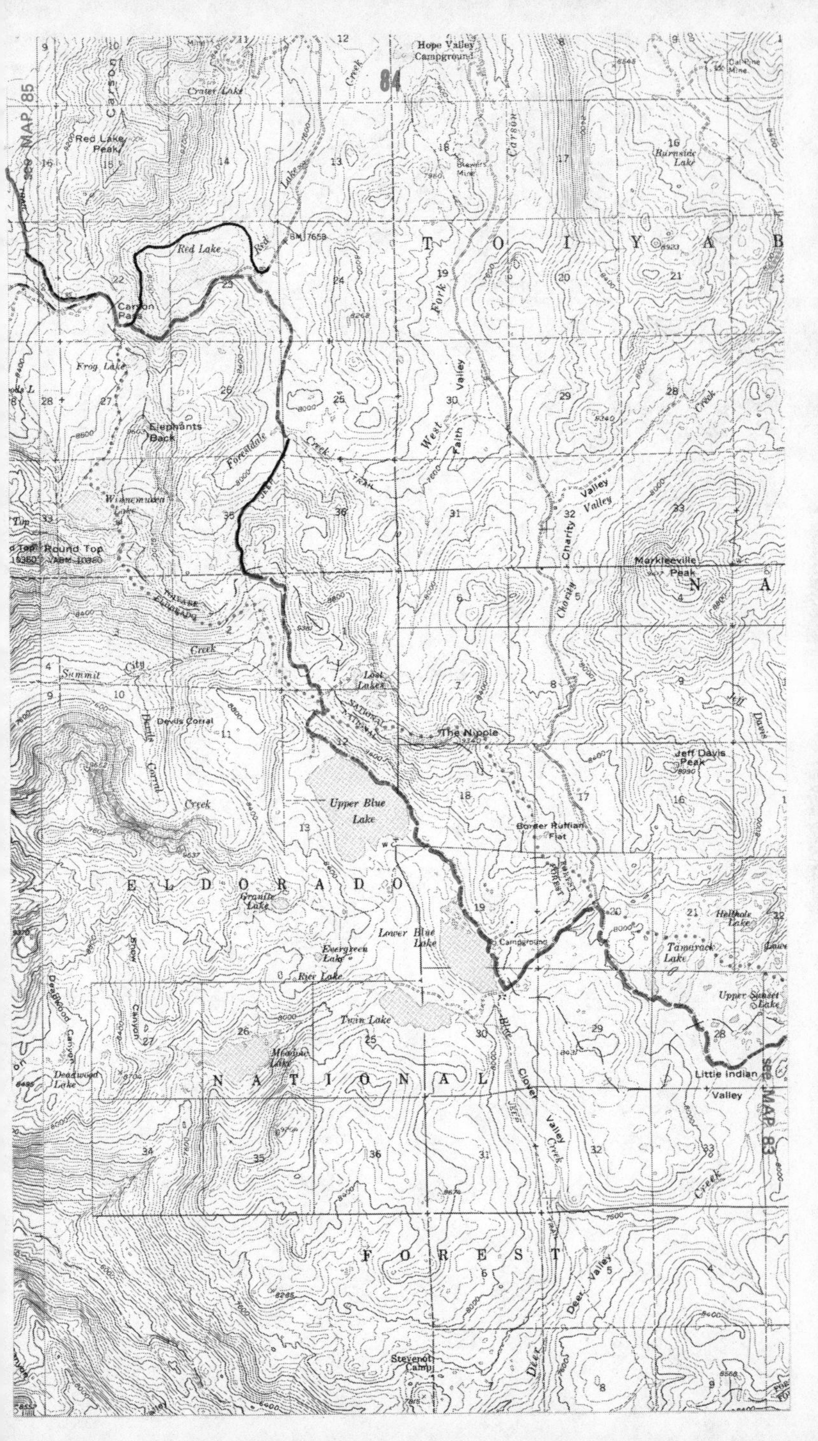

84
MAP 85
see MAP 83
Hope Valley Campground
Crater Lake
Red Lake Peak
Carson
Red Lake
Carson Pass
Frog Lake
Elephants Back
Winnemucca Lake
Round Top
Summit City
Devils Corral
Lost Lakes
The Nipple
Upper Blue Lake
Lower Blue Lake
Border Ruffian Flat
Campground
Granite Lake
Evergreen Lake
Twin Lake
Meadow Lake
Deadwood Lake
Markleeville Peak
Jeff Davis Peak
Burnside Lake
Charity Valley
Faith Valley
West Fork Carson
Tamarack Lake
Hellhole Lake
Upper Sunset Lake
Little Indian Valley
Clover Valley Creek
Deer Valley
Stevenot Camp
T O I Y A B
N A
E L D O R A D O
N A T I O N A L
F O R E S T

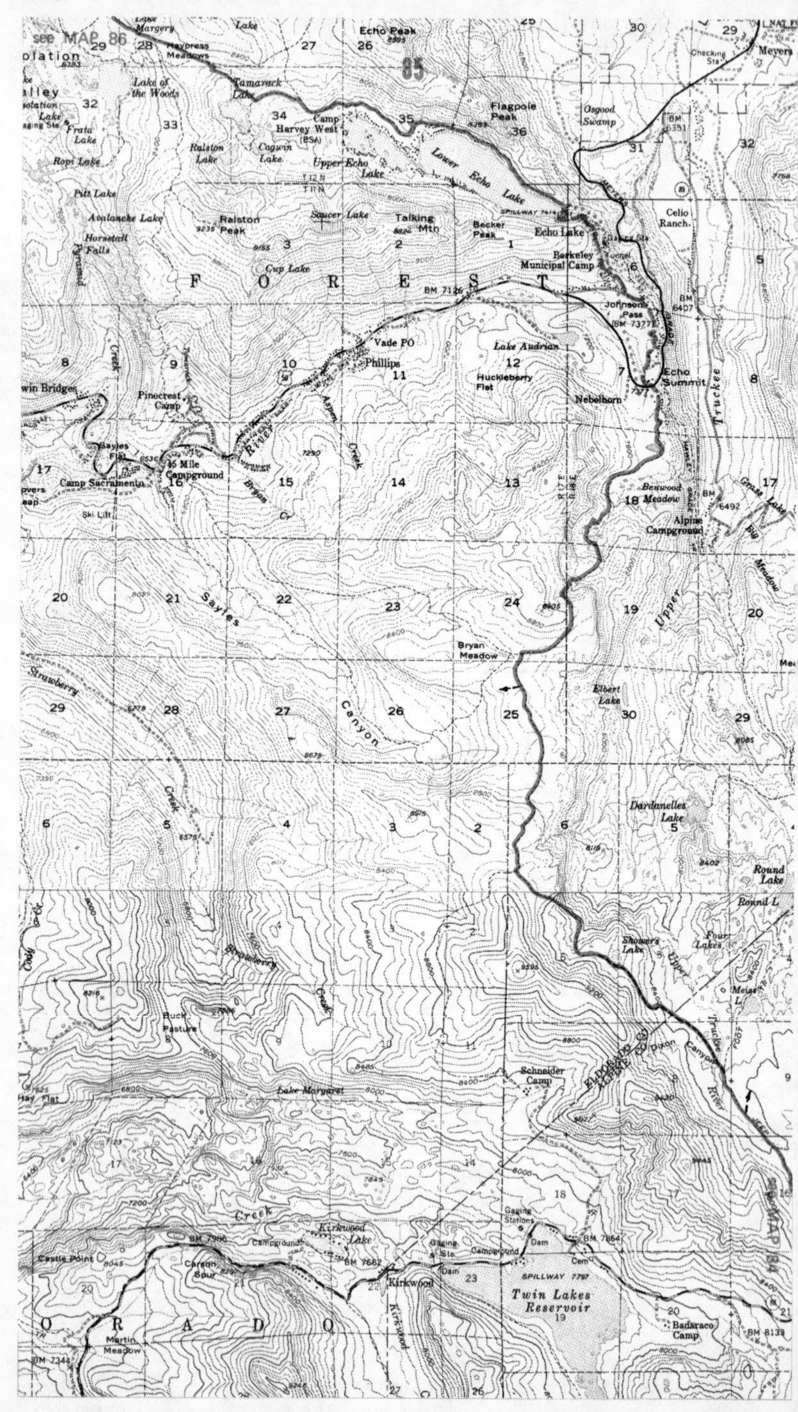

see MAP 86
Echo Peak
Haypress Meadows
Lake of the Woods
Tamarack Lake
Camp Harvey West (BSA)
Cagwin Lake
Ralston Lake
Upper Echo Lake
Lower Echo Lake
Flagpole Peak
Osgood Swamp
Meyers
Checking Sta
Ropi Lake
Pitt Lake
Avalanche Lake
Horsetail Falls
Ralston Peak
Saucer Lake
Talking Mtn
Becker Peak
Echo Lake
Berkeley Municipal Camp
Celio Ranch
Cup Lake
F O R E S T
BM 7126
Johnson Pass
Lake Audrian
Vade PO
Phillips
Huckleberry Flat
Echo Summit
Nebelhorn
Twin Bridges
Pinecrest Camp
Sayles Flat
16 Mile Campground
Camp Sacramento
Ski Lift
Aspen Creek
Bryan Cr
Benwood Meadow
Alpine Campground
Grass Lake
Big Meadow
Upper Truckee
Sayles Canyon
Bryan Meadow
Strawberry
Elbert Lake
Dardanelles Lake
Round Lake
Showers Lake
Four Lakes
Meiss L
Buck Pasture
Strawberry Creek
Schneider Camp
Lake Margaret
Hay Flat
ELDORADO CO
ALPINE CO
Dixon Canyon
Truckee River
Kirkwood Lake
Campground
Gaging Stations
Dam
BM 7864
Castle Point
Carson Spur
BM 7662
Kirkwood
SPILLWAY 7797
Twin Lakes Reservoir
Badaraco Camp
BM 8139
Martin Meadow
BM 7344
O R A D O
see MAP 84

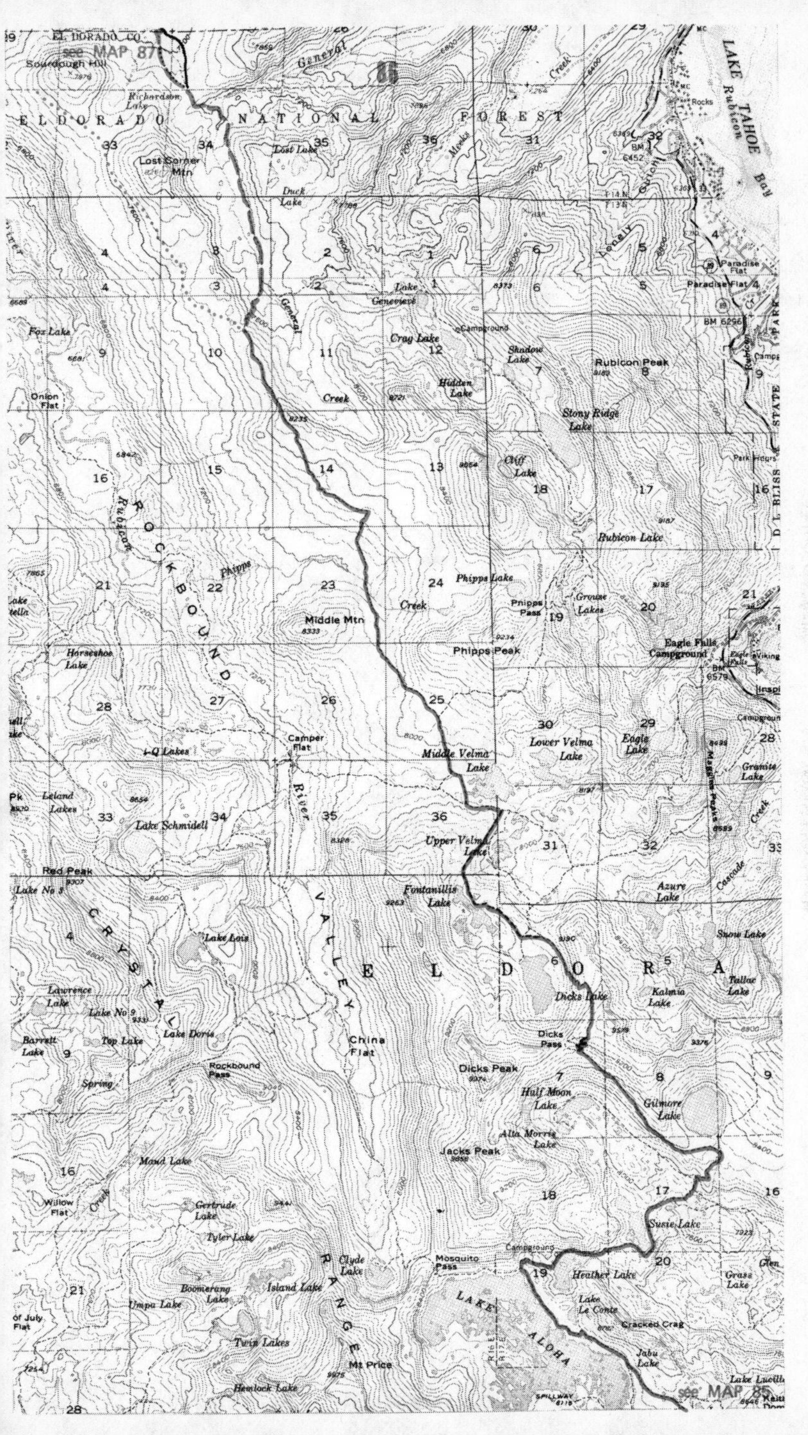

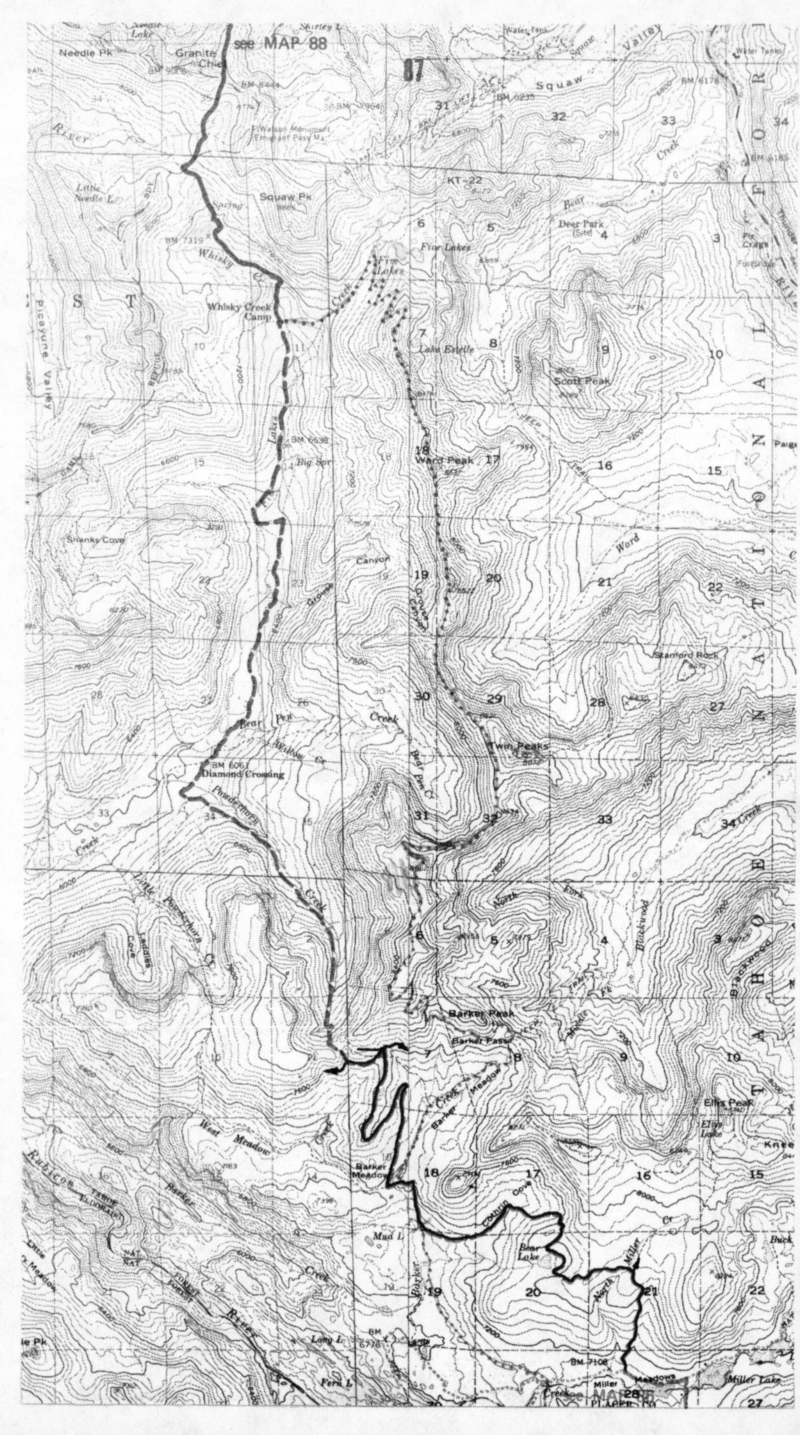

see MAP 88
87
Needle Pk
Granite Chief
Squaw Valley
Squaw Pk
Whisky Creek Camp
Five Lakes
Lake Estelle
Scott Peak
Deer Park
Ward Peak
Shanks Cove
Canyon
Stanford Rock
Twin Peaks
Bear Pen
Diamond Crossing
Picayune Valley
Barker Peak
Barker Pass
Barker Meadow
Ellis Peak
Ellis Lake
Bear Lake
West Meadow
Mud L.
Long L.
Miller Meadows
Miller Lake
Rubicon

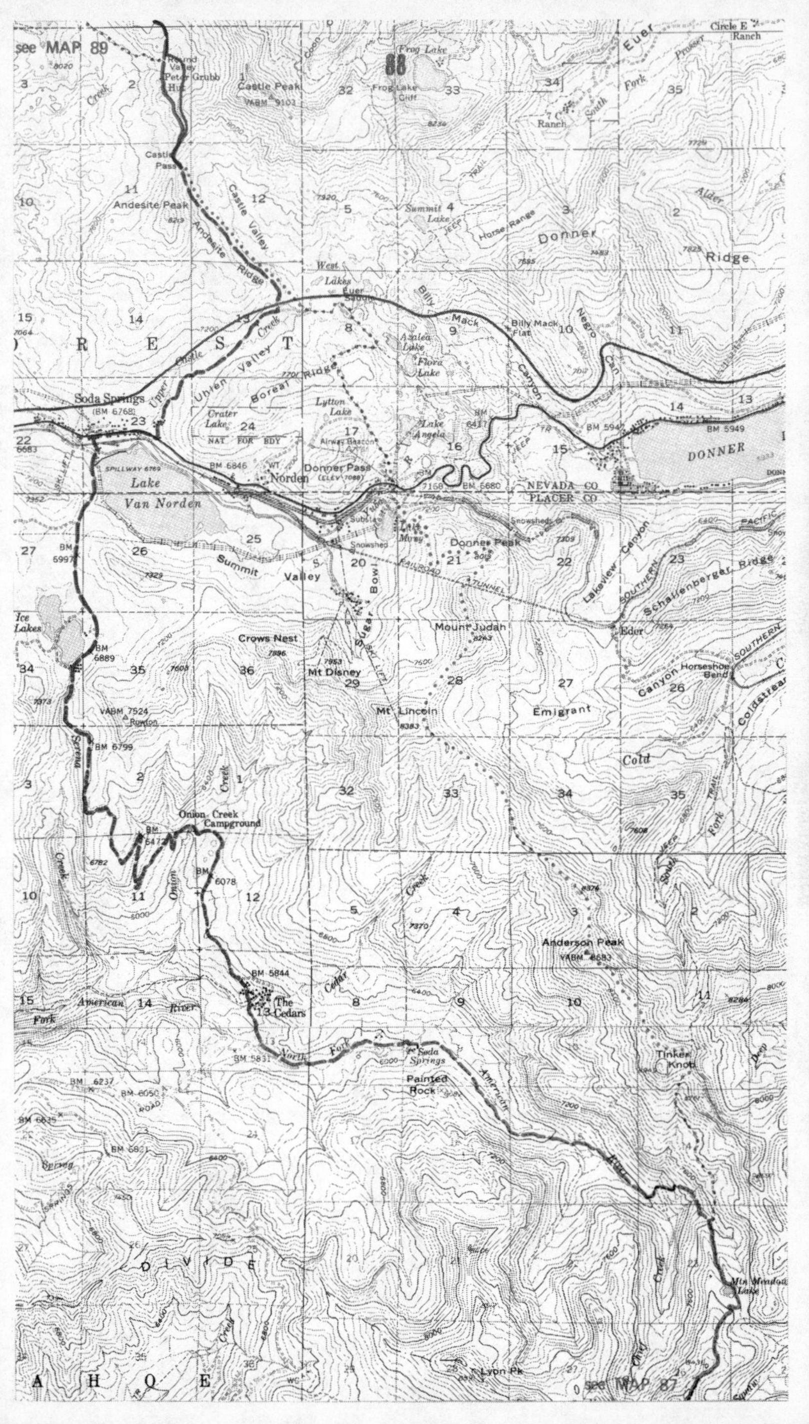

see MAP 89
88
Round Valley
Peter Grubb Hut
Castle Peak
VABM 9103
Frog Lake
Frog Lake Cliff
Circle E Ranch
7 C Ranch
Euer
South Fork
Prosser
Castle Pass
Andesite Peak
Andesite Ridge
Castle Valley
Summit Lake
Horse Range
Donner Ridge
Alder
West Lakes
Euer Saddle
Billy Mack
Billy Mack Flat
Negro Can
Canyon
Castle Creek
Upper Castle Creek
Union Valley
Boreal Ridge
Azalea Lake
Flora Lake
Lytton Lake
Crater Lake
Lake Angela
Soda Springs
(BM 6768)
NAT. FOR. BDY
Airway Beacon
Donner Pass
(ELEV 7088)
Norden
Spillway 6769
Lake Van Norden
NEVADA CO
PLACER CO
DONNER
Snowsheds
Donner Peak
Lakeview Canyon
Schallenberger Ridge
Summit Valley
Sugar Bowl
Ski Lift
Railroad Tunnel
Southern Pacific
Eder
Ice Lakes
Crows Nest
Mt Disney
Mount Judah
Mt Lincoln
Emigrant Canyon
Horseshoe Bend
Coldstream
VABM 7524
Rowton
Serena Creek
Cold
South Fork
Trail
Onion Creek Campground
Onion Creek
Anderson Peak
VABM 8683
The Cedars
Cedar Creek
American River
North Fork
Soda Springs
Painted Rock
Tinker Knob
Mtn Meadow Lake
Road
Divide
Lyon Pk
see MAP 87
T A H O E
F O R E S T

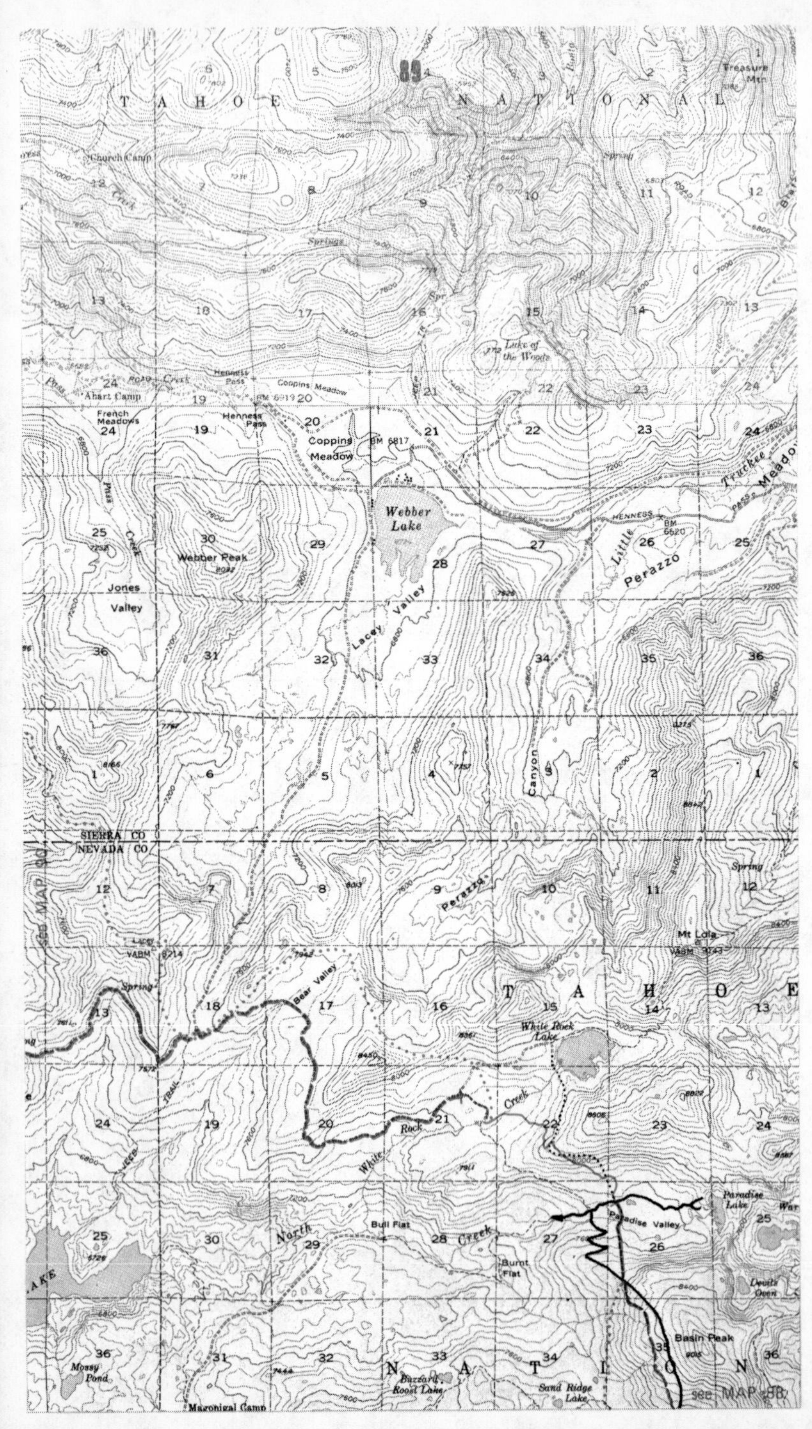
89
T A H O E N A T I O N A L
Treasure Mtn
Church Camp
Springs
Spr
Lake of the Woods
Henness Pass
Coppins Meadow
Ahart Camp
French Meadows
Webber Lake
Webber Peak
Jones Valley
Lacey Valley
Little Perazzo
Truckee
Canyon
SIERRA CO
NEVADA CO
see MAP 90
Perazzo
Mt Lola
Bear Valley
T A H O E
White Rock Lake
White Rock Creek
North Creek
Bull Flat
Burnt Flat
Paradise Valley
Paradise Lake
Devils Oven
Basin Peak
Mossy Pond
Buzzard Roost Lake
Sand Ridge Lake
Magonigal Camp
N A T I O N
see MAP 88

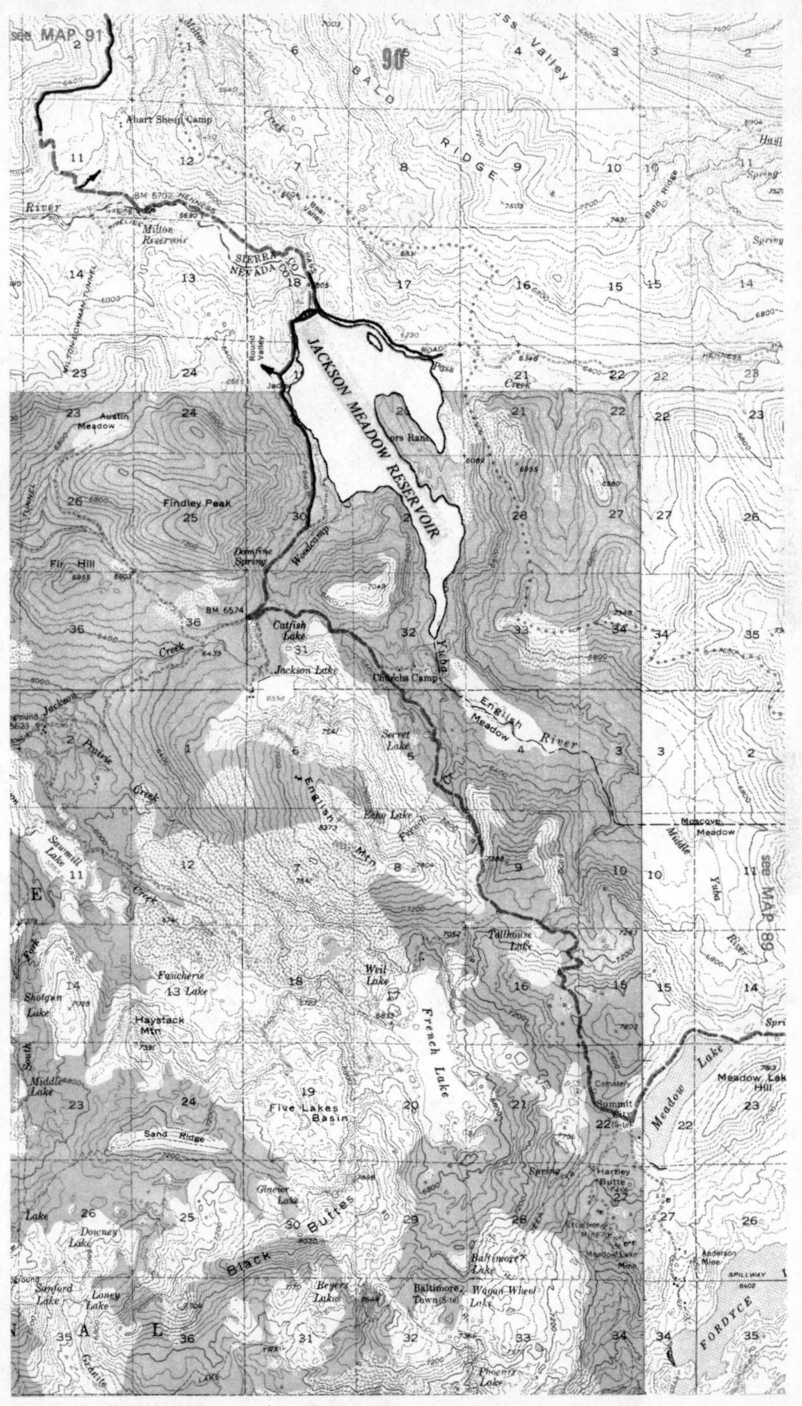

see MAP 91
90
BALD RIDGE
Jackson Meadow Reservoir
Findley Peak
English Mountain
French Lake
Five Lakes Basin
Black Buttes
Meadow Lake
Fordyce
see MAP 89

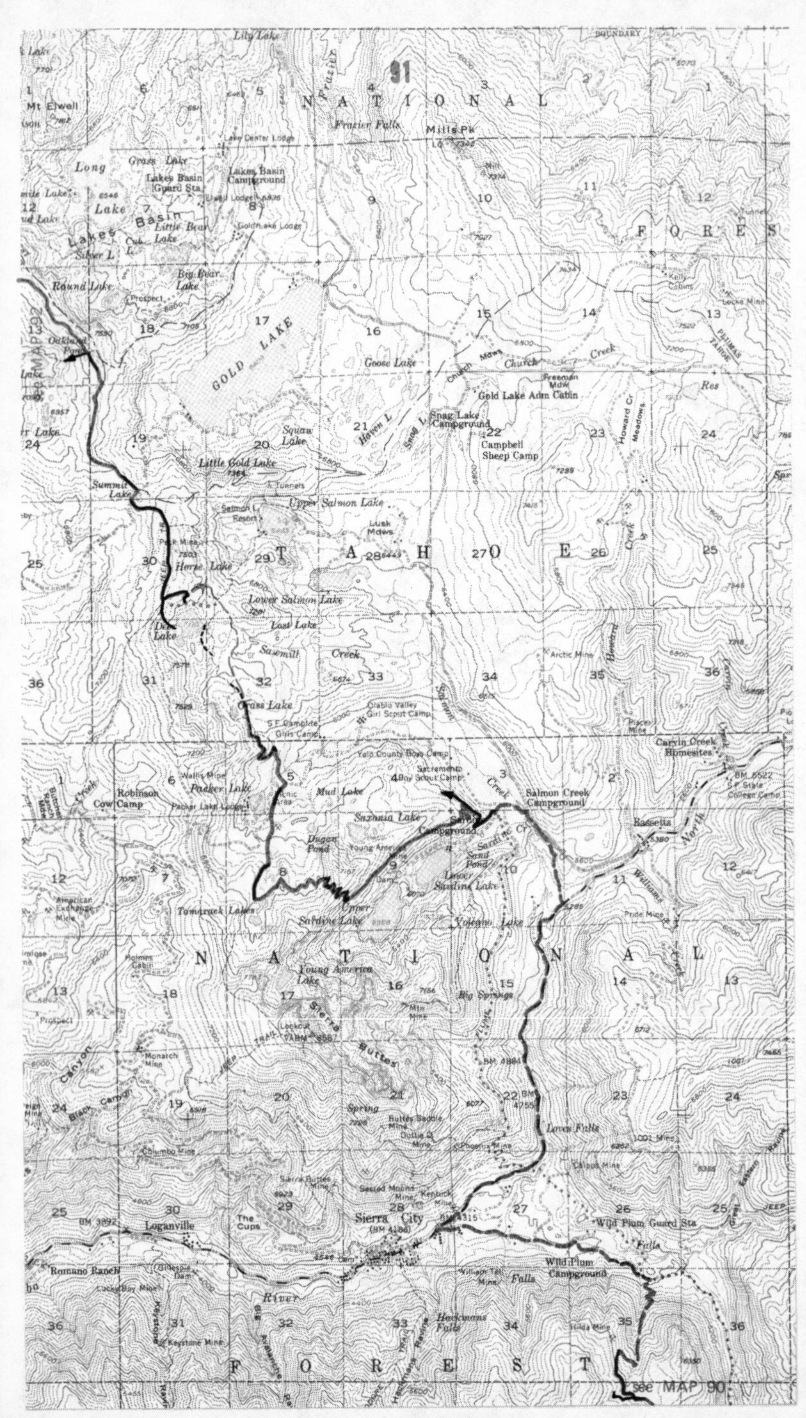

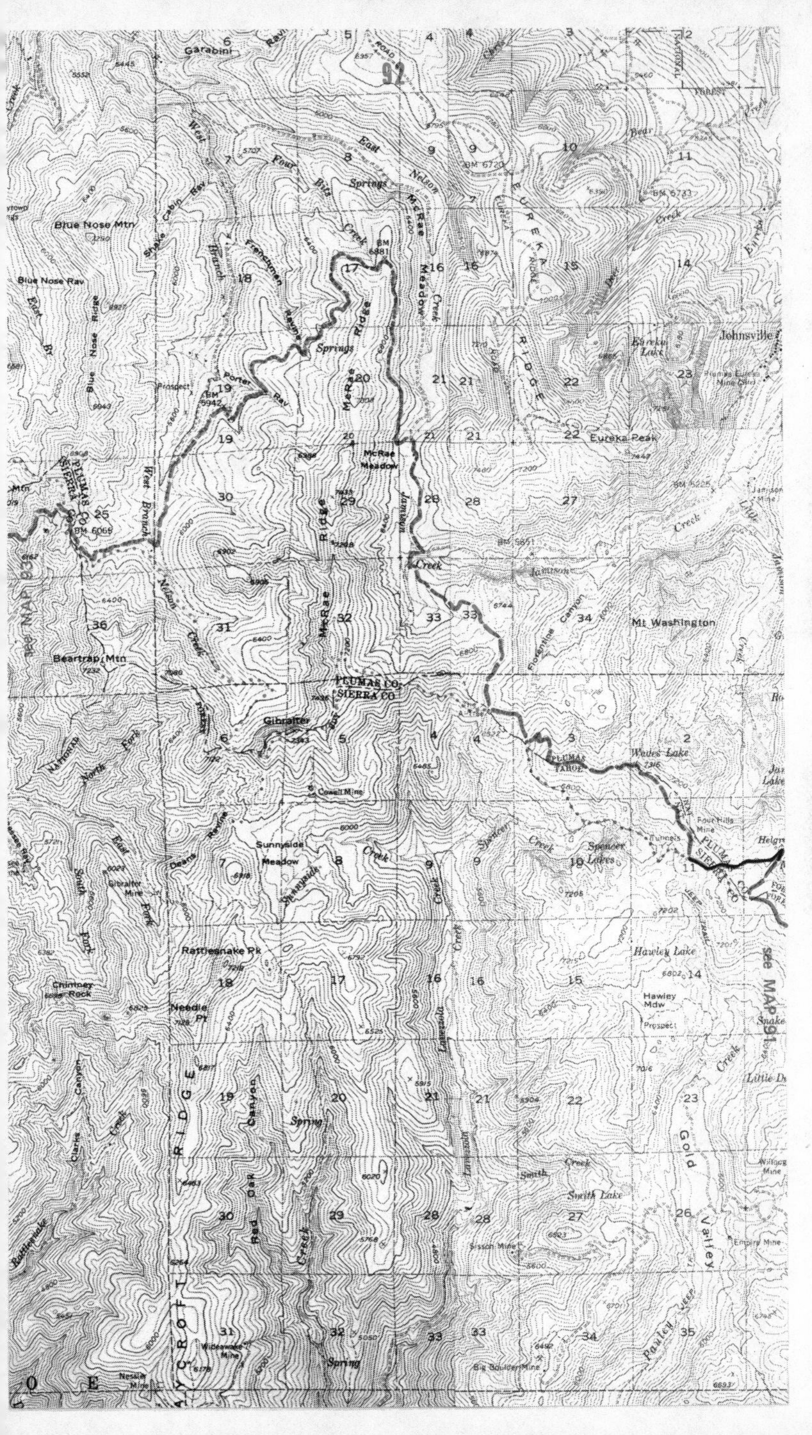
92
Garabini
Blue Nose Mtn
Blue Nose Rav
Blue Nose Ridge
East Nelson
Four Bits Creek
Springs
McRae
Frenchman Ravine
Snake Cabin Rav
West Branch
Porter Rav
Prospect
BM 5942
BM 6881
Meadow Creek
Springs Ridge
McRae Ridge
McRae Meadow
BM 6720
BM 6783
Bear
Creek
EUREKA RIDGE
Eureka Lake
Johnsville
Plumas Eureka Mine (Site)
Eureka Peak
BM 5225
Jamison Mine
Jamison Creek
Little
PLUMAS CO
SIERRA CO
BM 6066
see MAP 93
Nelson Creek
Florentine Canyon
Mt Washington
Beartrap Mtn
PLUMAS CO
SIERRA CO
Gibralter
Cowell Mine
Wades Lake
PLUMAS TAHOE
Four Hills Mine
Tunnels
Spencer Lakes
Spencer Creek
PLUMAS
SIERRA CO
North Fork
East
South Fork
Gibralter Mine
Deans Ravine
Sunnyside Meadow
Sunnyside Creek
Rattlesnake Pk
Chimney Rock
Needle Pt
Hawley Lake
Hawley Mdw
Prospect
see MAP 91
Lavezzola Creek
Canyon
Clarks Canyon
Creek
RIDGE
Spring
Red Oak Creek
Smith Creek
Smith Lake
Sisson Mine
Gold Valley
Empire Mine
Rattlesnake
Wilbeawake Mine
Nessie Mine
Big Boulder Mine
Pauley Jeep
JEEP TRAIL
AYCROFT
O E

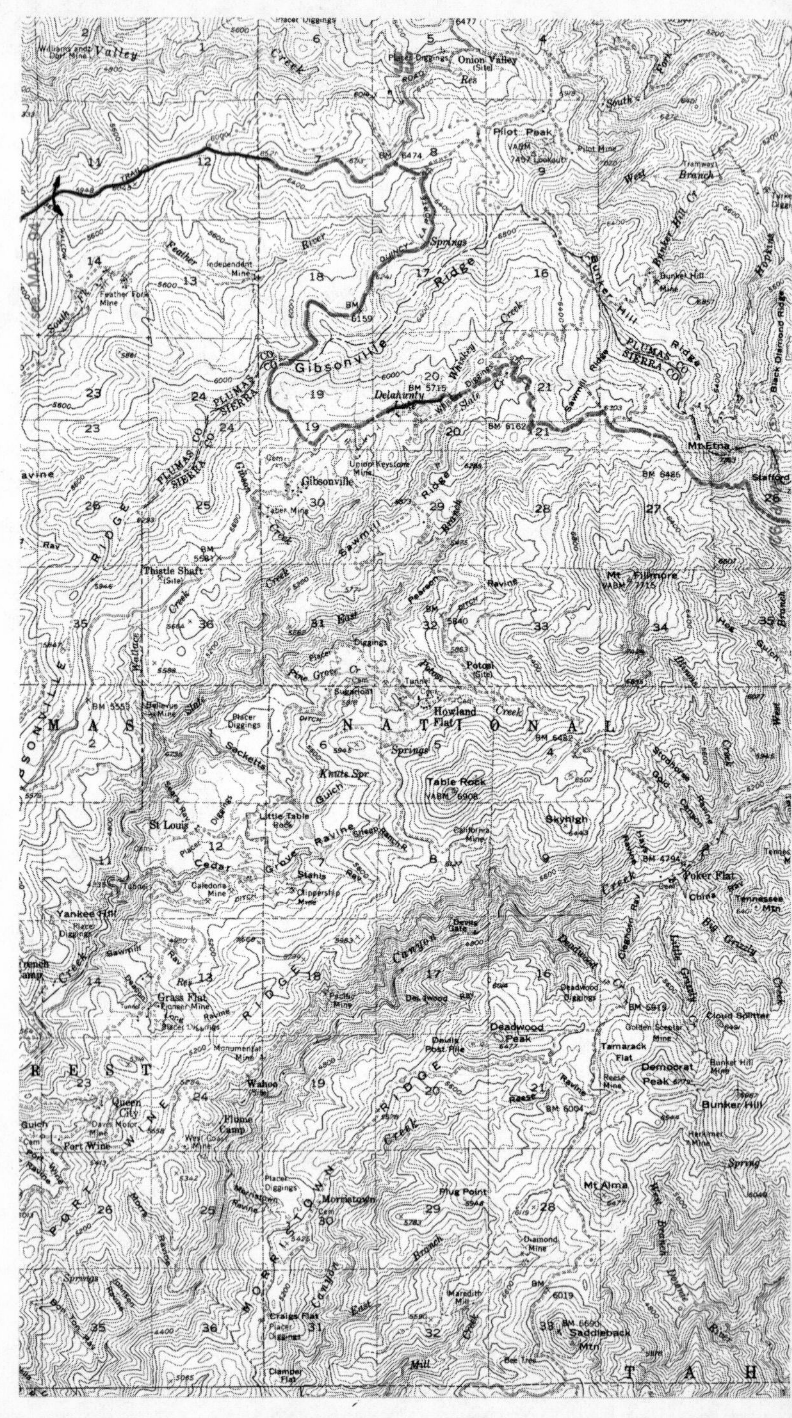

Placer Diggings
Onion Valley
(Site)
Res
Williams and Duff Mine
Valley
Creek
ROAD
Pilot Peak
VABM
7457 Lookout
Pilot Mine
South
Fork
West
Branch
Tramway
TRAIL
River
Feather
Independent Mine
Feather Fork Mine
South
QUINCY
LA PORTE
Springs
Ridge
Bunker Hill
Ridge
Bunker Hill Cr
Bunker Hill Mine
Hopkins
Black Diamond Ridge
Gibsonville
Whiskey
Creek
Whiskey Diggings
Slate
Cr
Delahunty
Lake
BM 5715
PLUMAS CO
SIERRA CO
Sawmill Ridge
BM 6162
Mt Etna
BM 6486
Stafford
BM 6159
Union Keystone Mine
Gibsonville
Cem
Taber Mine
Gibson
Creek
Sawmill
Branch
Ridge
BM 5581
Thistle Shaft
(Site)
Wallace
Creek
RIDGE
Pearson
Ravine
DITCH
BM 5840
Mt Fillmore
VABM 7715
East
Placer
Diggings
Pine Grove Cr
Potosi
Potosi
(Site)
Sugarloaf
Tunnel
Howland
Flat
Creek
Illinois
Hog
Gulch
Branch
BM 5559
Bellevue
Mine
Slate
Placer
Diggings
Sacketts
Gulch
Knuts Spr
Springs
M A S
N A T I O N A L
BM 6482
Table Rock
VABM 6908
Skyhigh
Stoddard
Gold
Canyon
Ravine
St Louis
Placer
Diggings
Little Table
Rock
Ravine
Sheep Ranch R
California
Mine
Cedar
Grove
Stahls
Caledonia
Mine
DITCH
Clippership
Mine
Yankee Hill
Placer
Diggings
Tunnel
BM 4794
Poker Flat
China
Tennessee
Mtn
Big
Grizzly
Creek
Little
Grizzly
Devils
Gate
Canyon
Deadwood
Deadwood
Diggings
Deadwood
Rav
Pacific
Mine
French
Camp
Creek
Sawmill
Rav
Res
Grass Flat
Pioneer Mine
Long
Ravine
Placer Diggings
R I D G E
BM 5919
Cloud Splitter
Golden Scepter
Mine
Deadwood
Peak
Devils
Post Pile
Tamarack
Flat
Democrat
Peak
Bunker Hill
Mine
Reese
Mine
Reese
Ravine
BM 6004
Bunker Hill
R E S T
Monumental
Mine
Wahoo
(Site)
R I D G E
Queen
City
Davis Motor
Mine
Flume
Camp
Fort Wine
West Coast
Mine
P O R T
W I N E
Harkimer
Mine
Spring
Placer
Diggings
Morristown
Ravine
Morristown
Cem
Plug Point
Mt Alma
West
Branch
Morris
Ravine
Diamond
Mine
M O R R I S T O W N
Canyon
Branch
East
Meredith
Mill
BM
6019
Springs
Bon Ton Rav
Craigs Flat
Placer
Diggings
Creek
Mill
BM 6690
Saddleback
Mtn
Bee Tree
Clamper
Flat
River
T A H

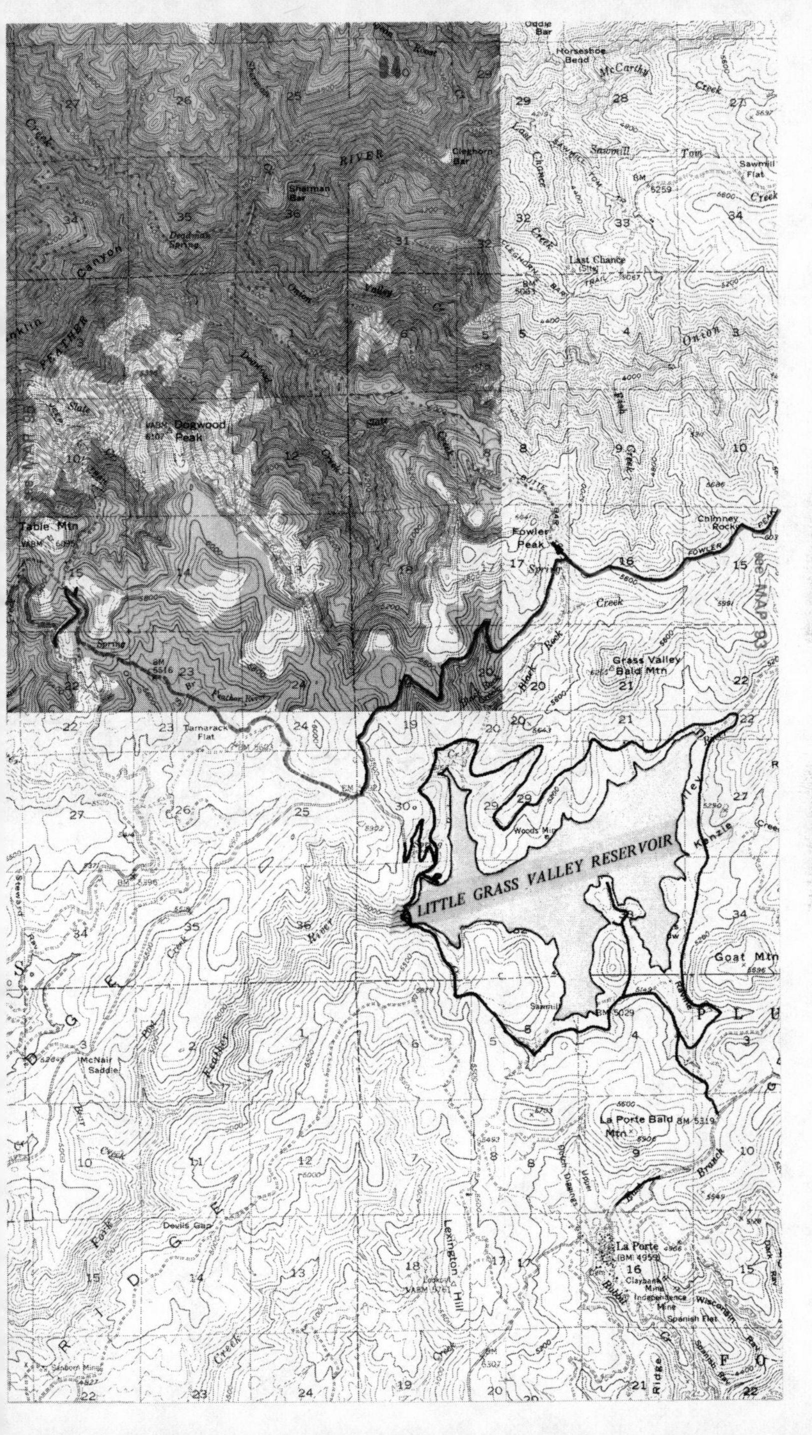
LITTLE GRASS VALLEY RESERVOIR
Dogwood Peak
Table Mtn
Fowler Peak
Grass Valley Bald Mtn
Goat Mtn
La Porte Bald Mtn
La Porte
Lexington Hill
Devils Gap
McNair Saddle
Tamarack Flat
Chimney Rock
Last Chance
Sherman Bar
Cleghorn Bar
Horseshoe Bend
Sawmill Flat
Spanish Flat
Independence Mine
Sanborn Mine
SEE MAP 93

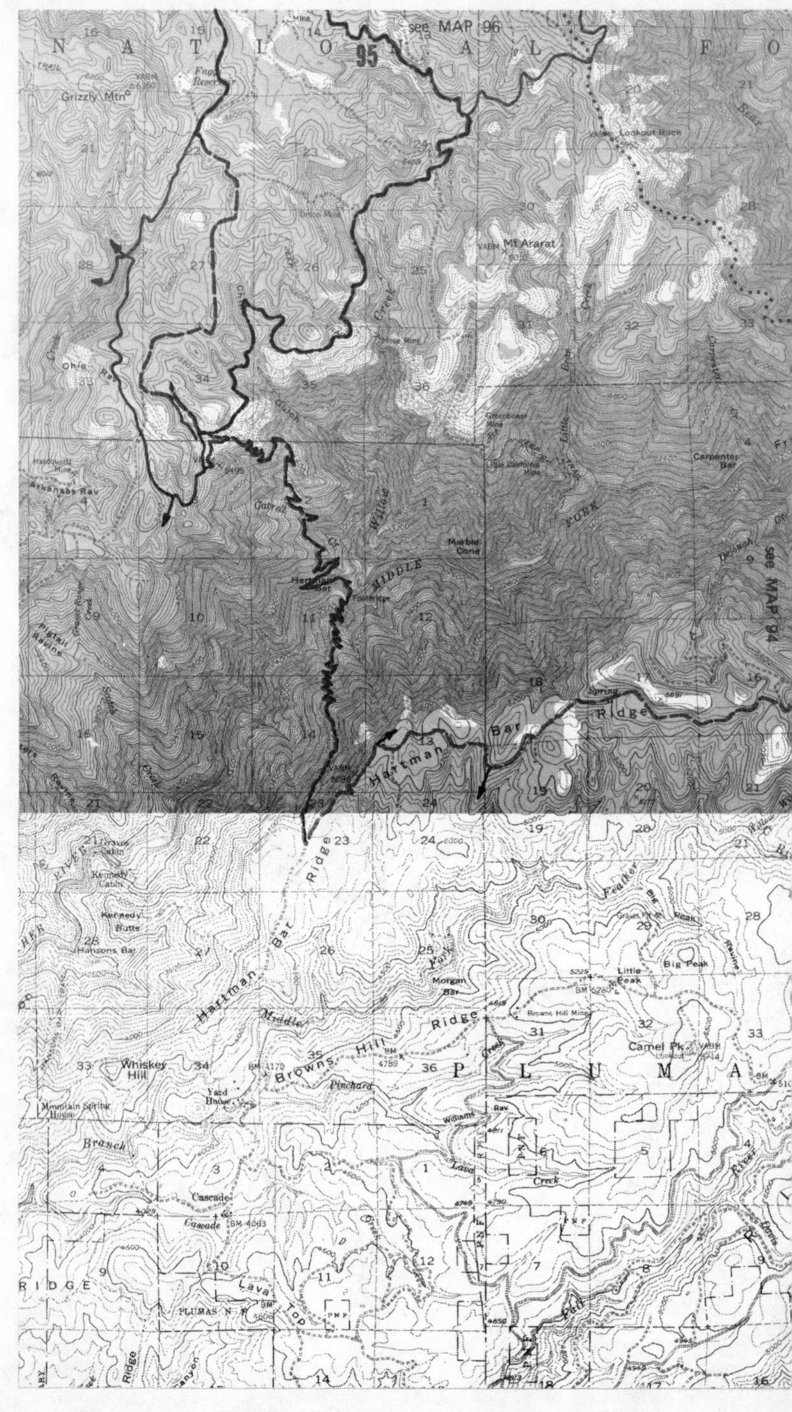
see MAP 96
95
Grizzly Mtn
Lookout Rock
Mt Ararat
Marble Cone
MIDDLE
FORK
Carpenter Bar
see MAP 94
Hartman Bar
Spring
Ridge
Hartman Bar Ridge
Kennedy Butte
Hansons Bar
Middle
Morgan Bar
Big Peak
Little Peak
Browns Hill Ridge
Camel Pk
Whiskey Hill
Mountain Spring House
Cascade
Lava Top
P L U M A S
R I D G E
PLUMAS N F

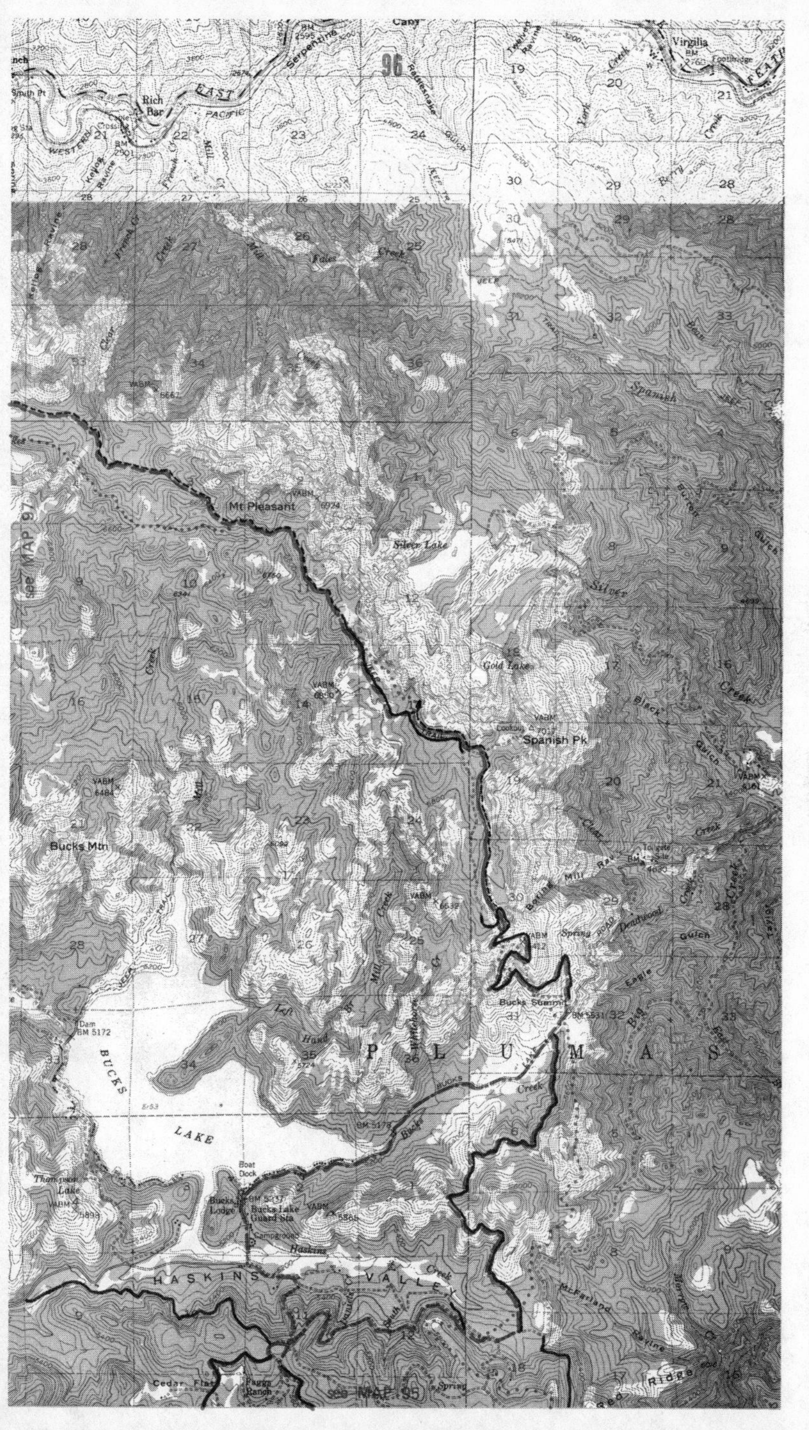

96
Rich Bar
EAST
PACIFIC
WESTERN
Serpentine
Vinglia
Mt Pleasant
SEE MAP 97
Silver Lake
Gold Lake
Spanish Pk
Bucks Mtn
Bucks Summit
BUCKS
LAKE
P L U M A S
Dam
BM 5172
Boat Dock
Bucks Lodge
Bucks Lake Guard Sta
Campground
HASKINS
VALLEY
Cedar Flat
SEE MAP 95
Spanish
Silver
Creek
Black
Quich
Gulch
Eagle
Haskins
McFarland
Ravine
Red Ridge

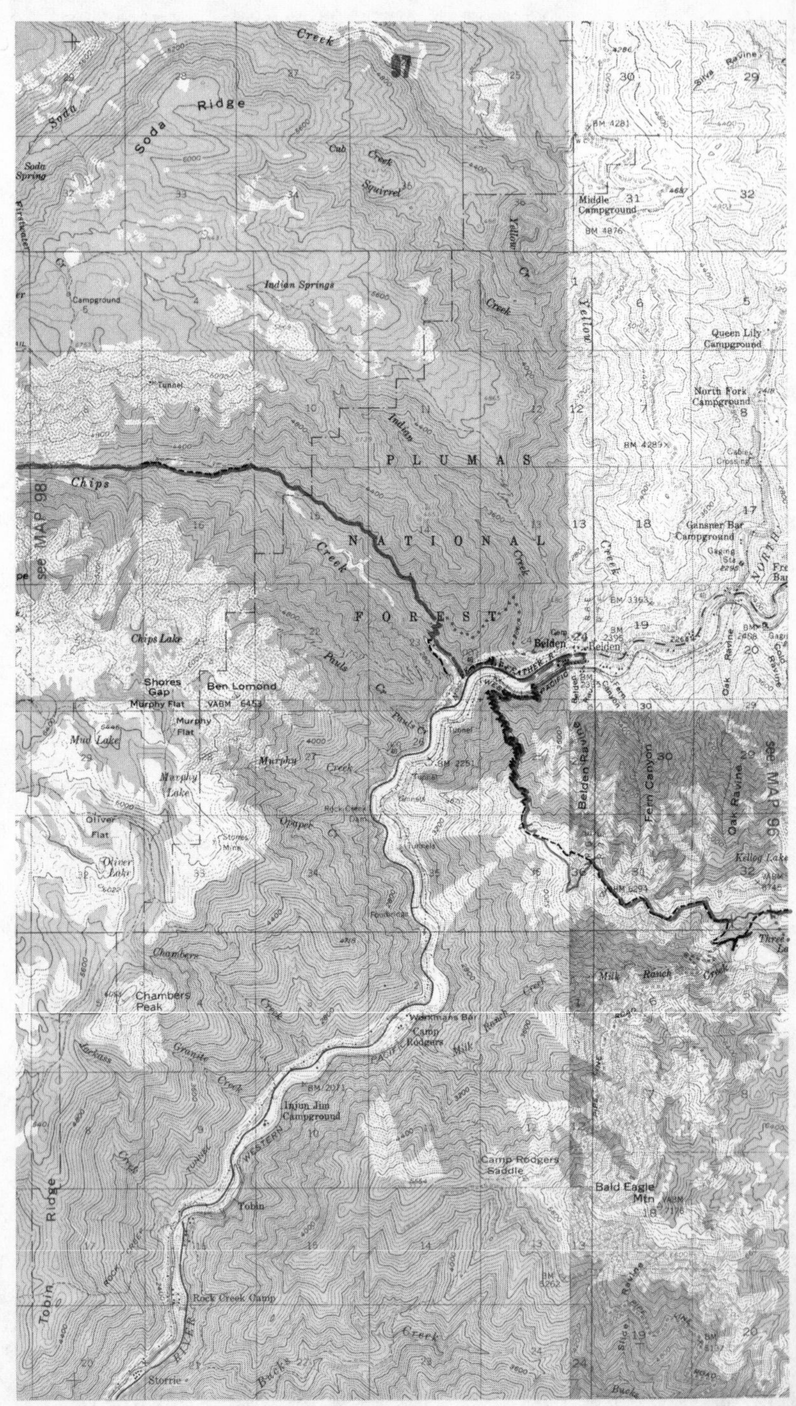
97
Creek
Soda
Ridge
Soda
Soda Spring
Cub
Creek
Squirrel
Yellow Cr
Middle Campground
BM 4281
BM 4876
Silva Ravine
Indian Springs
Campground
Creek
Yellow
Queen Lily Campground
North Fork Campground
Tunnel
Indian
BM 4289
Cable Crossing
PLUMAS
NATIONAL
FOREST
Chips
see MAP 98
Creek
Creek
Gansner Bar Campground
BM 3363
Chips Lake
Pauls
Belden
BM 2395
Shores Gap
Ben Lomond
Murphy Flat
VABM 6453
Murphy Flat
Mud Lake
Pauls Cr
Tunnel
BM 2251
Murphy
Creek
Murphy Lake
Belden Ravine
Fern Canyon
Oak Ravine
see MAP 96
Oliver Flat
Opapee
Cr
Tunnels
Oliver Lake
Kellog Lake
Footbridge
Chambers
Chambers Peak
Milk
Ranch
Creek
Workmans Bar
Camp Rodgers
Milk
Ranch
Creek
Granite
Creek
BM 2071
Injun Jim Campground
WESTERN
Camp Rodgers Saddle
Bald Eagle Mtn
VABM 7116
Ridge
Tobin
Creek
Rock Creek Camp
Tobin
BM 3262
Slide Ravine
Creek
RIVER
Bucks
Storrie

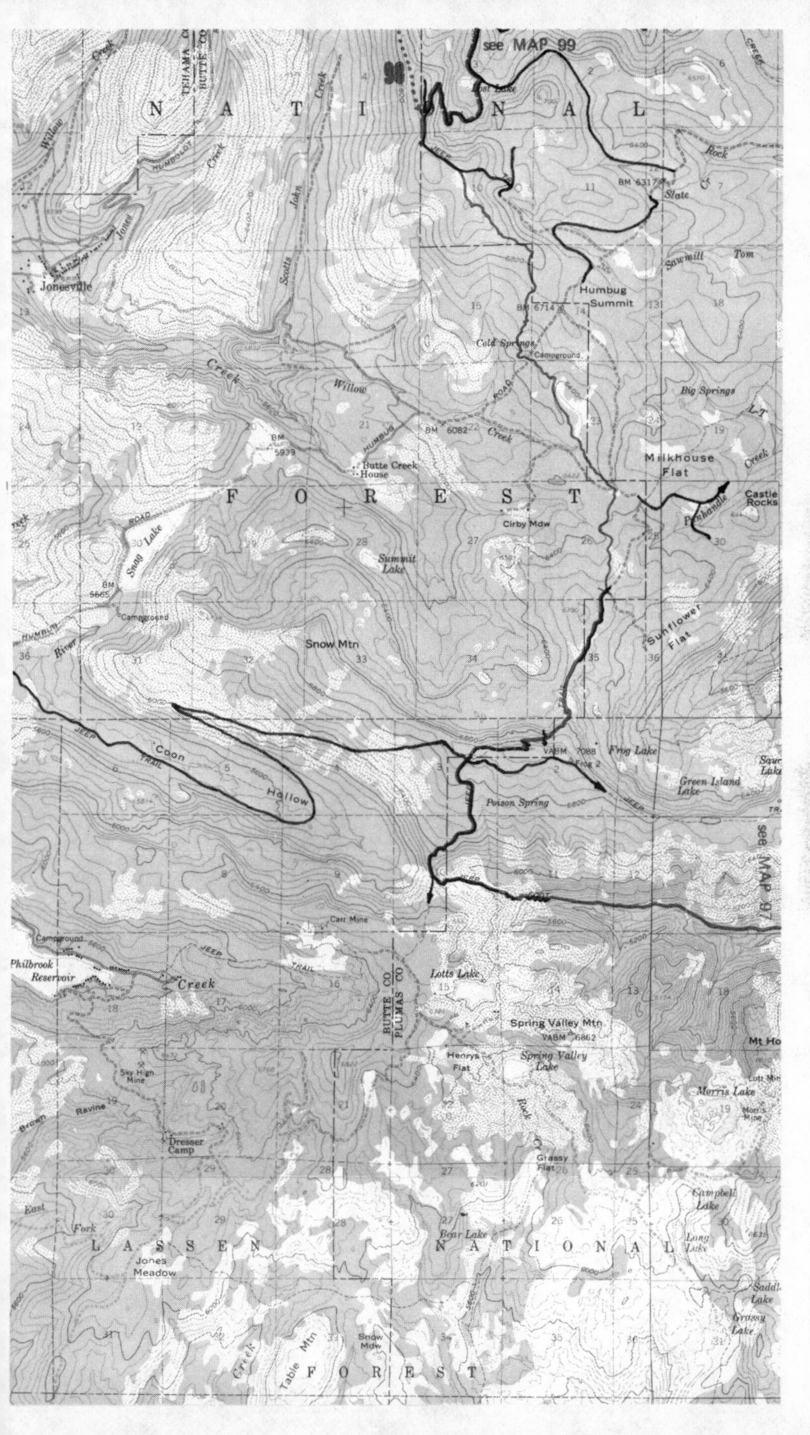

see MAP 99
N A T I O N A L
Joneville
Humbug Summit
Cold Springs
Willow
Butte Creek House
Milkhouse Flat
Castle Rocks
F O R E S T
Cirby Mdw
Snag Lake
Summit Lake
Snow Mtn
Sunflower Flat
Coon Hollow
Frog Lake
Green Island Lake
Poison Spring
see MAP 97
Carr Mine
Philbrook Reservoir
Lotts Lake
Spring Valley Mtn
Spring Valley Lake
Henrys Flat
Sky High Mine
Dresser Camp
Morris Lake
Grassy Flat
Campbell Lake
Bear Lake
L A S S E N N A T I O N A L
Jones Meadow
Long Lake
Table Mtn
Snow Mdw
F O R E S T

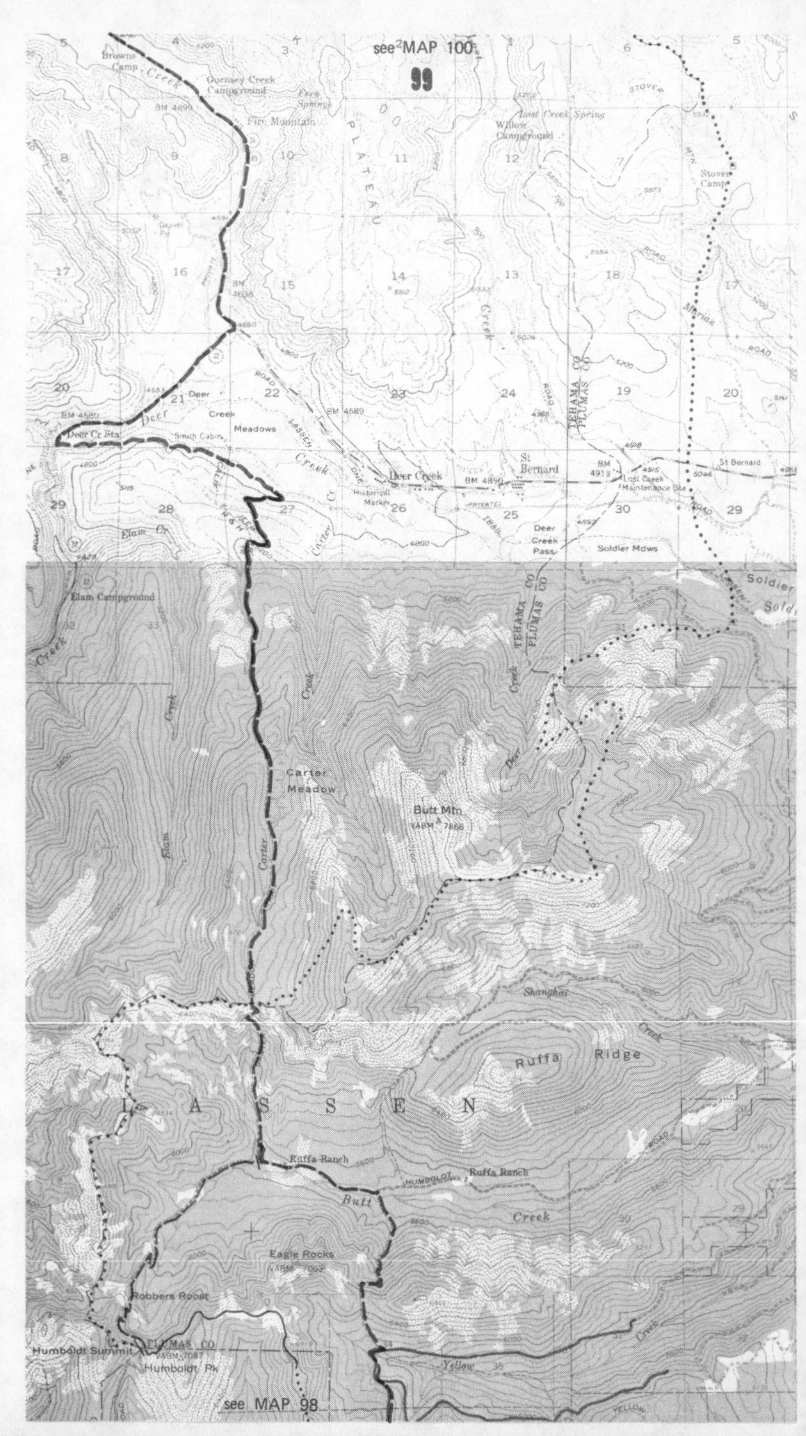
see MAP 100
99
Browns Camp
Gurnsey Creek Campground
Fern Spring
Fire Mountain
PLATEAU
Lost Creek Spring
Willow Campground
STOVER MTN.
Stover Camp
Gravel Pit
Marian
ROAD
Deer Creek Meadows
Deer Cr Sta
Smith Cabin
LASSEN
Deer Creek
Historical Marker
St Bernard
Lost Creek Maintenance Sta
TEHAMA CO
PLUMAS CO
Deer Creek Pass
Soldier Mdws
Elam Cr
Elam Campground
Carter Meadow
Butt Mtn
Shanghai
Ruffa Ridge
L A S S E N
Ruffa Ranch
HUMBOLDT ROAD
Butt Creek
Eagle Rocks
Robbers Roost
Humboldt Summit
PLUMAS CO
Humboldt Pk
Yellow Creek
see MAP 98

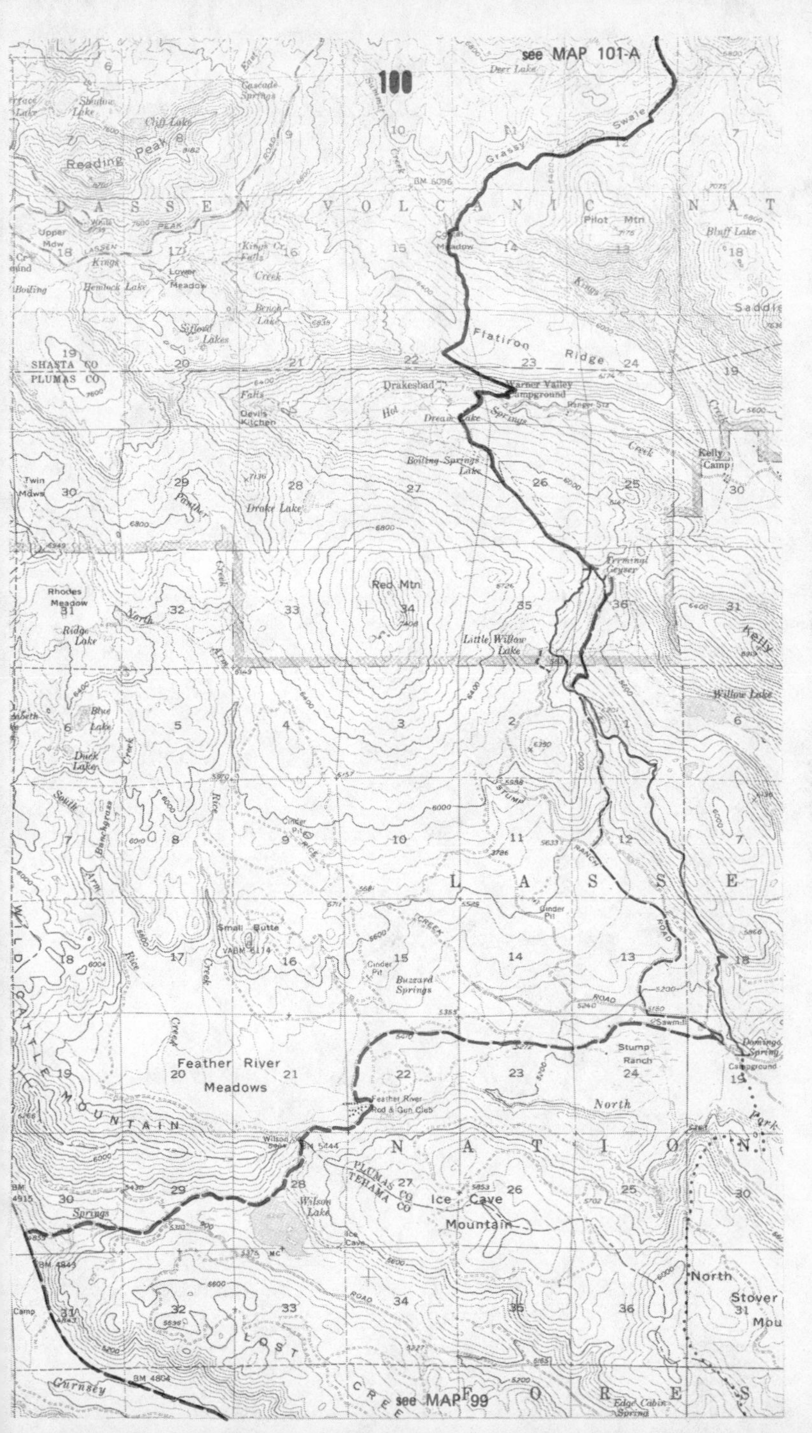

see MAP 101-A
100
Reading Peak
Cliff Lake
Shadow Lake
Cascade Springs
Deer Lake
Grassy Swale
Pilot Mtn
Bluff Lake
Upper Mdw
Lower Meadow
Kings Cr. Falls
Kings Creek
Hemlock Lake
Bench Lake
Siffleur Lakes
Corral Meadow
Flatiron Ridge
Saddle
SHASTA CO
PLUMAS CO
Drakesbad
Warner Valley Campground
Ranger Sta
Devils Kitchen
Hot Springs
Dream Lake
Boiling Springs Lake
Kelly Camp
Twin Mdws
Drake Lake
Terminal Geyser
Red Mtn
Little Willow Lake
Rhodes Meadow
Ridge Lake
Willow Lake
Blue Lake
Duck Lake
Cinder Pit
Small Butte
Buzzard Springs
Sawmill
Stump Ranch
Domingo Spring
Campground
Feather River Meadows
Feather River Rod & Gun Club
Wilson Lake
Ice Cave Mountain
Ice Cave
PLUMAS CO
TEHAMA CO
North Stover Mou
Edge Cabin Spring
Gurnsey
see MAP 99

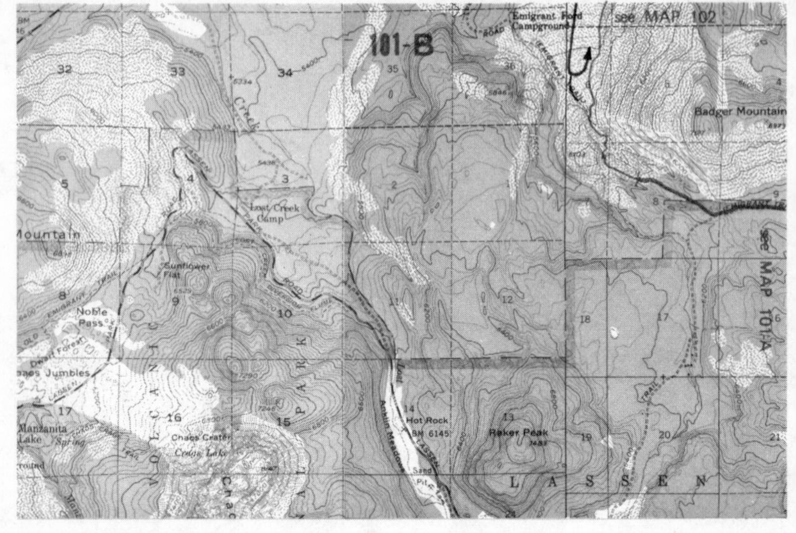

101-B
see MAP 102
Emigrant Ford Campground
Badger Mountain
Lost Creek Camp
Sunflower Flat
Noble Pass
Dwarf Forest
Chaos Jumbles
Mountain
Manzanita Lake
Chaos Crater
Crags Lake
Hot Rock
BM 6145
Raker Peak
Sand Pits
L A S S E N
V O L C A N I C
P A R K
see MAP 101-A

101-A
see MAP 102
VABM 6225
Bathtub
Bathtub Lake
Ranger Sta
Prospect Peak
Badger Flat
Gate
Soap Lake
Emigrant Lake
Cold Spring
Cinder Cone
Painted Dunes
Fantastic Lava Beds
see MAP 101-B
V O L C A N I C   N A T I O N A L   P
Cluster Lakes
Big Bear Lake
Silver Lake
Feather Lake
Little Bear Lake
Fairfield Peak
Rainbow Lake
Panther Spring
Snag Lake
SHASTA CO
LASSEN CO
Hat Mountain
Lower Twin Lake
Upper Twin Lake
Echo Lake
Swan Lake
Summit Lake
Campground
Crater Butte
Hidden Lake
see MAP 100

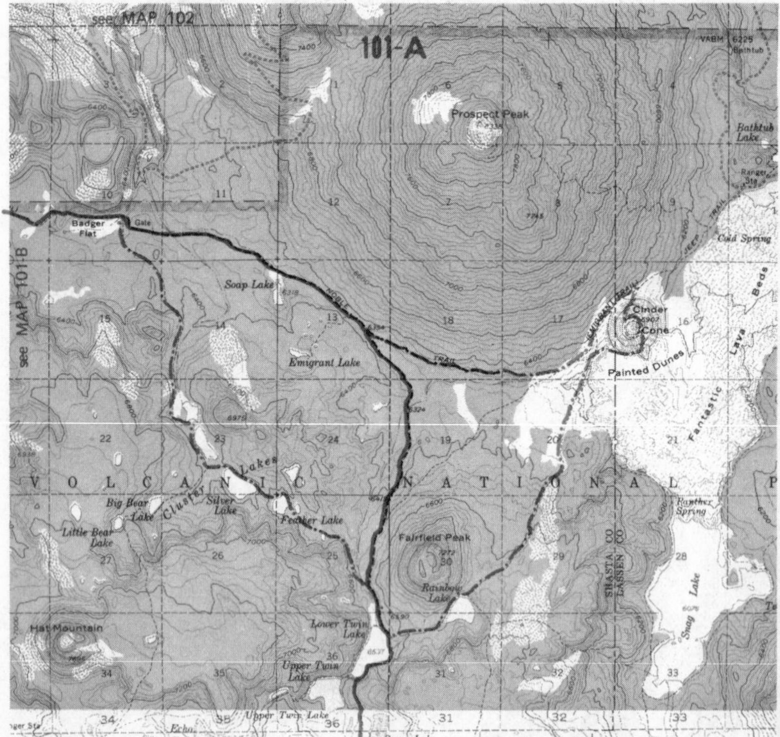

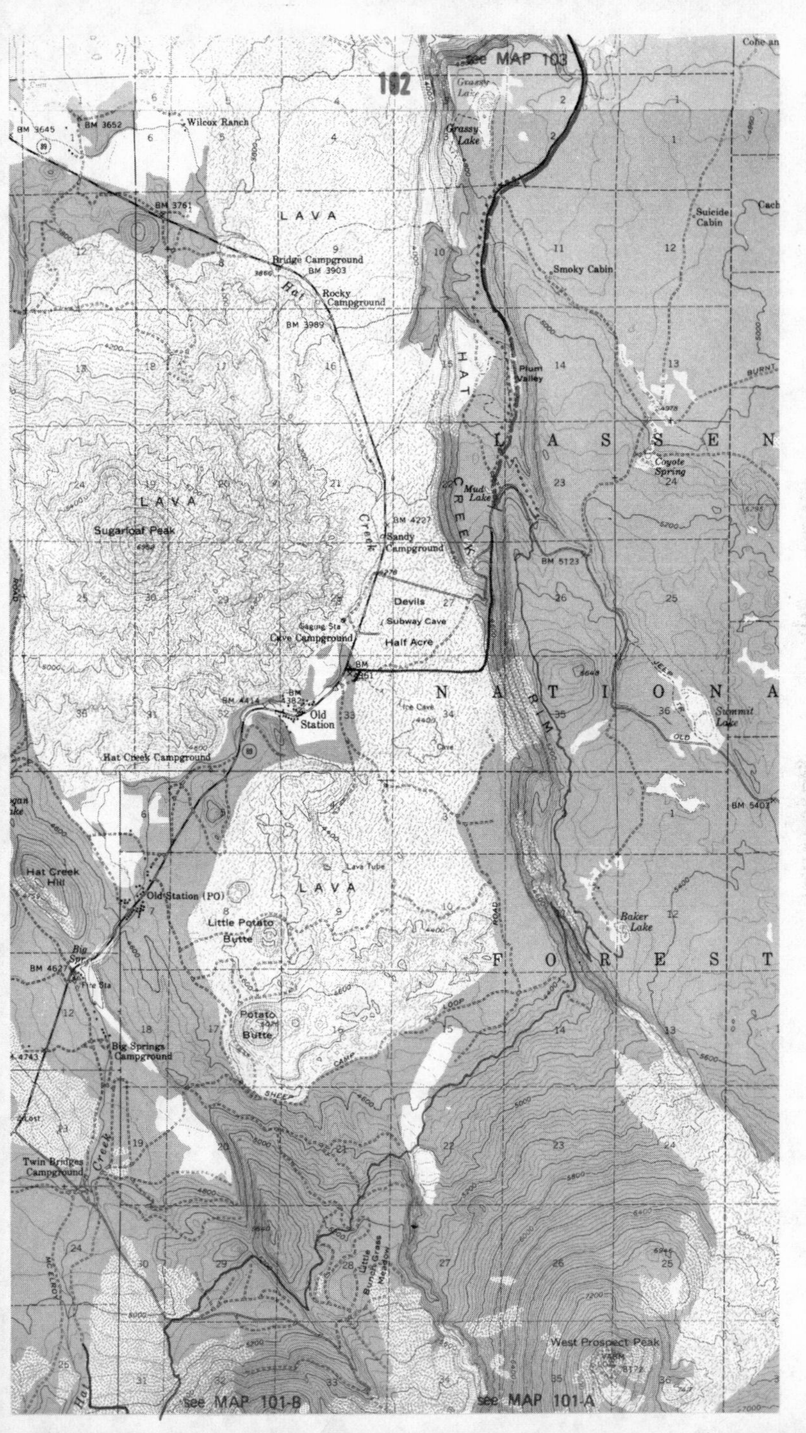

see MAP 103
102
Grassy Lake
Wilcox Ranch
BM 3645
BM 3652
BM 3761
LAVA
Suicide Cabin
Bridge Campground
BM 3903
Smoky Cabin
Hat
Rocky Campground
BM 3989
HAT
Plum Valley
BURNT
L A S S E N
Coyote Spring
Mud Lake
CREEK
LAVA
Sugarloaf Peak
Creek
BM 4227
Sandy Campground
BM 5123
Devils
Subway Cave
Gaging Sta
Cave Campground
Half Acre
N A T I O N A
RIM
JEEP
Summit Lake
OLD
BM 4414
Old Station
Ice Cave
Cave
Hat Creek Campground
BM 5401
Hat Creek Hill
Lava Tube
LAVA
Old Station (PO)
Little Potato Butte
Baker Lake
ROAD
F O R E S T
BM 4627
Fire Sta
Potato Butte
LOOP
Big Springs Campground
CAMP
SHEEP
Twin Bridges Campground
Creek
Little Bunch Grass Meadow
McELROY
West Prospect Peak
Hat
see MAP 101-B
see MAP 101-A

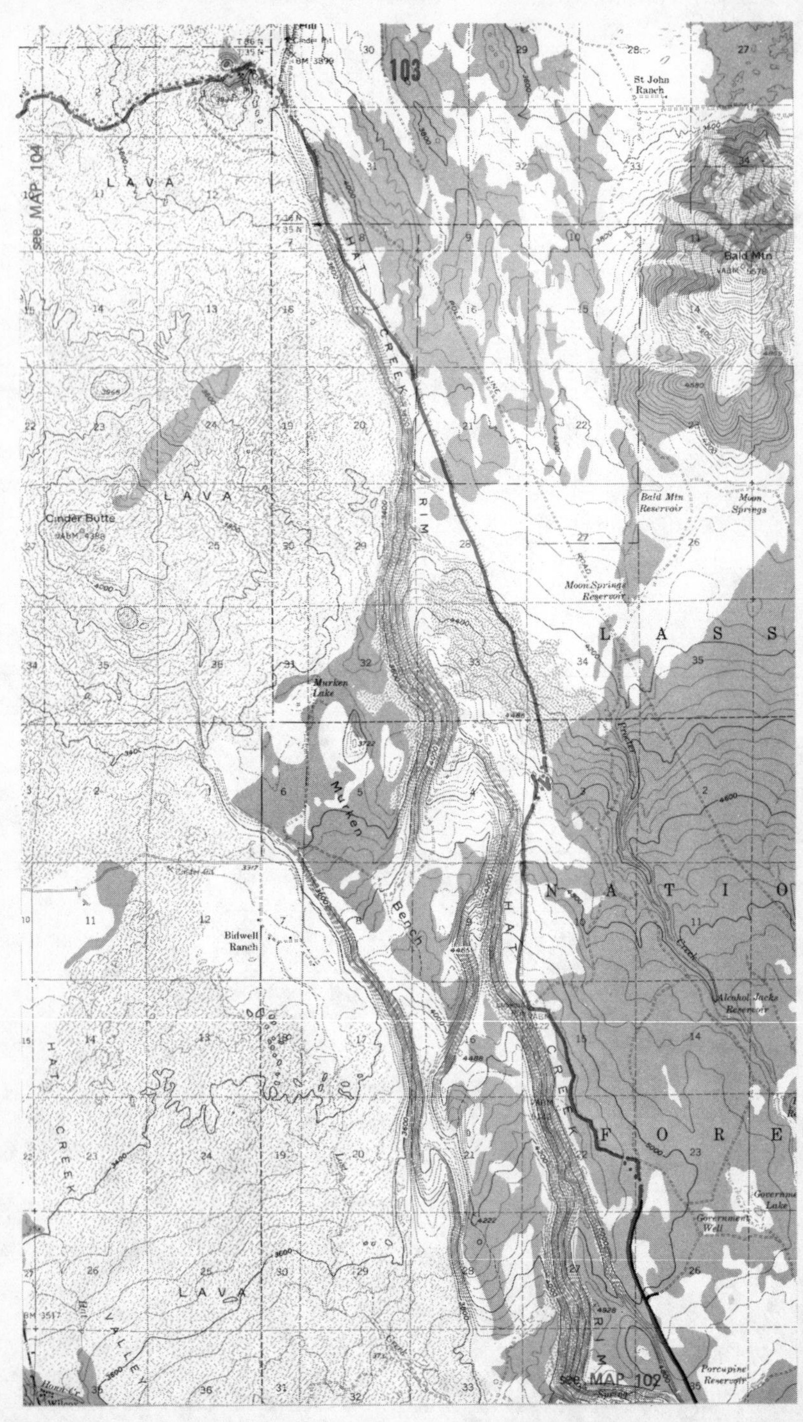

103
see MAP 104
LAVA
St John Ranch
Bald Mtn
HAT CREEK RIM
Cinder Butte
Bald Mtn Reservoir
Moon Springs
Moon Springs Reservoir
LASS
Murken Lake
Murken
Bench
Bidwell Ranch
NATIO
Alcohol Jacks Reservoir
HAT CREEK
FORE
Government Well
LAVA VALLEY
Porcupine Reservoir
see MAP 102

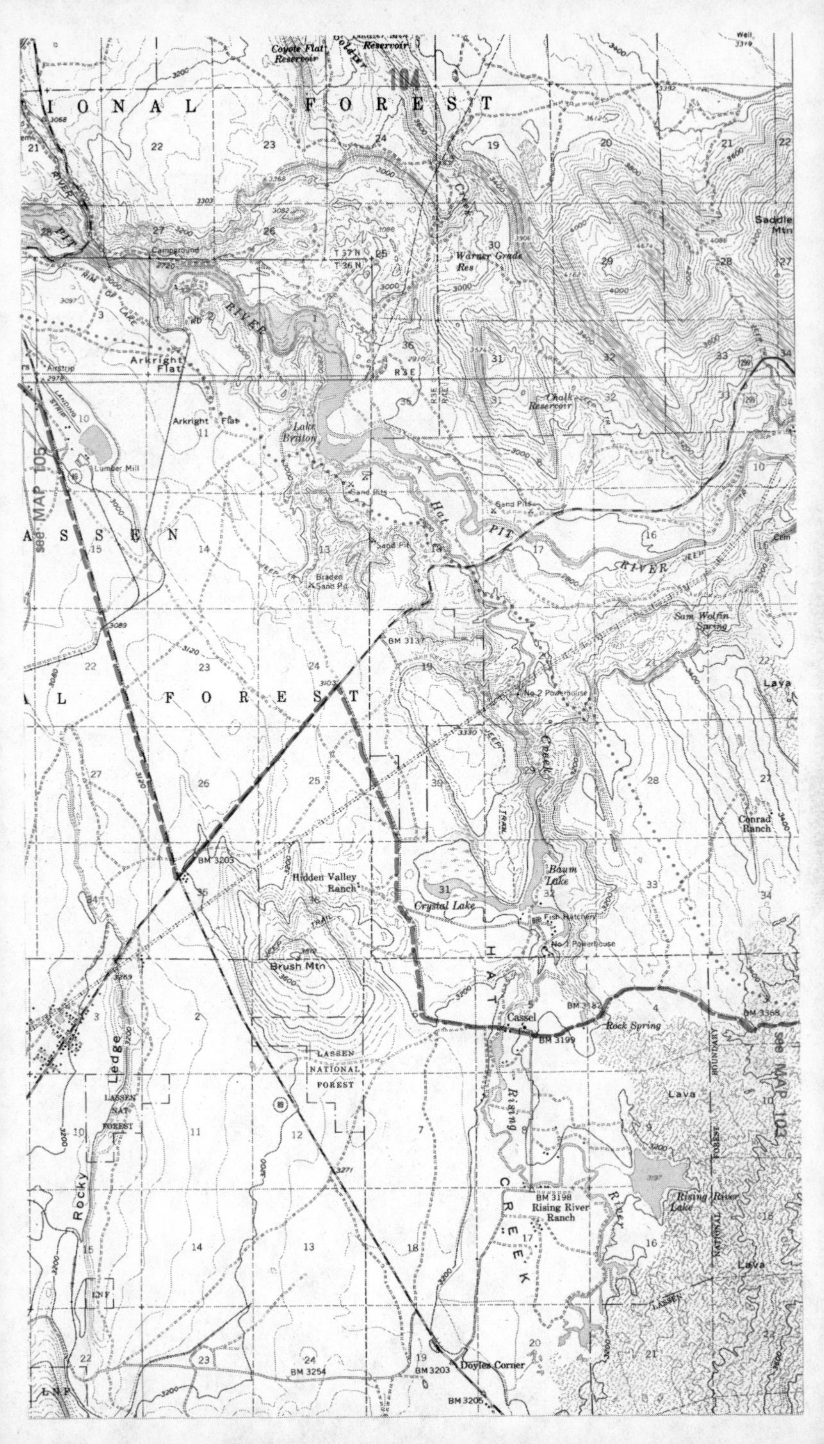

Coyote Flat Reservoir
Reservoir
IONAL FOREST
Saddle Mtn
Campground
Warner Grade Res
RIM OF LAKE RD
RIVER
PIT
Arkright Flat
Airstrip
LANDING STRIP
Lake Britton
Chalk Reservoir
Lumber Mill
SEE MAP 105
Sand Pits
Sand Pit
Hat
PIT RIVER
Braden Sand Pit
ASSEN
Sam Wolfin Spring
BM 3137
L FOREST
No 2 Powerhouse
Lava
Creek
Conrad Ranch
BM 3203
Hidden Valley Ranch
Baum Lake
Crystal Lake
Fish Hatchery
No 1 Powerhouse
Brush Mtn
Cassel
BM 3182
Rock Spring
BM 3368
BM 3199
LASSEN NATIONAL FOREST
Ledge
LASSEN NAT FOREST
Rising
SEE MAP 103
Rocky
BM 3198
Rising River Ranch
Rising River Lake
CREEK
River
LNF
Doyles Corner
BM 3254
BM 3203
BM 3205

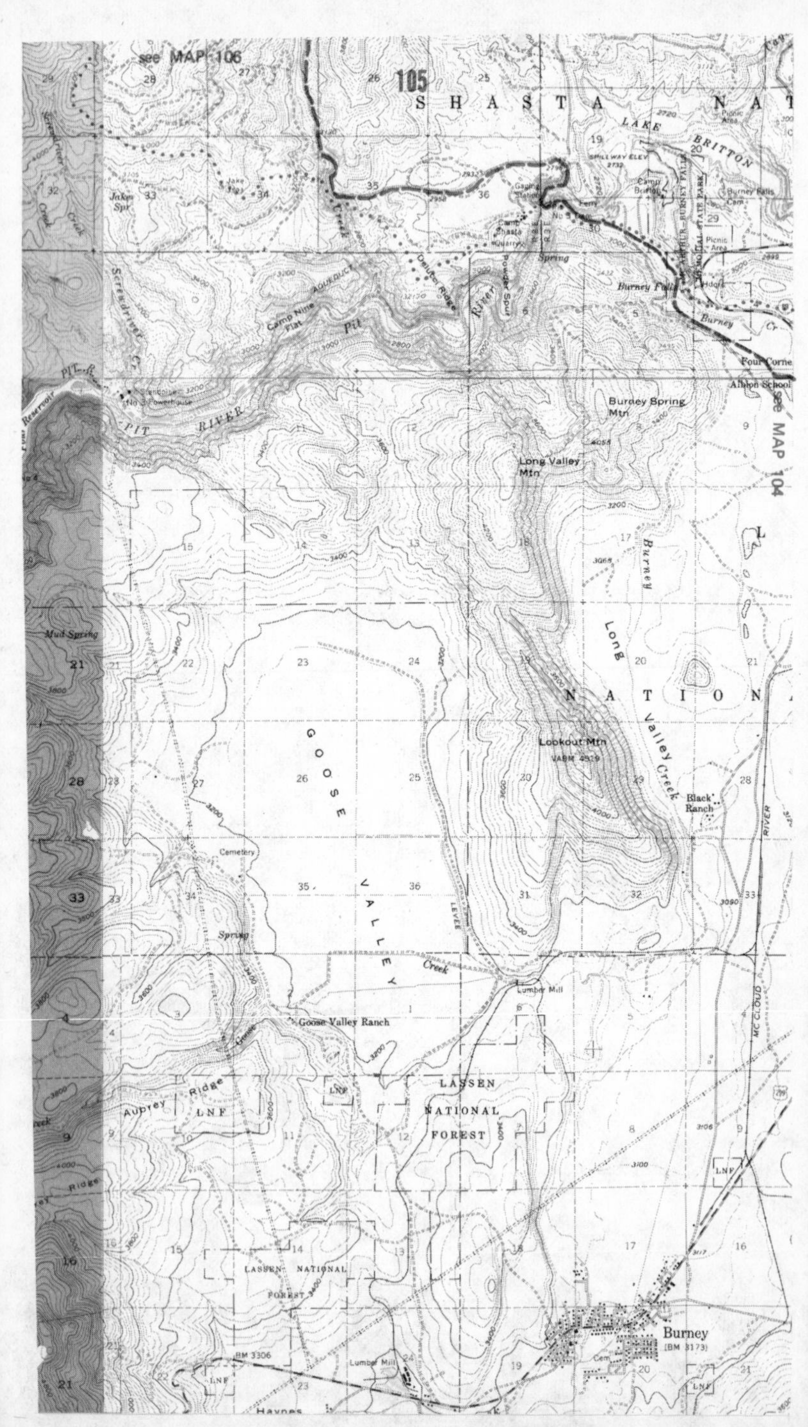
see MAP 106
105
SHASTA NAT
LAKE BRITTON
Camp Britton
Burney Falls
Pit River
Camp Nine Flat
AQUEDUCT
Powder Spur
Spring
PIT RIVER
Screwdriver Cr
Burney Spring Mtn
Long Valley Mtn
see MAP 104
Long Valley Creek
NATIONAL
Lookout Mtn
Black Ranch
GOOSE VALLEY
Creek
Cemetery
Spring
Mud Spring
Lumber Mill
Goose Valley Ranch
Aubrey Ridge
LNF
LASSEN NATIONAL FOREST
Burney
Lumber Mill
Haynes
MC CLOUD RIVER

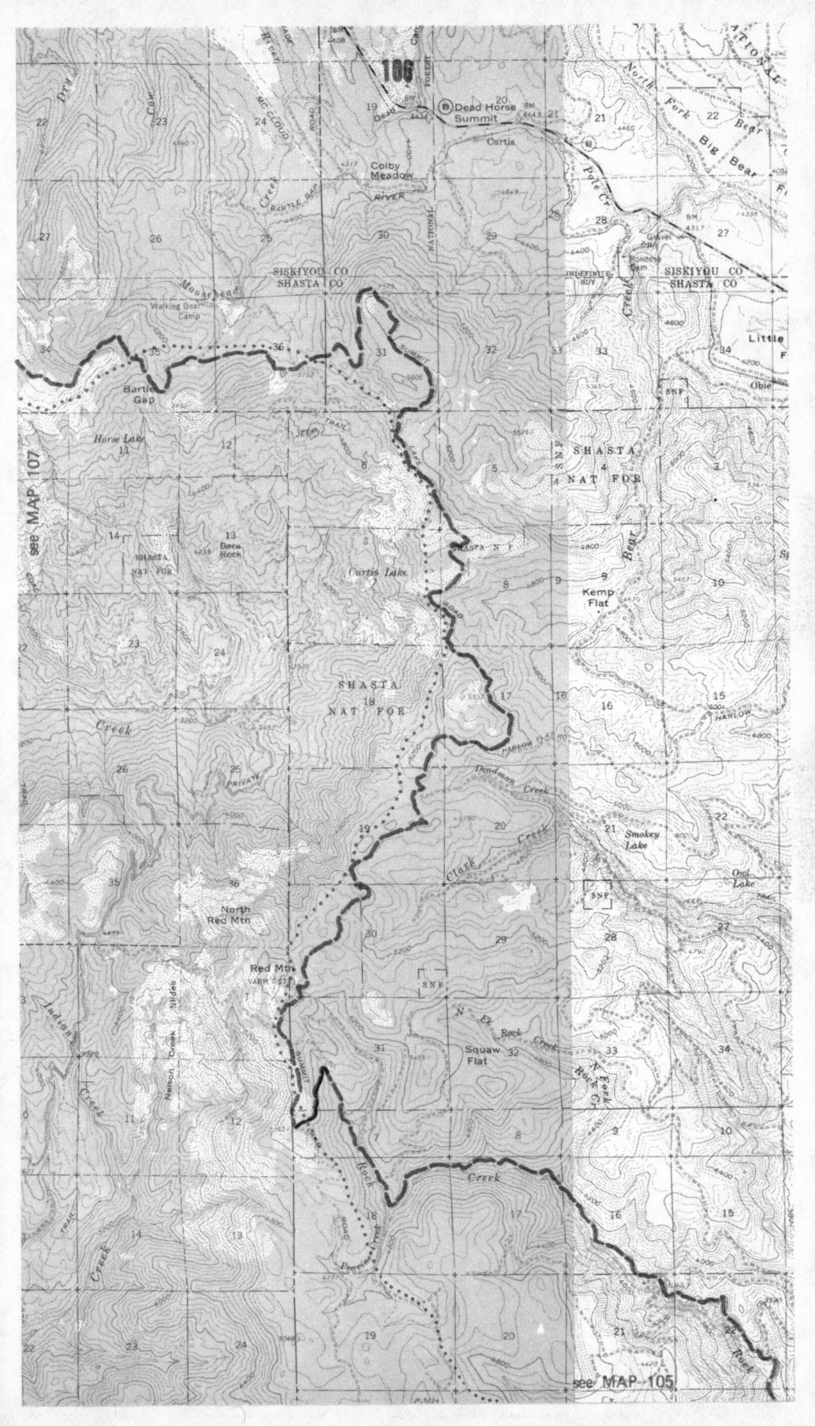

106
Dead Horse Summit
Colby Meadow
Curtis
SISKIYOU CO
SHASTA CO
Walking Bear Camp
Bartle Gap
Horse Lake
see MAP 107
Bear Rock
SHASTA NAT FOR
Curtis Lake
SHASTA NAT FOR
Kemp Flat
Deadman Creek
Smokey Lake
Owl Lake
Clark Creek
North Red Mtn
Red Mtn
Squaw Flat
N Fk Rock Creek
Nelson Creek Slides
Indian Creek
Rock Creek
North Fork Big Bear
Pole Cr
Obie
see MAP 105

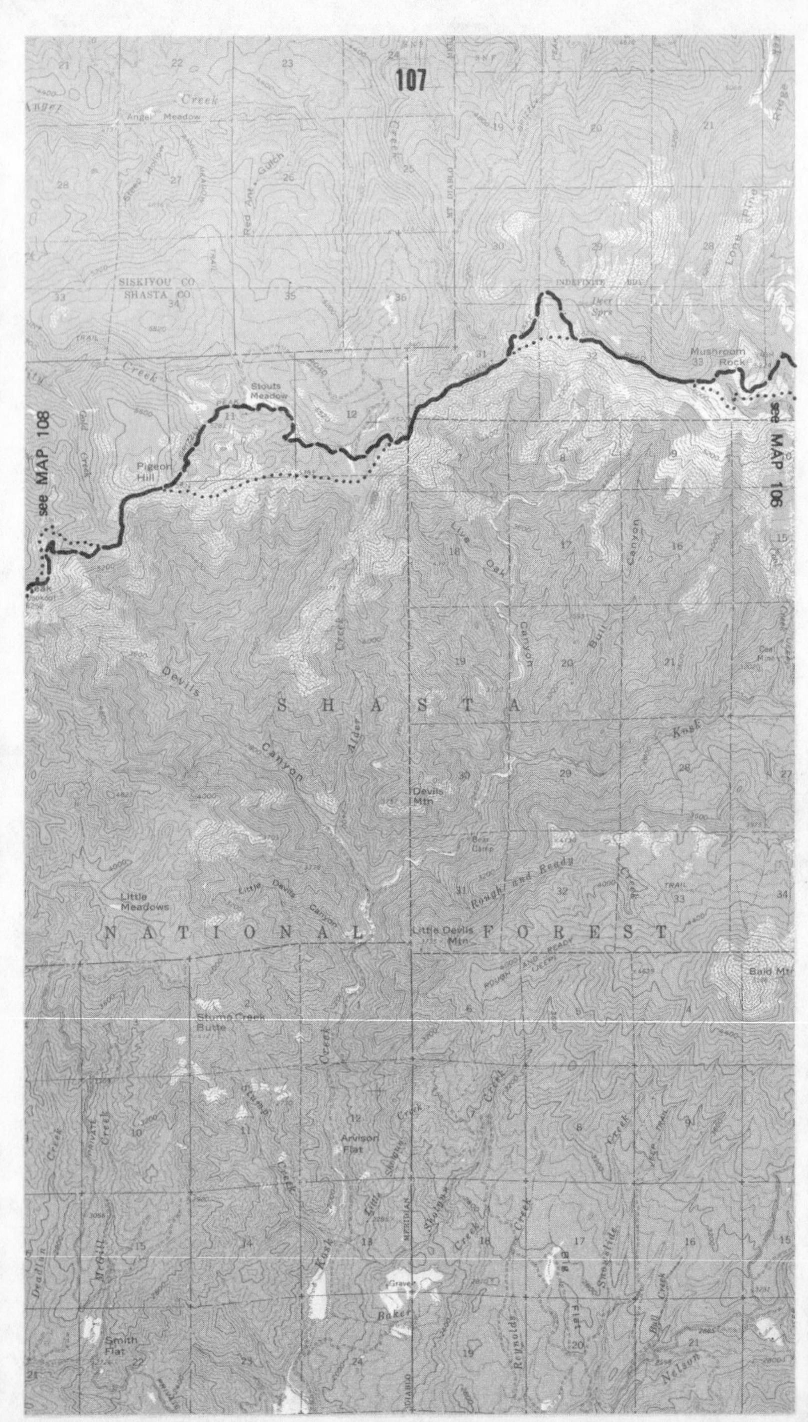

107
see MAP 108
see MAP 106
Angel Meadow
Stouts Meadow
Pigeon Hill
Mushroom Rock
SISKIYOU CO
SHASTA CO
S H A S T A
N A T I O N A L F O R E S T
Devils Mtn
Little Devils Mtn
Little Meadows
Stump Creek Butte
Arvison Flat
Smith Flat
Bald Mtn

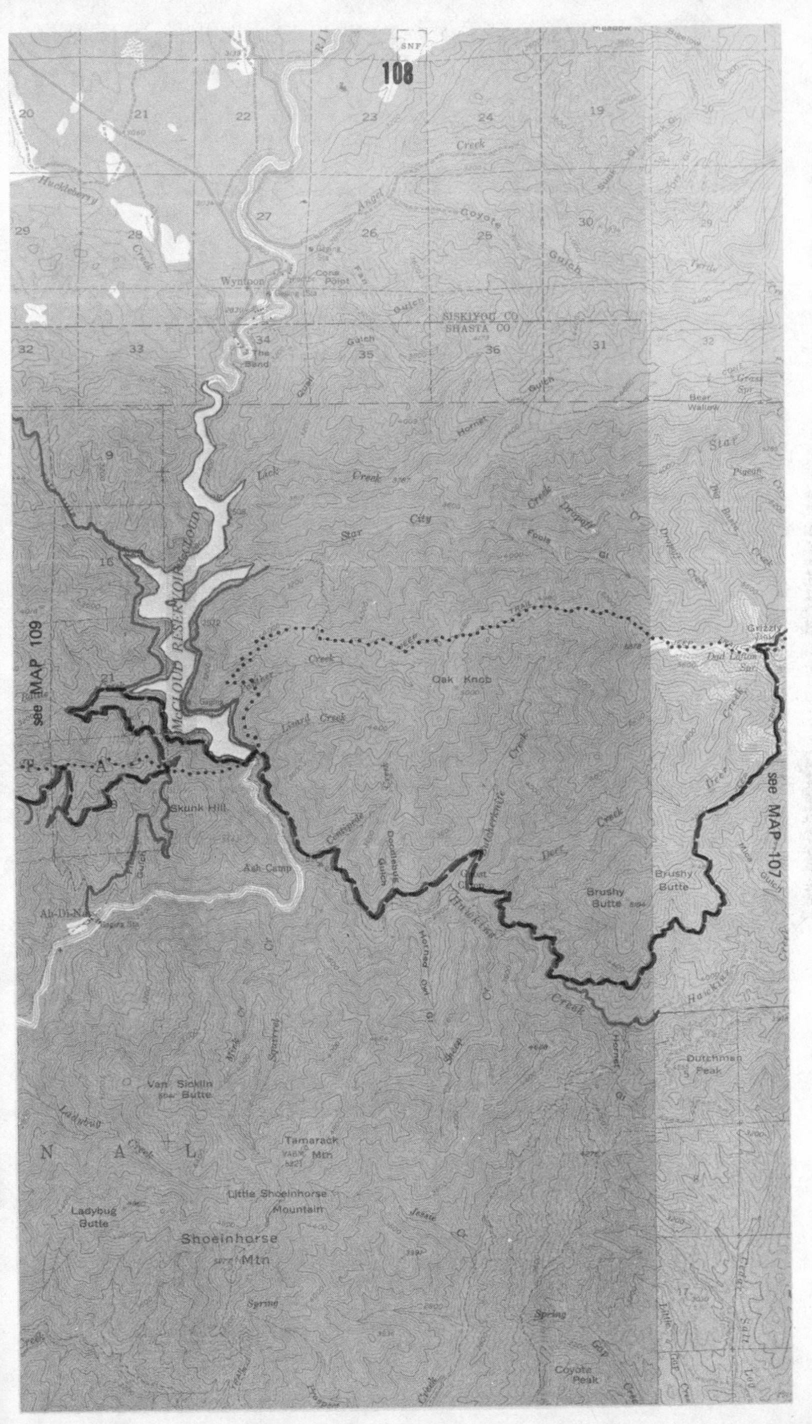

108
see MAP 109
see MAP 107
McCLOUD RESERVOIR
Wyntoon
Cone Point
SISKIYOU CO
SHASTA CO
The Bend
Skunk Hill
Ash Camp
Ah-Di-Na
Oak Knob
Brushy Butte
Dutchman Peak
Van Sicklin Butte
Tamarack Mtn
Little Shoeinhorse Mountain
Ladybug Butte
Shoeinhorse Mtn
Coyote Peak

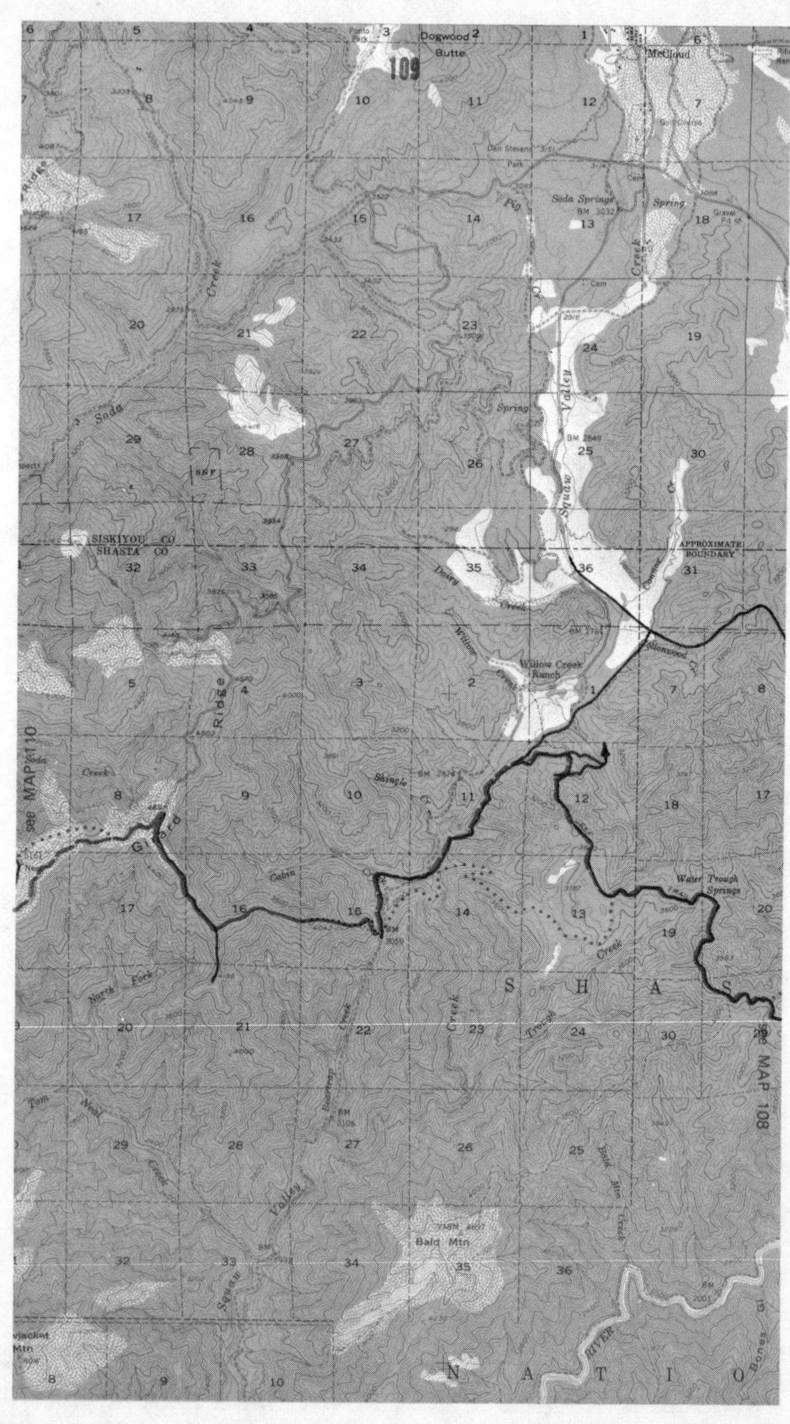
109
Dogwood Butte
McCloud
Golf Course
Dan Stevens Park
Soda Springs
Spring
Pig Cr
Squaw Valley Creek
Soda Creek
Spring
SISKIYOU CO
SHASTA CO
APPROXIMATE BOUNDARY
Dairy Creek
Willow Creek
Cottonwood Cr
Willow Creek Ranch
Ridge
see MAP 110
Soda Creek
Girard
Shingle Cr
Cabin Cr
Water Trough Springs
Trough Creek
North Fork
S H A S
see MAP 108
Tom Neal Creek
Bald Mtn Creek
Squaw Valley
Bald Mtn
RIVER
N A T I O

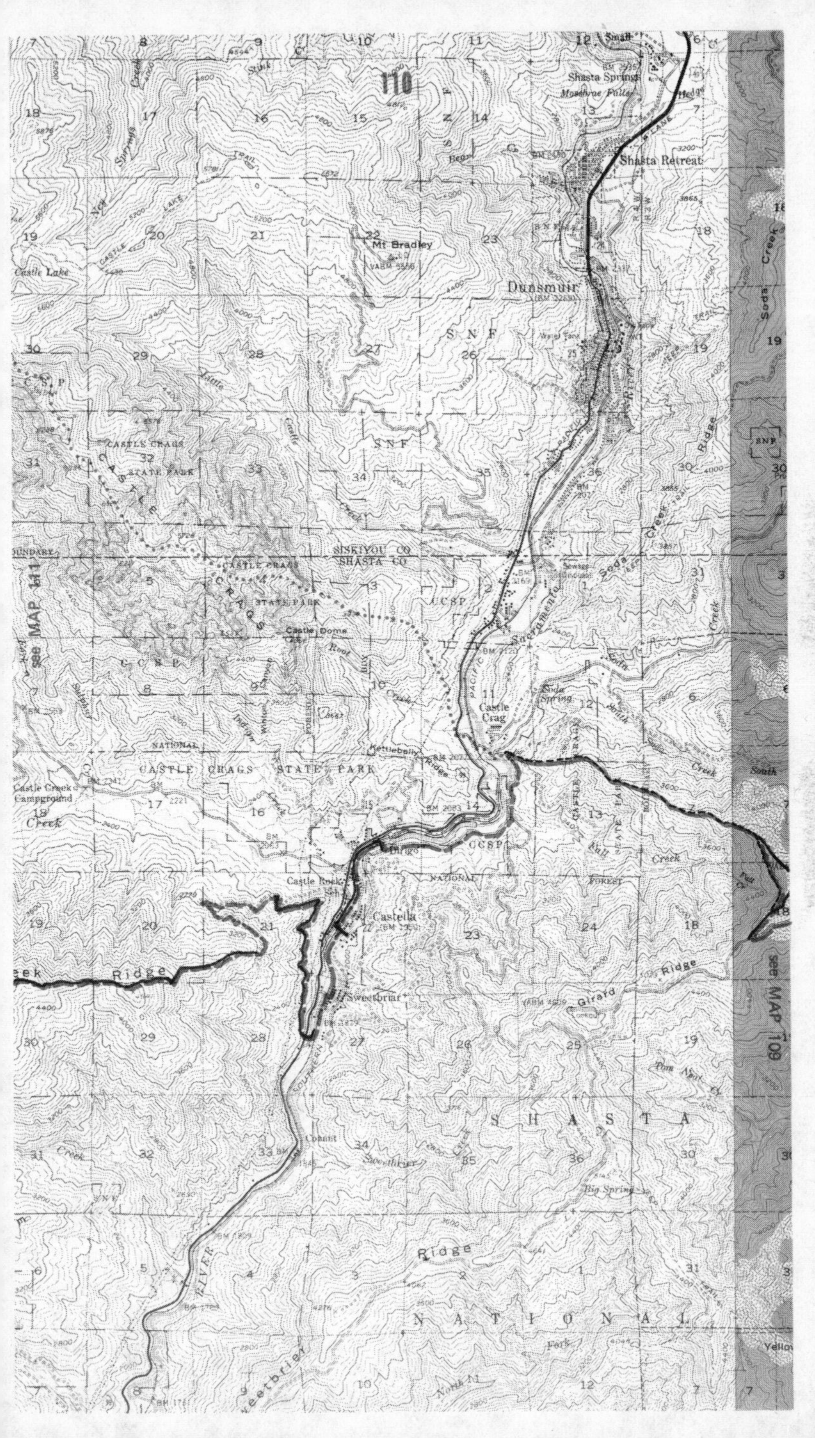

110
Shasta Springs
Mossbrae Falls
Shasta Retreat
Mt Bradley
Castle Lake
Dunsmuir
S N F
SNF
CASTLE CRAGS
STATE PARK
SISKIYOU CO
SHASTA CO
C C S P
Castle Dome
see MAP 111
Sacramento
Soda Spring
Castle Crag
Kettlebelly
Ridge
NATIONAL
CASTLE CRAGS STATE PARK
Castle Creek
Campground
Creek
Dirigo
Castle Rock
Castella
FOREST
Ridge
Sweetbriar
Girard
Soda Creek
South
see MAP 109
Conant
S H A S T A
Big Spring
Ridge
N A T I O N A L
RIVER

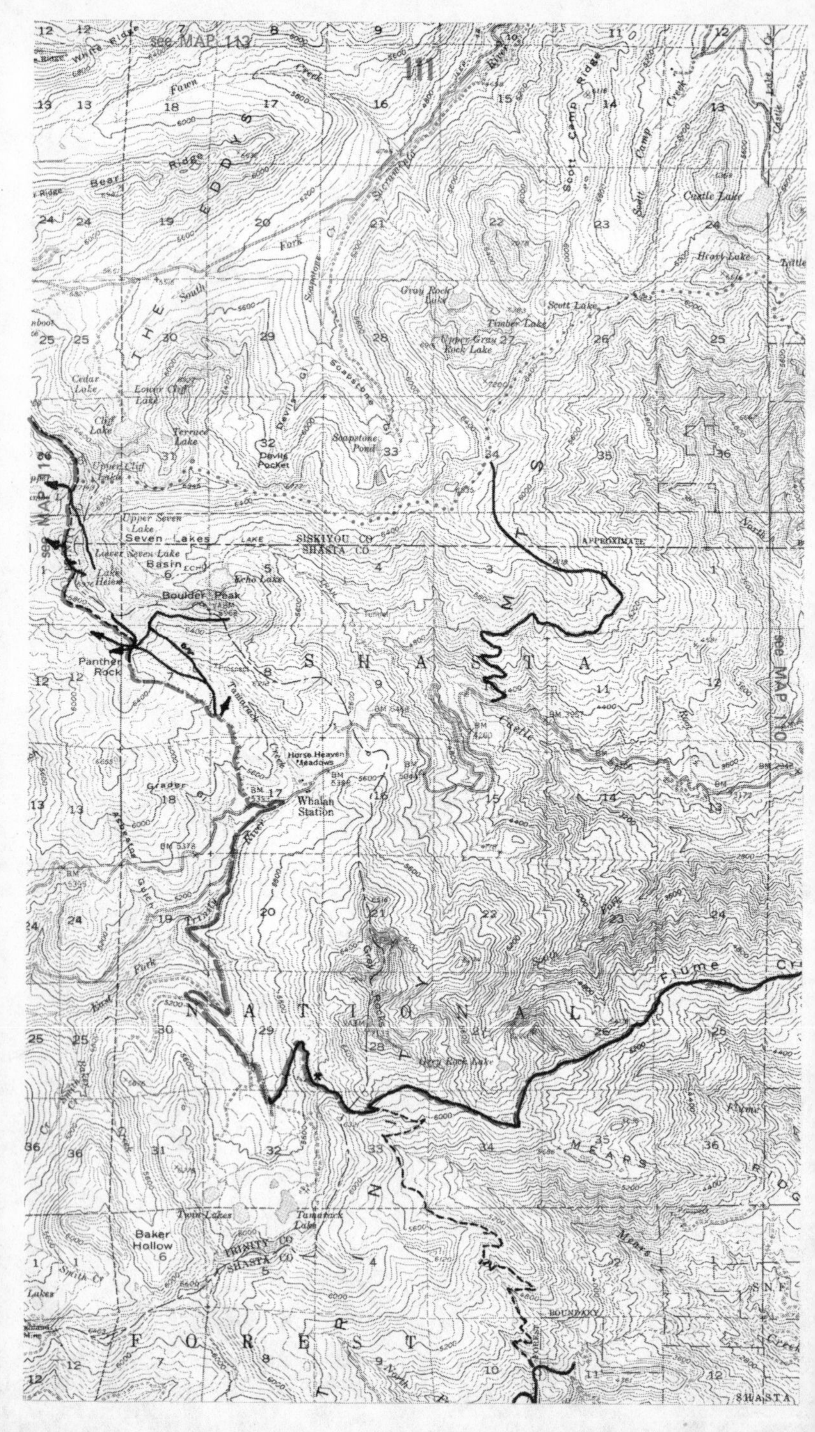
see MAP 113
111
THE EDDYS
Bear Ridge
Scott Camp Ridge
Castle Lake
Heart Lake
Scott Lake
Gray Rock Lake
Timber Lake
Upper Gray Rock Lake
Cedar Lake
Lower Cliff Lake
Cliff Lake
Terrace Lake
Upper Cliff Lake
Devils Pocket
Soapstone Pond
Upper Seven Lake
Seven Lakes
Lower Seven Lake
Basin
Lake Helen
Echo Lake
Boulder Peak
SISKIYOU CO
SHASTA CO
APPROXIMATE
see MAP 110
Panther Rock
SHASTA
Horse Heaven Meadows
Whalan Station
Grader
NATIONAL
Flume Cr
Grey Rock Lake
MEARS
Twin Lakes
Tamarack Lake
Baker Hollow
TRINITY CO
SHASTA CO
BOUNDARY
FOREST
S.N.F.
SHASTA

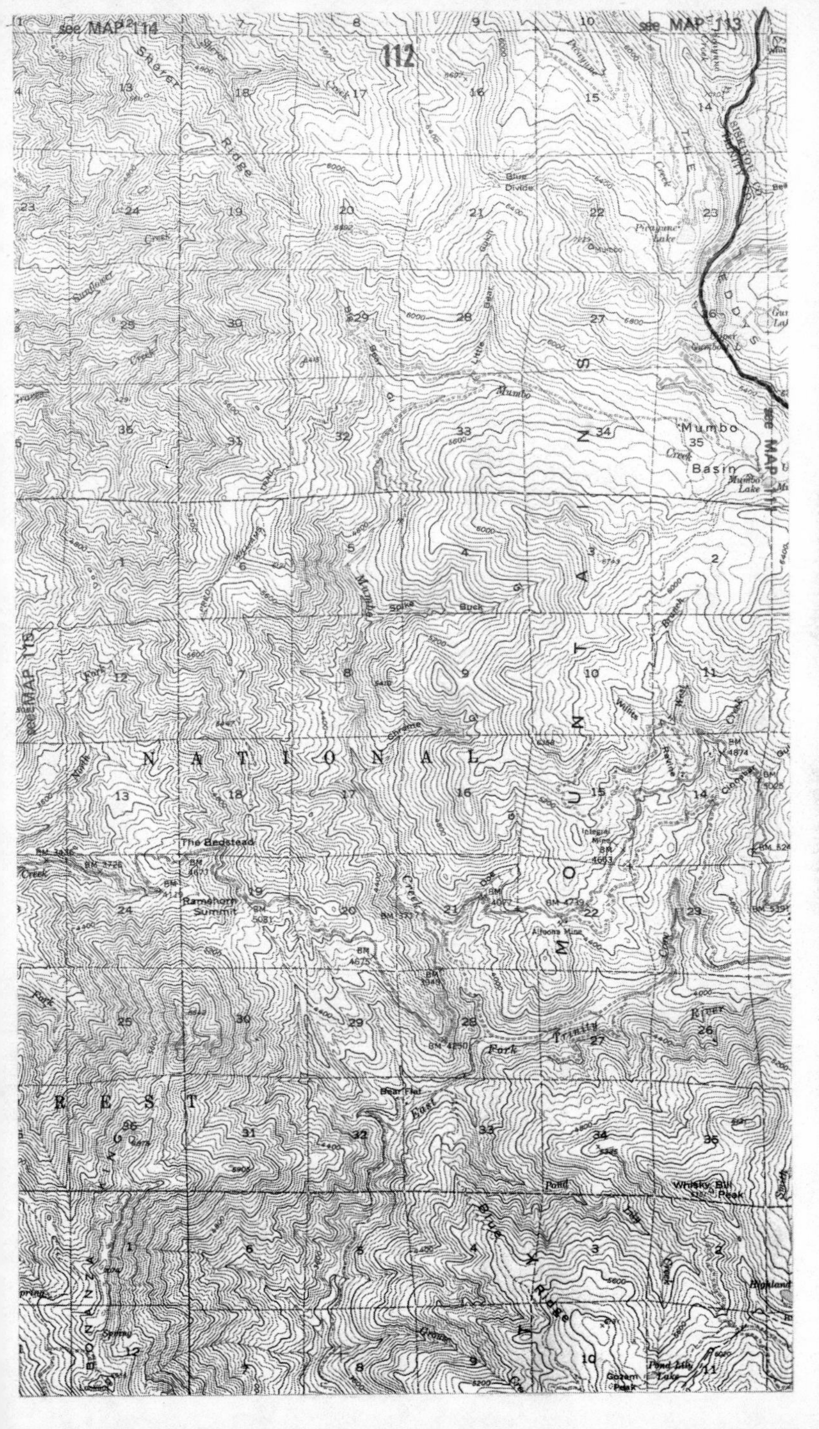
see MAP 114
112
see MAP 113
Shasta Ridge
Blue Divide
Picayune Lake
Mumbo Creek
Mumbo Basin
Mumbo Lake
see MAP 111
see MAP 115
Spike Buck
N A T I O N A L
The Bedstead
Ramshorn Summit
Integral Mine
Altoona Mine
East Fork Trinity River
Bear Flat
R E S T
M O U N T A I N S
T H E
Whisky Bill Peak
Blue Ridge
Pond Lily Lake
Gozem Peak
Highland

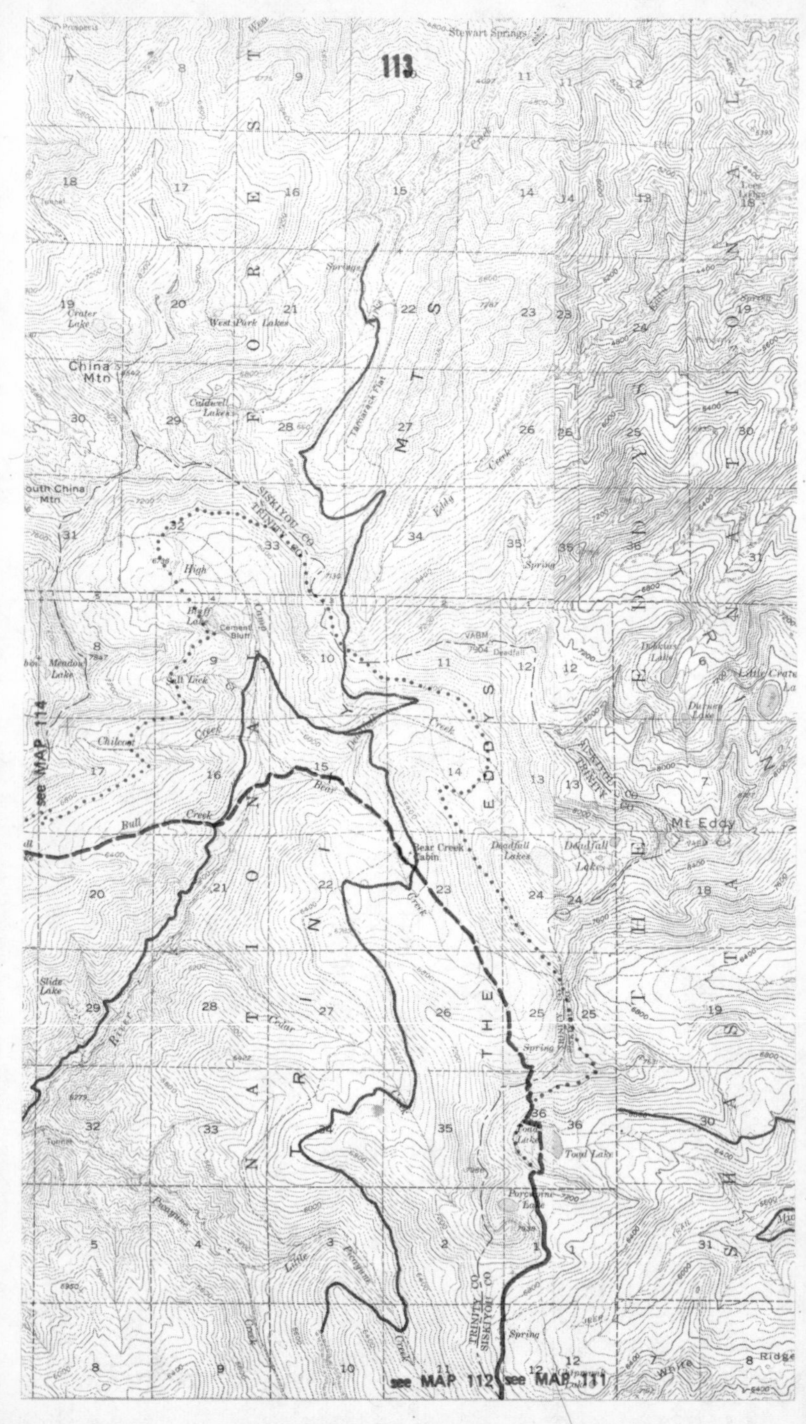
113
Stewart Springs
China Mtn
South China Mtn
Crater Lake
West Park Lakes
Caldwell Lakes
Tamarack Flat
Eddy Creek
SISKIYOU CO
TRINITY CO
High
Bluff Lake
Cement Bluff
Camp
Salt Lick
Meadow Lake
Chilcoot
Creek
Bull Creek
Bear Creek Cabin
Deadfall
Deadfall Lakes
Dobkins Lake
Durney Lake
Little Crater Lake
Mt Eddy
Slide Lake
River
Cedar
Spring
Toad Lake
Porcupine Lake
Little Picayune Creek
Tunnel
White Ridge
Lees Lodge
Prospects
see MAP 114
see MAP 112
see MAP 111
THE EDDYS
TRINITY NATIONAL FOREST
MTS
SHASTA NATIONAL FOREST

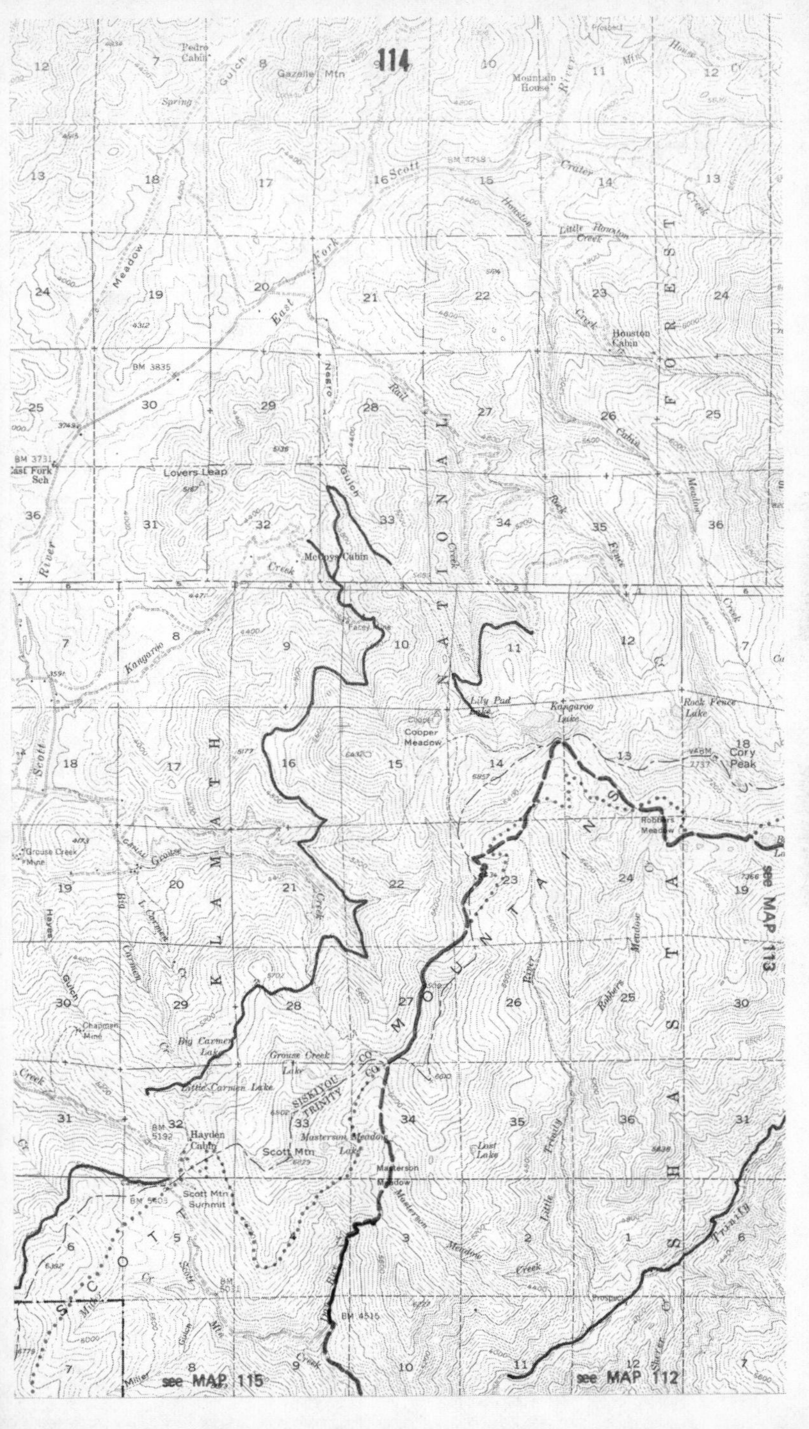

Pedro Cabin
Gazelle Mtn
Mountain House
Scott River
East Fork
Crater Creek
Houston Creek
Little Houston Creek
Houston Cabin
Meadow
Lovers Leap
McCoys Cabin
Negro Gulch
Rail Creek
Cabin Creek
Rock Fence Creek
Kangaroo Creek
Lily Pad Lake
Kangaroo Lake
Rock Fence Lake
Cooper Meadow
Cory Peak
Robbers Meadow
Grouse Creek Myne
Big Carmen Lake
Little Carmen Lake
Grouse Creek Lake
Chapman Mine
Hayden Cabin
Scott Mtn
Scott Mtn Summit
Masterson Meadow Lake
Masterson Meadow
Lost Lake
Little Trinity River
Trinity River
SISKIYOU CO
TRINITY CO
KLAMATH NATIONAL FOREST
SHASTA NATIONAL FOREST
SCOTT MOUNTAINS
see MAP 113
see MAP 115
see MAP 112

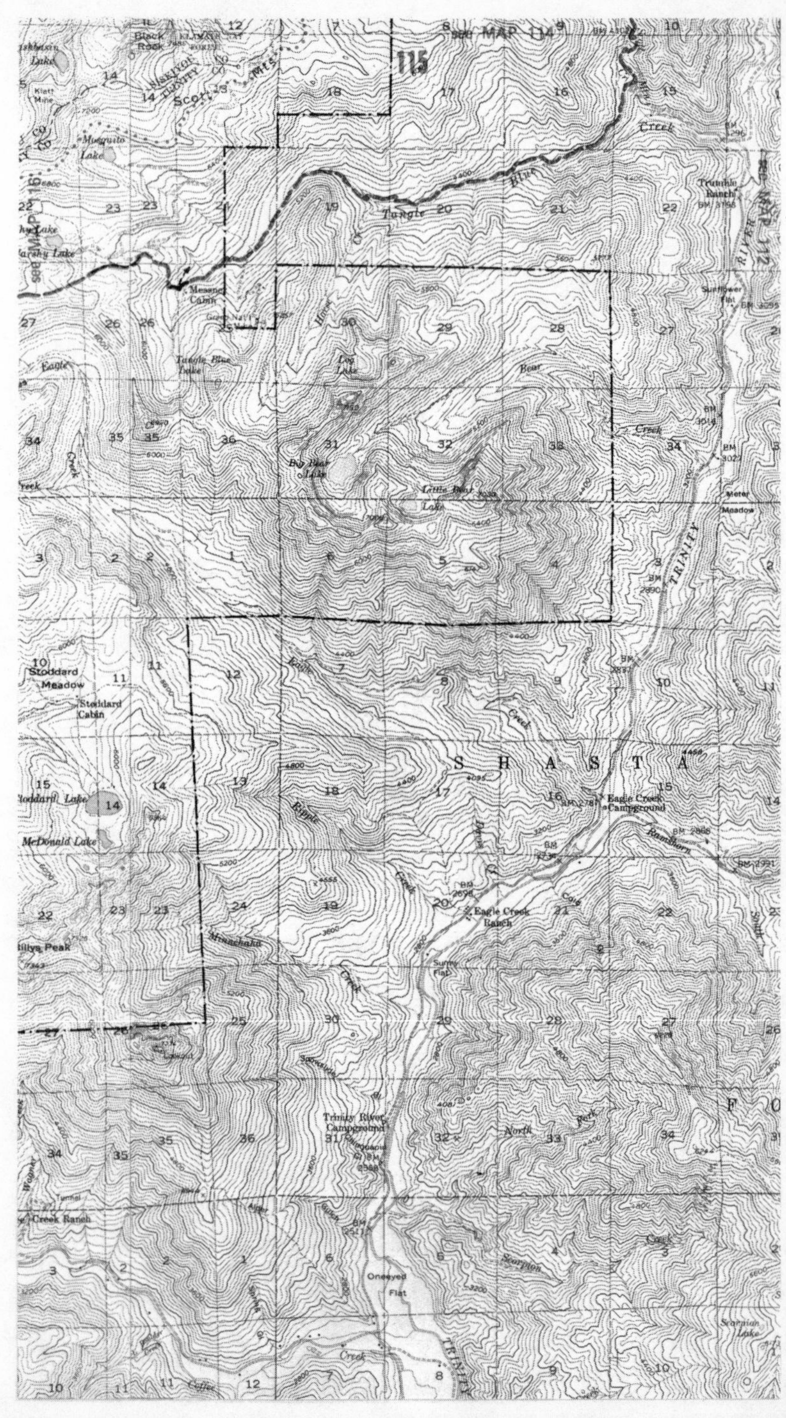

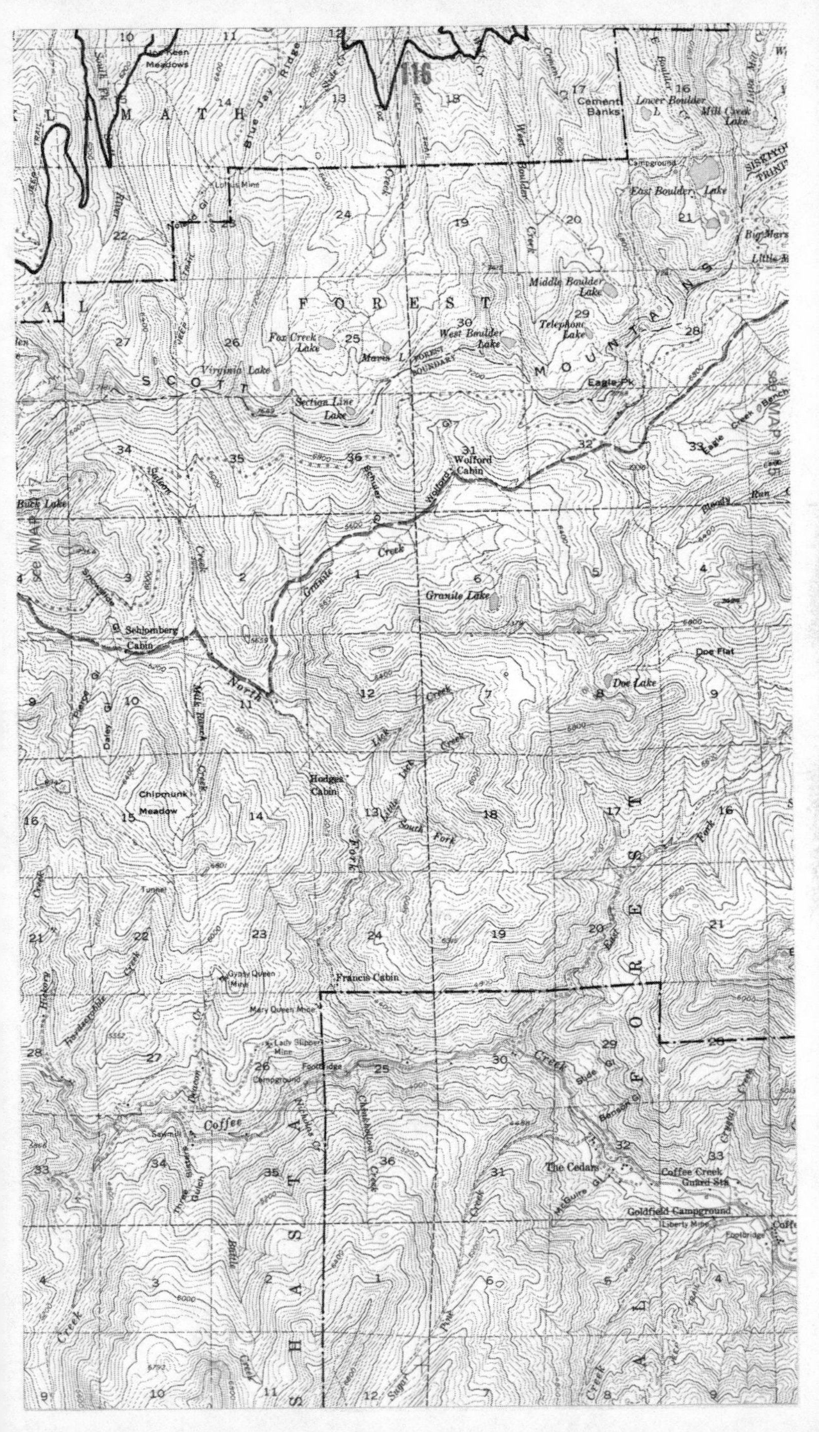

McKeen Meadows
Blue Jay Ridge
Cement Banks
Lower Boulder L
Mill Creek Lake
Campground
East Boulder Lake
Big Marsh
Little Marsh
Middle Boulder Lake
Telephone Lake
West Boulder Lake
Fox Creek Lake
Maria L
FOREST BOUNDARY
Virginia Lake
Section Line Lake
Eagle Pk
Eagle Creek Bench
SEE MAP 115
K L A M A T H
A L
F O R E S T
S C O T T
M O U N T A I N S
Wolford Cabin
Buck Lake
SEE MAP 117
Granite Creek
Granite Lake
Schlomberg Cabin
Doe Flat
Doe Lake
North
Lick Creek
Hodges Cabin
Chipmunk Meadow
South Fork
Tunnel
Gypsy Queen Mine
Francis Cabin
Mary Queen Mine
Lady Slipper Mine
Footbridge
Campground
Coffee
Sawmill
Three Sisters Gulch
The Cedars
Coffee Creek Guard Sta
Goldfield Campground
Liberty Mine
Footbridge
S H A S T A
T R I N I T Y

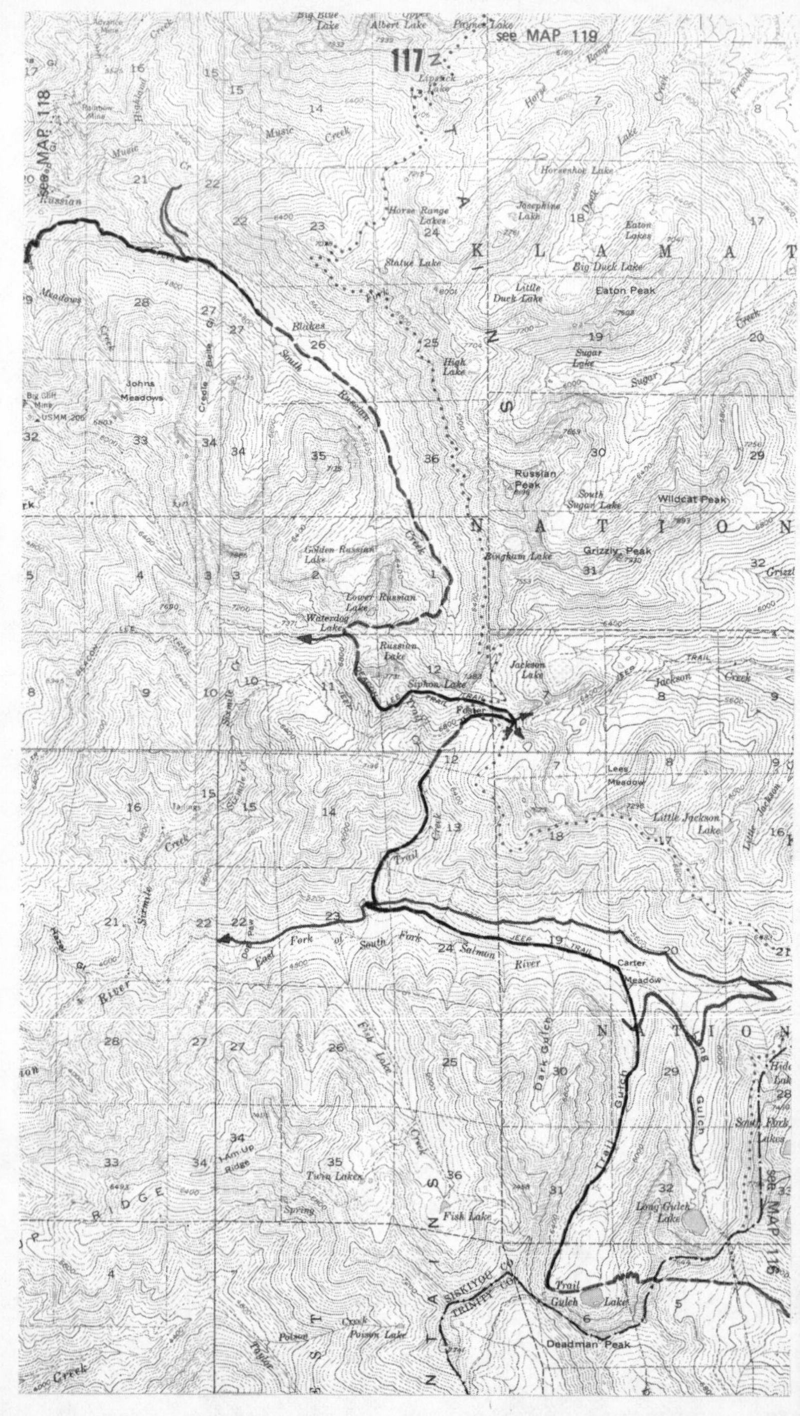
117
see MAP 119
see MAP 118
see MAP 116
Big Blue Lake
Upper Albert Lake
Paynes Lake
Lipstick Lake
Horse Range Lakes
Statue Lake
Josephine Lake
Horseshoe Lake
Eaton Lakes
Big Duck Lake
Little Duck Lake
Eaton Peak
Sugar Lake
High Lake
Blakes Fork
South Russian Creek
Johns Meadows
Big Cliff Mine
Russian Peak
South Sugar Lake
Wildcat Peak
Grizzly Peak
Bingham Lake
Golden Russian Lake
Lower Russian Lake
Waterdog Lake
Russian Lake
Siphon Lake
Jackson Lake
Jackson Creek
Foster Lake
Lees Meadow
Little Jackson Lake
East Fork of South Fork Salmon River
Carter Meadow
Dark Gulch
Trail Gulch
Long Gulch
Long Gulch Lake
Trail Gulch Lake
Deadman Peak
Twin Lakes
Fish Lake
Poison Lake
I-Am-Up Ridge
South Fork Lakes
SISKIYOU CO
TRINITY CO
K L A M A T H
N A T I O N A L
S I S K I Y O U
JEEP TRAIL

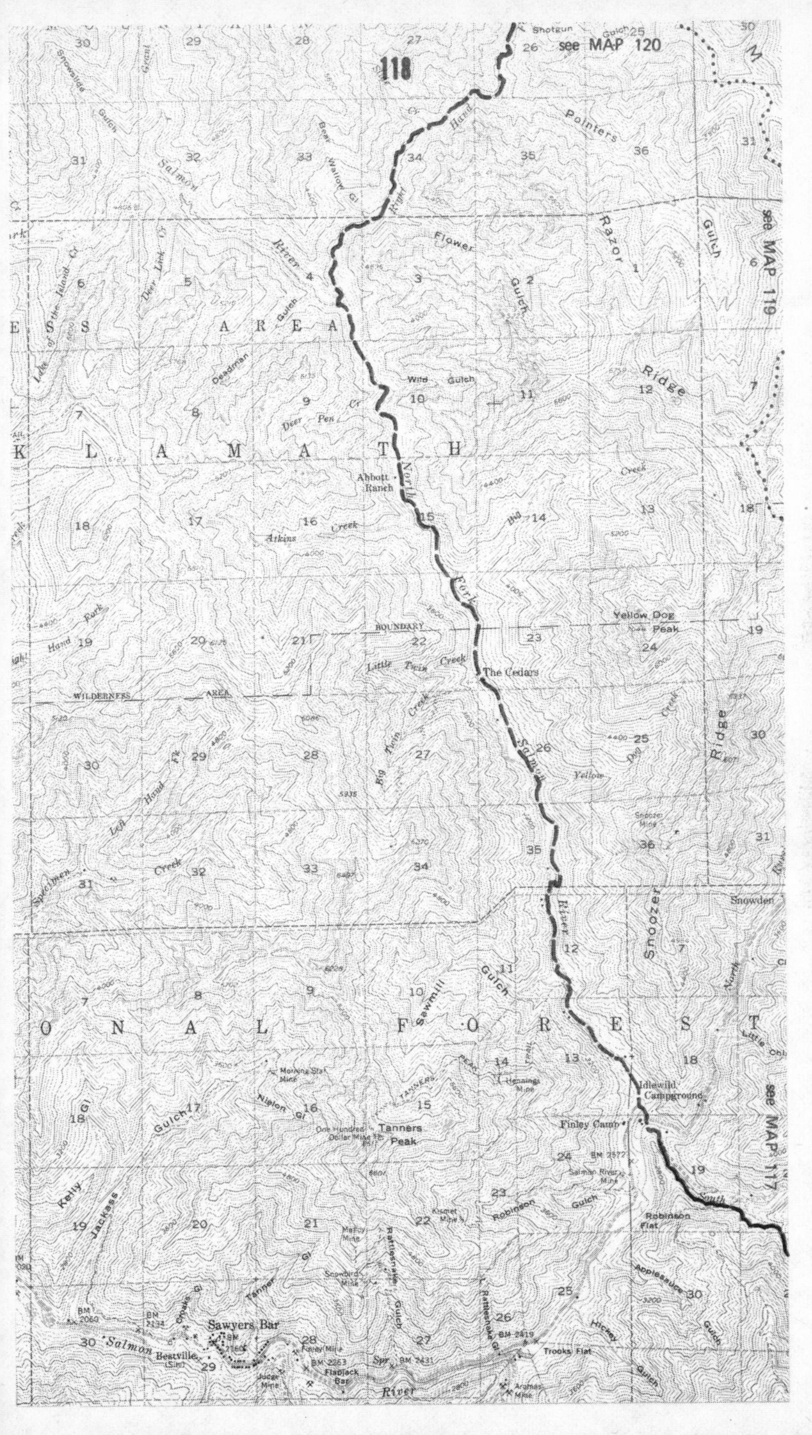

118
see MAP 120
see MAP 119
see MAP 117
Shotgun Gulch
Pointers
Razor
Gulch
Flower
Gulch
Ridge
Wild Gulch
Deer Pen Cr
Abbott Ranch
North Fork
Salmon River
Atkins Creek
Bear Wallow Gl
Deer Lick Cr
Deadman Gulch
Snowslide Gulch
Yellow Dog Peak
The Cedars
Little Twin Creek
Big Twin Creek
Yellow Dog Creek
Snoozer Mine
Hand Fork
Left Hand Fk
Specimen Creek
K L A M A T H
E S S A R E A
WILDERNESS AREA
BOUNDARY
O N A L F O R E S T
Snoozer Ridge
Snowden
Sawmill Gulch
Morning Star Mine
Nigion Gl
Hennings Mine
Tanners Peak
One Hundred Dollar Mine
Idlewild Campground
Finley Camp
Salmon River Mine
Robinson Gulch
Robinson Flat
Kismet Mine
Kelly
Jackass
Gulch
Rattlesnake Gl
Rattlesnake Gulch
Snowbird Mine
Applesauce Gulch
Hickey Gulch
Sawyers Bar
Bestville (Site)
Salmon River
Flapjack Bar
Judge Mine
Trooks Flat
Arumas Mine
South
Little North

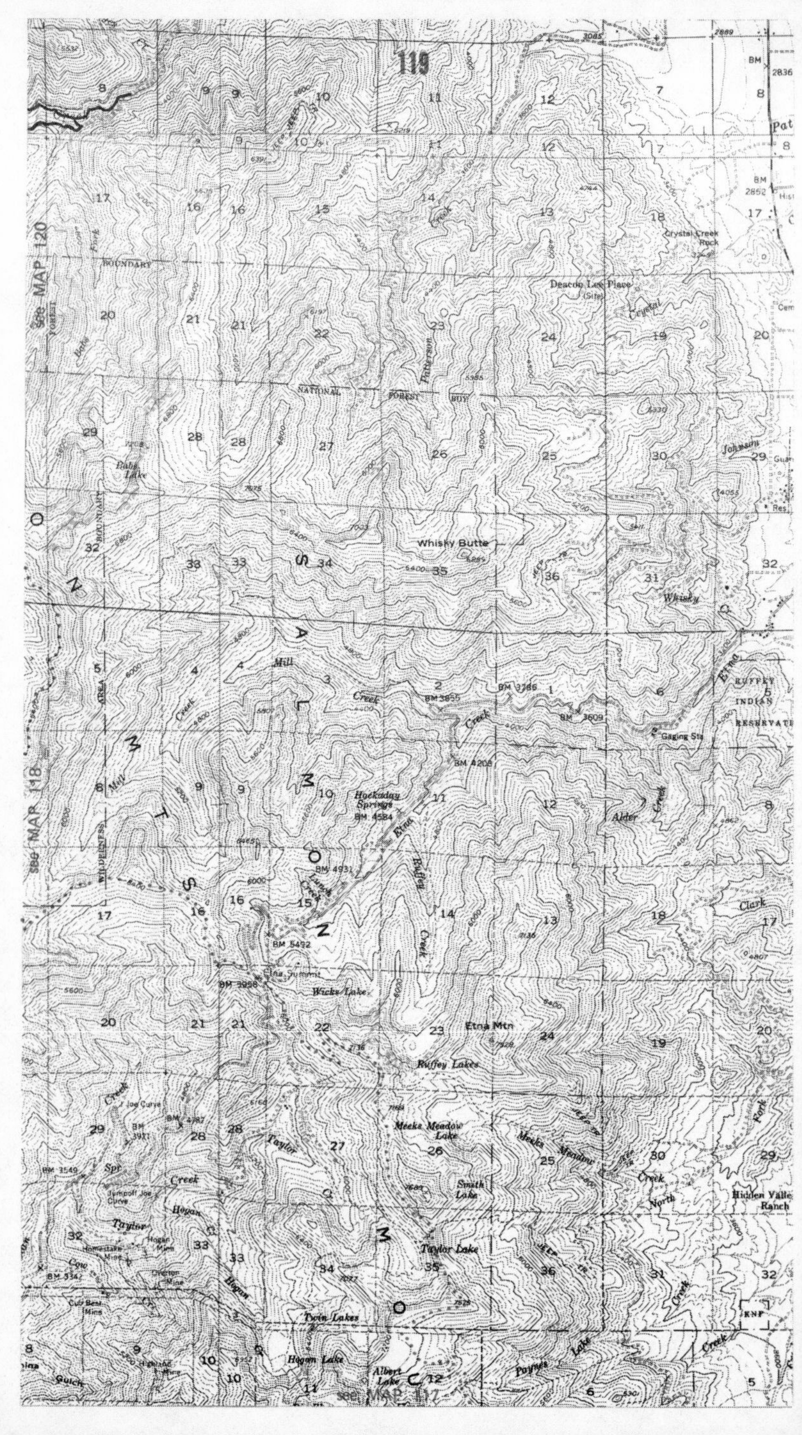

119
see MAP 120
see MAP 118
see MAP 117
Deacon Lee Place (Site)
Crystal Creek Rock
Whisky Butte
Patterson Creek
NATIONAL FOREST BDY
Babe Lake
Mill Creek
Etna Creek
Hockaday Springs
Lunch Creek
Ruffey Creek
Alder Creek
Clark
Etna Summit
Wicks Lake
Etna Mtn
Ruffey Lakes
RUFFEY INDIAN RESERVATION
Gaging Sta
Meeks Meadow Lake
Smith Lake
Taylor Lake
Twin Lakes
Hogan Lake
Albert Lake
Paynes Lake
Taylor Creek
Hogan Creek
Jumpoff Joe Curve
Homestake Mine
Hogan Mine
Cut Best Mine
Hidden Valley Ranch
North Fork
Whisky
Johnson
KNF
MOUNTAINS

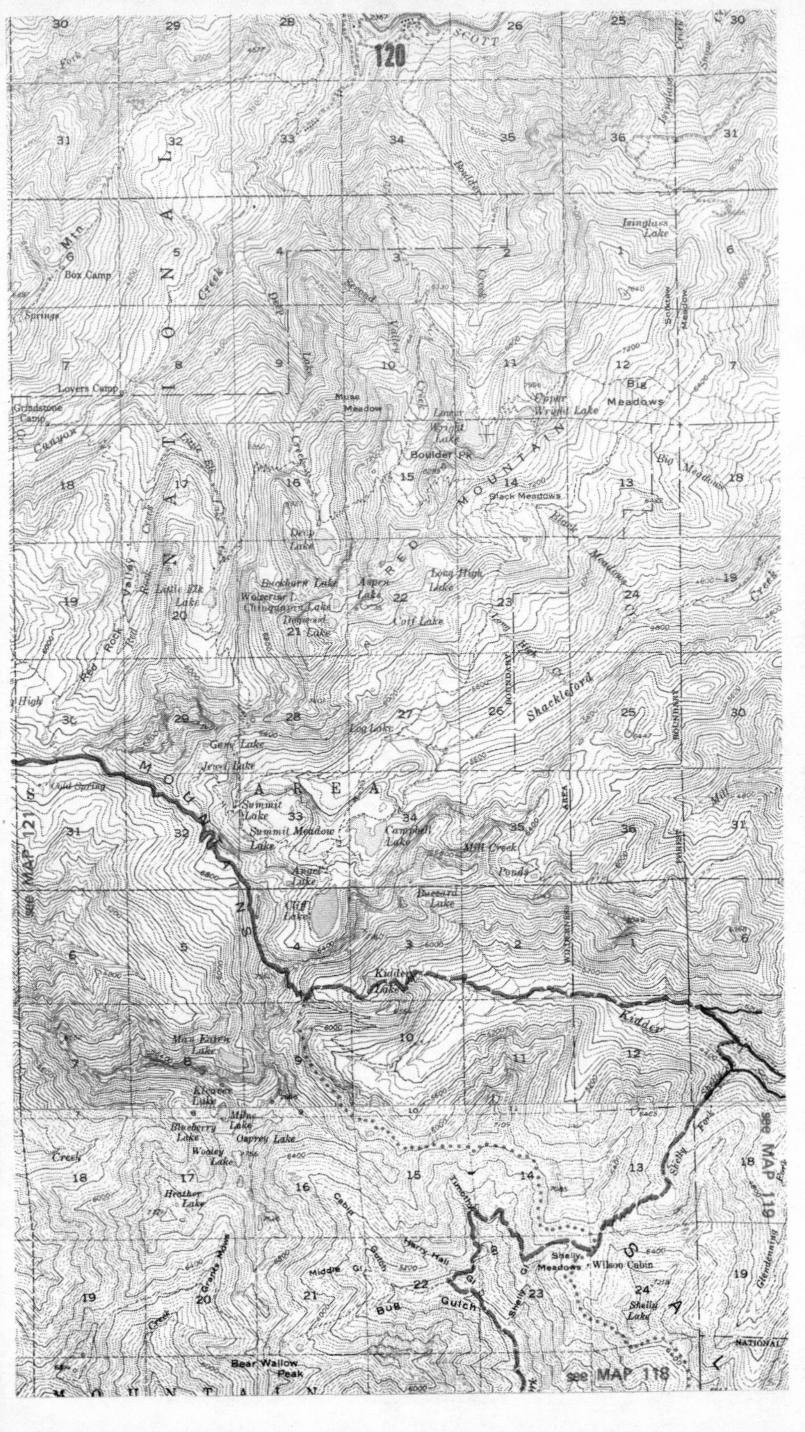

120
SCOTT
Box Camp
Springs
Lovers Camp
Grindstone Camp
Canyon
Muse Meadow
Second Valley
Deep Lake
Lower Wright Lake
Upper Wright Lake
Boulder Pk
Big Meadows
Isinglass Lake
Black Meadows
RED MOUNTAIN
Buckhorn Lake
Aspen Lake
Long High Lake
Little Elk Lake
Wolverine L.
Chinquapin Lake
Dogwood Lake
Calf Lake
Red Rock Valley
Shackleford
Log Lake
Gem Lake
Jewel Lake
AREA
Summit Lake
Summit Meadow Lake
Campbell Lake
Mill Creek Ponds
Angel Lake
Cliff Lake
Buzzard Lake
Kidder Lake
Kidder
Man Eaten Lake
Kleaver Lake
Milne Lake
Blueberry Lake
Osprey Lake
Wooley Lake
Heather Lake
Bear Wallow Peak
Middle Gl
Harry Hall
Bug Gulch
Shelly Meadows
Wilson Cabin
Shelly Lake
Shelly Fork
see MAP 121
see MAP 119
see MAP 118
NATIONAL
WILDERNESS AREA
FOREST BOUNDARY

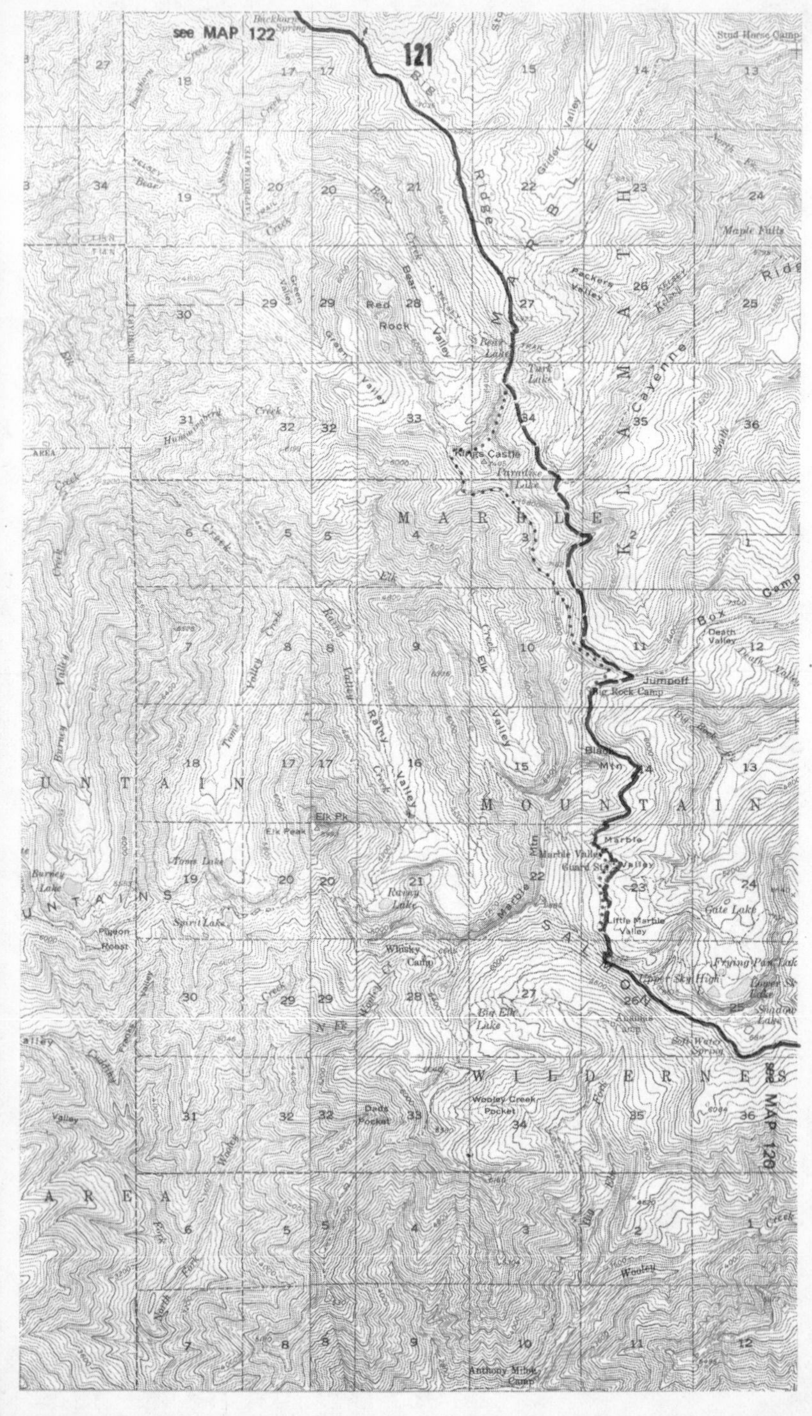
see MAP 122
121
see MAP 120
Big Ridge
Marble Mountain
Kings Castle
Paradise Lake
Black Mtn
Jumpoff
Big Rock Camp
Marble Valley Guard Sta
Little Marble Valley
Elk Peak
Wooley Creek Pocket
Anthony Milne Camp
Dads Pocket
Whisky Camp
Stud Horse Camp
Death Valley

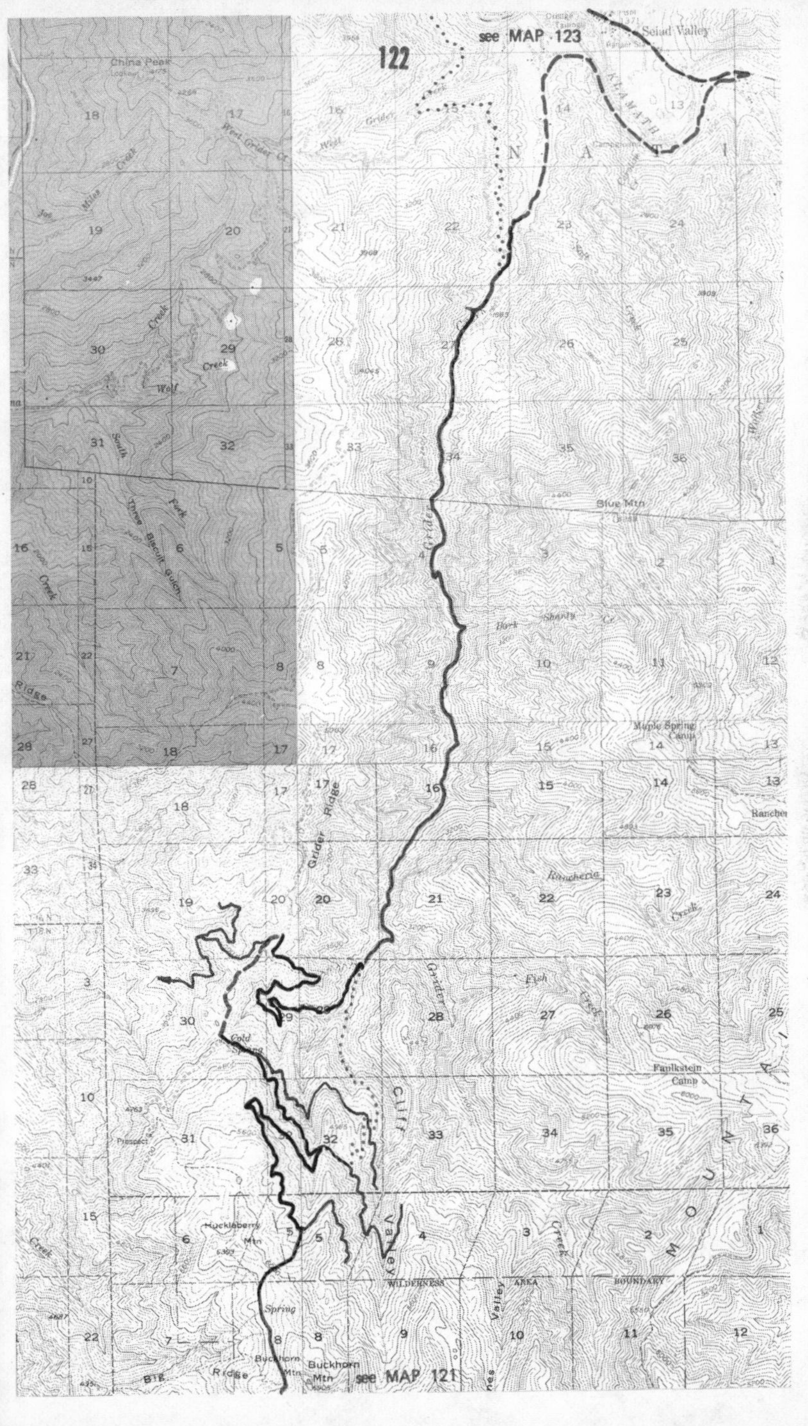

122
see MAP 123
Seiad Valley
China Peak
West Grider Cr
Joe Miles Creek
KLAMATH
N A T I
Creek
Wolf
South Fork
Three Biscuit Gulch
Creek
Ridge
Grider
Blue Mtn
Bark Shanty Cr
Maple Spring Camp
Grider Ridge
Rancheria Creek
Fish Creek
Grider
Cold Spring
Cliff
Valley
Faulkstein Camp
Prospect
Huckleberry Mtn
Creek
Spring
WILDERNESS AREA BOUNDARY
M O U N T A
Valley
Big Ridge
Buckhorn Mtn
Buckhorn Mtn
see MAP 121

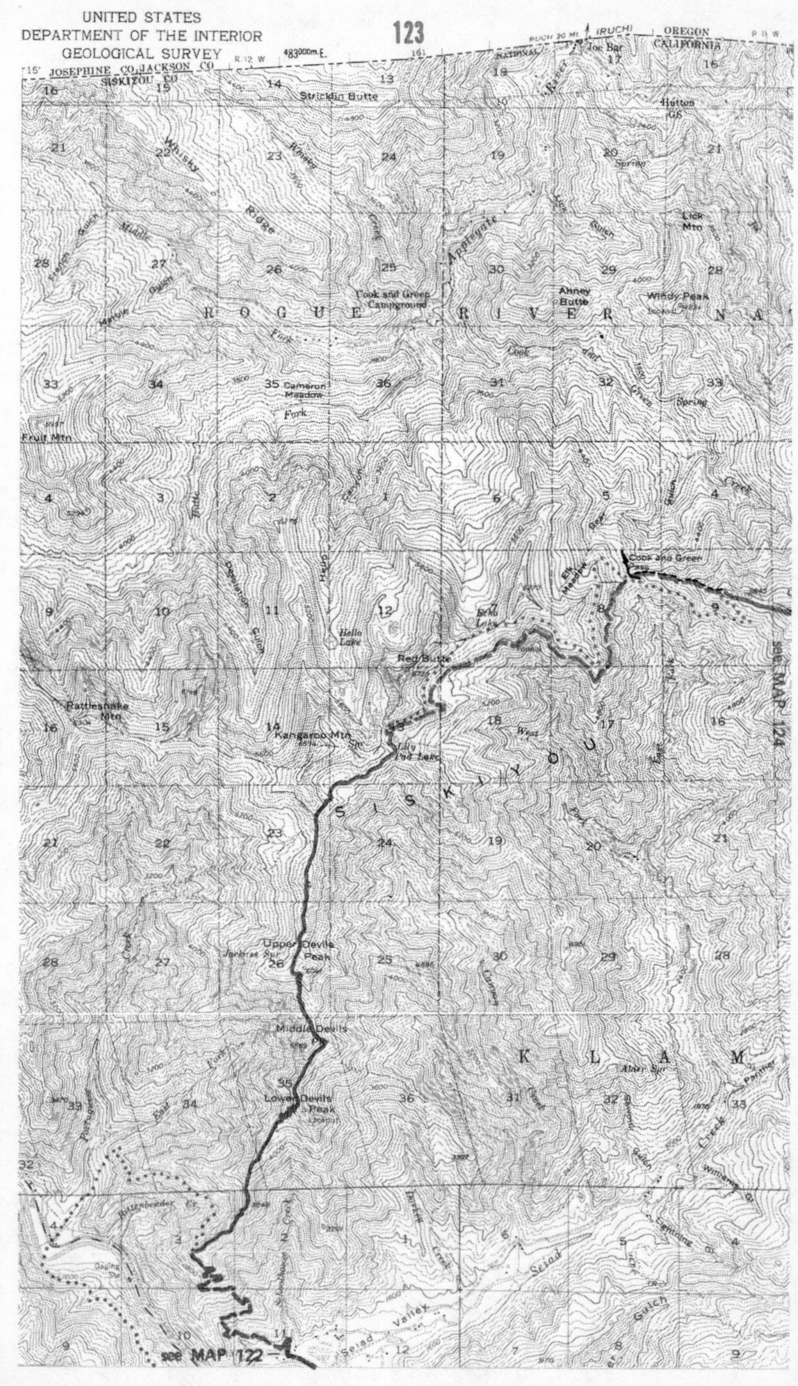

UNITED STATES
DEPARTMENT OF THE INTERIOR
GEOLOGICAL SURVEY
JOSEPHINE CO
JACKSON CO
SISKIYOU CO
OREGON
CALIFORNIA
Joe Bar
Stricklin Butte
Hutton GS
Whisky
Ridge
Applegate
River
Lick Mtn
Cook and Green Campground
Ahney Butte
Windy Peak
R O G U E   R I V E R   N A
Cameron Meadow
Fruit Mtn
Cook and Green Pass
Elk Meadow
Echo Lake
Hello Lake
Red Butte
Rattlesnake Mtn
Kangaroo Mtn
Lily Pad Lake
see MAP 124
S I S K I Y O U
Upper Devils Peak
Middle Devils Pk
Lower Devils Peak
K L A M
Seiad Valley
see MAP 122

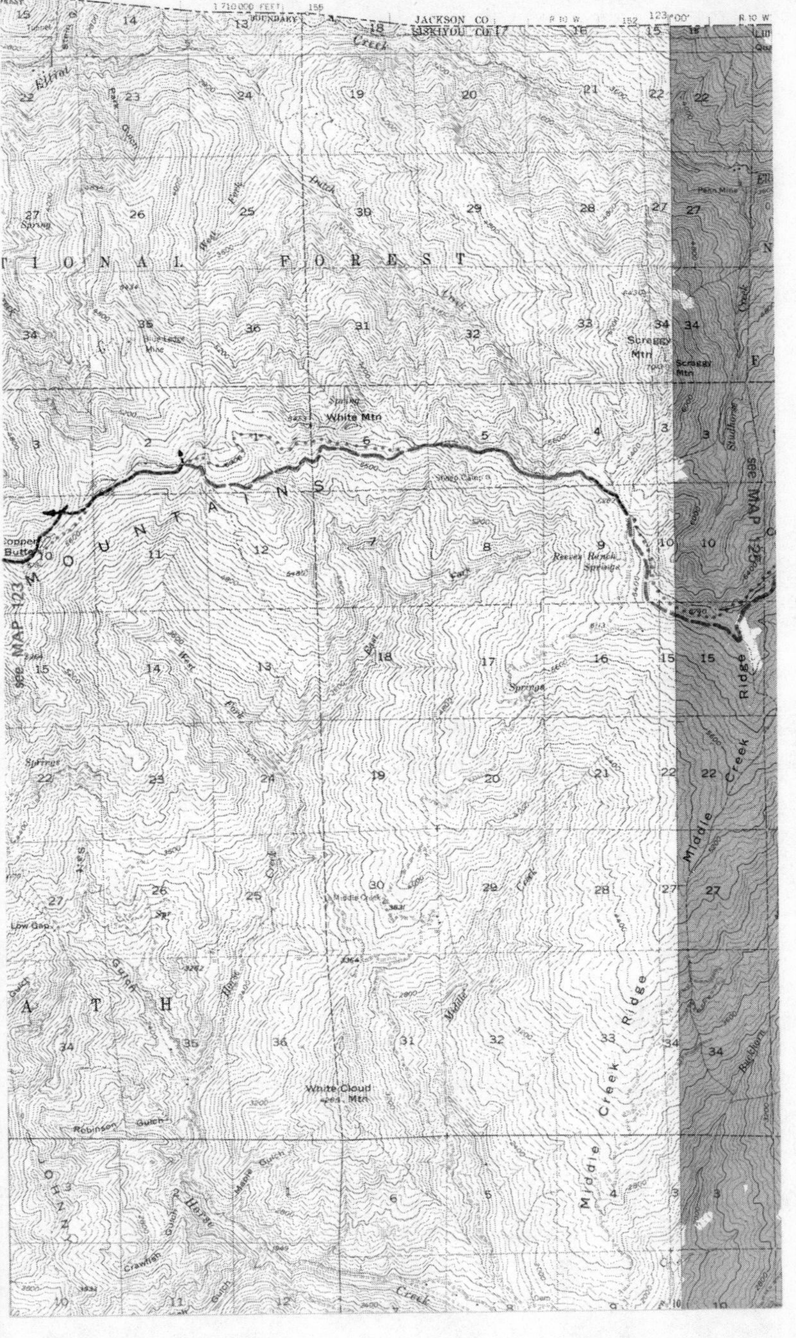
JACKSON CO
SISKIYOU CO
White Mtn
Scraggy Mtn
Copper Butte
Reeves Ranch Springs
White Cloud Mtn
Middle Creek Ridge
Robinson Gulch
Low Gap
Crawfish
Maple Gulch
Blue Ledge Mine
Penn Mine
see MAP 123
see MAP 125

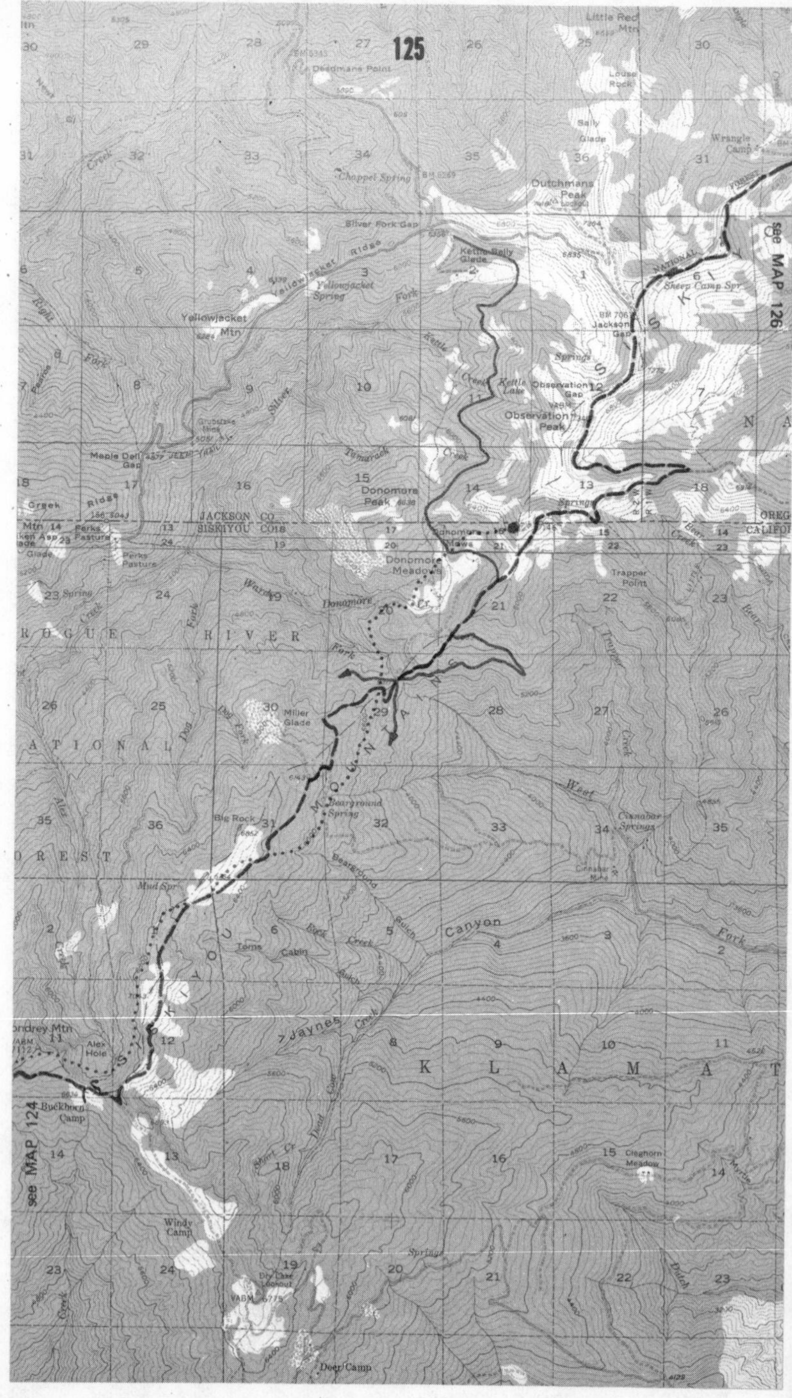


see MAP 126

see MAP 124

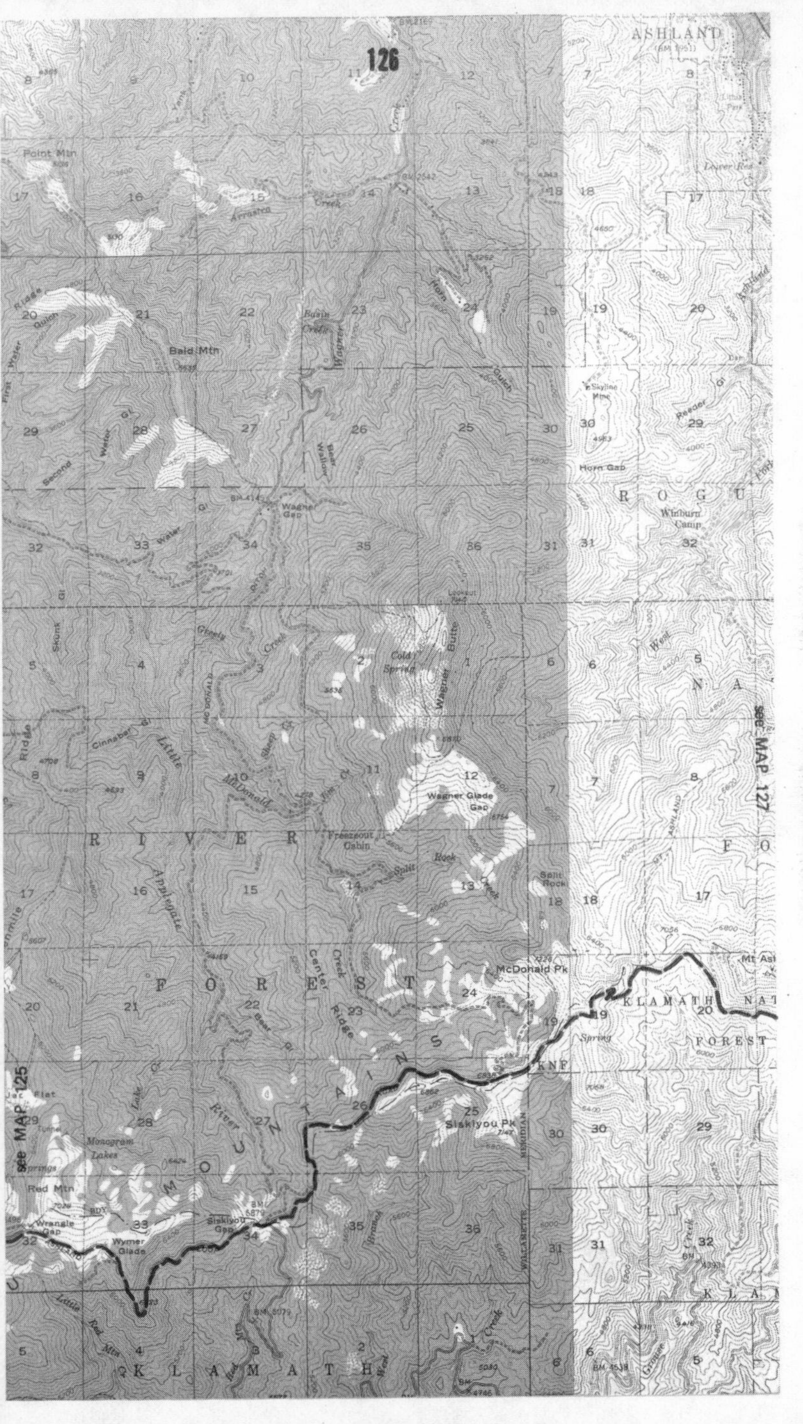

126
ASHLAND
Point Mtn
Arrastra Creek
Bald Mtn
Basin Creek
Wagner Gap
Skyline Mine
Horn Gap
Winburn Camp
Cold Spring
Wagner Butte
Wagner Glade Gap
Freezeout Cabin
Split Rock
McDonald Pk
Siskiyou Pk
Siskiyou Gap
Wymer Glade
Wrangle Gap
Red Mtn
Monogram Lakes
R O G U E
R I V E R
F O R E S T
N A
F O
M O U N T A I N S
K L A M A T H
KLAMATH NAT
FOREST
KNF
see MAP 127
see MAP 125

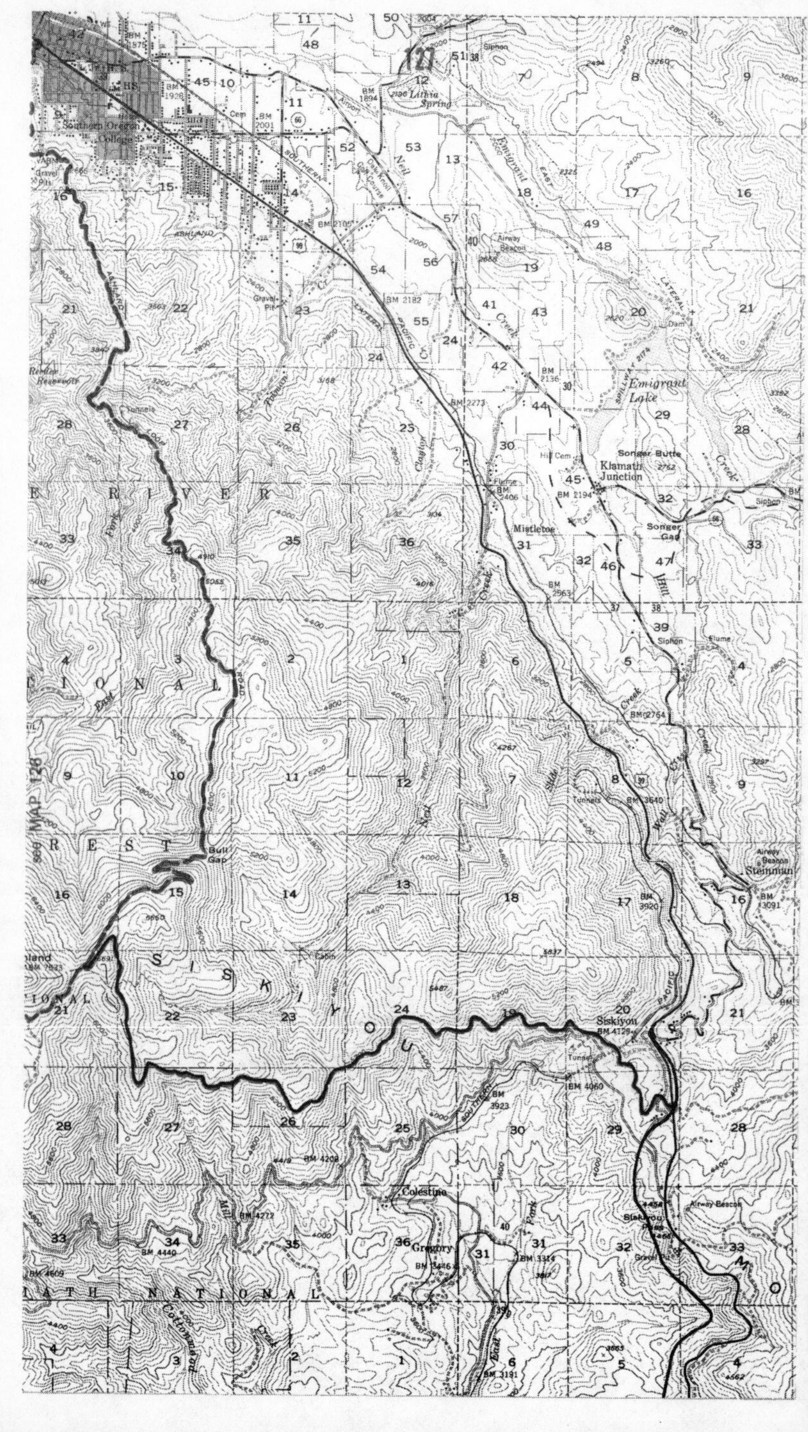

# 1975 Supplement to The Pacific Crest Trail, Volume 1: California

Many segments of the Pacific Crest Trail in California were not yet constructed when this book was published in 1973, and many are still not constructed. But some new segments of the final route have been constructed since then, and some portions of the temporary route have been rerouted.

So for this 1975 edition of the guide, there follows a page-by-page updating of the trail description. In addition, the red part of the maps in the back of the book has been changed to conform to the situation as it existed in November 1974. You can recognize the changed red lines because they have been made with a finer point.

In the way of general advice, you should consider whether snow will be a problem on your trek. If you begin at Mexico in early April, you will encounter snow on Mt. San Jacinto, on Mt. San Gorgonio, in the High Sierra and in the northern Sierra. If you do the trail in segments here and there, be aware that snow can be a problem on Mt. San Jacinto in April, on San Gorgonio into May, in the High Sierra through June and in the northern Sierra through mid-July of a typical year. In the northern Sierra snow merely presents route-finding problems, but in the other places it can be dangerous where steep and icy, and you may need an ice ax, crampons, or even rope.

**p. 46, line 6:** Yellow Rose Spring. A sign cautions against drinking the spring water, but there is creek water in the springtime.

**p. 46, line 33:** Water at Burnt Rancheria Campground. Water is available here *when* the campground is open.

**p. 46, line 43:** Horse Heaven Campground. Water is available here *when* the campground is open.

**p. 47, line 6:** Road 15S23. All of this road that the route follows is now paved.

**p. 47, line 44:** Horsemen's Group Camp. The correct elevation is 4710' and there is water here now.

**p. 48, line 15:** Unnamed fork. There is now a sign *Banner* here.

**p. 48, line 21:** Paralleling San Felipe Valley Road. Don't cross the highway and follow the trail, but instead follow the road, to avoid cactus.

**p. 48, line 24:** Ascending the San Felipe Valley. There is water at a highway-maintenance station at elevation 3048'.

**p. 49, line 21:** Twin Lakes. These lakes are on private land, and the owners may not want people to camp at them.

**p. 49, line 26:** Durasna Valley. In this valley there is a ranch with a water tower, and the owner lets hikers use this water. He may pipe it to the trail.

**p. 50, lines 4-6:** State Highway 74. Between this highway and Herkey Creek Camp there was a bad fire.

**p. 52, line 11:** The descent to Hurley Flat. A bad fire burned over three miles of the route, and it is hard to follow the trail through the burn.

**p. 56, line 31, to p. 57, line 11:** Onyx Summit. A new PCT section has been completed northwest of here. As your trail descends north, then northwest from the summit, notice the influence of the desert on this side of the divide — pinyon pine, juniper and sagebrush become predominant. Your trail drops into the head of Arrastre Creek, and follows the shady creek, crossing and recrossing it several times, down to a junction (7430-3.3) with a dirt road descending Balky Horse Canyon. You cross the road and climb northward around a pinyon-covered ridge, leaving Arrastre Creek far below, with expansive views out over the desert. The recently constructed trail turns northwest and crosses a low point in the ridge, then climbs over an open area before descending through pinyon and juniper to a junction with Forest Service Road 2NO2 (6760-3.1). You continue northwest, climbing and contouring along the desert-facing slope of Nelson Ridge, before finally dropping to an intersection with **State Highway 18 (6830-3.3).** The new trail crosses the highway and climbs again, then contours along the northeastern, desert-facing slope of the ridge. You pass three lonely Jeffrey pines that stand out conspicuously above the pinyon forest before your trail intersects.

**Doble Dump Road (6830-1.8).** The permanent PCT from here west to Van Dusen Canyon is scheduled for construction in 1975, so your temporary route utilizes Forest Service Road 3N16. Turn left (southwest) and follow Doble Dump Road 0.3 mile south-southwest to its intersection with 3N16. Turn right onto 3N16 and follow the dirt road as it climbs up to a saddle on the northeast ridge of Gold Mountain. After a short walk south, you pass, on your left, the ruins of Lucky Baldwin's *Doble Mine* (7250 – 1.2). Your road swings west, crosses another saddle and contours around the head of Chicopee Canyon to Arrastre Flat (7500 – 2.2), where the pinyon-juniper forest abruptly turns to

Jeffrey pine. You continue west into **Upper Holcomb Valley** (7352 – 2.2), a pine-dotted basin once the scene of a frenzied gold rush. A permanent section of the PCT from Van Dusen Canyon around Bertha Peak to Poligue Canyon has been completed (October 1974), starting three-fourths mile southeast down the Van Dusen Canyon Road. Until adjoining sections are constructed in 1975, however, you should take the temporary route through Holcomb Valley.

**p. 61, bottom line, to p. 62, line 13:** Lone Pine Canyon. After less than a mile on pavement, you pass the Sharpless Ranch (3940 – 0.0) and reach a junction with Forest Road 3N29, on your left, marked by a small wooden sign. Turn left (southwest) and follow this narrow dirt road as it winds to the top of Upper Lytle Creek Ridge and a junction with 3N31 (5200 – 2.3). Proceed northwest along the ridgetop road, through open terrain with panoramic views southwest to the peaks of the Cucamonga Wilderness and north over the tawny desert, passing a junction with 3N33, on your left, to a junction with 3N30 (6300 – 3.9). Go left and follow the dirt road around the mountainside, through a forest of pine and fir, to its end at a saddle (6450 – 0.6). Here you meet a newly constructed Blue Ridge section of the PCT. Proceed along the trail — a welcome change after miles of road walking — as it winds up the ridge, alternately through forest and open chaparral, and around the north slope of Wright Mountain to Guffy Campground (8250 – 5.7).

**p. 64, line 34:** Water at Messenger Flat Campground. There is water here.

**p. 66, line 41, to p. 70, line 25:** Two undesirable routes. The temporary route now follows the alternate route we described on page 67, lines 8 through 30. Then follow the description on page 69, lines 33 through 44, which is the aqueduct segment from Tehachapi-Willow Springs Road to Oak Creek Road. Here you can trod east to Mojave, should you need supplies. The temporary route, however, continues northeast alongside the aqueduct to

**State Highway 58 (3165 – 6.2).** For the next several miles, ribs roughly a foot apart and just as high stick out from the almost-buried old aqueduct. You must follow one of two dirt roads parallel to it and heading northeast. Keep the aqueduct roof in sight as you dip into numerous washes — small, medium and large — and pass an unsigned junction (3173 – 1.0) with paved Randsburg Cutoff. Don't leave the old aqueduct until you come to the service road for the new one, onto which you veer right at an **unsigned scissors junction** (3175 – 4.7). From here on, look for the capped pipes mentioned in the text. There are 300 yards apart and have *Jawbone Pipeline* stenciled on them, where the paint hasn't peeled. Look also for protruding cisterns with locked-on manhole covers, and make sure the road you take runs in a wide swath of "cultivated" ground. The best campsites along this route are generally northwest, toward the mouths of canyons. You'll be passing through many 3- and 4-way intersections with other dirt roads, some well-travelled. Roll over a few steep hills to find the aqueduct above ground and on stilts to avoid the wash from Lone Tree Canyon, then pass some distance below a habitation surrounded by the rusty hulks of junked cars. Once you see the buildings of Sprague's (formerly Tokiwa's) restaurant and gas station, wait until your road is at a 90° angle from them (2210 – 8.9) before crossing the desert in-between. The water cooler at Cinco (2135 – 0.5) is so attractive that most everyone will want to join the route described in the text (page 70, line 25) at this point.

**p. 70, lines 26–27:** Next water. Recently a spigot signed *DRINKING WATER* has been adapted to a hydrant on the old L.A. Aqueduct where it's crossed by Jawbone Canyon Road.

**p. 70, lines 33–35:** Secluded campsites. The spur road to these campsites has been washed out, and the bouldery wash you turn south on to reach the campsites is 0.1 mile west past the start of Hoffman Well Road, on Jawbone Canyon Road. The campsite is 200 yards from the pavement, at the candy-striped mouth of a canyon highly suitable for rock-climbing practice. Other campsites developed by motorcyclists, whose trails you'll see everywhere, are better for groups larger than three. They are scattered along Hoffman Well Road, where enforcement of the "no camping" rule has been ineffective.

As Hoffman Well Road is now impassable to all except high-clearance vehicles, it sometimes resembles just another motorcycle speedway. This makes pathfinding difficult; pay close attention to the map.

**p. 70, bottom line (photo caption):** *California,* not Los Angeles, Aqueduct.

**p. 72, line 36, to p. 73, line 22:** Alternate route. This route is no longer recommended due to the obliteration of the Bright Star Trail and the refusal of the owners of the Leibel Ranch to let anyone cross their property. However, those wishing to resupply at Kernville, where the selection is greater, can hook up with this alternate route upon reaching the junction of State Highway 178 and Kern River Road near Weldon (see correction for page 74, lines 17 – 27), and following the latter 13.2 miles around the north side of Lake Isabella to Kernville. Detouring to Kernville means you'll be hiking 12 miles farther than you would if you stuck to the temporary PCT.

**p. 73, lines 25 – 28:** Cannell Trail. The first 1.5 miles of trail have been abandoned and a sign immediately south of Camp Owens indicates that you take a dirt road over the saddle mentioned to the new trailhead. This adds perhaps 0.1 mile to the total distance; the dirt road begins 0.9 mile north of the 4-lane turnoff to Kernville on Kern River Road.

**p. 73, line 31:** Kern Canyon, not Rincon, Fault.

**p. 73, lines 34–35:** Cannell Meadow Trail. The old trail via Caldwell Creek and Tunnel Spring has been abandoned. Its number, 33E32, is now the designation for the Cannell Trail, not 33E49.

**p. 74, line 6:** Saddle. The jeep road beyond here has been closed off and returned to nature.

**p. 74, lines 17–27:** Dry Meadows Trail. This is the most used path in the Piutes, not the least, and for PCT trekkers, the most direct and desirable. New switchbacks added to the old trail into South Fork Valley now ease the grade. But there is no sign where you hit State Highway 178, 0.1 mile west of the K.O.A. Hiking east on 178, you'll find its store and motel on a spur road to the south, a signed junction with the Kern River Road heading north, a signed junction with Kelso Valley Road heading southeast, and the Weldon post office at a signed junction (2651-3.1) with Fay Ranch Road, which you follow north.

**p. 74, line 28, to p. 75, line 5:** Woolstalf Trail. This is not a better alternative. A new alignment was surveyed and cleared of brush, but Richard Hulbert, the Havilah ranger whose enthusiasm was responsible for most of the rebuilding of Greenhorn District trails taking place in the last 10 years, was transferred before a tread could be cut in the switchbacks down to Kelso Creek valley. Thus the pathfinding along the new alignment, which adds 1.4 miles to the total, is more difficult. There are no buildings occupied at Roberts Ranch, so you needn't fear shotgun-armed people here.

**p. 75, line 13:** Quarter Circle Five Ranch. The foreman's name is Robinson, and he's moved. Instead, ask his wife, who is the postmaster at Weldon.

**p. 75, lines 17–24:** Little Cannell Cow Driveway. This excruciatingly steep path has been abandoned. New signs posted where Fay Ranch Road dips to ford Fay Creek direct you to follow Cane Meadow Trail up onto the Kern Plateau. You go past Cane

Meadow to a pile of vandalized signs where, for 0.1 mile in crossing a gully, you join an abandoned logging road, now the Bartolas Country Trail. At the west side of the gully you have a choice: you can follow the PCT shields posted along the northern extension of the Cane Meadow Trail, and leave it after 1.1 miles to follow trail 34E22 0.3 miles southwest, then Cherry Hill Road 0.3 miles southwest, *or* you can continue northwest on this logging road, crossing Fay Creek and heading up the next gully to the west to hit Cherry Hill Road (1.3 miles). The latter is the easier and more direct. A jeep trail from the turn-around where Cherry Hill Road ends (6800 – 0.3) bypasses Little Cannell Meadow and brings you to a signed junction (6900 – 0.7) with the Little Cannell Cow Driveway, on which you turn north. Just over a low ridge is Fay Creek (7420–0.7) and a good campsite.

**p. 76, lines 7–13:** Mosquito Meadow. A new timber sale has taken the virgin forest from Mosquito to Durrwood meadows, and a dirt road has taken the place of your trail between those points. The paved Sherman Pass Road now crosses Sherman Pass and goes a mile beyond, north. You can pick up the northbound Curliss Trail (temporary PCT) at the pass.

**p. 76, lines 28–31:** Curliss Meadows Guard Station. This collapsed under the heavy snowfall of 1969; the wreckage was taken away. The temporary PCT was rerouted here to avoid the meadow. Now it forms a 0.6-mile-long hypotenuse of a crumpled right triangle, the other two legs being the first lateral you come to, which is a short one crossing the meadow, and a second lateral you meet at a saddle on the watershed divide.

**p. 76, lines 31–37:** Bonita Meadows. Cross the recently constructed Sherman Pass Road at an unsigned junction immediately after fording Bonita Creek.

**p. 76, line 41, to p. 78, line 8:** Beach Meadows. Recent logging has superseded the trail from the next saddle north of this to the spur ridge immediately south of Beach Meadows with an abandoned road. Hike north on it to this spur ridge, where the road is open to automobiles, then find a trail heading left to the edge of Beach Meadows, then paralleling them north. Halfway across an arm of Beach Meadows, PCT shields indicate that you turn west, cross the main part of the meadow and Beach Creek, and parallel the meadow, heading north onto the Bonita Flat Trail, the Little Horse Trail, Road 20542, and finally, at a sign beside Beach Creek, the signed *Beach Trail*.

**p. 78, lines 9–11:** Logging road. These logging roads have been "returned to nature" — parts have been sloughed off by bulldozer; in other places huge water bars have been thrown up; and culverts have been removed. It's surprising to see such care taken so far from the eyes of the road-bound public, and commendable.

**p. 79, lines 1–8:** Long Canyon Creek. The trail has been rerouted here. Cross Long Canyon Creek at the former southern junction with the Beer Keg Trail, pass a new, signed junction (8640 – 0.4) with the Beer Keg Trail, turn southeast and then curve sharply northeast on what was formerly a spur of the Beer Keg Trail. Here is a junction (8660 – 0.6) mentioned in the text where the temporary PCT used to join your route from the east.

**p. 79, line 36:** Mulkey Meadows Trail. Experienced pathfinders interested in taking a newly constructed section of permanent PCT from Trail Pass to Siberian Pass can hook up with it by using the Mulkey Meadows and Trail Pass trails. The first 3.2 miles of pathfinding along the Mulkey Meadows Trail are difficult, as the trail has disappeared under hundreds of minutely interlacing cowpaths. After a wade-across ford of the South Fork Kern River, close adherence to the route shown on the topographic map is best, particularly for finding the tread once you leave Ramshaw Meadows for good. Head up the third of four prominent canyons. Later, when you reach a signed junction with a multilaned east-west path in Mulkey Meadows, turn west for 100 yards and then northeast on the Trail Pass Trail (9360 – 7.3). The junction with the Pacific Crest Trail is directly at Trail Pass (10,500 – 2.3); turn northwest here. Pass Poison Meadow (10,780 – 1.6), a signed junction with the Cottonwood Pass Trail (11,180 – 2.6) and a lateral to campsites by Chicken Spring Lake (11,270 – 0.6). Then enter Sequoia National Park at a spur ridge 430 feet above the level of Siberian Pass. Continue northwest to a junction with the Siberian Pass Trail (10,990 – 3.7). See the High Sierra Hiking Guide to *Kern Peak-Olancha* for a complete description of these trails.

**p. 80, lines 34–35:** Siberian Pass. Instead of meeting the permanent Pacific Crest Trail at a junction directly on top of the pass (westbound), and another junction 0.1 mile to the north (eastbound), the temporary PCT now extends to a 4-way junction 0.8 mile north of the pass, because the permanent PCT was recently rerouted out of Siberian Outpost.

**p. 82, line 9:** Chute. Rejoin the chute coming down from Mt. Irvine, follow it down for 100 yards, and diagonal down to the flats at the outlet of Consultation Lake. There are cliffs hidden at the edge of the lake which you should stay high to avoid.

**p. 82, line 12:** Traverse west, not east.

**p. 94, lines 39–45:** Sierra Club Camp. The Sierra Club deeded its private campground in Tuolumne Meadows to the National Park Service. Yosemite authorities closed the dirt road to vehicles south of the stables. Mile 0.0 of the Tahoe-Yosemite Trail is now at the point of this road closure.

**p. 103, line 23:** Nobel Lake area. The Forest Service expects construction of the final PCT from a point ½ mile southeast of Nobel Lake to the Ebbetts Pass Highway to be complete by July 1975. However, the continuation of the PCT north from the highway will not be constructed until sometime later, so the temporary route down past Silver Creek Campground remains the preferred route.

**p. 106, lines 24—34:** Sayles Canyon. The Sayles Canyon Trail has been rebuilt. You now reach its junction on a saddle 0.9 trail miles south of Bryan Meadow. The Crystal Range is not seen. From Bryan Meadow, the PCT makes both a short climb and descent before the "climb awhile." The descent in "several forested stages" is very steep — up to 35°. It could be dangerous in early season snow. Beyond Benwood Meadow, the trail climbs a low ridge, dips to a creek, and then climbs to the roadend.

**p. 106, lines 38–44:** Highway maintenance station. Several temporary routes are possible; some are confusing. The easiest route to Echo Lake Resort is to head north up the road that starts from the west side of the maintenance station. After 0.9 mile, at Johnson Pass, you reach a paved road which you follow west 0.2 mile to a signed *Echo Lakes* junction, from where you climb northwest 1.2 miles on another paved road which takes you to the resort.

**p. 107, lines 8–13:** There are now more trails in this section than the book indicates. Some trail junctions have been recently relocated. Junctions and mileages from Echo Lake Resort are: spur trail left down to public pier, 2.7; faint trail right up to Triangle Lake saddle, 3.2; trail left down to Tamarack Lake, 3.8 (also, the old PCT starts west here, paralleling our newer trail segment above it); second trail right to Triangle Lake saddle, 4.5; fork left through Haypress Meadows toward Lake of the Woods, 4.6; trail left up to Ralston Peak, 5.1 (also, in less than 100 yards, trail right down to Lake Lucille); fork left down to Lake Aloha, 5.5; second trail right to Lake Lucille, 5.7; Lake Aloha, 6.2.

**p. 107, line 23:** Susie Lake campsites. Best campsites are on a small forested flat about 80 yards down the lake's outlet creek.

**p. 107, line 28:** Two consecutive junctions. Now just one intersection, left to Half Moon Lake, right to Fallen Leaf Lake Resort, store and post office, and ahead to Dicks Pass.

**p. 110, lines 16–20:** Squaw Valley Village. Stores and a post office are here. From Whisky Creek Camp, signed trails plus a dirt road lead you 4.7 miles down to a large Squaw Valley parking lot, from which you walk north on a paved road 0.3 mile to a junction at the fire station. From here the village is 0.4 mile east on Squaw Valley Road. Starting at the east side of the fire station, a trail ascends 3.4 miles up to a junction with the PCT at a point just southeast of Mountain Meadow Lake.

**p. 111, lines 24–29:** Tinker Knob. A faint, obvious ridge trail strikes north from the knob, but it eventually dies out. The ensuing cross-country route, although excellent at first, eventually takes you down to patrolled ski areas trespassing on which is frowned upon, to put it mildly. Therefore, this alternate route is no longer recommended.

**p. 111, line 42:** Onion Creek Campground. No longer maintained. Camp beside or near Onion Creek.

**p. 112, line 39, and p. 113, lines 9–18:** Cross country begins here. Luckily, it doesn't. A few yards northwest of this trail/road junction a faint 1.7-mile-long trail starts a climb north, curves westward up to a ridge, then winds down to White Rock Creek. The trail here is obscure, but the crossing — a wide, open stretch just below some forest-bound rapids — is essentially east-west. From it, head west-southwest 0.2 mile to the spur road of line 17, p. 113. The trail meets this road where it turns from south to west, less than 100 yards before it dead-ends at a camp by the creek. You hike north on this road, then northwest, for a 0.3-mile stretch to the White Rock Lake Jeep Road of line 18.

**p. 116, lines 20–22:** Grass Lake Creek. On a flat which is 0.6 trail miles north of this creek crossing, a faint 0.3-mile-long trail bears east along a ridge and down its gentle north slope to the *real* Grass Lake. Just 60 yards farther north along the flat, we encounter the Deer Lake spur trail, on our left, which heads northwest up a gully.

**p. 121:** Temporary route. The Forest Service has established a temporary route which differs from ours. Take your choice. You also have a similar choice of routes farther north, just beyond the Lake Britton area, page 131.

**p. 122, line 42, to p. 123, line 11:** Shallow lake. At the east end of this shallow lake — really a pond — the cryptic California Riding and Hiking Trail departs south to Bucks Lake. Continuing west, you won't reach the Three Lakes Road, but rather you'll meet, after hiking 0.9 mile, a junction where a new PCT trail segment forks right. This segment contours 0.4 mile to a junction at a sharp curve one-third mile up the Belden Trail (page 123, line 3).

Follow this trail — actually an old jeep road — westward 1.8 miles to the start of the real trail and the descent. This trail was reconstructed in 1974 so that it is now 0.5 mile longer but less steep. The new upper segment has two trickling springs. From 5200 feet and lower, your descent route is essentially unchanged.

**p. 124, line 12, to p. 125, line 22:** Sunflower Flat spur road. A new trail segment has been constructed from this junction. Perhaps by the end of summer 1976, you will be able to walk on permanent PCT all the way from the Spanish Peak area, near Bucks Lake, north through Lassen Park to the Hat Creek Rim Fire Lookout (pages 122 – 130). At the junction where the Sunflower Flat spur road branches southeast, the PCT makes a somewhat confusing descent north gently down through a partly logged over area, then around a forested slope to two crossings of an old jeep road. 150 yards north of the second crossing, the trail segment ends on the road's east side, and you walk 50 yards north-northeast on it to a junction where the east-west trending

**Road 26N02 (6380 – 1.0)** intersects the north-south trending Humbug Ridge Road. From the northwest corner we follow a signed trail segment 0.3 mile northwest to an old road and walk northwest on it less than 100 yards, to where it starts to curve northeast. Here a short trail segment bears northwest to the south end of a long, mule-eared meadow. Rather than taking an obvious, but erroneous, short trail north, we follow PCT diamonds west across the south edge of the meadow, and, 30 yards into a lodgepole forest on an old westward logging road, we reach another new trail segment. Following it north, we parallel at a distance the long meadow's west edge. Our trail ends at another old logging road, and on this we hike north, still paralleling the meadow, then leave it on another trail segment that climbs above the meadow's northwest corner, switchbacks west and reaches, on a low ridge, yet another old logging road. This we follow one-quarter mile west to an intersection of the

**Humbug Road (27N01) (6450 – 1.7)** at Cold Springs Campground, one-half mile southwest and below Humbug Summit (6714), a saddle. The well-signed spring, among the aspens just west of the road, should be considered a key campsite area for both north and southbound PCT trekkers. The PCT follows the spring's creeklet about 100 yards southwest, crosses it, and then climbs northward 0.3 mile to an old road that heads southeast 0.2 mile back to the Humbug Road. After another 0.3 mile northward climb, the trail segment ends at a road junction. A minor dirt road starts northwest before quickly aborting. Our route is the jeep road from the southeast. (Since the trail from Cold Springs to this road junction is hard to find when snow-patches prevail through June, you can reach it by walking from the springs northeast 0.5 mile up the Humbug Road to a road junction, on your left, just 120 yards before the signed *Humbug Summit*. Traverse west 0.3 mile along this good jeep road to the PCT junction.) At the road/trail junction, the jeep road turns north, and we climb up it to a ridge where, at another junction (6850 – 1.2), our jeep road curves eastward. We take the other jeep road northwestward up a ridge on which it diminishes to a trail, and we continue upward. Soon, a break in the forest appears and we can see Lake Almanor for the first time. Our gentle, broad ridge curves west, and the trail along it becomes very faint just before joining a **road** (7110 – 0.9) immediately southeast of a flat summit area. (Southbound hikers: Where this road ends, look for telltale PCT diamonds. If you can't find them, or the trail, head east along the ridge and both should become evident in about 100 yards.) Our road makes a short climb out of the red-fir forest and on to the level, open summit area just south of and above a flat with a seasonal pond. Our road at first is lined with lupines as it makes a short descent to the flat, but soon the route becomes quite barren as we approach a **junction** (7000 – 0.3) with another road, striking east. We take the road striking northwest, which climbs slightly and provides us with views of Lassen Peak and Lake Almanor, then we descend on it to a saddle, where just beyond it a **spur road** (7010 – 0.8) descends rather steeply to Lost Lake. This descent is part of the old temporary route.

In 0.1 mile, our ridge road north ends, and a new PCT segment begins. As of October 1974 the first 1.2 miles were still in a brushy construction stage, but this stretch should be hikable by midsummer 1975. Should you encounter this stretch before its completion, you might consider following the temporary Lost Lake route to the Carter Meadow Trail (page 125, lines 4 – 22). Otherwise, follow this ridgecrest-hugging stretch north down to a saddle, long and narrow like the previous one, then jog along the ridge to yet another long saddle, this one bending westward when just a quarter mile southwest of the dark, prominent, volcanic Eagle Rocks (7063). As we progress westward, we pass by two large volcanic pinnacles immediately to the north. The path west becomes faint in places as it winds past smaller volcanic pinnacles and blocks, but by staying close to the crest you can't lose the route. As the crest curves southwest, the trail sculptured into it becomes quite obvious, and our panoramic views disappear as we enter a forest on the northwest steep slope of Humboldt Peak (7087). Snowbound at least until early July, this stretch first drops, then climbs to the Humboldt Road at

**Humboldt Summit (6610 – 3.7).** From this saddle north to the

Domingo Springs area, a few miles south of Lassen Park, the permanent PCT is only flagged. The entire stretch should be completed by late summer 1976. In the meantime, proceed eastward 3.0 miles down the Humboldt Road to the temporary PCT at the start of the Carter Meadow Trail (page 125, line 22 through page 126, line 9).

**p. 126, lines 9–26:** Rice Creek Road. At this junction you can see a new trail about 20 feet above and east of the road. This 0.9-mile segment crosses the main east-west road about one-quarter mile east of the junction. For a minimum effort, join this segment by walking north 40 yards to a minor spur road forking right, and follow its northeast curving path 100 yards to the level trail at the base of the volcanic rubble slope. This segment starts close to the base, then climbs moderately to a closed road, up which you pace 80 yards — almost to a saddle — where the trail resumes. It switchbacks one-quarter mile up across a steeply ascending closed road (same one), then joins it where its gradient eases off to moderate. We now follow the road 0.4 mile, to where its gradient sharply increases and a trail branches off its west side. This 2.8-mile segment, somewhat shaded by ponderosa pine, sugar pine, white fir and incense cedar, climbs to the bear-and-deer-inhabited ridge, crosses it three times, then reaches the brink of an east-west trending secondary ridge, from which we can see Willow Lake northeast below us and Lassen Peak northwest above us. From this good vantage point we start a contour west, descend to a saddle on the main ridge, cross it and traverse its slope northwest. Up the canyon to our west, a private logging road climbs to a broad saddle, where our now-descending trail almost touches it, then finally joins it after a 0.1-mile paralleling descent northwest (5960–4.1). We follow the road 50 yards to where it forks. A few paces farther, an obvious trail starts from the west side of the west (left) fork, parallels it toward the Little Willow Lake outlet creek, then climbs steeply up beside this seasonal creek to a junction along the east fringe of swampy

**Little Willow Lake (6100 – 0.7).** Immediately across the outlet creek we encounter the narrow trail that descends steeply east along the creek to the private logging road (the unused road of page 126, line 18). From our outlet creek junction, the PCT winds north-northeast, first up, then down, through a shady, dense, pine-marten-inhabited white-fir forest and finally reaches a junction (6000 – 1.0) with the old PCT route. This junction is 200 yards northwest above the 80-yard-long spur trail to the Terminal Geyser Overlook (page 126, line 26).

For the late-season hiker, the entire stretch just described is almost entirely devoid of fresh water. For the early-season hiker, it is hard to follow due to a snowpack that lasts, in places, until June. An easier route to follow is to walk from the first junction (p. 126, line 9) to that with the Stump Ranch Road (5150 – 0.7, line 12), then follow it 2.2 miles to a junction where the private logging road, mentioned earlier, forks right (northeast) (5540 – 2.2). Hike up this road to the previously mentioned broad saddle, then northwest 0.1 mile down to the PCT intersection (5960 – 1.6). Fifty yards farther, where the road forks, take the right fork and follow it northward to the poorly marked Terminal Geyser Trail (5840 – 1.2, line 22), then up it 0.3 mile to the junction with the new PCT route. Not only is this recommended route shorter than the new 5.8-mile PCT stretch, but it involves a lot less climbing, crosses spring-fed creeklets and avoids early-season snow problems.

**p. 128, lines 10–33:** Emigrant Trail. This footpath is no longer well hidden; a PCT diamond marks its departure from the now-closed Badger Flat Road (now you can drive north on it from State Highway 89 only down to the Hat Creek cossing). Since 1972 the trail has been modified and extended north to State Highway 44. Beyond State 44, the permanent route has been flagged, and it may be completed as far north as Lake Britton by late 1977. The first 0.8 mile of route is the same old Emigrant Trail: down a shallow gully, then down along a ridge. But then the new PCT continues along the ridge, providing you with views of Lassen Peak, whereas the more conspicuous old Emigrant Trail funnels you down a deep gully on the north side of the ridge. Beware! If you don't see Lassen before descending north into a gully, you're in the wrong gully. After about 0.3 mile of ridge descent, with views south of Lassen above and a dry gorge below, our manzanita-and-tobacco-bush-bordered PCT curves north and descends to a reunion with the scrubby, overgrown Emigrant Trail. In about 200 yards we reach the

**Plantation Loop Road (5580 – 1.8).** (The route meets this road about ⅓ mile southeast of where the black arrow in Map 101B takes off.) We turn right (east) and follow this shadeless road as it arcs north along the base of raped, desolate Badger Mountain. Eventually our road angles north-northwest in a moderate descent to a junction (5120 – 1.3) at the edge of a shady forest. We start west on a lateral road, but in 30 yards turn right and follow a trail north which stays within the forest's fringe. Soon our trail intersects

**Road 32N12 (5010 – 0.5)** at its bend, 1¼ miles southeast of its Hat Creek crossing. Back at the last junction, had you continued north on the Plantation Loop Road, you would have intersected

Road 32N12 just 40 yards east of the PCT. Consider: you haven't seen a drop of fresh water since Lower Twin Lake, about 11 miles back. The PCT route ahead is just as dry, though much longer. To obtain water, you'll have to hike out of your way to reach stagnant ponds. The author (Schaffer) still maintains the best route to follow is north on State Highway 89, as recommended in the original edition. His only change is to start hiking along the highway sooner by heading northwest 1.5 miles on 32N12 to just beyond the Lost Creek bridge, then north 1.3 miles on Road 32N13, paralleling the creek to Big Pine Campground ("Big Springs Campground" on the map). From here you walk west 0.5 mile to a junction with Highway 89, and follow it north 4.8 miles to the Highway 44 junction, where the original alternate route began. The advantages of starting the alternate route sooner are that you parallel Hat Creek sooner and that you pass two more stores, two more campgrounds and two more picnic grounds, including one beside unbelievably large Big Spring, which, by itself, doubles the volume of Hat Creek.

If you are a purist or a desert rat, then stick to the newly constructed PCT. There will be some rewarding views to justify your trials. The trail's grade is sympathetic to your struggle: it is mostly level in either direction. From Road 32N12, head east-northeast through a selectively logged forest, crossing several old roads before finally reaching a more used one (5160 – 1.1) just below a saddle southwest of point 5640. Up this road we walk but 40 yards, almost to atop the saddle, where we locate our trail once again as it starts a very long, gentle switchback leg southeast. Along this leg the avid photographer will stop many times to capture the beauty of Lassen's north face exquisitely framed by trailside ponderosa, Jeffrey and sugar pines, plus white firs and incense cedars. Don't use up all your film here, for there are more views to come. Eventually we reach a low point (5290 – 0.8) atop this up-faulted escarpment of Pliocene andesite lavas. Now our trail becomes cryptic. Watch for ducks, blazes, PCT diamonds, anything (!) over the next mile or so. Numerous roads in various states of disuse are crossed. From the escarpment we start a traverse north to a low ridge (5360 – 0.5), then make a winding descent to a usually dry creek. Beyond it we walk northeast through chaparral — mostly chest-high manzanita — for about 200 yards to a major east-west heavily used **logging road** (4690 – 1.9). Our trail ends here and we follow a hot, dusty, drivable (this is the *permanent* PCT?) road north. In about 250 yards a similar road, emerging northwest from the forest, joins ours. We continue our sunny, gentle descent north, begin a curve northeast, enter the forest's fringe and soon make contact with the **PCT** again (4520 – 0.6). Now our route is a long, winding traverse past some steeply descending logging spur roads. Along this traverse the observant hiker will notice a subtle change in forest vegetation: the typical forest understory shrubs are now largely displaced by bitterbrush, a woody shrub indicative of drier soils. Another addition to the forest's ledger is the Douglas fir, which has crept up from the Hat Creek valley floor. Just after we cross the last logging road (4440 – 1.6), which descends only moderately, we commence a series of long, easy-graded switchbacks that take us almost effortlessly up the faulted Hat Creek Rim escarpment. Once again we see to the south Lassen Peak and its subordinate associate, Chaos Crags. Below us to our west lie the basaltic Potato Buttes and related, sparsely vegetated lava flows that may be only several thousand years old. The third switchback leg takes us north up to Hat Creek Rim, and we quickly reach a gate across a well-maintained

**Logging Road (5260 – 2.0).** Since your first good dependable water won't be until the Hat Creek Rim Fire Lookout (page 130, line 7), 15.4 thirsty miles distant, you had best head for Baker Lake and camp there for the night. Hike southeast 0.4 mile along this road to where it curves south. Here a smaller road strikes east. Start along it about 50 yards, then follow a north fork about 100 yards to campsites at the lake's southwest corner. Don't expect excellent water or fishing, though, for this fairly large permanent lake is hardly more than a foot deep in its deeper sections. Back at the gate, head north 20 yards along the road, at which point the PCT branches northwest from the road, then parallels it a brief distance before meandering over to the escarpment. This we parallel about five miles before turning east and then descending north to a spur road along

**State Highway 44** (4980 – 5.5). Along the escarpment you'll see the familiar Jeffrey, ponderosa and sugar pines, but also will notice the appearance of drought-tolerant species: juniper, mountain mahogany, bitterbrush, rabbitbrush and sagebrush. Also for the first time, you'll see Mt. Shasta, as well as Lassen Peak. This rim traverse between these two imposing volcanic monarchs is a taste of the Cascade scenery you'll see farther north, where you're often between two dominating volcanoes, such as between Mts. Jefferson and Hood in Oregon or Mts. Adams and Rainier in Washington.

If the PCT doesn't continue beyond Highway 44 at the time you reach it, then follow it or its old dirt predecessor northwest 0.7 mile to the resumption of the temporary route, which starts north on Road 33N21 (page 130, line 3).

**p. 141, line 27, to p. 142, line 13:** Shelly Meadows. During the summer of 1974 a trail segment was under construction from this area northwest to the ridge above Kidder Lake. It is likely to be completed by the time you hike it.